The Clamour for Glamour

FAIRIES T

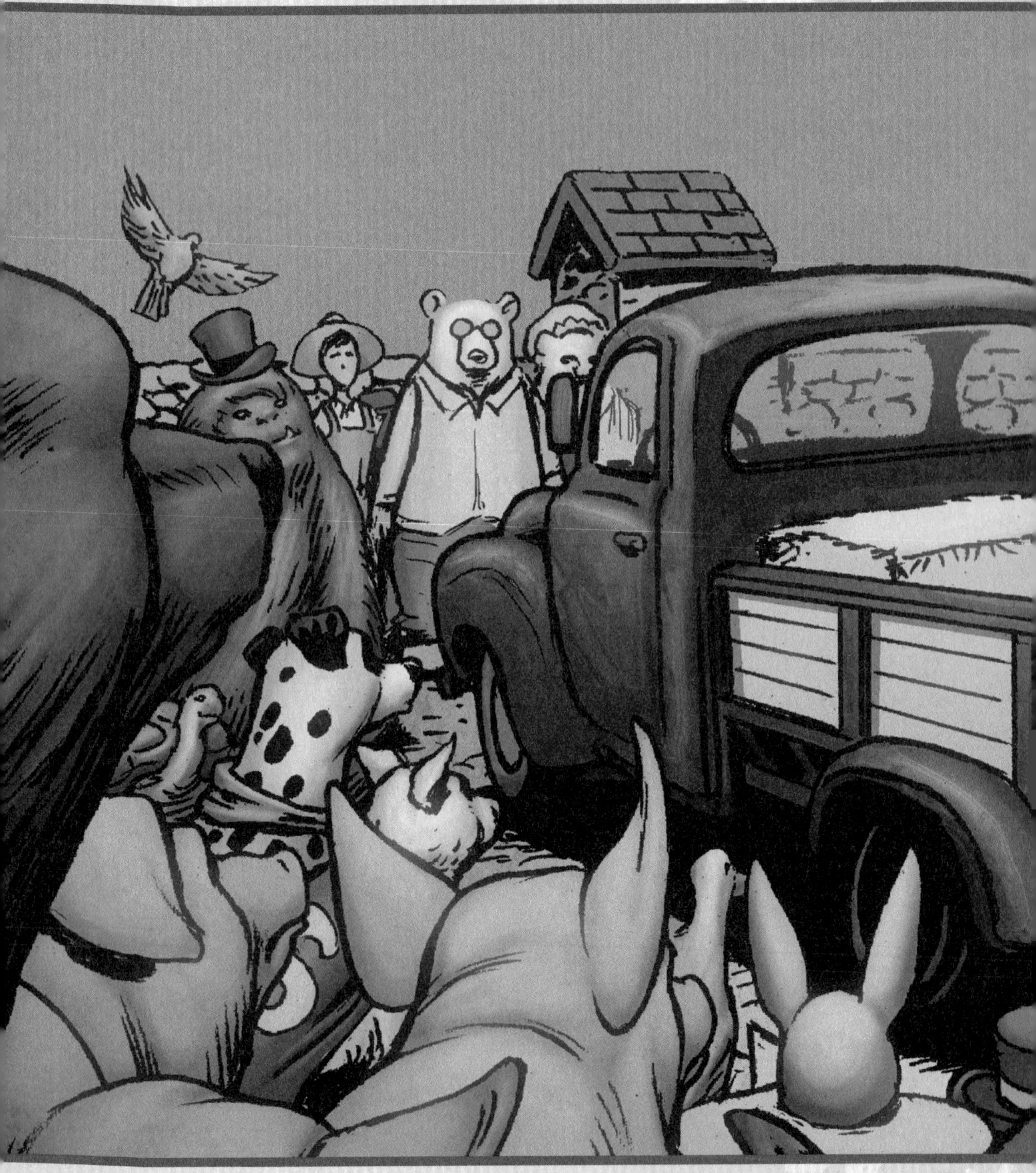

FAIREST

The Clamour for Glamour

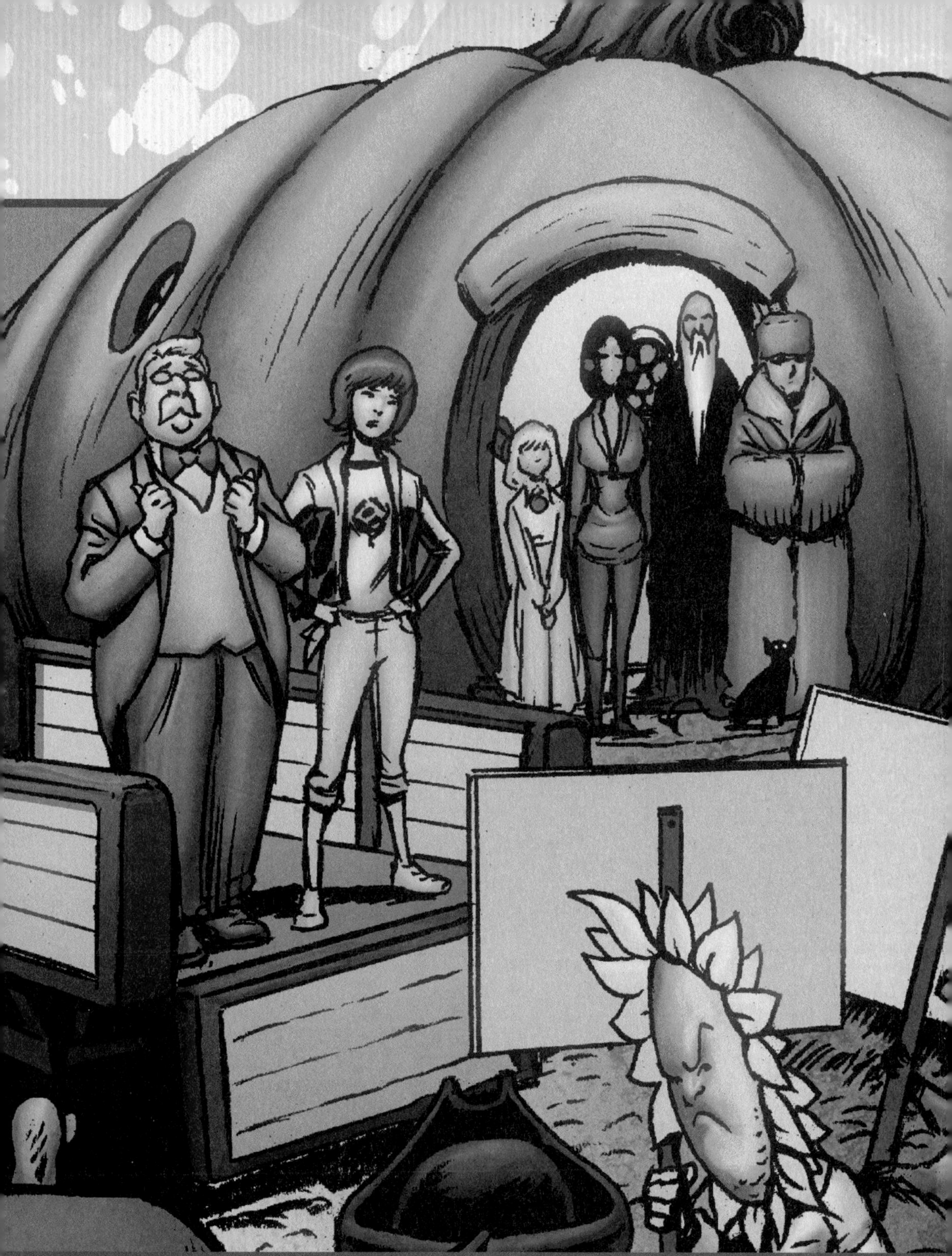

Mark Buckingham
Bill Willingham
WRITERS

Russ Braun
Meghan Hetrick
Andrew Pepoy
ARTISTS

Andrew Dalhouse
Lee Loughridge
Guy Major
COLORISTS

Todd Klein
LETTERER

Adam Hughes
COVER ART AND ORIGINAL SERIES COVERS

FAIREST CREATED BY **Bill Willingham**

FAIREST: THE CLAMOUR FOR GLAMOUR

Published by DC Comics. Copyright © 2015 Bill Willingham and DC Comics. All Rights Reserved.

Originally published in single magazine form in FAIREST 27-33. Copyright © 2014, 2015 Bill Willingham and DC Comics. All Rights Reserved. All characters, their distinctive likenesses and related elements featured in this publication are trademarks of Bill Willingham. VERTIGO is a trademark of DC Comics. The stories, characters and incidents featured in this publication are entirely fictional. DC Comics does not read or accept unsolicited submissions of ideas, stories or artwork.

DC Comics, 4000 Warner Blvd., Burbank, CA 91522
A Warner Bros. Entertainment Company.
Printed in the USA. First Printing.
ISBN: 978-1-4012-5426-1.

Library of Congress Cataloging-in-Publication Data

Buckingham, Mark, author.
Fairest. Volume 5, The Clamour for Glamour / Mark Buckingham ; Russ Braun.
    pages cm
ISBN 978-1-4012-5426-1 (paperback)
 1. Fairy tales—Comic Books, strips, etc. 2. Graphic novels. I. Braun, Russell, illustrator. II. Title. III. Title: The Clamour for Glamour
PN6728.F255B83 2015
741.5'973—dc23

2015008032

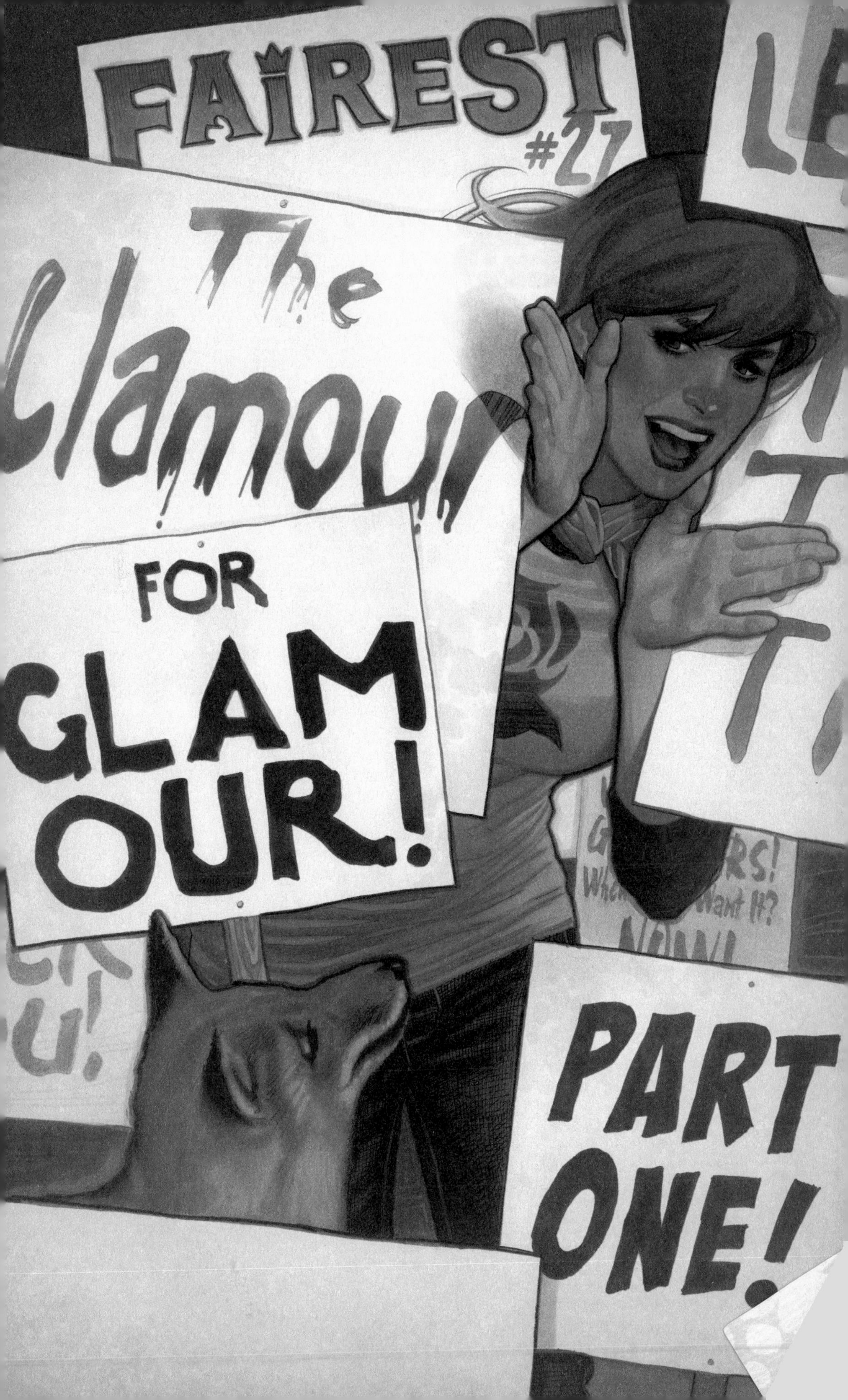
FAIREST
#27
The Glamour
FOR
GLAM
OUR!
PART
ONE!

"Did I mention I'm a knight and you're not?"

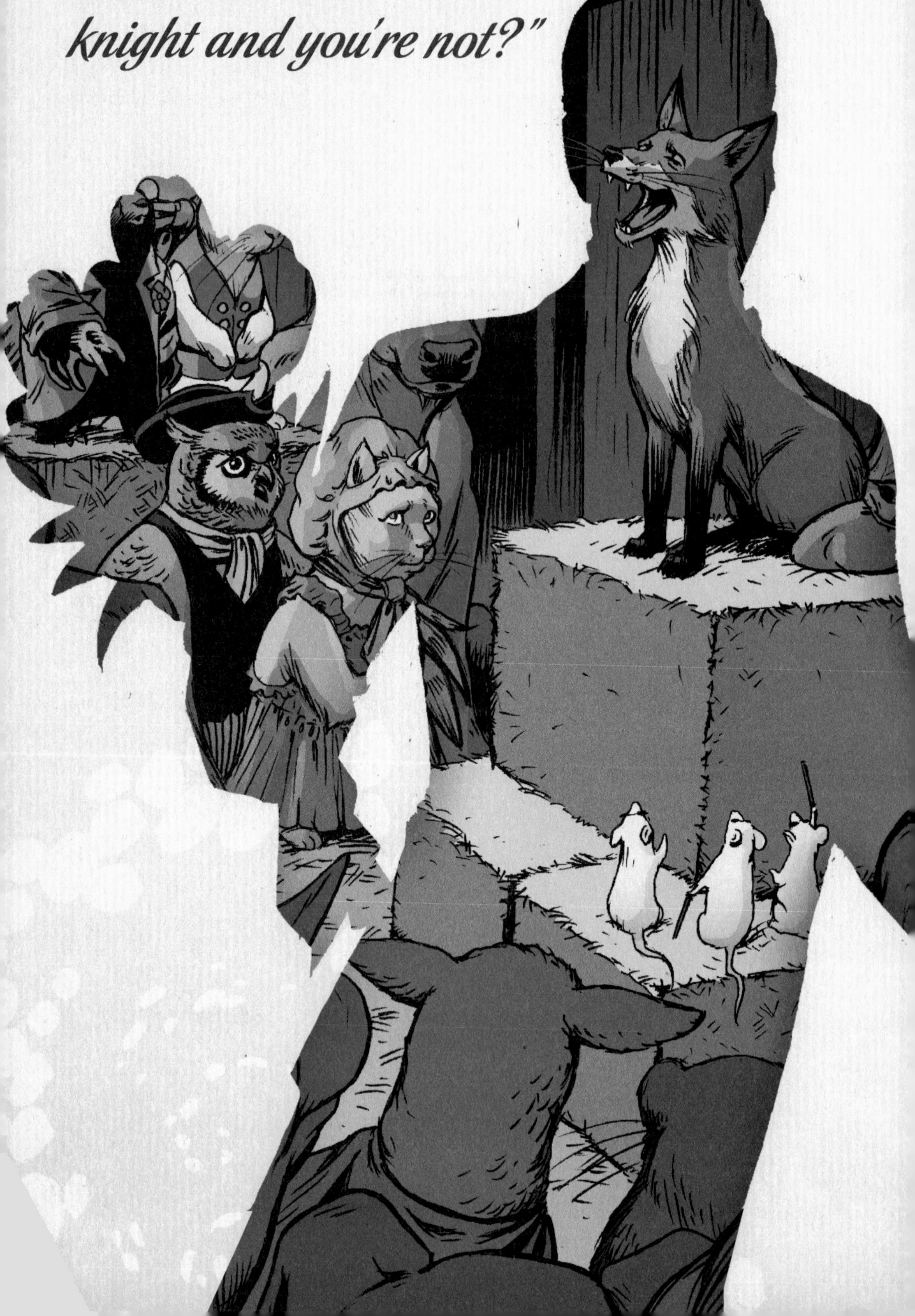

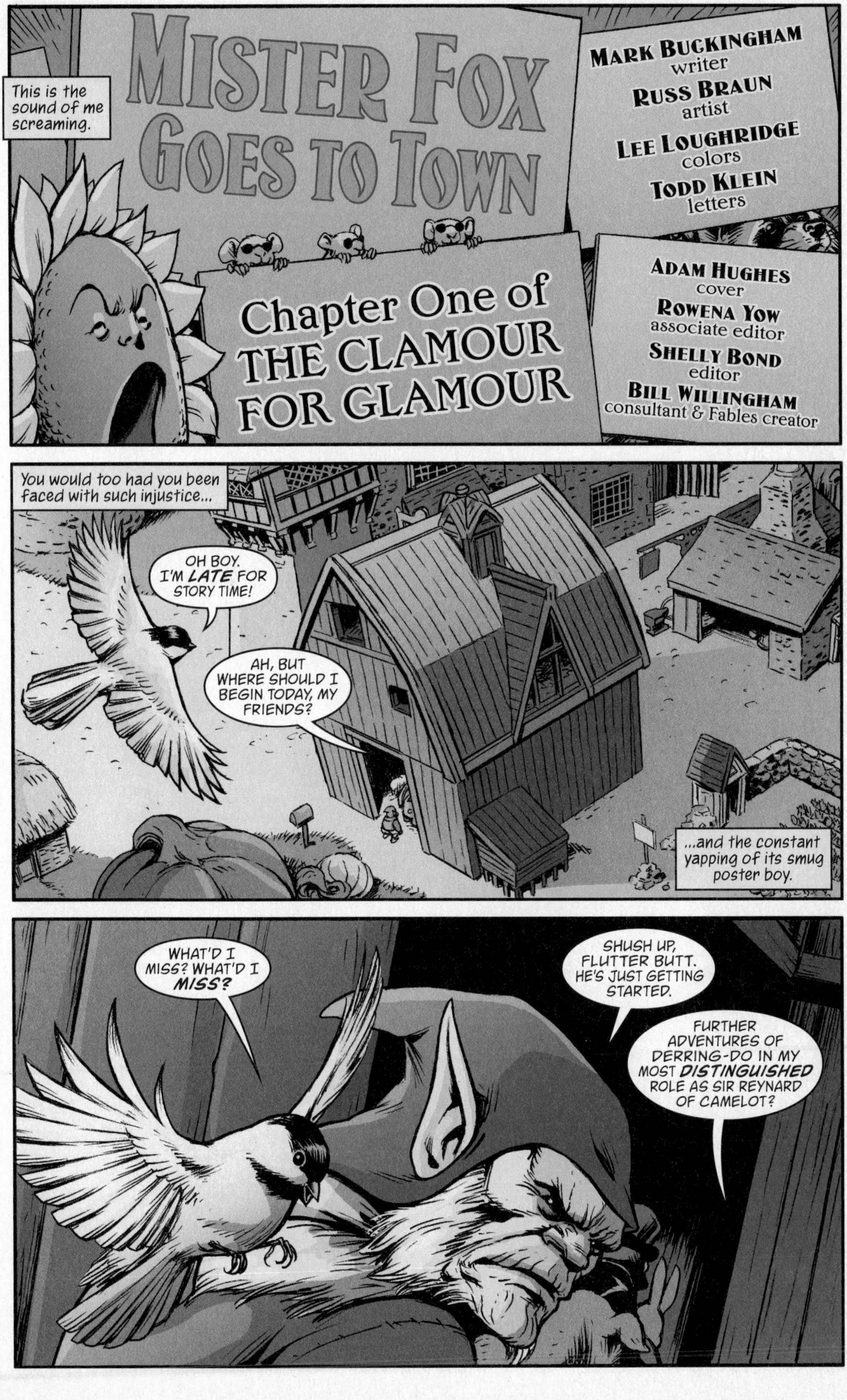

This is the sound of me screaming.
MISTER FOX GOES TO TOWN
MARK BUCKINGHAM writer
RUSS BRAUN artist
LEE LOUGHRIDGE colors
TODD KLEIN letters
Chapter One of THE CLAMOUR FOR GLAMOUR
ADAM HUGHES cover
ROWENA YOW associate editor
SHELLY BOND editor
BILL WILLINGHAM consultant & Fables creator
You would too had you been faced with such injustice...
OH BOY. I'M LATE FOR STORY TIME!
AH, BUT WHERE SHOULD I BEGIN TODAY, MY FRIENDS?
...and the constant yapping of its smug poster boy.
WHAT'D I MISS? WHAT'D I MISS?
SHUSH UP, FLUTTER BUTT. HE'S JUST GETTING STARTED.
FURTHER ADVENTURES OF DERRING-DO IN MY MOST DISTINGUISHED ROLE AS SIR REYNARD OF CAMELOT?

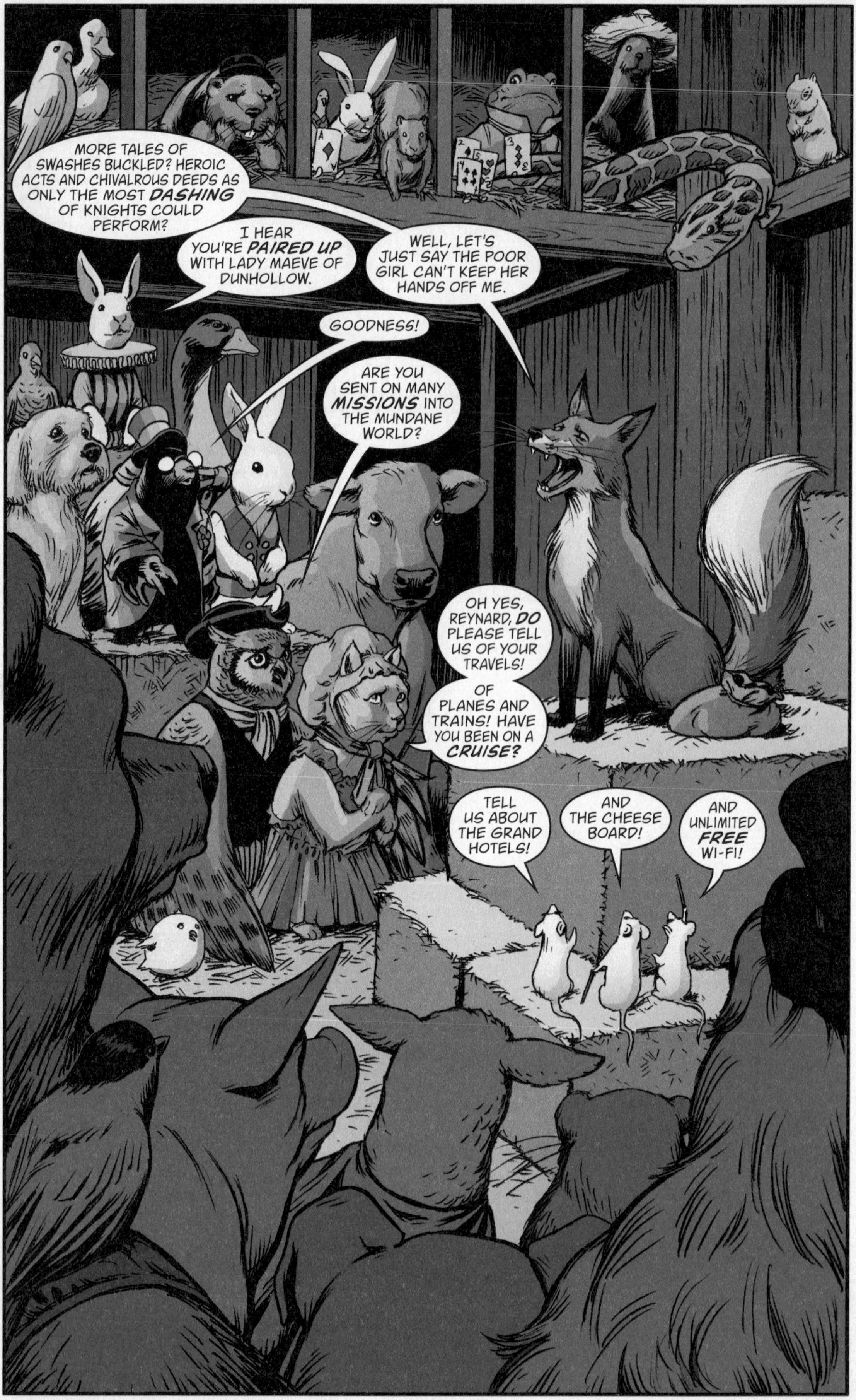
MORE TALES OF SWASHES BUCKLED? HEROIC ACTS AND CHIVALROUS DEEDS AS ONLY THE MOST DASHING OF KNIGHTS COULD PERFORM?
I HEAR YOU'RE PAIRED UP WITH LADY MAEVE OF DUNHOLLOW.
WELL, LET'S JUST SAY THE POOR GIRL CAN'T KEEP HER HANDS OFF ME.
GOODNESS!
ARE YOU SENT ON MANY MISSIONS INTO THE MUNDANE WORLD?
OH YES, REYNARD, DO PLEASE TELL US OF YOUR TRAVELS!
OF PLANES AND TRAINS! HAVE YOU BEEN ON A CRUISE?
TELL US ABOUT THE GRAND HOTELS!
AND THE CHEESE BOARD!
AND UNLIMITED FREE WI-FI!

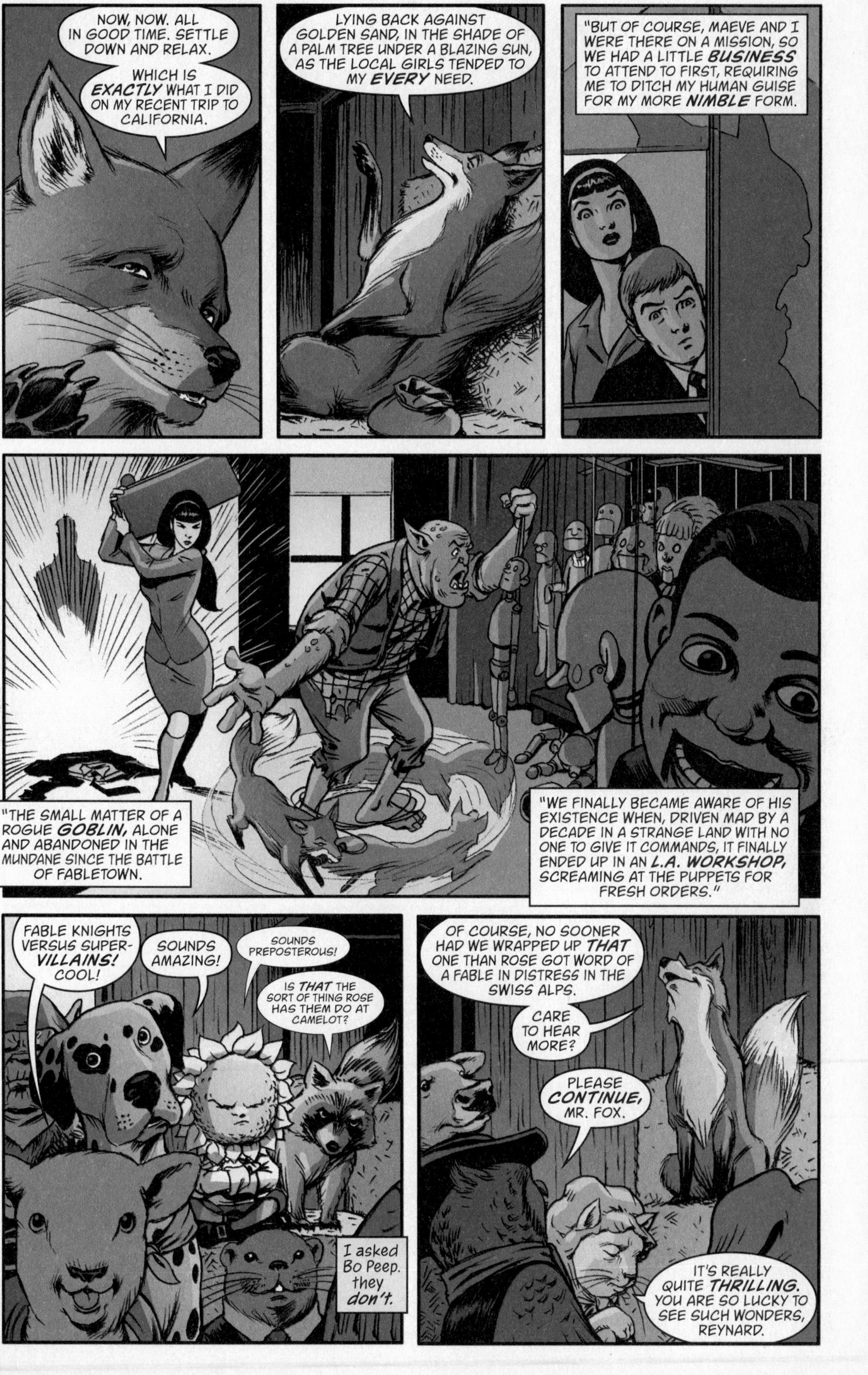
NOW, NOW. ALL IN GOOD TIME. SETTLE DOWN AND RELAX.
WHICH IS EXACTLY WHAT I DID ON MY RECENT TRIP TO CALIFORNIA.
LYING BACK AGAINST GOLDEN SAND, IN THE SHADE OF A PALM TREE UNDER A BLAZING SUN, AS THE LOCAL GIRLS TENDED TO MY EVERY NEED.
"BUT OF COURSE, MAEVE AND I WERE THERE ON A MISSION, SO WE HAD A LITTLE BUSINESS TO ATTEND TO FIRST, REQUIRING ME TO DITCH MY HUMAN GUISE FOR MY MORE NIMBLE FORM.
"THE SMALL MATTER OF A ROGUE GOBLIN, ALONE AND ABANDONED IN THE MUNDANE SINCE THE BATTLE OF FABLETOWN.
"WE FINALLY BECAME AWARE OF HIS EXISTENCE WHEN, DRIVEN MAD BY A DECADE IN A STRANGE LAND WITH NO ONE TO GIVE IT COMMANDS, IT FINALLY ENDED UP IN AN L.A. WORKSHOP, SCREAMING AT THE PUPPETS FOR FRESH ORDERS."
FABLE KNIGHTS VERSUS SUPER-VILLAINS! COOL!
SOUNDS AMAZING!
SOUNDS PREPOSTEROUS!
IS THAT THE SORT OF THING ROSE HAS THEM DO AT CAMELOT?
I asked Bo Peep. they don't.
OF COURSE, NO SOONER HAD WE WRAPPED UP THAT ONE THAN ROSE GOT WORD OF A FABLE IN DISTRESS IN THE SWISS ALPS.
CARE TO HEAR MORE?
PLEASE CONTINUE, MR. FOX.
IT'S REALLY QUITE THRILLING. YOU ARE SO LUCKY TO SEE SUCH WONDERS, REYNARD.

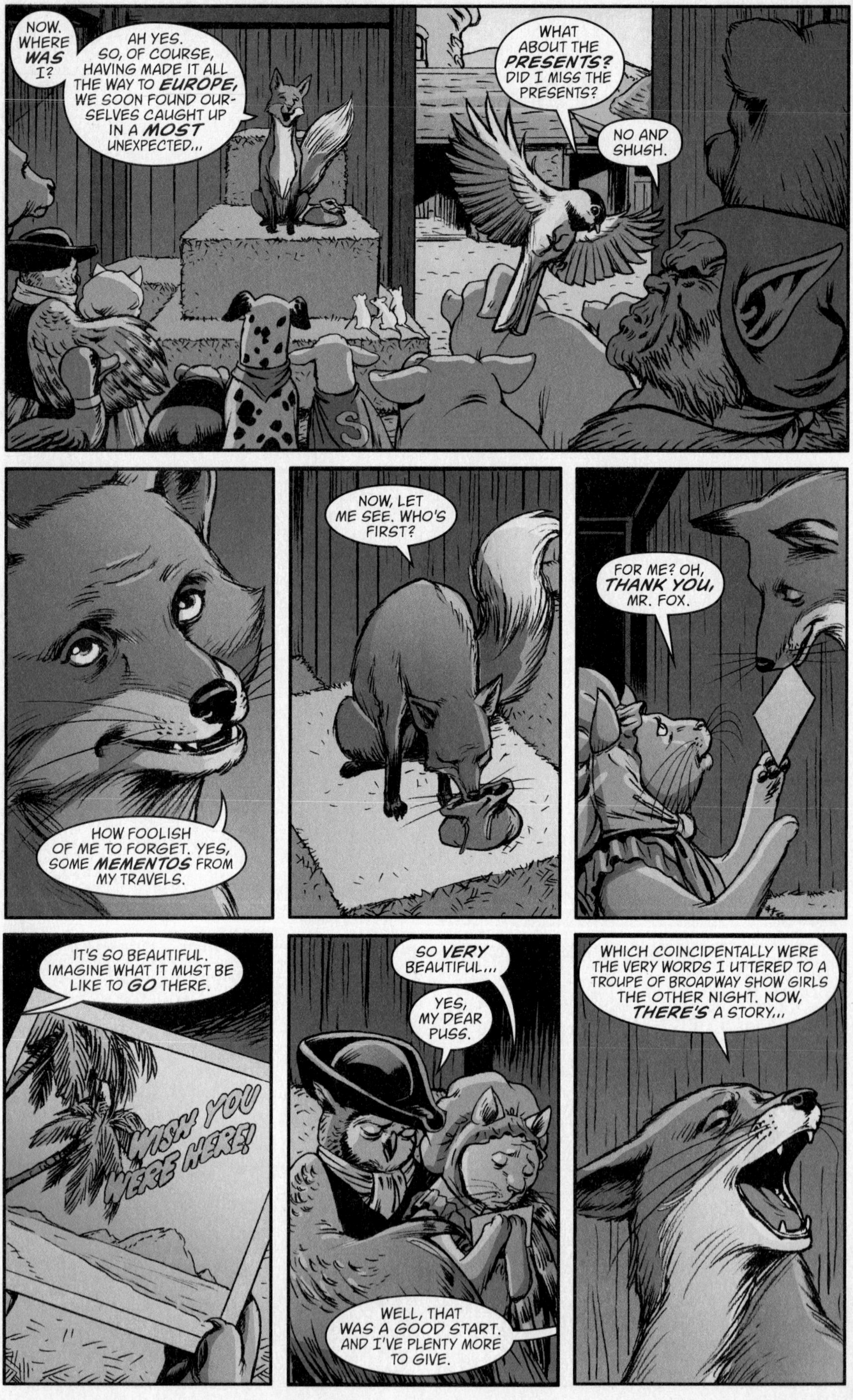
NOW. WHERE WAS I?
AH YES. SO, OF COURSE, HAVING MADE IT ALL THE WAY TO EUROPE, WE SOON FOUND OURSELVES CAUGHT UP IN A MOST UNEXPECTED...
WHAT ABOUT THE PRESENTS? DID I MISS THE PRESENTS?
NO AND SHUSH.
HOW FOOLISH OF ME TO FORGET. YES, SOME MEMENTOS FROM MY TRAVELS.
NOW, LET ME SEE. WHO'S FIRST?
FOR ME? OH, THANK YOU, MR. FOX.
IT'S SO BEAUTIFUL. IMAGINE WHAT IT MUST BE LIKE TO GO THERE.
WISH YOU WERE HERE!
SO VERY BEAUTIFUL...
YES, MY DEAR PUSS.
WELL, THAT WAS A GOOD START. AND I'VE PLENTY MORE TO GIVE.
WHICH COINCIDENTALLY WERE THE VERY WORDS I UTTERED TO A TROUPE OF BROADWAY SHOW GIRLS THE OTHER NIGHT. NOW, THERE'S A STORY...

THREE HOURS LATER...

THAT'S IT. I NEED A BREAK FROM REYNARD'S *INCESSANT* BOASTING.

I DON'T KNOW HOW THE OTHERS CAN *TAKE* IT.

DID YOU SEE THE WAY SUNFLOWER AND RACCOON WERE FUMING?

SIMMERING IN JEALOUSY.

ROASTING WITH RESENTMENT.

I SWEAR THEY'RE JUST ONE BRAG AWAY FROM HACKING THAT *SMUG* LITTLE SO-AND-SO INTO *BITS.*

STILL, I DON'T *BLAME* THEM FOR BEING ENVIOUS.

NOW THAT GLAMOURS ARE AVAILABLE FOR A SELECT FEW THAT THE HUMANS DEEM *WORTHY,* BUT WE'RE STILL *OVER-LOOKED.*

GLAMOURS. IT WAS ANNOYING ENOUGH WHEN OZMA GAVE REYNARD ONE IN FRONT OF US ALL.

NOW MISS RED IS HANDING THEM OUT TO ANY OF HER CAMELOT *KNIGHTS* WHO NEEDS THEM.

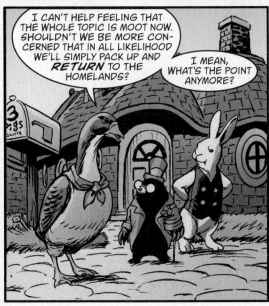

I CAN'T HELP FEELING THAT THE WHOLE TOPIC IS MOOT NOW. SHOULDN'T WE BE MORE CON-CERNED THAT IN ALL LIKELIHOOD WE'LL SIMPLY PACK UP AND *RETURN* TO THE HOMELANDS?

I MEAN, WHAT'S THE POINT ANYMORE?

ISN'T IT *ALL* GOING AWAY?

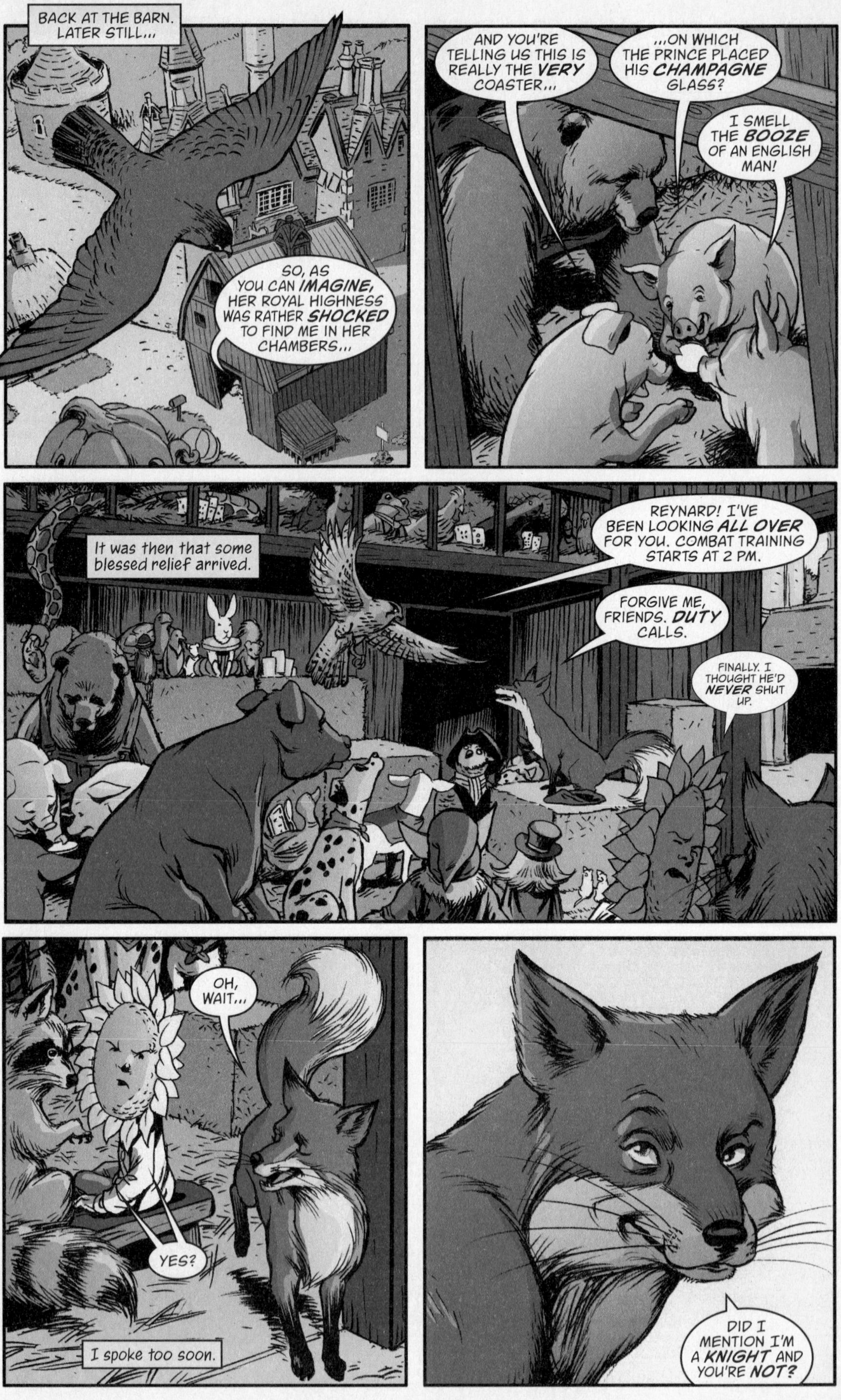
BACK AT THE BARN. LATER STILL...
SO, AS YOU CAN IMAGINE, HER ROYAL HIGHNESS WAS RATHER SHOCKED TO FIND ME IN HER CHAMBERS...
AND YOU'RE TELLING US THIS IS REALLY THE VERY COASTER...
...ON WHICH THE PRINCE PLACED HIS CHAMPAGNE GLASS?
I SMELL THE BOOZE OF AN ENGLISH MAN!
It was then that some blessed relief arrived.
REYNARD! I'VE BEEN LOOKING ALL OVER FOR YOU. COMBAT TRAINING STARTS AT 2 PM.
FORGIVE ME, FRIENDS. DUTY CALLS.
FINALLY. I THOUGHT HE'D NEVER SHUT UP.
OH, WAIT...
YES?
I spoke too soon.
DID I MENTION I'M A KNIGHT AND YOU'RE NOT?

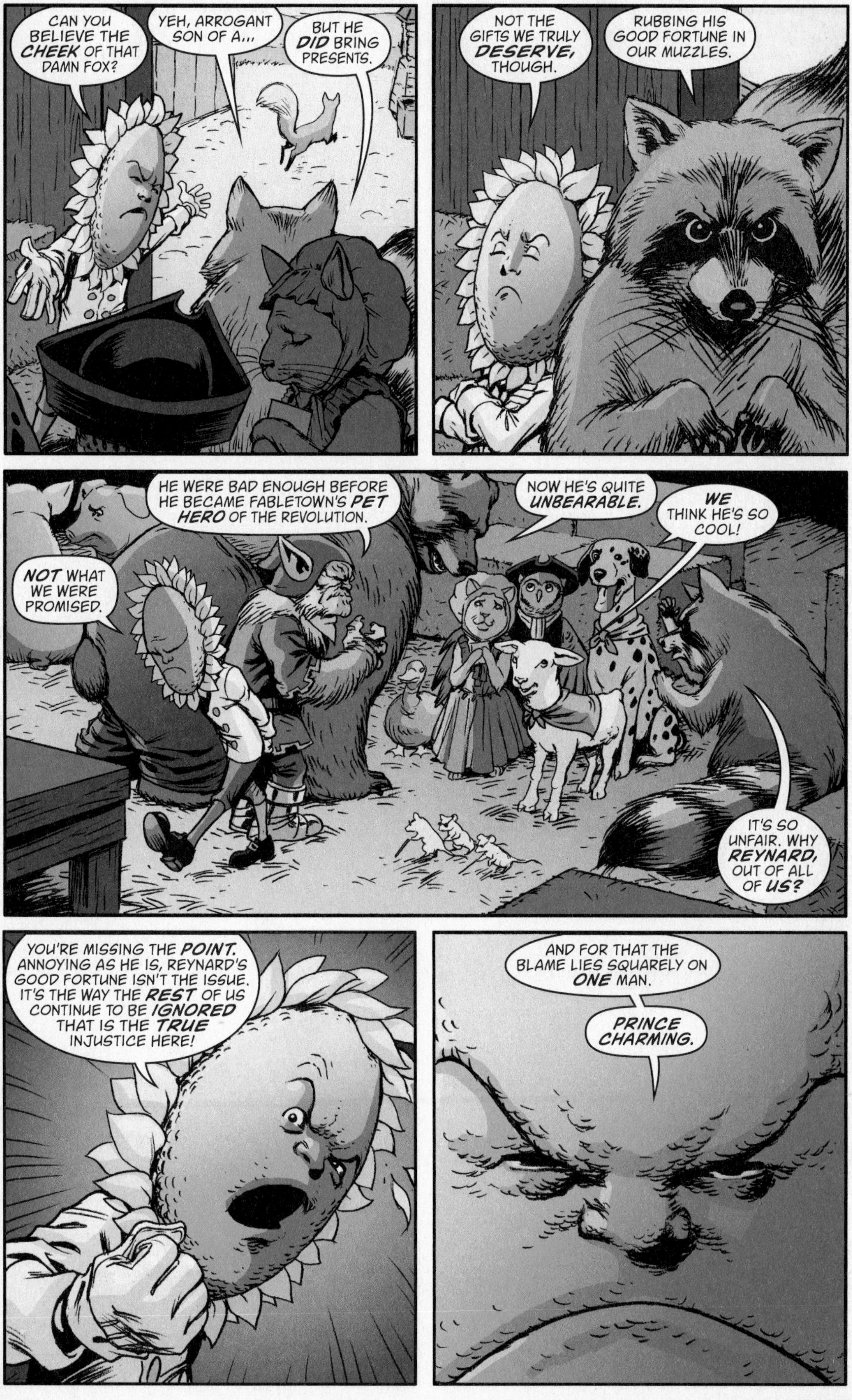

CAN YOU BELIEVE THE CHEEK OF THAT DAMN FOX?
YEH, ARROGANT SON OF A...
BUT HE DID BRING PRESENTS.
NOT THE GIFTS WE TRULY DESERVE, THOUGH.
RUBBING HIS GOOD FORTUNE IN OUR MUZZLES.
HE WERE BAD ENOUGH BEFORE HE BECAME FABLETOWN'S PET HERO OF THE REVOLUTION.
NOW HE'S QUITE UNBEARABLE.
WE THINK HE'S SO COOL!
NOT WHAT WE WERE PROMISED.
IT'S SO UNFAIR. WHY REYNARD, OUT OF ALL OF US?
YOU'RE MISSING THE POINT. ANNOYING AS HE IS, REYNARD'S GOOD FORTUNE ISN'T THE ISSUE. IT'S THE WAY THE REST OF US CONTINUE TO BE IGNORED THAT IS THE TRUE INJUSTICE HERE!
AND FOR THAT THE BLAME LIES SQUARELY ON ONE MAN.
PRINCE CHARMING.

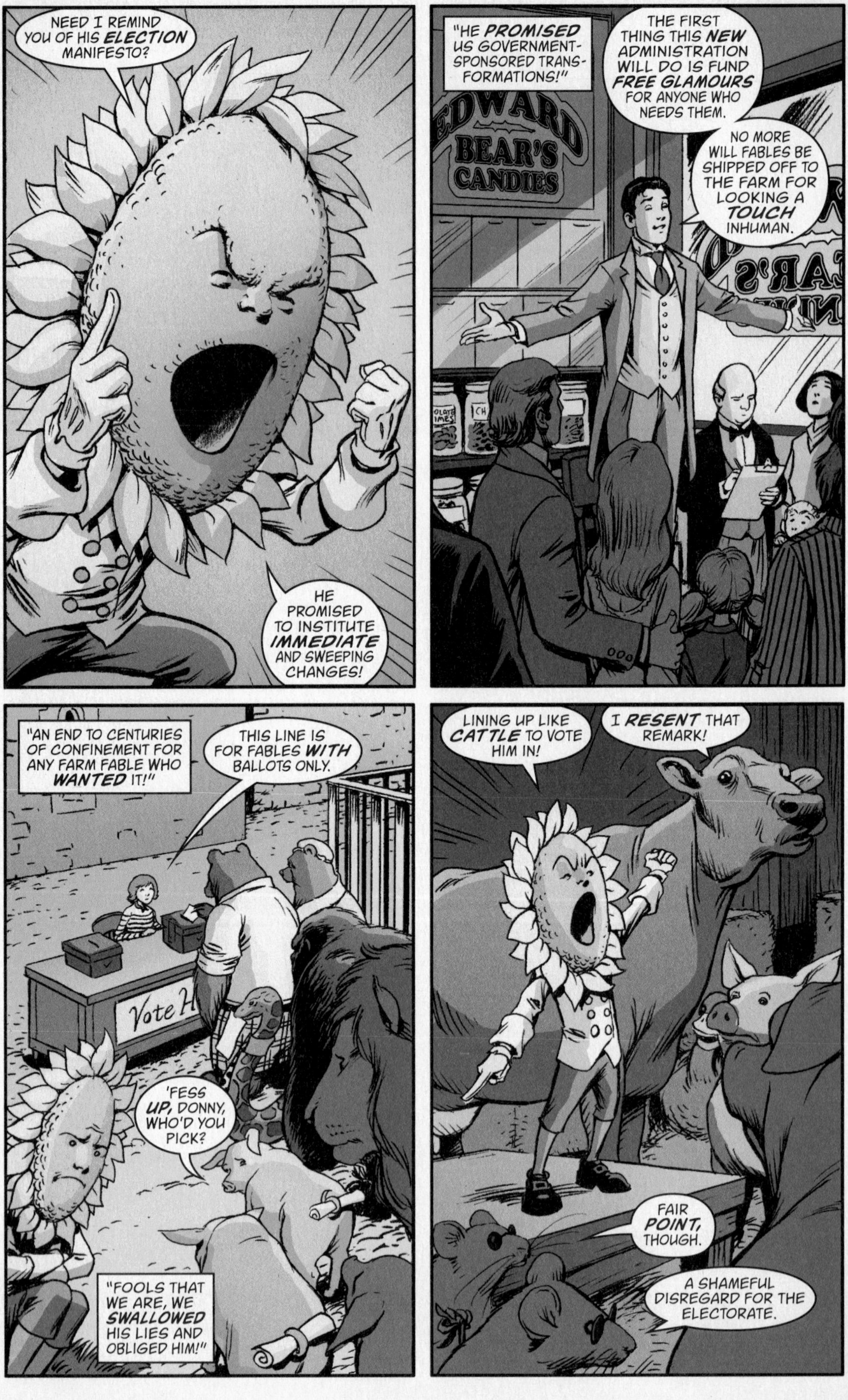
NEED I REMIND YOU OF HIS ELECTION MANIFESTO?
HE PROMISED TO INSTITUTE IMMEDIATE AND SWEEPING CHANGES!
"HE PROMISED US GOVERNMENT-SPONSORED TRANS-FORMATIONS!"
THE FIRST THING THIS NEW ADMINISTRATION WILL DO IS FUND FREE GLAMOURS FOR ANYONE WHO NEEDS THEM.
NO MORE WILL FABLES BE SHIPPED OFF TO THE FARM FOR LOOKING A TOUCH INHUMAN.
EDWARD BEAR'S CANDIES
"AN END TO CENTURIES OF CONFINEMENT FOR ANY FARM FABLE WHO WANTED IT!"
THIS LINE IS FOR FABLES WITH BALLOTS ONLY.
'FESS UP, DONNY, WHO'D YOU PICK?
"FOOLS THAT WE ARE, WE SWALLOWED HIS LIES AND OBLIGED HIM!"
LINING UP LIKE CATTLE TO VOTE HIM IN!
I RESENT THAT REMARK!
FAIR POINT, THOUGH.
A SHAMEFUL DISREGARD FOR THE ELECTORATE.

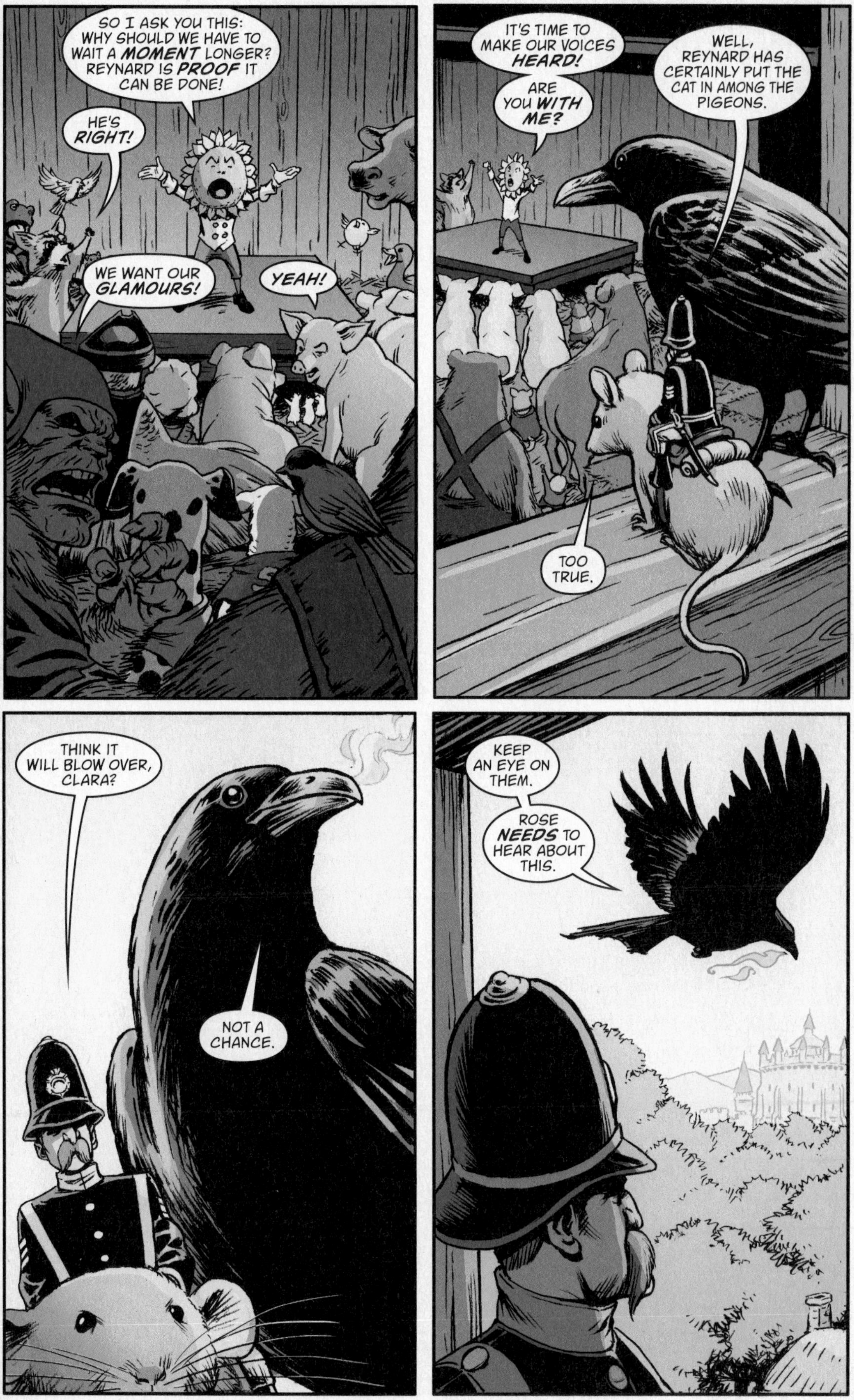
SO I ASK YOU THIS: WHY SHOULD WE HAVE TO WAIT A **MOMENT** LONGER? REYNARD IS **PROOF** IT CAN BE DONE!
HE'S **RIGHT!**
WE WANT OUR **GLAMOURS!**
YEAH!
IT'S TIME TO MAKE OUR VOICES **HEARD!**
ARE YOU **WITH ME?**
WELL, REYNARD HAS CERTAINLY PUT THE CAT IN AMONG THE PIGEONS.
TOO TRUE.
THINK IT WILL BLOW OVER, CLARA?
NOT A CHANCE.
KEEP AN EYE ON THEM.
ROSE **NEEDS** TO HEAR ABOUT THIS.

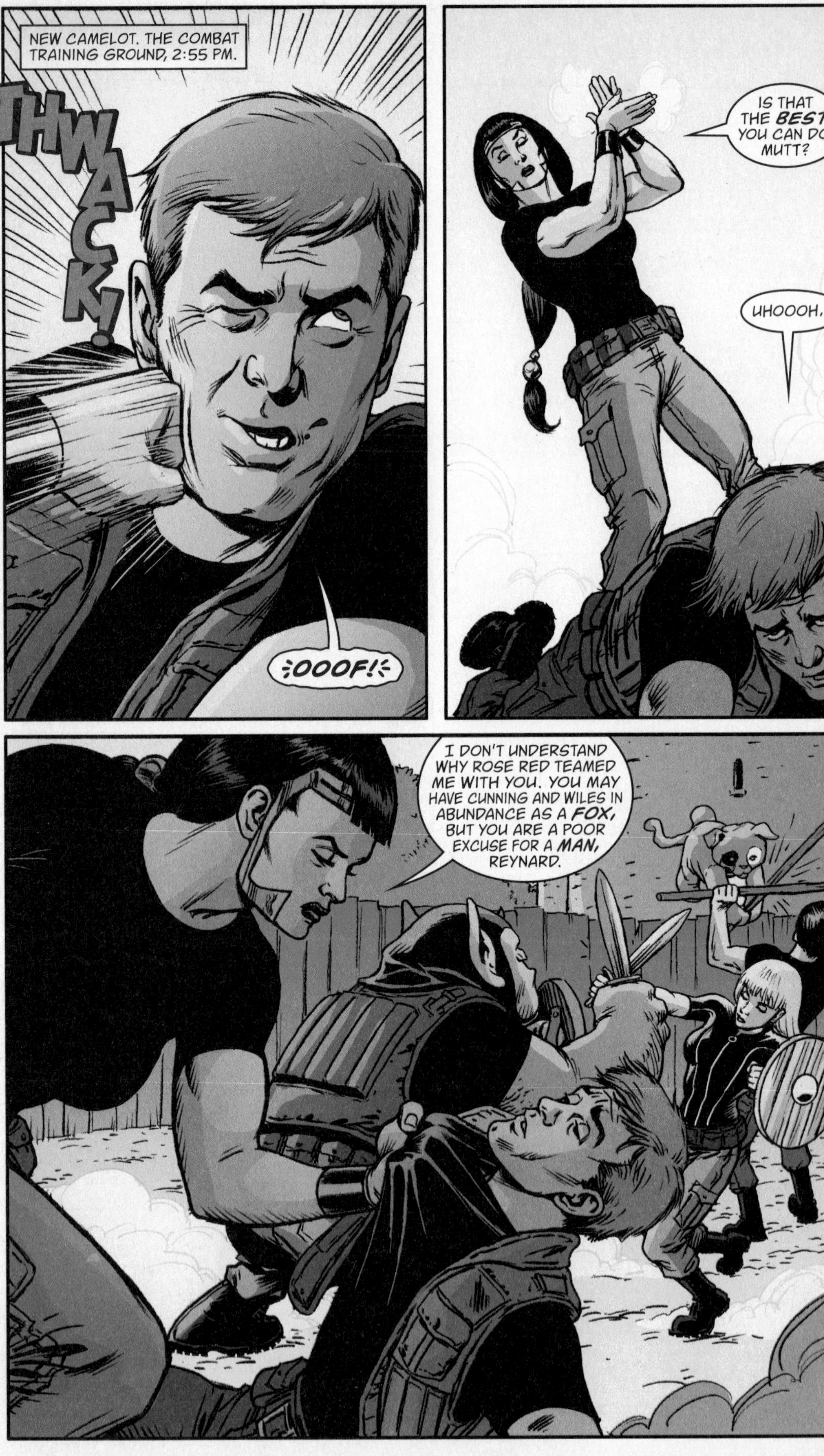

NEW CAMELOT. THE COMBAT TRAINING GROUND, 2:55 PM.
THWACK!
OOOF!
IS THAT THE BEST YOU CAN DO, MUTT?
UHOOOH...
I DON'T UNDERSTAND WHY ROSE RED TEAMED ME WITH YOU. YOU MAY HAVE CUNNING AND WILES IN ABUNDANCE AS A FOX, BUT YOU ARE A POOR EXCUSE FOR A MAN, REYNARD.

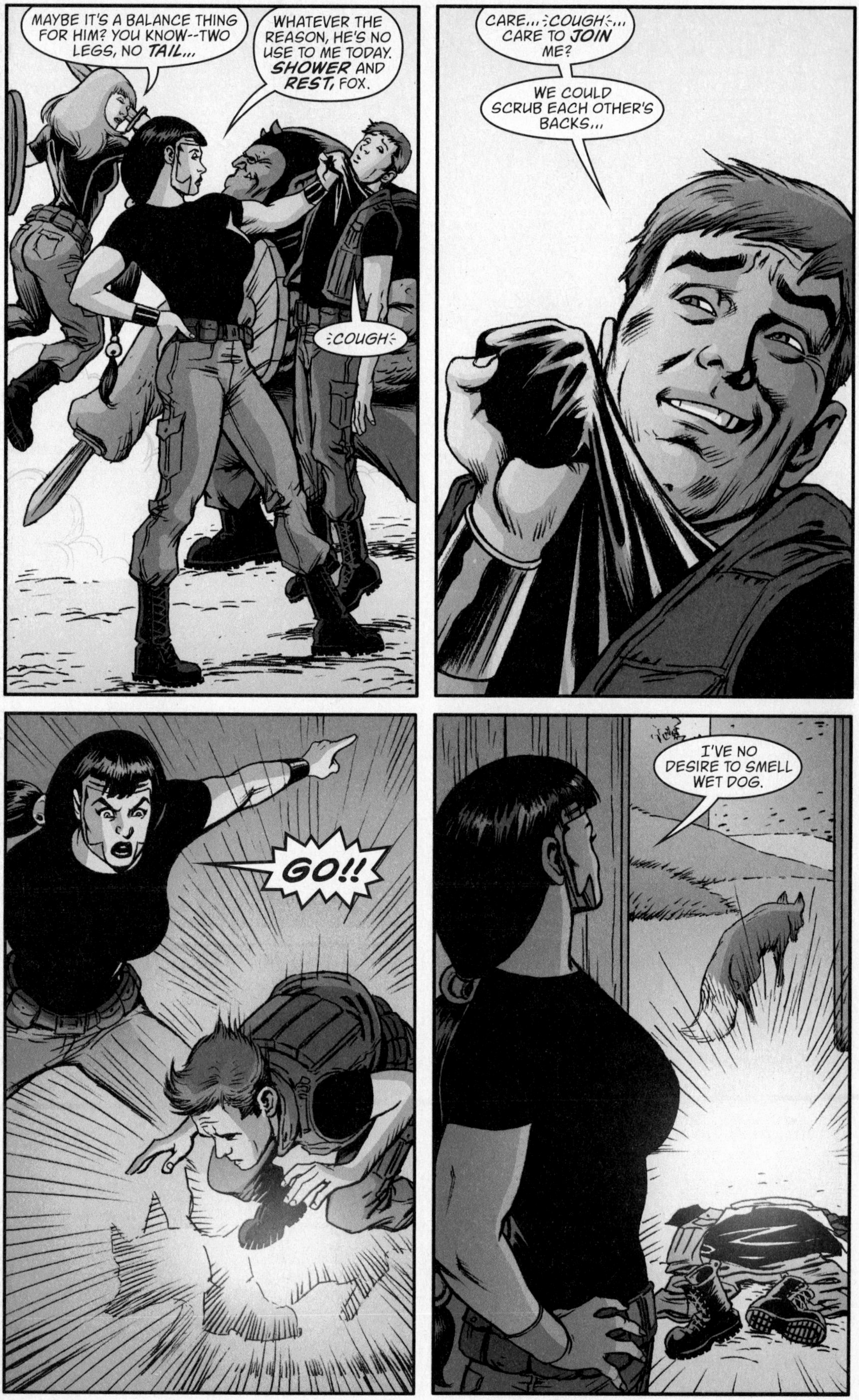
MAYBE IT'S A BALANCE THING FOR HIM? YOU KNOW--TWO LEGS, NO TAIL...
WHATEVER THE REASON, HE'S NO USE TO ME TODAY. SHOWER AND REST, FOX.
COUGH
CARE... COUGH... CARE TO JOIN ME?
WE COULD SCRUB EACH OTHER'S BACKS...
GO!!
I'VE NO DESIRE TO SMELL WET DOG.

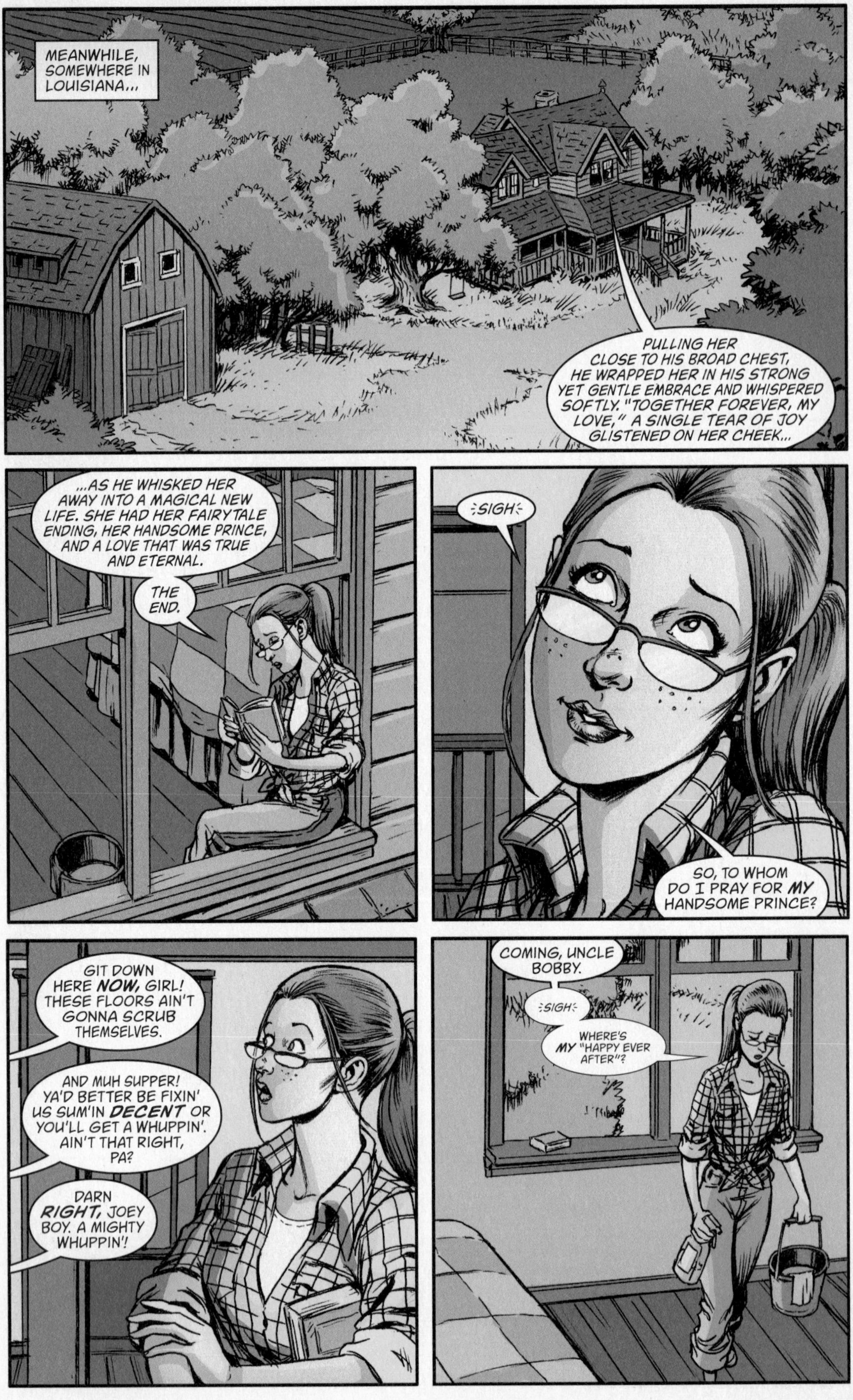
MEANWHILE, SOMEWHERE IN LOUISIANA...
PULLING HER CLOSE TO HIS BROAD CHEST, HE WRAPPED HER IN HIS STRONG YET GENTLE EMBRACE AND WHISPERED SOFTLY. "TOGETHER FOREVER, MY LOVE," A SINGLE TEAR OF JOY GLISTENED ON HER CHEEK...
...AS HE WHISKED HER AWAY INTO A MAGICAL NEW LIFE. SHE HAD HER FAIRYTALE ENDING, HER HANDSOME PRINCE, AND A LOVE THAT WAS TRUE AND ETERNAL.
THE END.
SIGH
SO, TO WHOM DO I PRAY FOR MY HANDSOME PRINCE?
GIT DOWN HERE NOW, GIRL! THESE FLOORS AIN'T GONNA SCRUB THEMSELVES.
AND MUH SUPPER! YA'D BETTER BE FIXIN' US SUM'IN DECENT OR YOU'LL GET A WHUPPIN'. AIN'T THAT RIGHT, PA?
DARN RIGHT, JOEY BOY. A MIGHTY WHUPPIN'!
COMING, UNCLE BOBBY.
SIGH
WHERE'S MY "HAPPY EVER AFTER"?

NEW CAMELOT.

:SIGH:

WHO AM I KIDDING?

I'M NO KNIGHT. NO GLOBE-TROTTING ADVENTURER. I'M A *FOX* MASQUERADING AS A MAN.

I PUT ON THIS SUIT OF PINK FLESH AND WATCH MY CUNNING AND GUILE *EVAPORATE* AS I BECOME ONE OF THOSE LUMBERING, HAIRLESS APES. NO OFFENSE MEANT TO *APES,* OF COURSE.

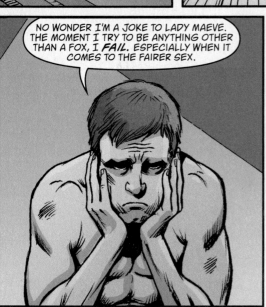

NO WONDER I'M A JOKE TO LADY MAEVE. THE MOMENT I TRY TO BE ANYTHING OTHER THAN A FOX, I *FAIL.* ESPECIALLY WHEN IT COMES TO THE FAIRER SEX.

"THE CLOSEST THING TO BEING WITH A WOMAN I'VE EXPERIENCED WAS DINNER WITH *PRINCESS ALDER.* RETCHING AFTER KISSING A PLANT THAT TASTED LIKE *MANURE* CAN HARDLY BE SEEN AS SUCCESS IN THAT DEPARTMENT EITHER."

IF ONLY I COULD HARNESS MY TRUE NATURE IN THIS FORM. TO FIND A WOMAN WHO TRULY *INSPIRES* MY CONFIDENCE, MY HEROISM, BUT I CAN THINK OF NO ONE,,,

,,,EXCEPT OF COURSE FOR,,,

,,,FOR,,,

,,,NO. I COULDN'T,,,

,,,COULD I?

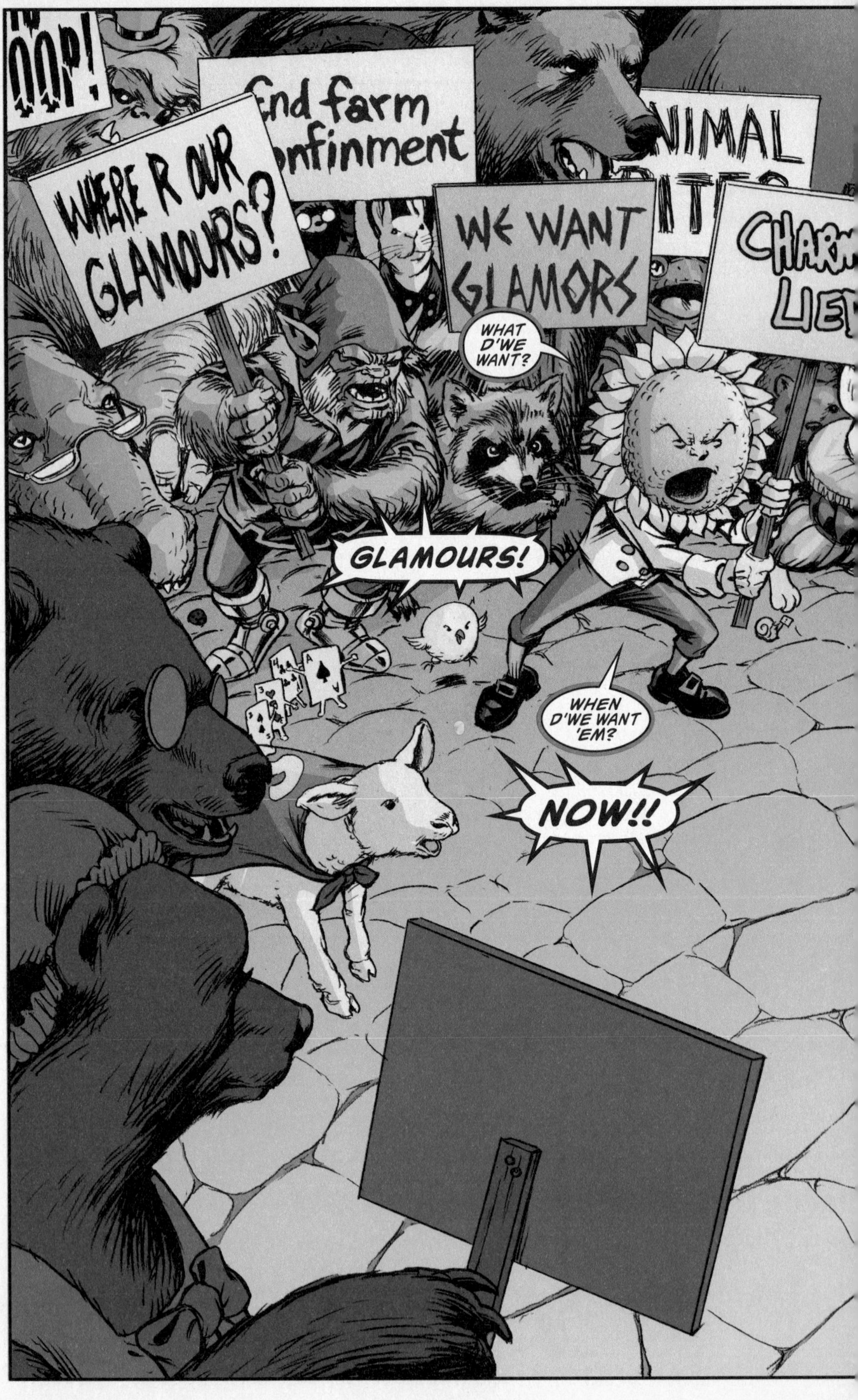
OOP!
End farm confinment
WHERE R OUR GLAMOURS?
WE WANT GLAMORS
CHARM LIE
WHAT D'WE WANT?
GLAMOURS!
WHEN D'WE WANT 'EM?
NOW!!

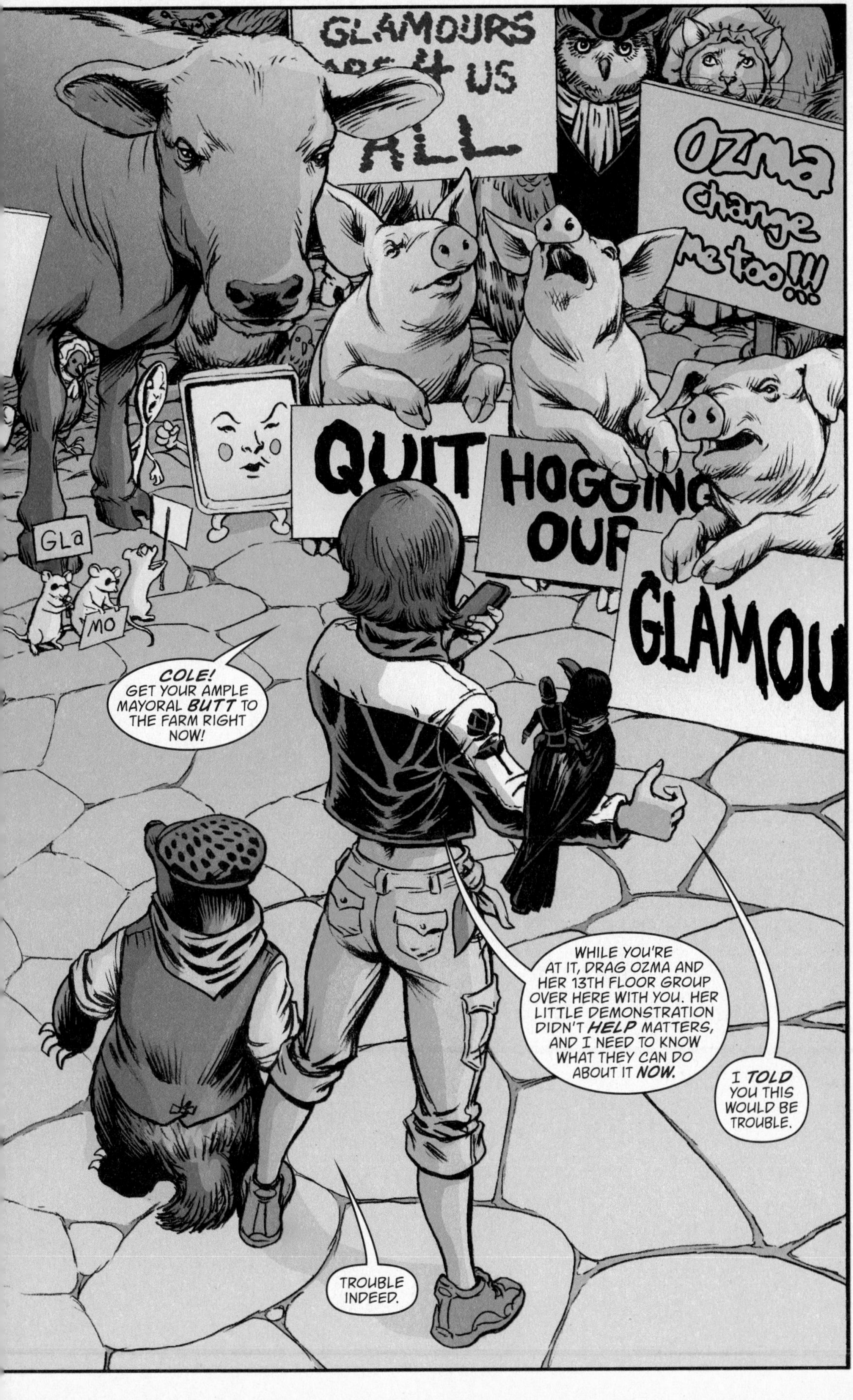
GLAMOURS
4 US
ALL
OZMA
change
me too!!!
Gla
MO
QUIT
HOGGING
OUR
GLAMOU
COLE! GET YOUR AMPLE MAYORAL BUTT TO THE FARM RIGHT NOW!
WHILE YOU'RE AT IT, DRAG OZMA AND HER 13TH FLOOR GROUP OVER HERE WITH YOU. HER LITTLE DEMONSTRATION DIDN'T HELP MATTERS, AND I NEED TO KNOW WHAT THEY CAN DO ABOUT IT NOW.
I TOLD YOU THIS WOULD BE TROUBLE.
TROUBLE INDEED.

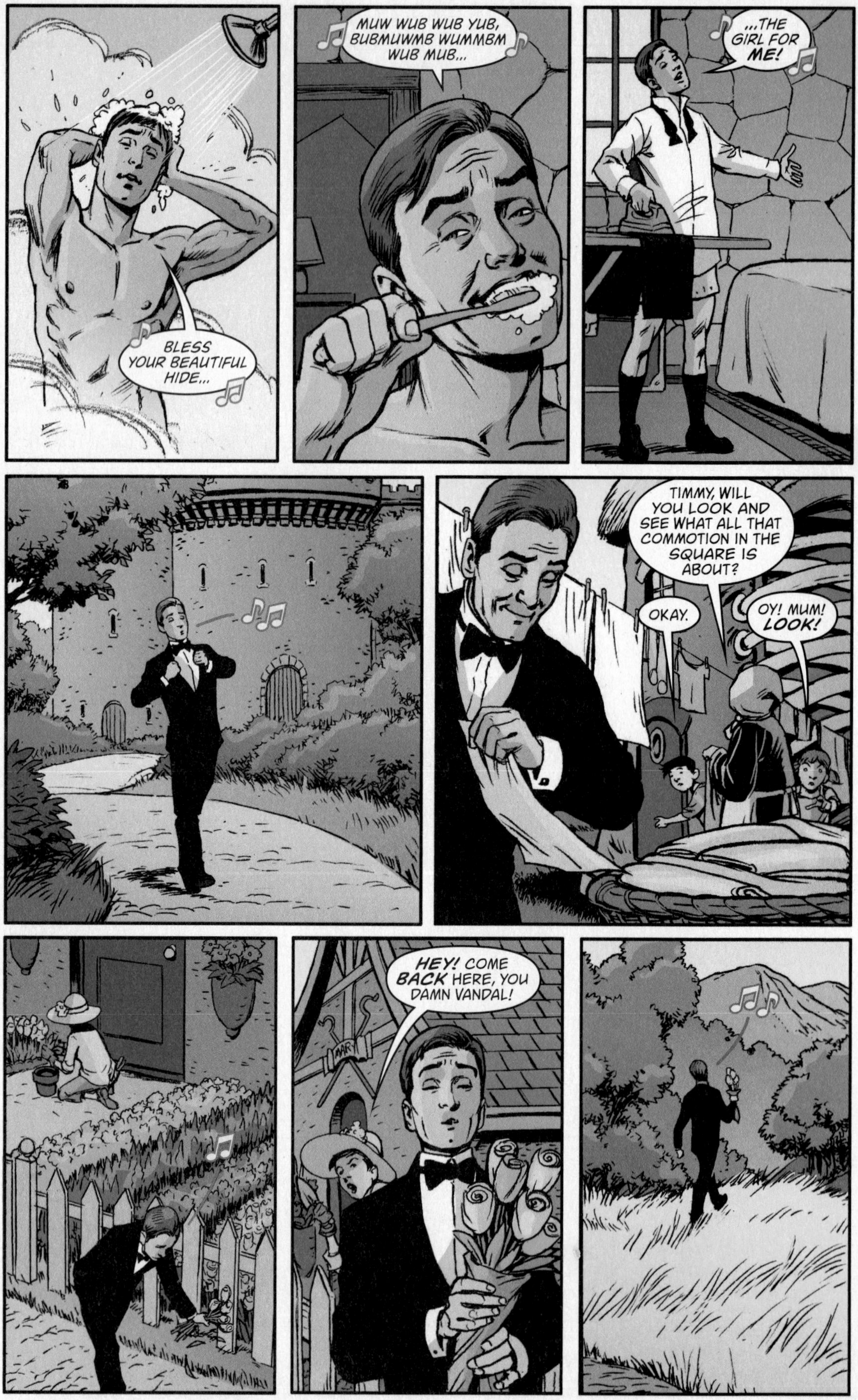
BLESS YOUR BEAUTIFUL HIDE...
MUW WUB WUB YUB, BUBMUWMB WUMMBM WUB MUB...
...THE GIRL FOR ME!
TIMMY, WILL YOU LOOK AND SEE WHAT ALL THAT COMMOTION IN THE SQUARE IS ABOUT?
OKAY.
OY! MUM! LOOK!
HEY! COME BACK HERE, YOU DAMN VANDAL!

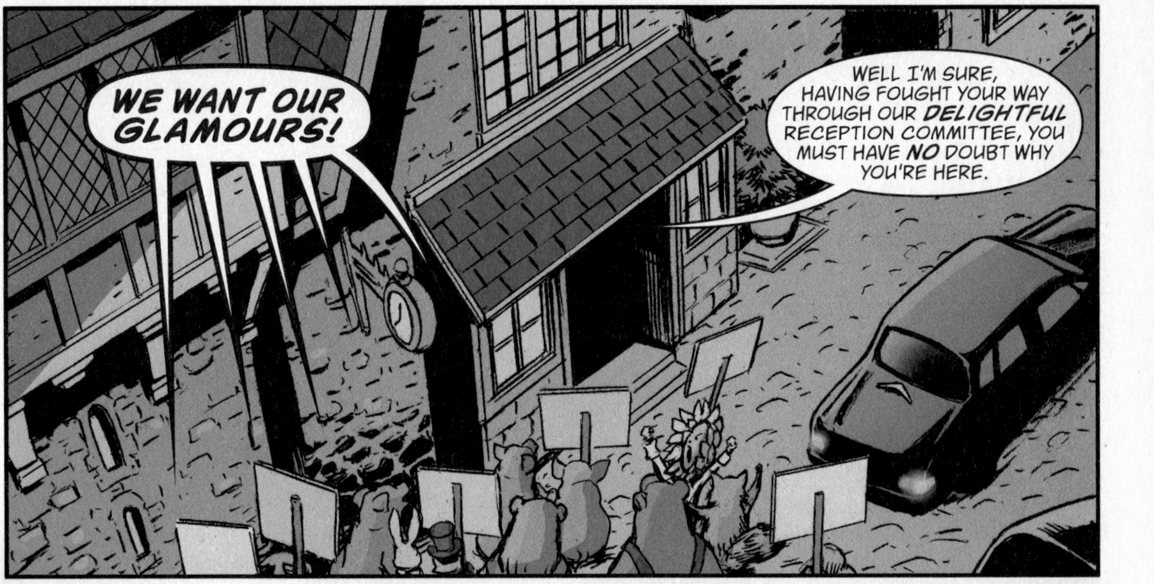
WE WANT OUR GLAMOURS!
WELL I'M SURE, HAVING FOUGHT YOUR WAY THROUGH OUR DELIGHTFUL RECEPTION COMMITTEE, YOU MUST HAVE NO DOUBT WHY YOU'RE HERE.

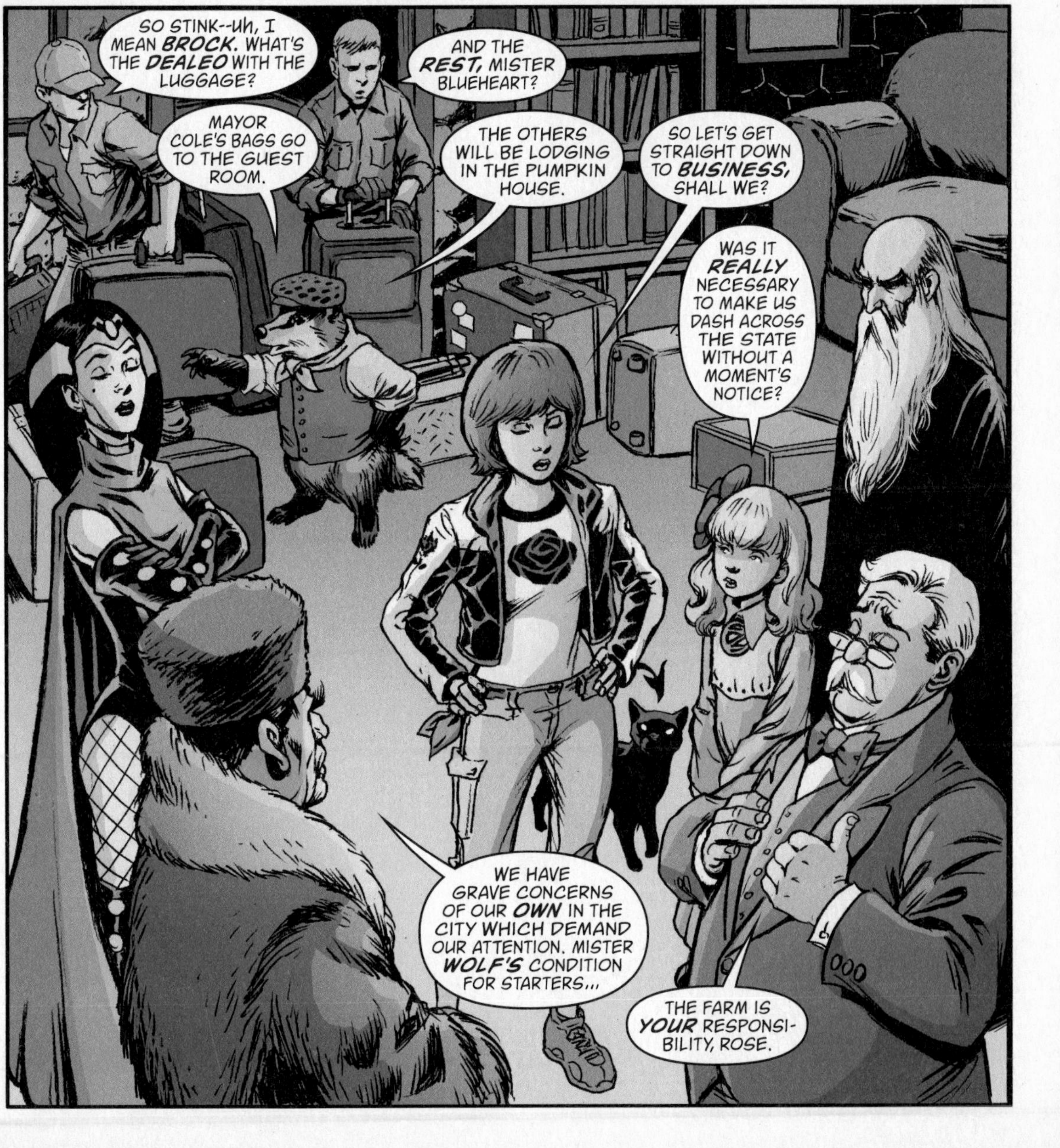
SO STINK--uh, I MEAN BROCK. WHAT'S THE DEALEO WITH THE LUGGAGE?
MAYOR COLE'S BAGS GO TO THE GUEST ROOM.
AND THE REST, MISTER BLUEHEART?
THE OTHERS WILL BE LODGING IN THE PUMPKIN HOUSE.
SO LET'S GET STRAIGHT DOWN TO BUSINESS, SHALL WE?
WAS IT REALLY NECESSARY TO MAKE US DASH ACROSS THE STATE WITHOUT A MOMENT'S NOTICE?
WE HAVE GRAVE CONCERNS OF OUR OWN IN THE CITY WHICH DEMAND OUR ATTENTION. MISTER WOLF'S CONDITION FOR STARTERS...
THE FARM IS YOUR RESPONSI-BILITY, ROSE.

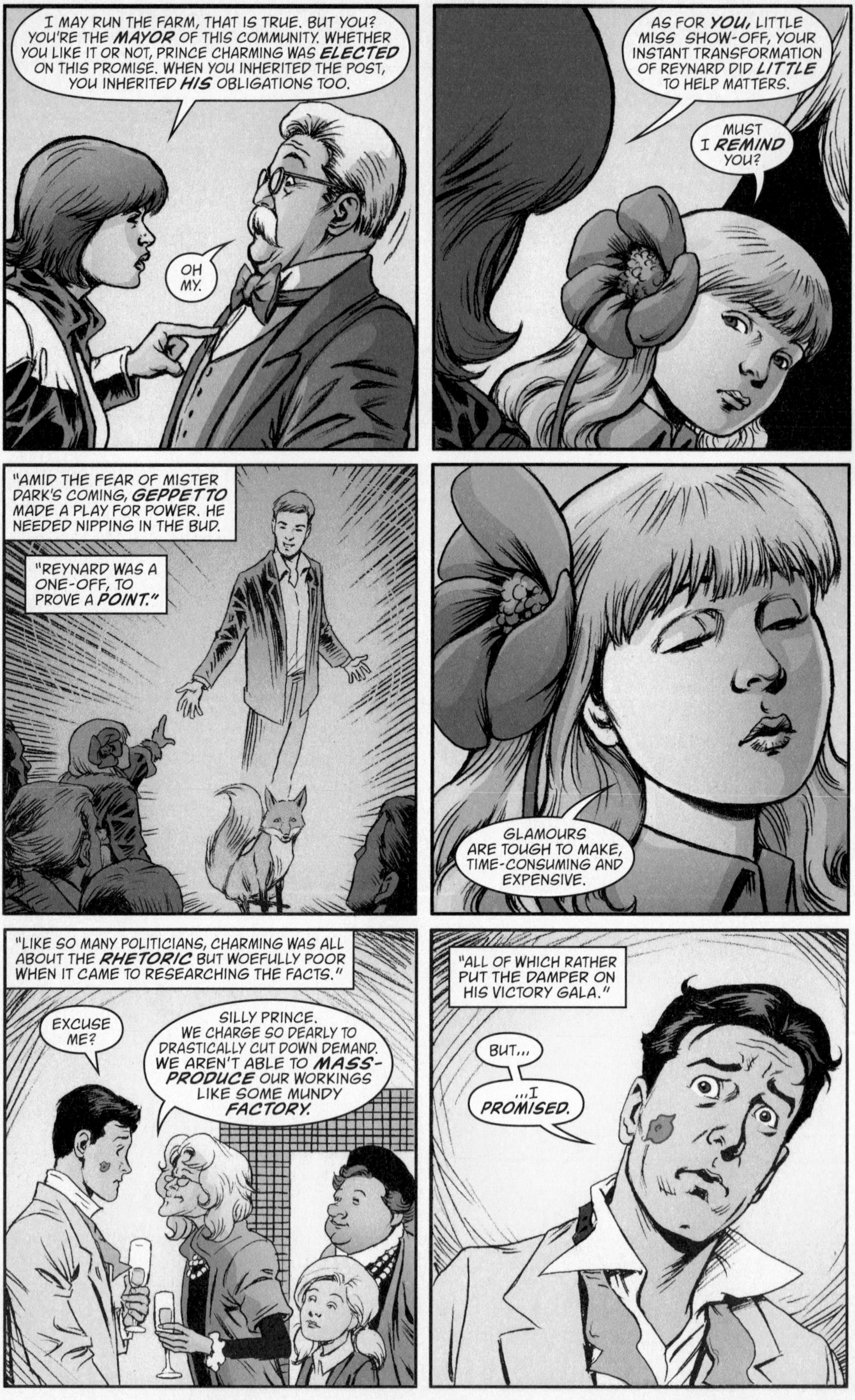
I MAY RUN THE FARM, THAT IS TRUE. BUT YOU? YOU'RE THE MAYOR OF THIS COMMUNITY. WHETHER YOU LIKE IT OR NOT, PRINCE CHARMING WAS ELECTED ON THIS PROMISE. WHEN YOU INHERITED THE POST, YOU INHERITED HIS OBLIGATIONS TOO.
OH MY.
AS FOR YOU, LITTLE MISS SHOW-OFF, YOUR INSTANT TRANSFORMATION OF REYNARD DID LITTLE TO HELP MATTERS.
MUST I REMIND YOU?
"AMID THE FEAR OF MISTER DARK'S COMING, GEPPETTO MADE A PLAY FOR POWER. HE NEEDED NIPPING IN THE BUD.
"REYNARD WAS A ONE-OFF, TO PROVE A POINT."
GLAMOURS ARE TOUGH TO MAKE, TIME-CONSUMING AND EXPENSIVE.
"LIKE SO MANY POLITICIANS, CHARMING WAS ALL ABOUT THE RHETORIC BUT WOEFULLY POOR WHEN IT CAME TO RESEARCHING THE FACTS."
EXCUSE ME?
SILLY PRINCE. WE CHARGE SO DEARLY TO DRASTICALLY CUT DOWN DEMAND. WE AREN'T ABLE TO MASS-PRODUCE OUR WORKINGS LIKE SOME MUNDY FACTORY.
"ALL OF WHICH RATHER PUT THE DAMPER ON HIS VICTORY GALA."
BUT...
...I PROMISED.

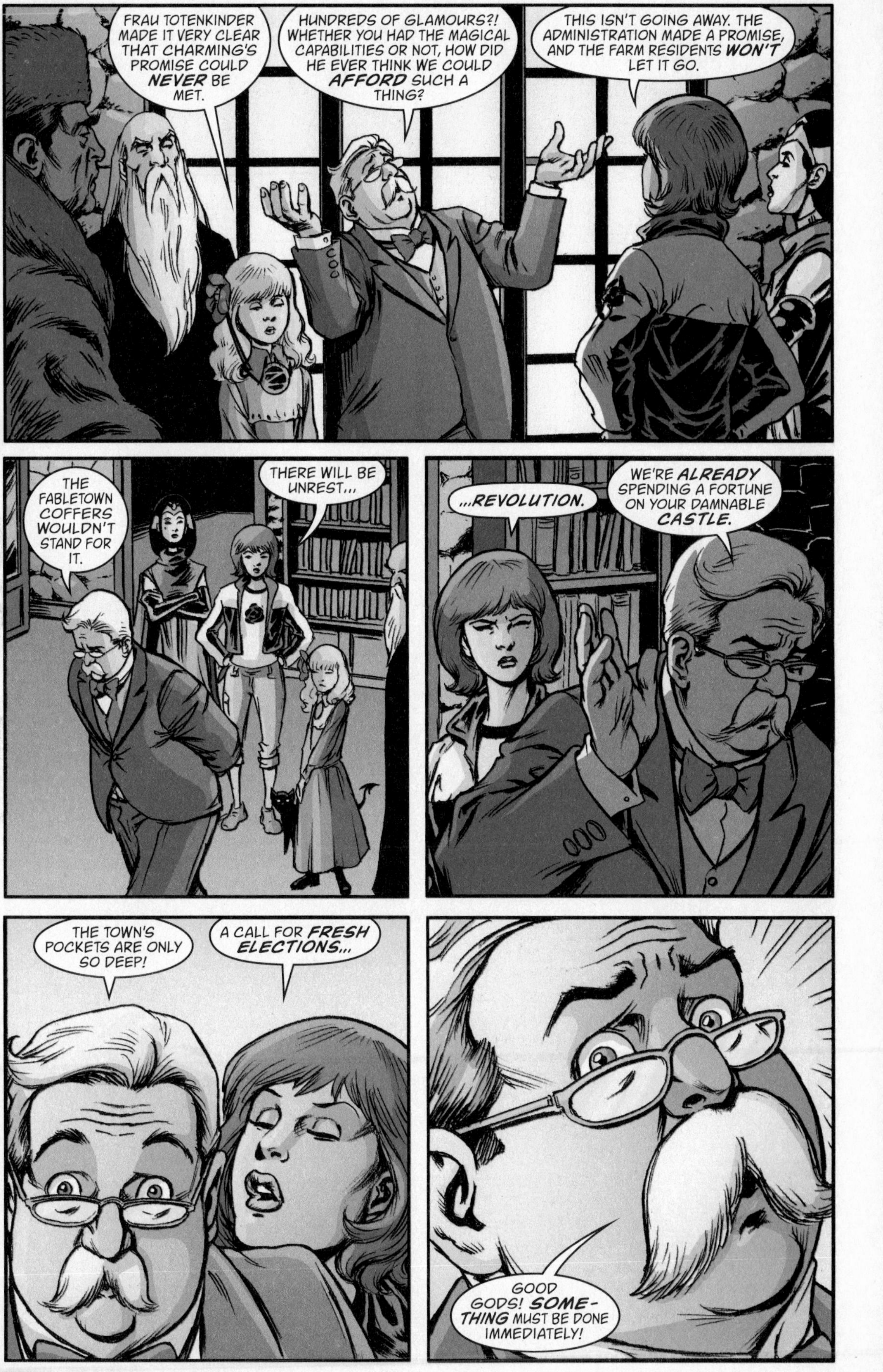
FRAU TOTENKINDER MADE IT VERY CLEAR THAT CHARMING'S PROMISE COULD NEVER BE MET.
HUNDREDS OF GLAMOURS?! WHETHER YOU HAD THE MAGICAL CAPABILITIES OR NOT, HOW DID HE EVER THINK WE COULD AFFORD SUCH A THING?
THIS ISN'T GOING AWAY. THE ADMINISTRATION MADE A PROMISE, AND THE FARM RESIDENTS WON'T LET IT GO.
THE FABLETOWN COFFERS WOULDN'T STAND FOR IT.
THERE WILL BE UNREST...
...REVOLUTION.
WE'RE ALREADY SPENDING A FORTUNE ON YOUR DAMNABLE CASTLE.
THE TOWN'S POCKETS ARE ONLY SO DEEP!
A CALL FOR FRESH ELECTIONS...
GOOD GODS! SOME-THING MUST BE DONE IMMEDIATELY!

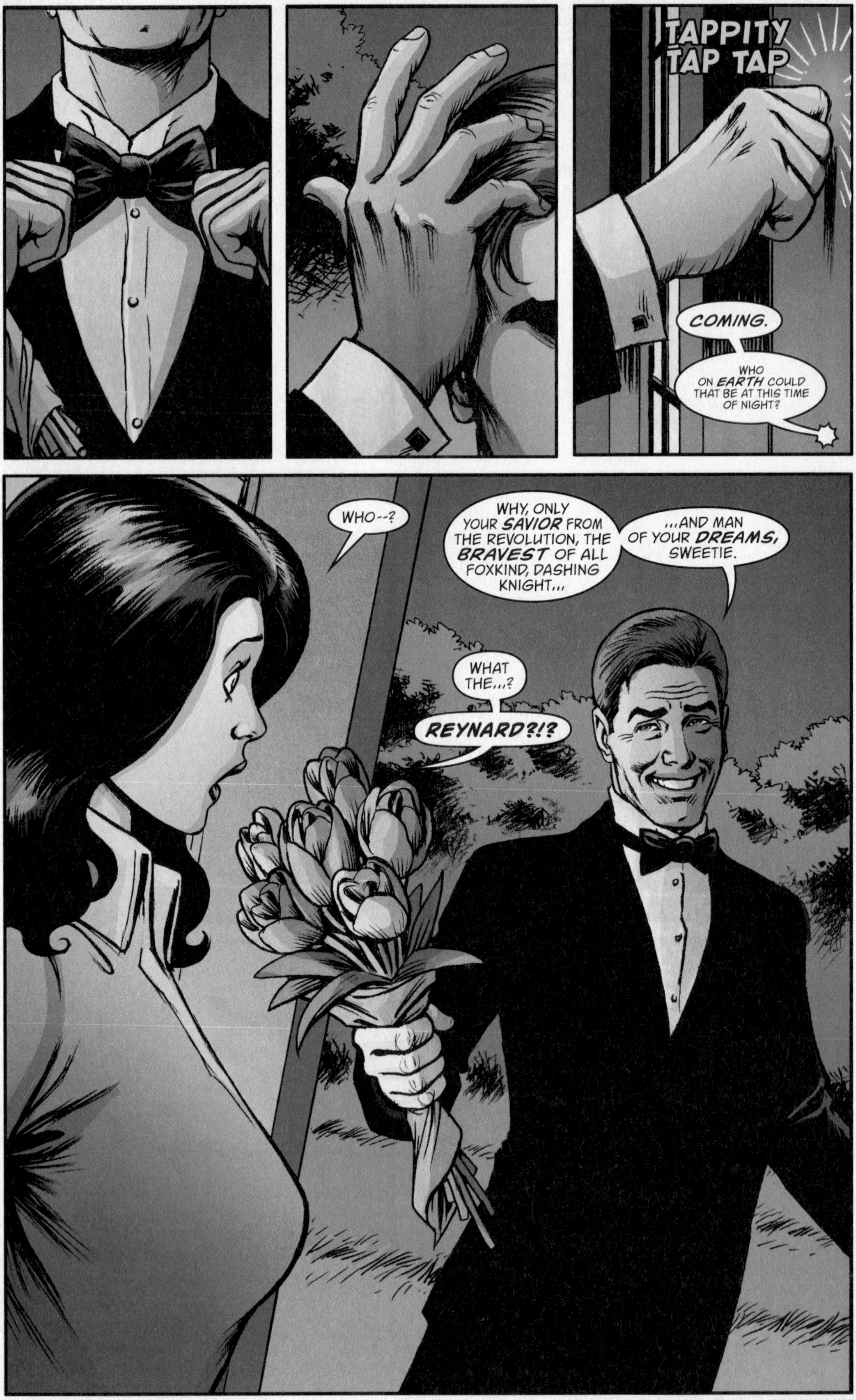
TAPPITY TAP TAP
COMING.
WHO ON EARTH COULD THAT BE AT THIS TIME OF NIGHT?
WHO--?
WHY, ONLY YOUR SAVIOR FROM THE REVOLUTION, THE BRAVEST OF ALL FOXKIND, DASHING KNIGHT...
...AND MAN OF YOUR DREAMS, SWEETIE.
WHAT THE...?
REYNARD?!?

NEXT: LIFE IS A LOTTERY!

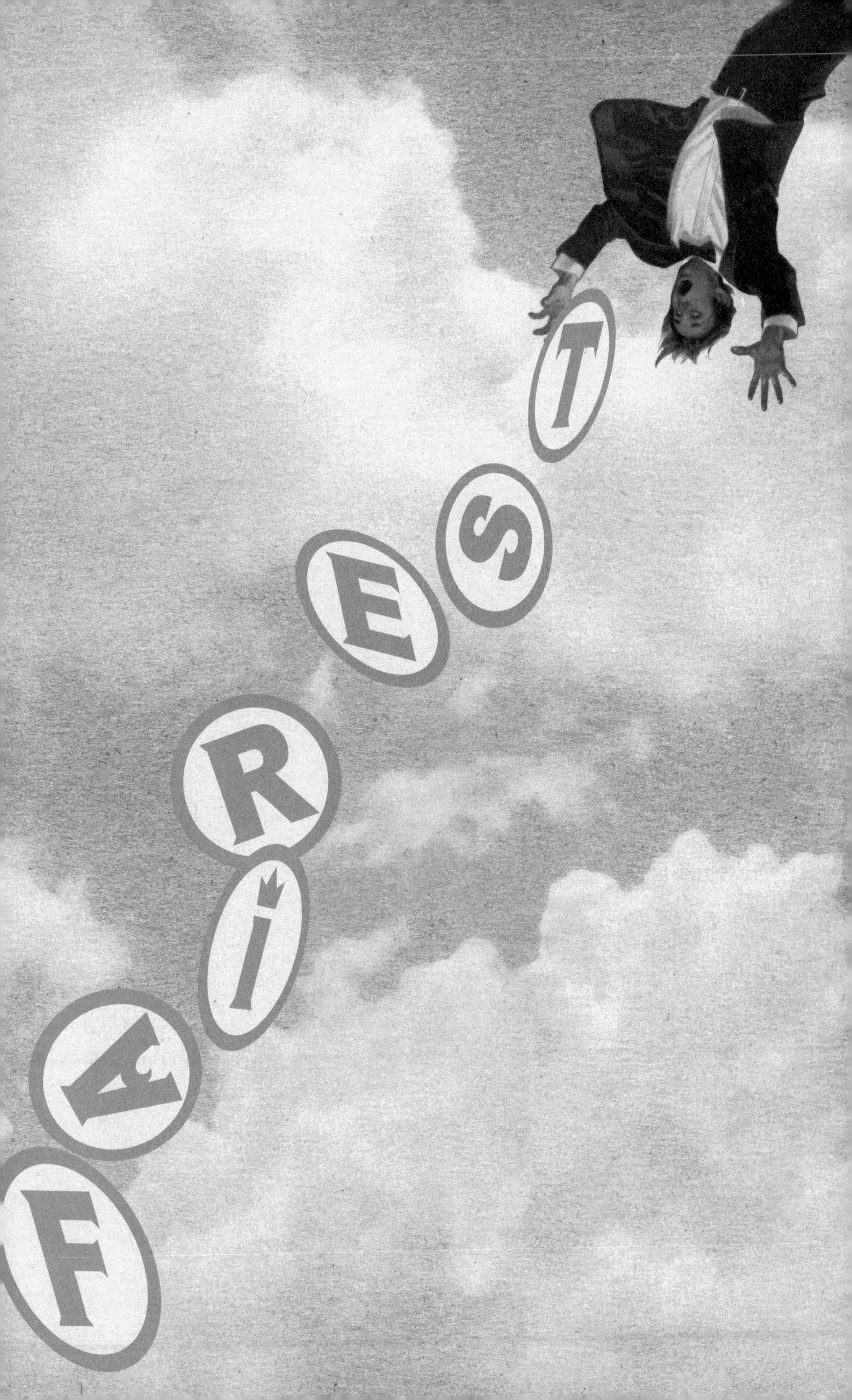
FAIREST

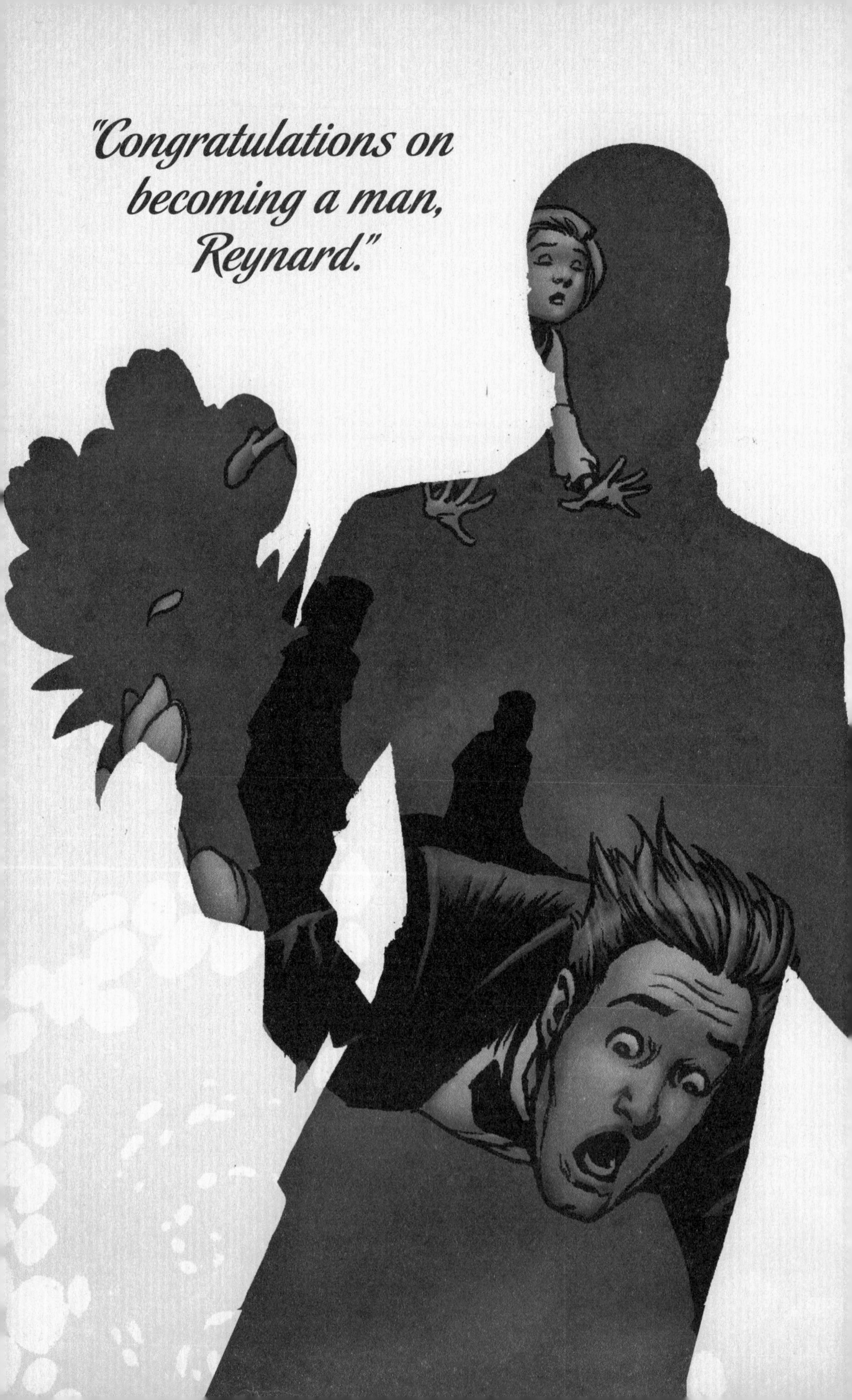
"Congratulations on becoming a man, Reynard."

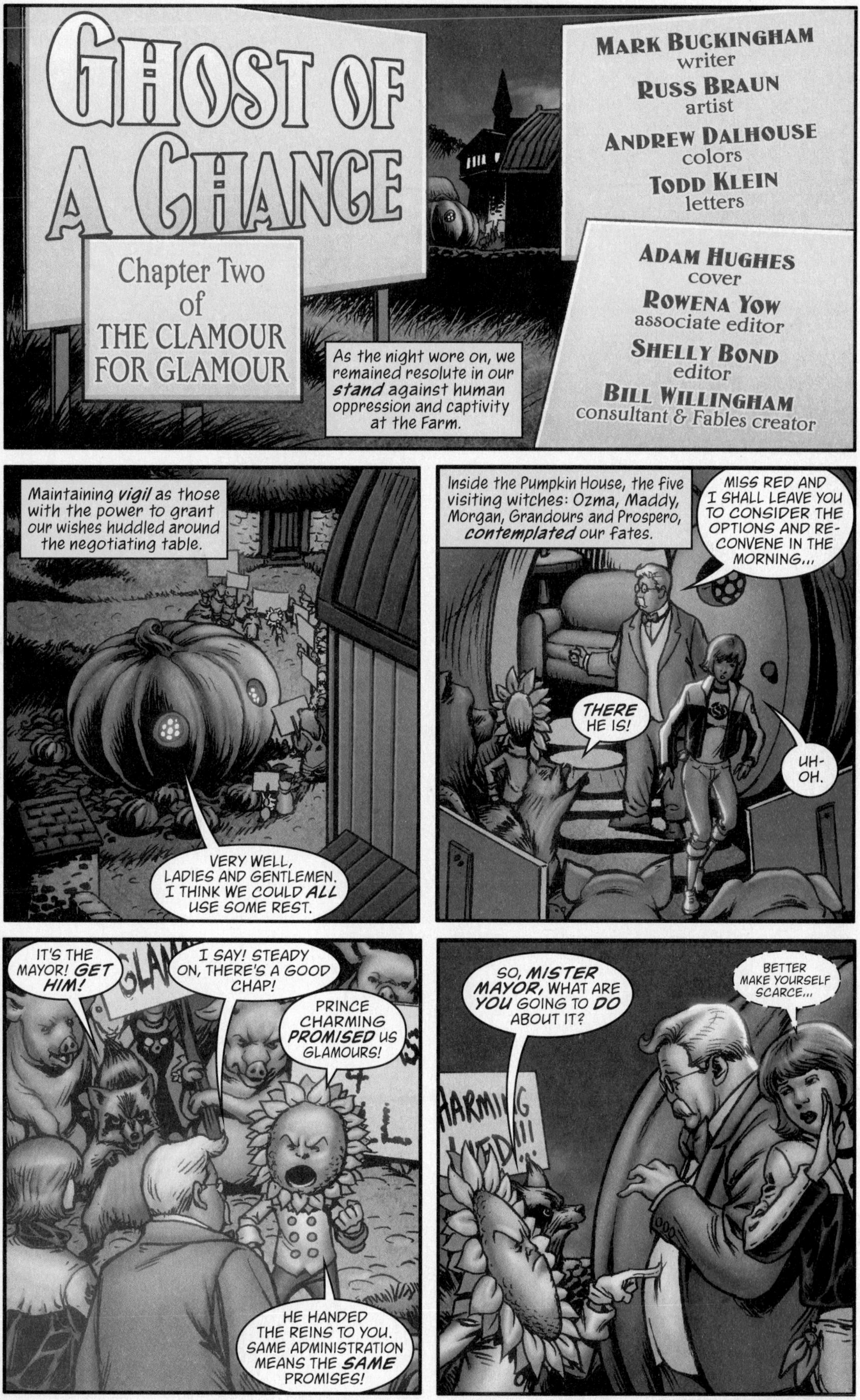
GHOST OF A CHANCE
Chapter Two of THE CLAMOUR FOR GLAMOUR
As the night wore on, we remained resolute in our *stand* against human oppression and captivity at the Farm.
MARK BUCKINGHAM writer
RUSS BRAUN artist
ANDREW DALHOUSE colors
TODD KLEIN letters
ADAM HUGHES cover
ROWENA YOW associate editor
SHELLY BOND editor
BILL WILLINGHAM consultant & Fables creator
Maintaining *vigil* as those with the power to grant our wishes huddled around the negotiating table.
VERY WELL, LADIES AND GENTLEMEN. I THINK WE COULD *ALL* USE SOME REST.
Inside the Pumpkin House, the five visiting witches: Ozma, Maddy, Morgan, Grandours and Prospero, *contemplated* our fates.
MISS RED AND I SHALL LEAVE YOU TO CONSIDER THE OPTIONS AND RE-CONVENE IN THE MORNING...
THERE HE IS!
UH-OH.
IT'S THE MAYOR! *GET HIM!*
I SAY! STEADY ON, THERE'S A GOOD CHAP!
PRINCE CHARMING *PROMISED* US GLAMOURS!
HE HANDED THE REINS TO YOU. SAME ADMINISTRATION MEANS THE *SAME* PROMISES!
SO, *MISTER MAYOR,* WHAT ARE *YOU* GOING TO *DO* ABOUT IT?
BETTER MAKE YOURSELF SCARCE...

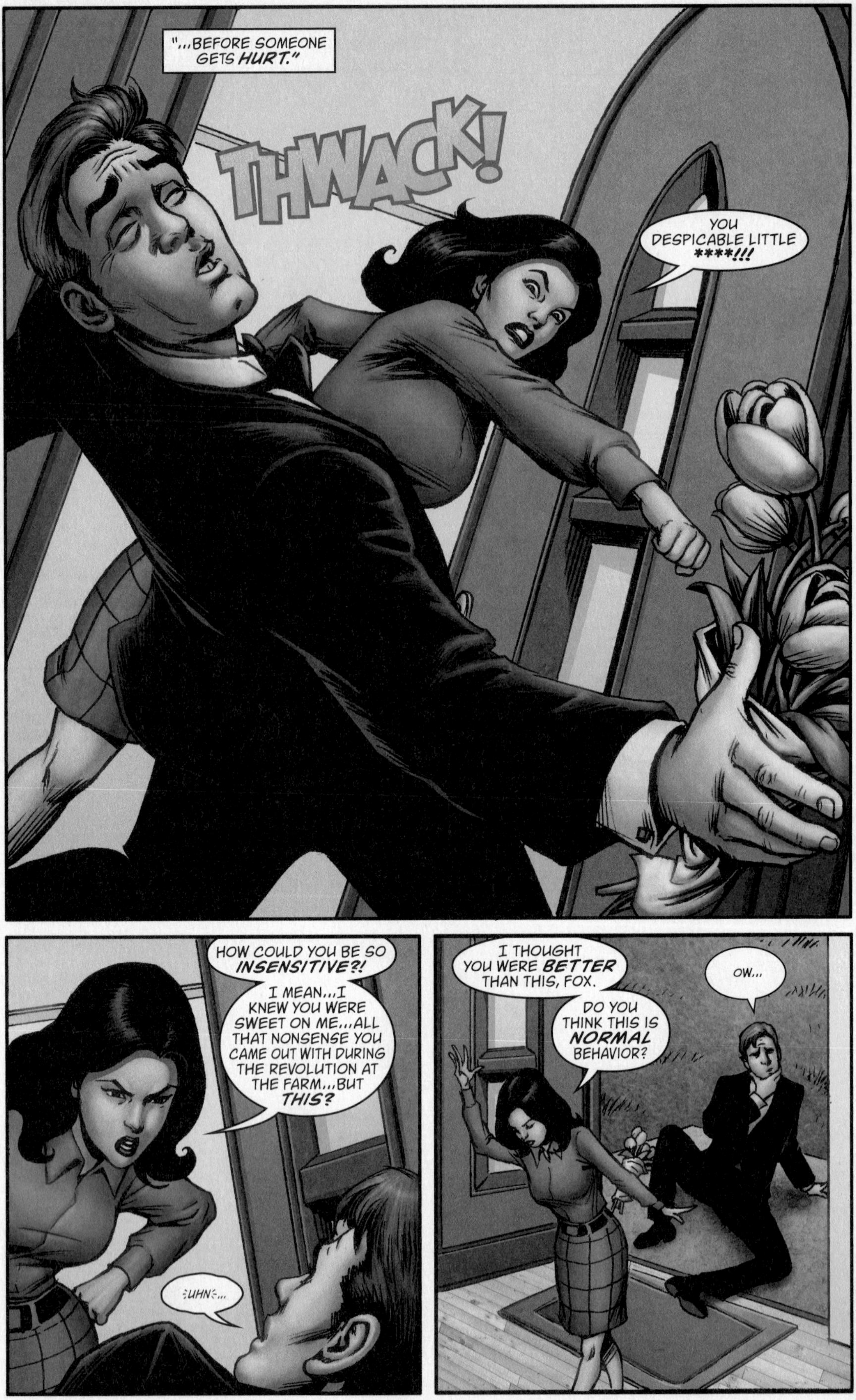
"...BEFORE SOMEONE GETS HURT."
THWACK!
YOU DESPICABLE LITTLE ****!!!
HOW COULD YOU BE SO INSENSITIVE?!
I MEAN...I KNEW YOU WERE SWEET ON ME...ALL THAT NONSENSE YOU CAME OUT WITH DURING THE REVOLUTION AT THE FARM...BUT THIS?
UHN...
I THOUGHT YOU WERE BETTER THAN THIS, FOX.
DO YOU THINK THIS IS NORMAL BEHAVIOR?
OW...

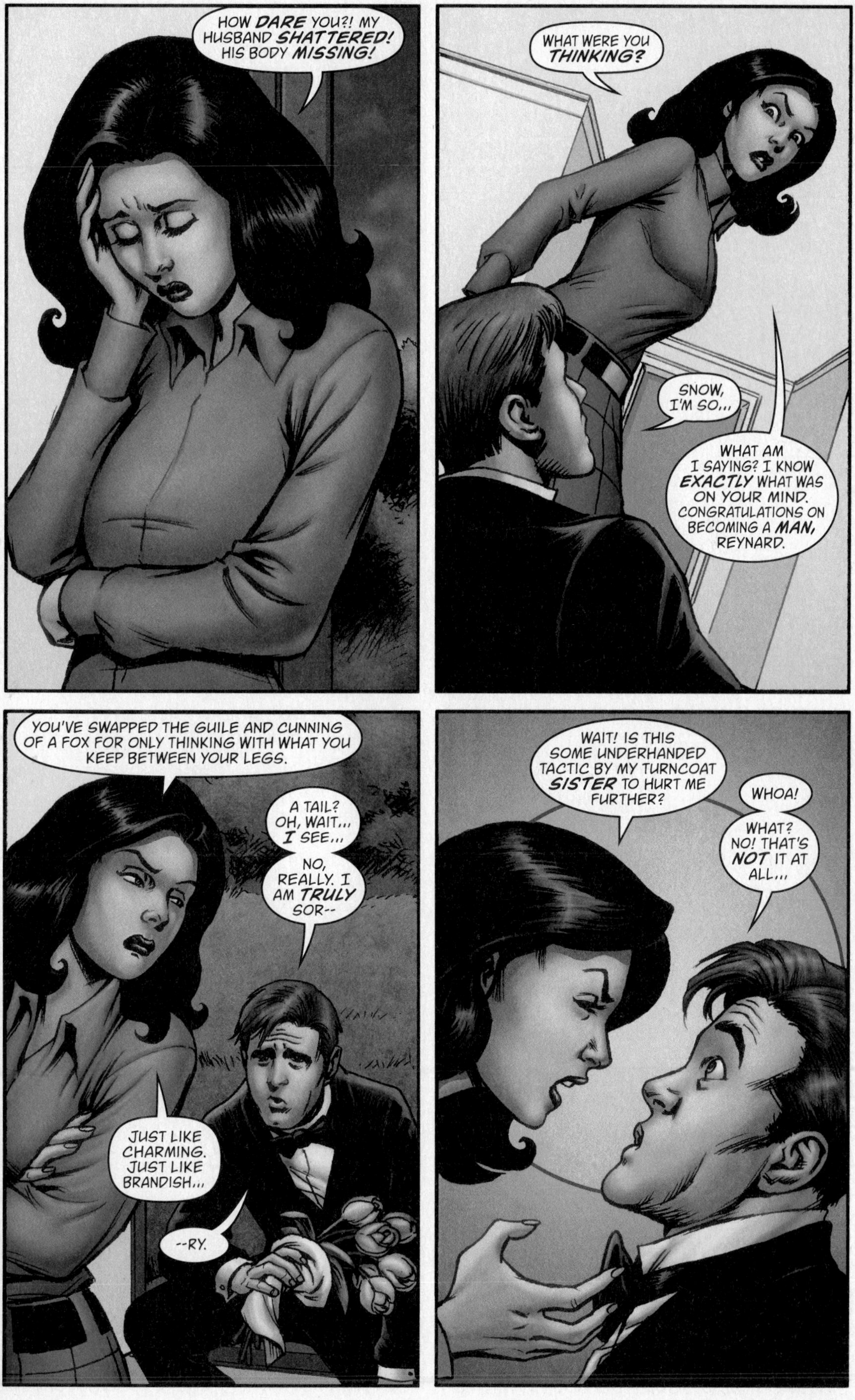

HOW DARE YOU?! MY HUSBAND SHATTERED! HIS BODY MISSING!
WHAT WERE YOU THINKING?
SNOW, I'M SO...
WHAT AM I SAYING? I KNOW EXACTLY WHAT WAS ON YOUR MIND. CONGRATULATIONS ON BECOMING A MAN, REYNARD.
YOU'VE SWAPPED THE GUILE AND CUNNING OF A FOX FOR ONLY THINKING WITH WHAT YOU KEEP BETWEEN YOUR LEGS.
A TAIL? OH, WAIT... I SEE...
NO, REALLY. I AM TRULY SOR--
JUST LIKE CHARMING. JUST LIKE BRANDISH...
--RY.
WAIT! IS THIS SOME UNDERHANDED TACTIC BY MY TURNCOAT SISTER TO HURT ME FURTHER?
WHOA!
WHAT? NO! THAT'S NOT IT AT ALL...

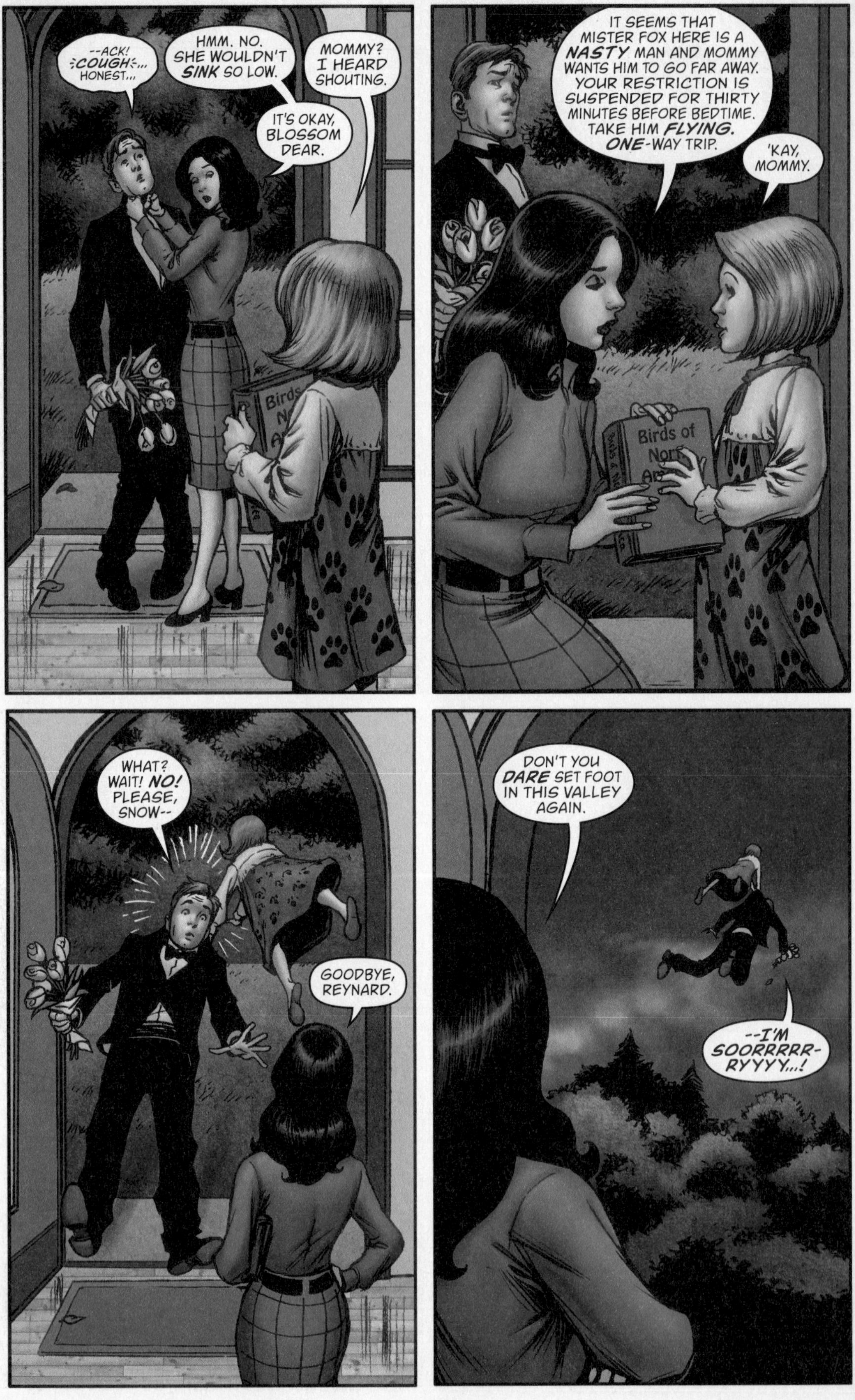
--ACK! *COUGH*... HONEST...
HMM. NO. SHE WOULDN'T **SINK** SO LOW.
IT'S OKAY, BLOSSOM DEAR.
MOMMY? I HEARD SHOUTING.
IT SEEMS THAT MISTER FOX HERE IS A **NASTY** MAN AND MOMMY WANTS HIM TO GO FAR AWAY. YOUR RESTRICTION IS SUSPENDED FOR THIRTY MINUTES BEFORE BEDTIME. TAKE HIM **FLYING. ONE**-WAY TRIP.
'KAY, MOMMY.
WHAT? WAIT! **NO!** PLEASE, SNOW--
GOODBYE, REYNARD.
DON'T YOU **DARE** SET FOOT IN THIS VALLEY AGAIN.
--I'M SOORRRRR-RYYYY...!

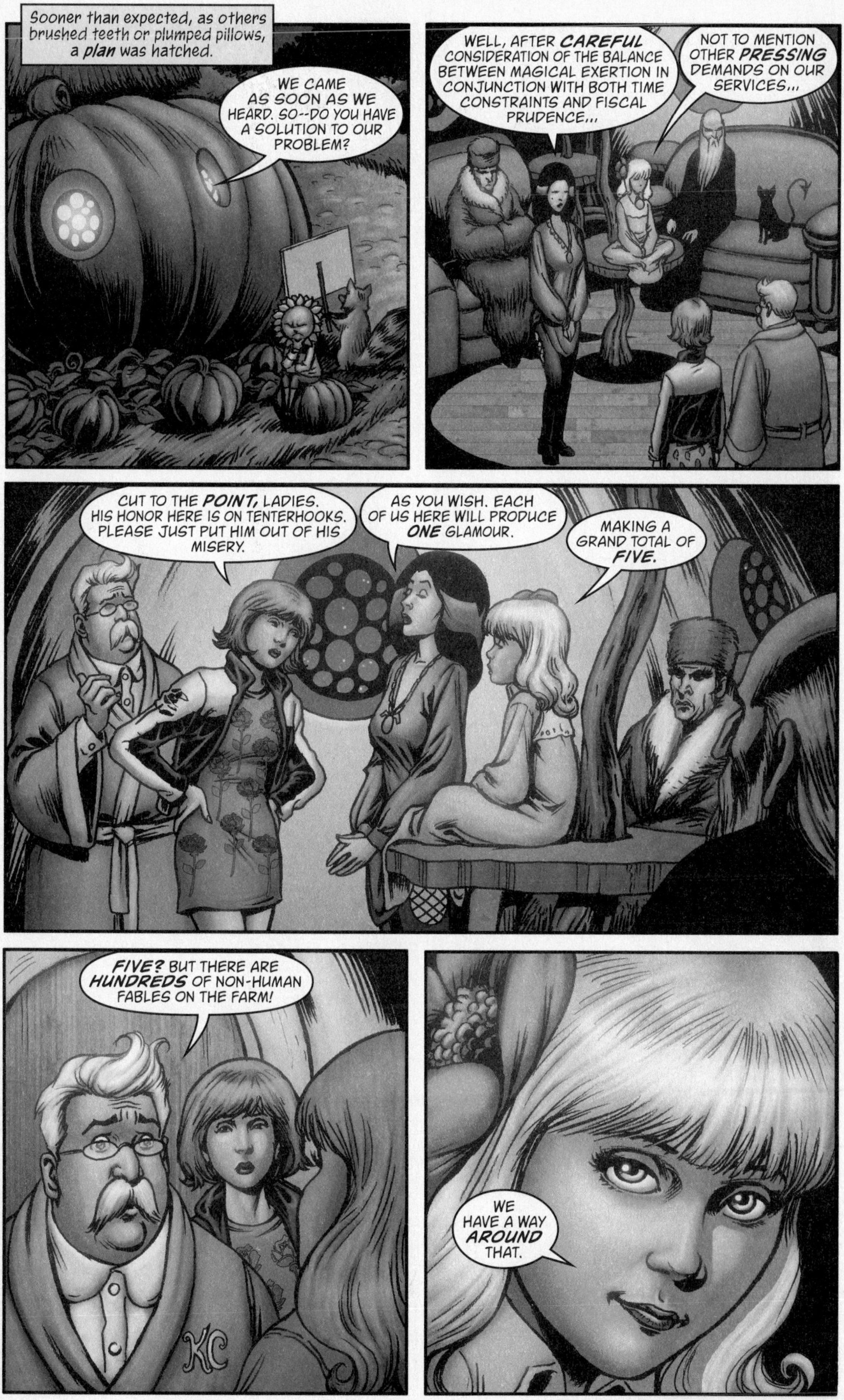
Sooner than expected, as others brushed teeth or plumped pillows, a *plan* was hatched.
WE CAME AS SOON AS WE HEARD. SO--DO YOU HAVE A SOLUTION TO OUR PROBLEM?
WELL, AFTER ***CAREFUL*** CONSIDERATION OF THE BALANCE BETWEEN MAGICAL EXERTION IN CONJUNCTION WITH BOTH TIME CONSTRAINTS AND FISCAL PRUDENCE...
NOT TO MENTION OTHER ***PRESSING*** DEMANDS ON OUR SERVICES...
CUT TO THE ***POINT,*** LADIES. HIS HONOR HERE IS ON TENTERHOOKS. PLEASE JUST PUT HIM OUT OF HIS MISERY.
AS YOU WISH. EACH OF US HERE WILL PRODUCE ***ONE*** GLAMOUR.
MAKING A GRAND TOTAL OF ***FIVE.***
FIVE? BUT THERE ARE ***HUNDREDS*** OF NON-HUMAN FABLES ON THE FARM!
WE HAVE A WAY ***AROUND*** THAT.

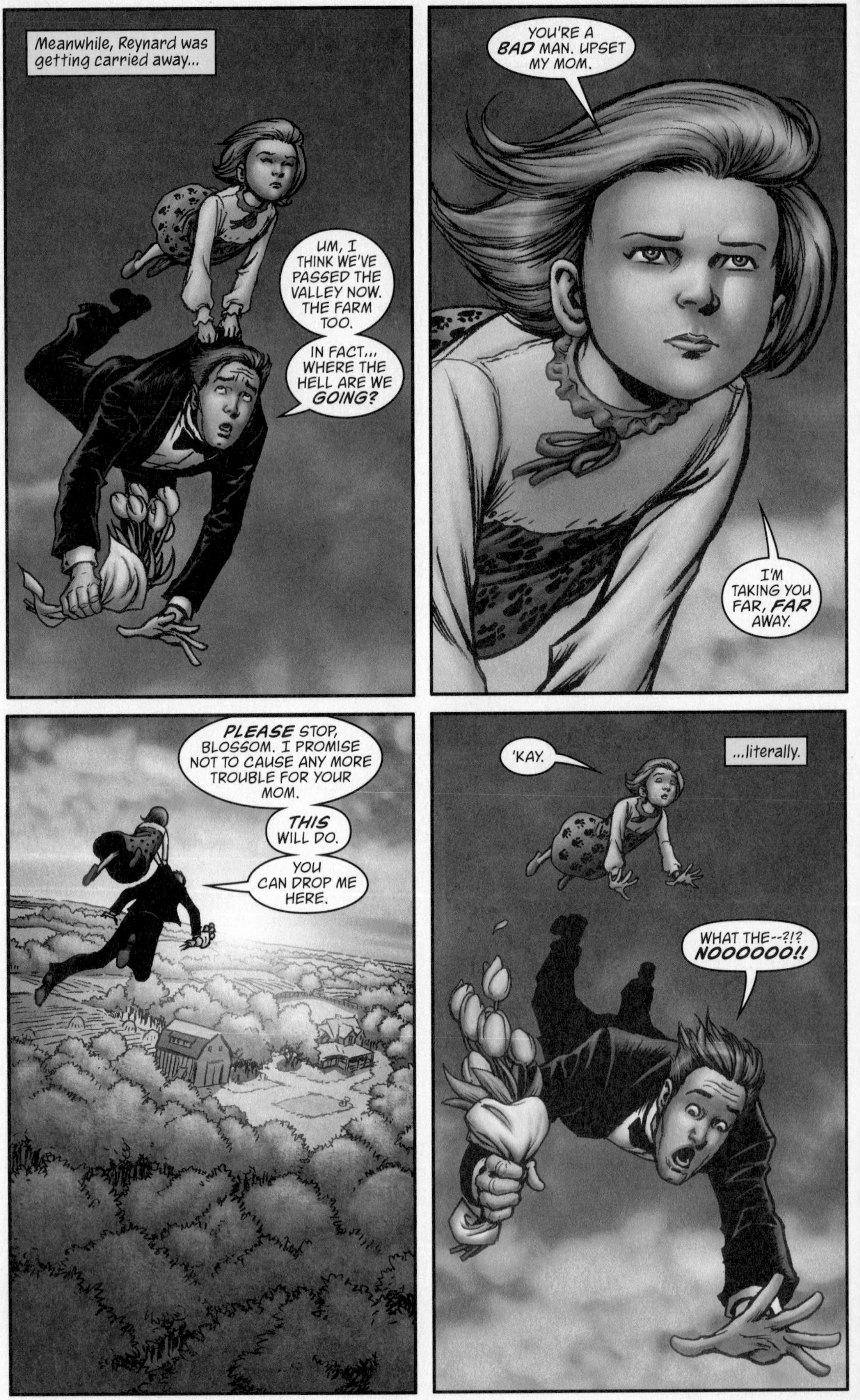
Meanwhile, Reynard was getting carried away...
UM, I THINK WE'VE PASSED THE VALLEY NOW. THE FARM TOO.
IN FACT... WHERE THE HELL ARE WE GOING?
YOU'RE A BAD MAN. UPSET MY MOM.
I'M TAKING YOU FAR, FAR AWAY.
PLEASE STOP, BLOSSOM. I PROMISE NOT TO CAUSE ANY MORE TROUBLE FOR YOUR MOM.
THIS WILL DO.
YOU CAN DROP ME HERE.
'KAY.
...literally.
WHAT THE--?!? NOOOOOO!!

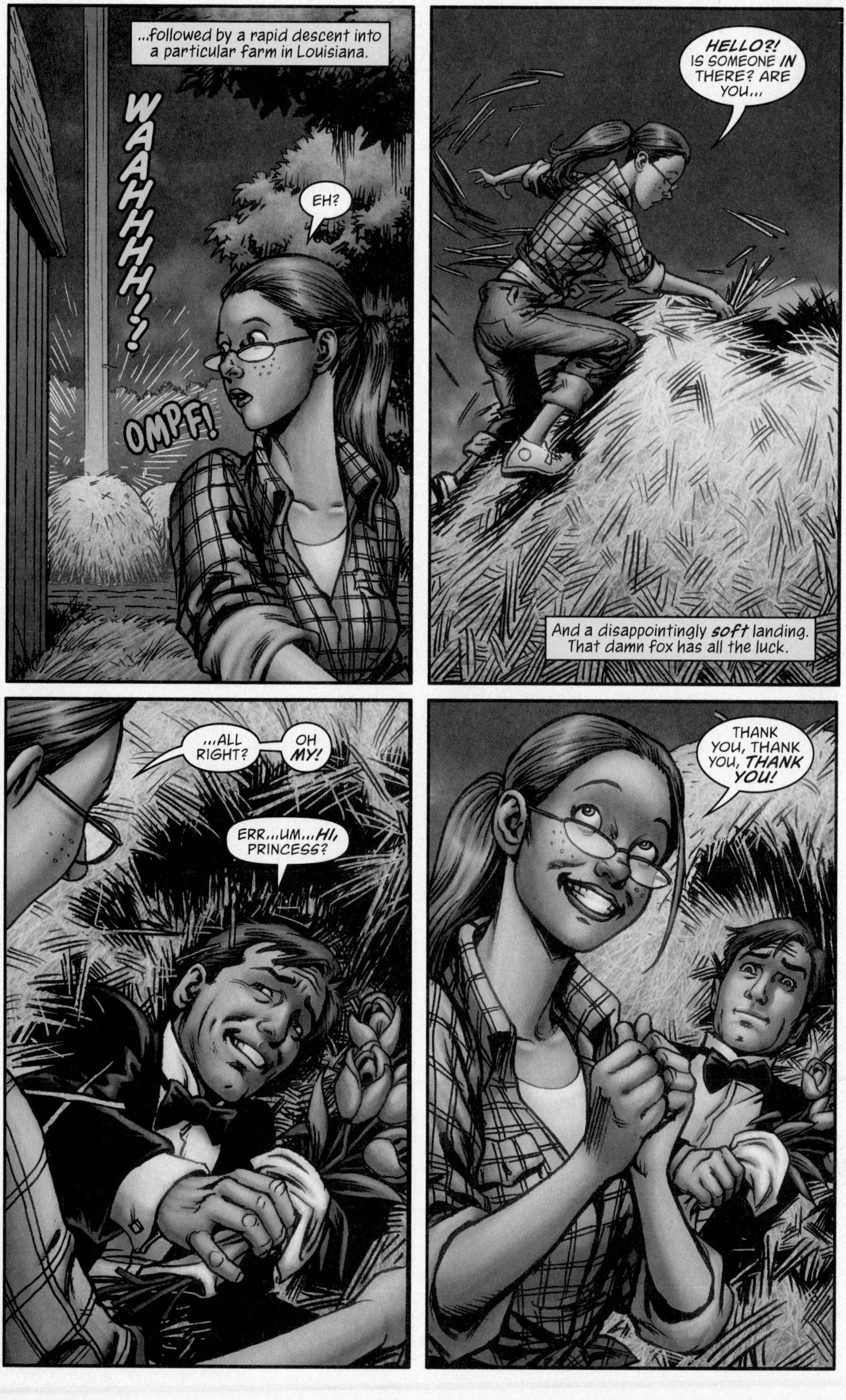
...followed by a rapid descent into a particular farm in Louisiana.
WAAHHHH!!
EH?
OMPF!
HELLO?! IS SOMEONE IN THERE? ARE YOU...
And a disappointingly soft landing. That damn fox has all the luck.
...ALL RIGHT?
OH MY!
ERR...UM...HI, PRINCESS?
THANK YOU, THANK YOU, THANK YOU!

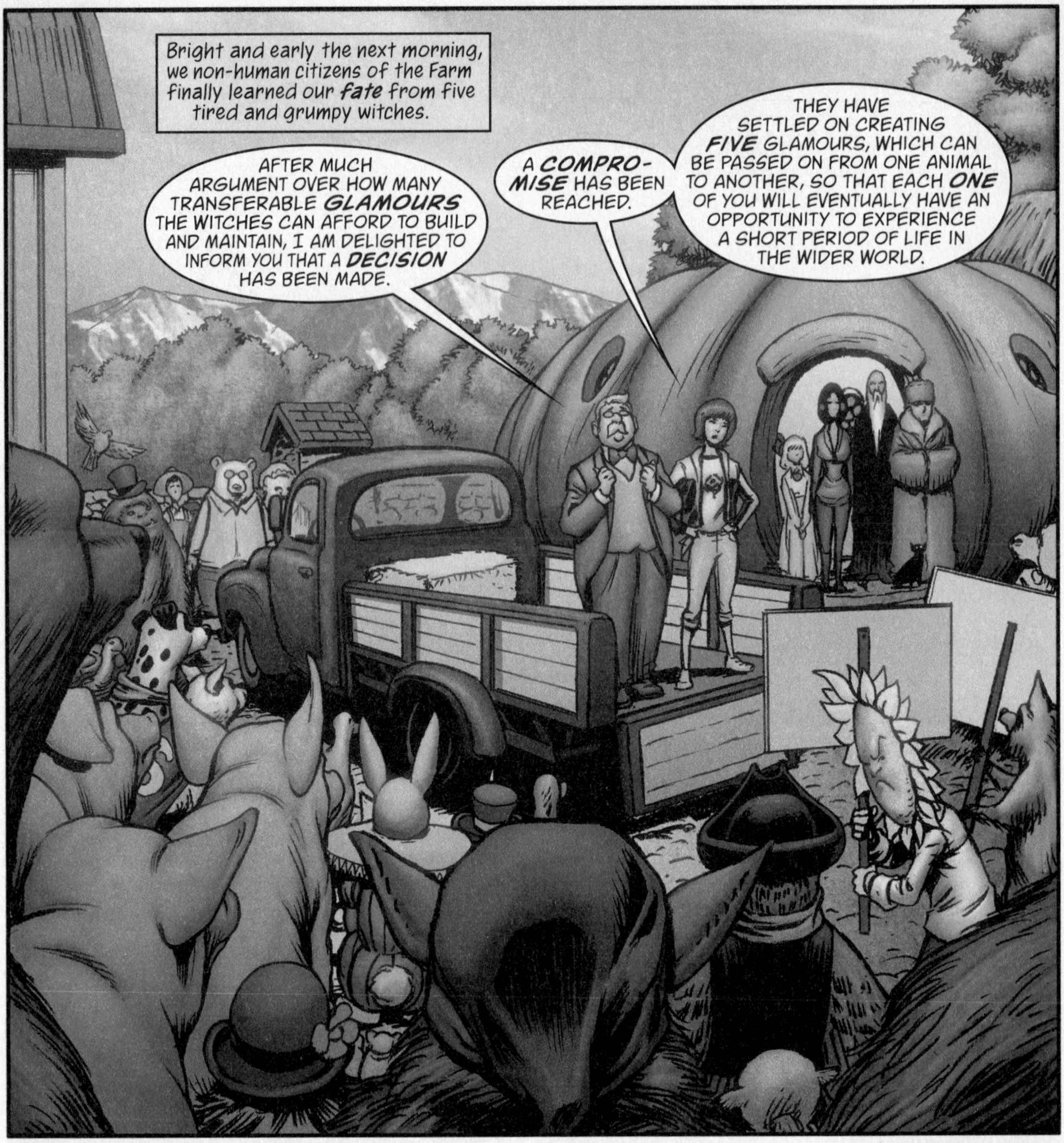
Bright and early the next morning, we non-human citizens of the Farm finally learned our fate from five tired and grumpy witches.
AFTER MUCH ARGUMENT OVER HOW MANY TRANSFERABLE GLAMOURS THE WITCHES CAN AFFORD TO BUILD AND MAINTAIN, I AM DELIGHTED TO INFORM YOU THAT A DECISION HAS BEEN MADE.
A COMPRO-MISE HAS BEEN REACHED.
THEY HAVE SETTLED ON CREATING FIVE GLAMOURS, WHICH CAN BE PASSED ON FROM ONE ANIMAL TO ANOTHER, SO THAT EACH ONE OF YOU WILL EVENTUALLY HAVE AN OPPORTUNITY TO EXPERIENCE A SHORT PERIOD OF LIFE IN THE WIDER WORLD.

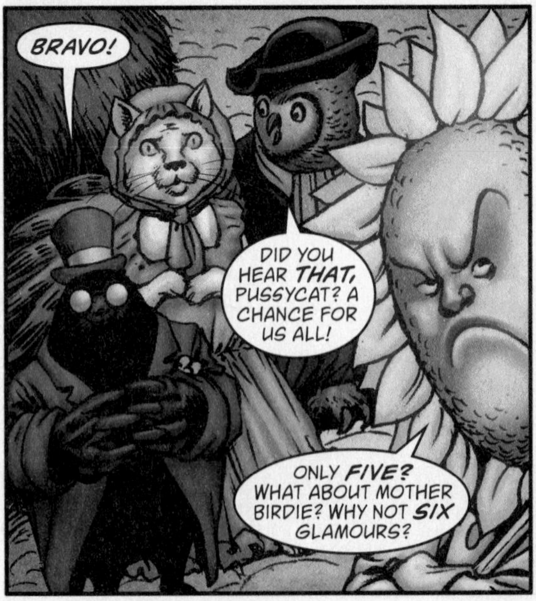
BRAVO!
DID YOU HEAR THAT, PUSSYCAT? A CHANCE FOR US ALL!
ONLY FIVE? WHAT ABOUT MOTHER BIRDIE? WHY NOT SIX GLAMOURS?

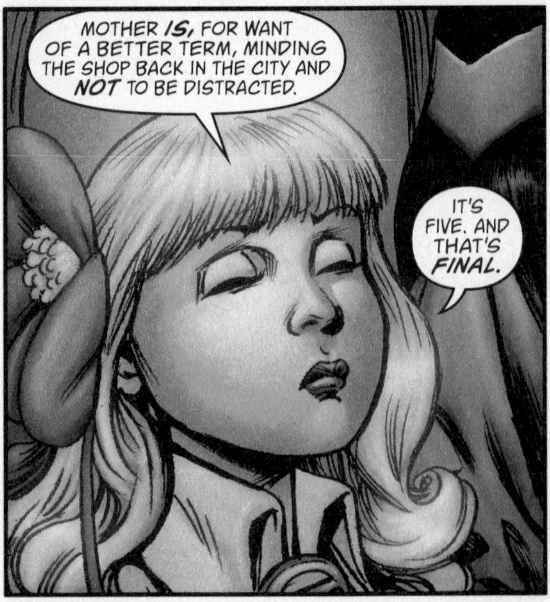
MOTHER IS, FOR WANT OF A BETTER TERM, MINDING THE SHOP BACK IN THE CITY AND NOT TO BE DISTRACTED.
IT'S FIVE. AND THAT'S FINAL.

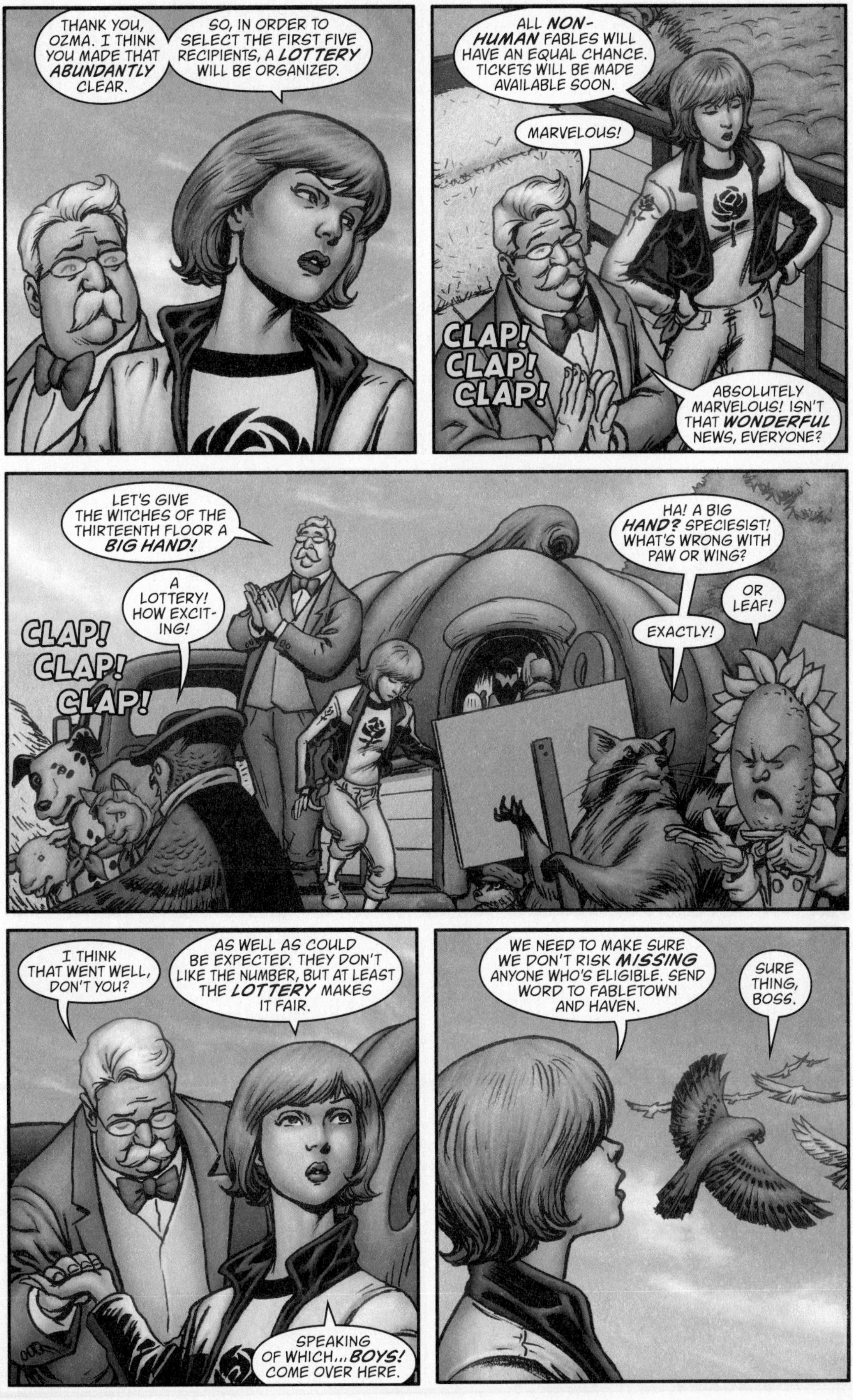
THANK YOU, OZMA. I THINK YOU MADE THAT ABUNDANTLY CLEAR.
SO, IN ORDER TO SELECT THE FIRST FIVE RECIPIENTS, A LOTTERY WILL BE ORGANIZED.
ALL NON-HUMAN FABLES WILL HAVE AN EQUAL CHANCE. TICKETS WILL BE MADE AVAILABLE SOON.
MARVELOUS!
CLAP! CLAP! CLAP!
ABSOLUTELY MARVELOUS! ISN'T THAT WONDERFUL NEWS, EVERYONE?
LET'S GIVE THE WITCHES OF THE THIRTEENTH FLOOR A BIG HAND!
A LOTTERY! HOW EXCIT-ING!
CLAP! CLAP! CLAP!
HA! A BIG HAND? SPECIESIST! WHAT'S WRONG WITH PAW OR WING?
EXACTLY!
OR LEAF!
I THINK THAT WENT WELL, DON'T YOU?
AS WELL AS COULD BE EXPECTED. THEY DON'T LIKE THE NUMBER, BUT AT LEAST THE LOTTERY MAKES IT FAIR.
SPEAKING OF WHICH... BOYS! COME OVER HERE.
WE NEED TO MAKE SURE WE DON'T RISK MISSING ANYONE WHO'S ELIGIBLE. SEND WORD TO FABLETOWN AND HAVEN.
SURE THING, BOSS.

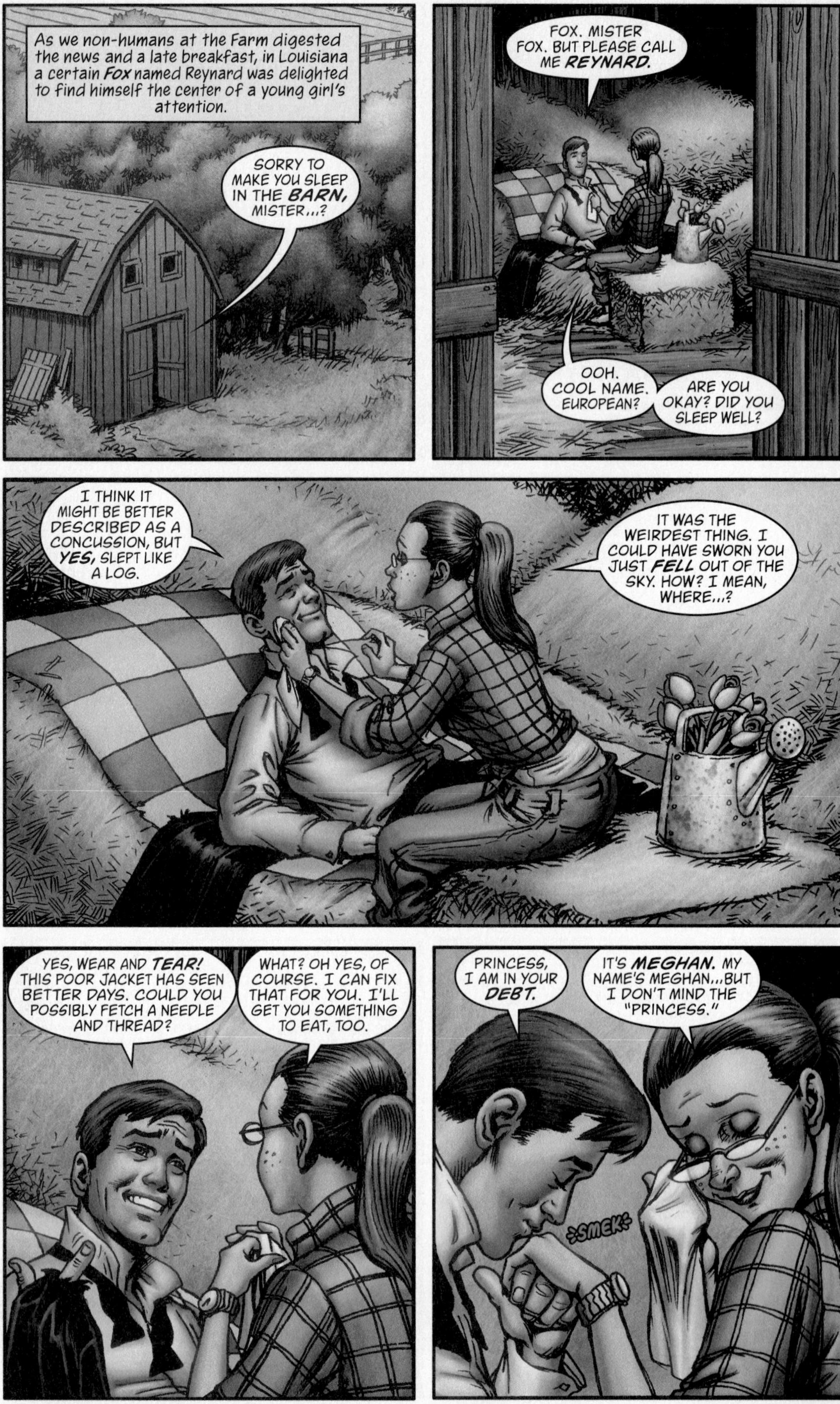
As we non-humans at the Farm digested the news and a late breakfast, in Louisiana a certain Fox named Reynard was delighted to find himself the center of a young girl's attention.
SORRY TO MAKE YOU SLEEP IN THE BARN, MISTER...?
FOX. MISTER FOX. BUT PLEASE CALL ME REYNARD.
OOH. COOL NAME. EUROPEAN?
ARE YOU OKAY? DID YOU SLEEP WELL?
I THINK IT MIGHT BE BETTER DESCRIBED AS A CONCUSSION, BUT YES, SLEPT LIKE A LOG.
IT WAS THE WEIRDEST THING. I COULD HAVE SWORN YOU JUST FELL OUT OF THE SKY. HOW? I MEAN, WHERE...?
YES, WEAR AND TEAR! THIS POOR JACKET HAS SEEN BETTER DAYS. COULD YOU POSSIBLY FETCH A NEEDLE AND THREAD?
WHAT? OH YES, OF COURSE. I CAN FIX THAT FOR YOU. I'LL GET YOU SOMETHING TO EAT, TOO.
PRINCESS, I AM IN YOUR DEBT.
SMEK
IT'S MEGHAN. MY NAME'S MEGHAN...BUT I DON'T MIND THE "PRINCESS."

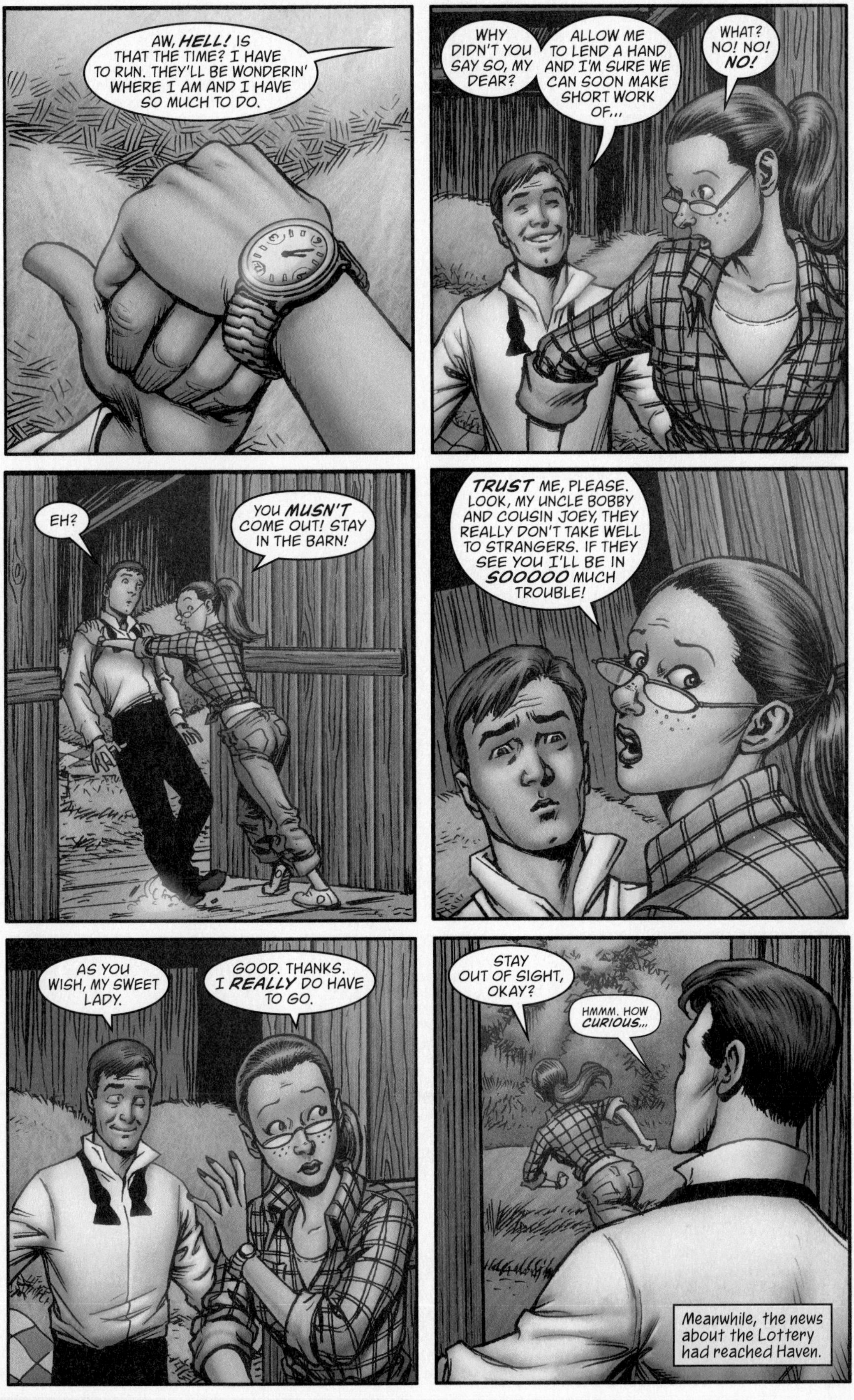
AW, HELL! IS THAT THE TIME? I HAVE TO RUN. THEY'LL BE WONDERIN' WHERE I AM AND I HAVE SO MUCH TO DO.
WHY DIDN'T YOU SAY SO, MY DEAR?
ALLOW ME TO LEND A HAND AND I'M SURE WE CAN SOON MAKE SHORT WORK OF...
WHAT? NO! NO! NO!
EH?
YOU MUSN'T COME OUT! STAY IN THE BARN!
TRUST ME, PLEASE. LOOK, MY UNCLE BOBBY AND COUSIN JOEY, THEY REALLY DON'T TAKE WELL TO STRANGERS. IF THEY SEE YOU I'LL BE IN SOOOOO MUCH TROUBLE!
AS YOU WISH, MY SWEET LADY.
GOOD. THANKS. I REALLY DO HAVE TO GO.
STAY OUT OF SIGHT, OKAY?
HMMM. HOW CURIOUS...
Meanwhile, the news about the Lottery had reached Haven.

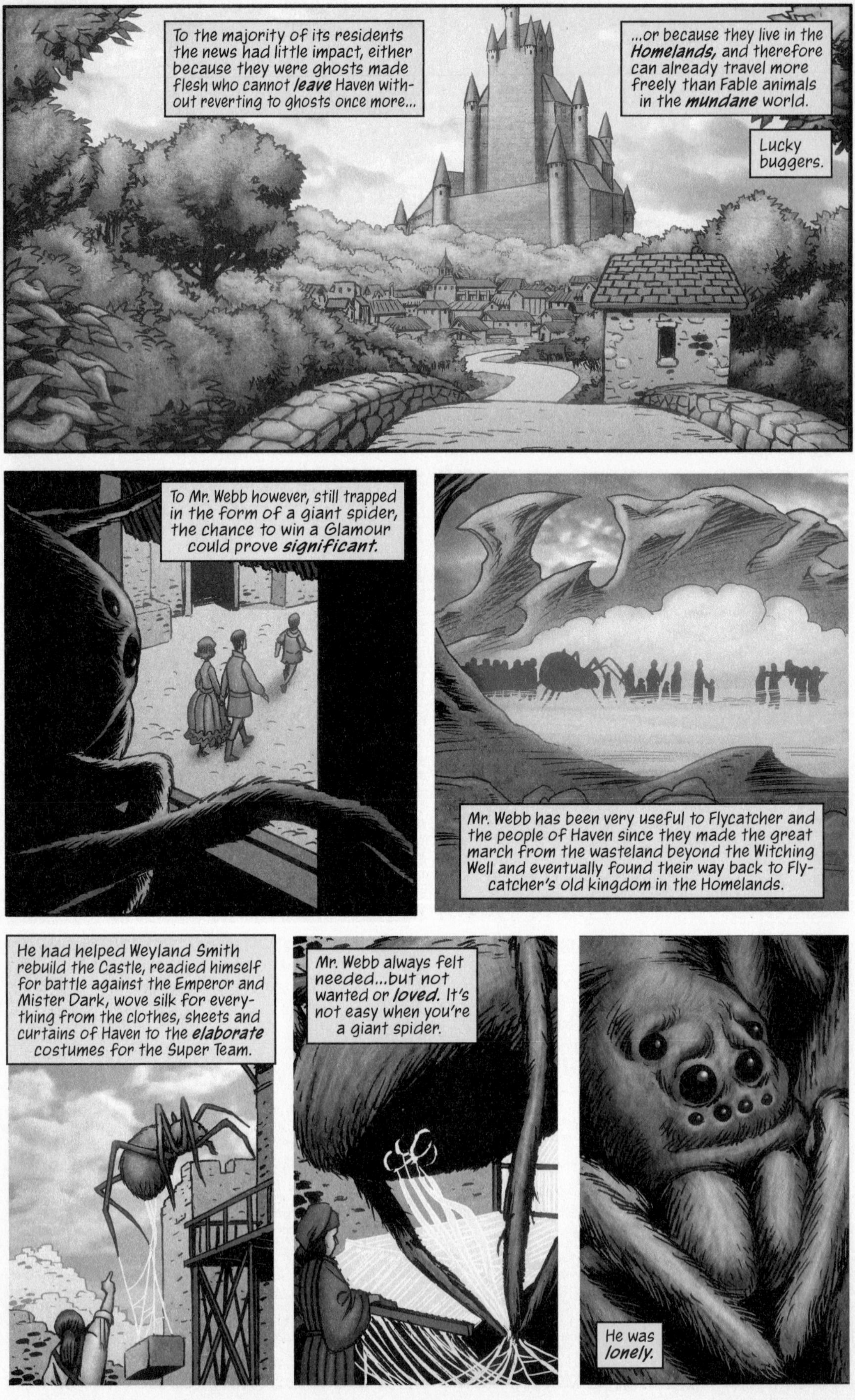

To the majority of its residents the news had little impact, either because they were ghosts made flesh who cannot *leave* Haven without reverting to ghosts once more...
...or because they live in the ***Homelands,*** and therefore can already travel more freely than Fable animals in the ***mundane*** world.
Lucky buggers.
To Mr. Webb however, still trapped in the form of a giant spider, the chance to win a Glamour could prove ***significant.***
Mr. Webb has been very useful to Flycatcher and the people of Haven since they made the great march from the wasteland beyond the Witching Well and eventually found their way back to Flycatcher's old kingdom in the Homelands.
He had helped Weyland Smith rebuild the Castle, readied himself for battle against the Emperor and Mister Dark, wove silk for everything from the clothes, sheets and curtains of Haven to the *elaborate* costumes for the Super Team.
Mr. Webb always felt needed...but not wanted or *loved.* It's not easy when you're a giant spider.
He was *lonely.*

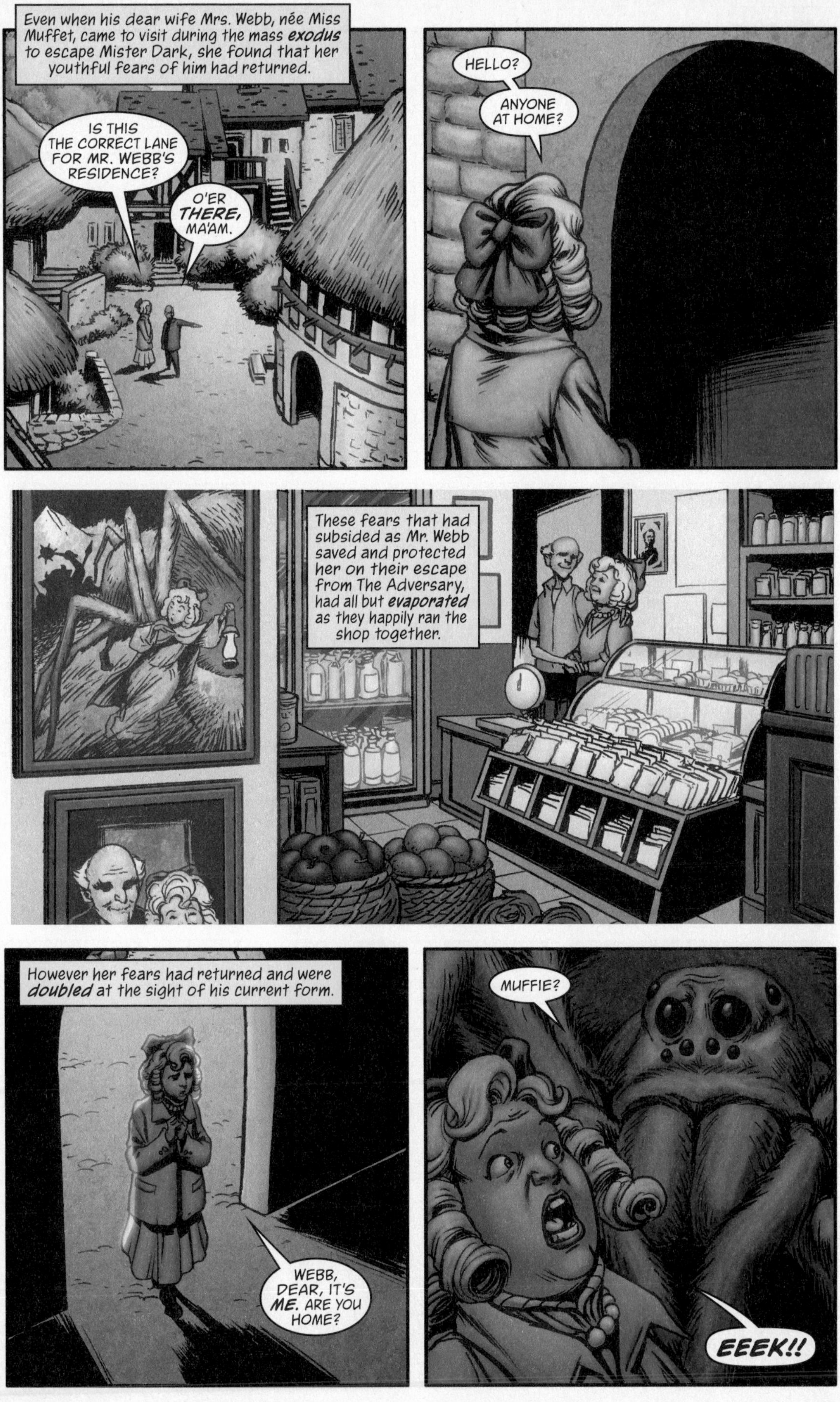

Even when his dear wife Mrs. Webb, née Miss Muffet, came to visit during the mass *exodus* to escape Mister Dark, she found that her youthful fears of him had returned.
IS THIS THE CORRECT LANE FOR MR. WEBB'S RESIDENCE?
O'ER *THERE,* MA'AM.
HELLO?
ANYONE AT HOME?
These fears that had subsided as Mr. Webb saved and protected her on their escape from The Adversary, had all but *evaporated* as they happily ran the shop together.
However her fears had returned and were *doubled* at the sight of his current form.
WEBB, DEAR, IT'S *ME.* ARE YOU HOME?
MUFFIE?
EEEK!!

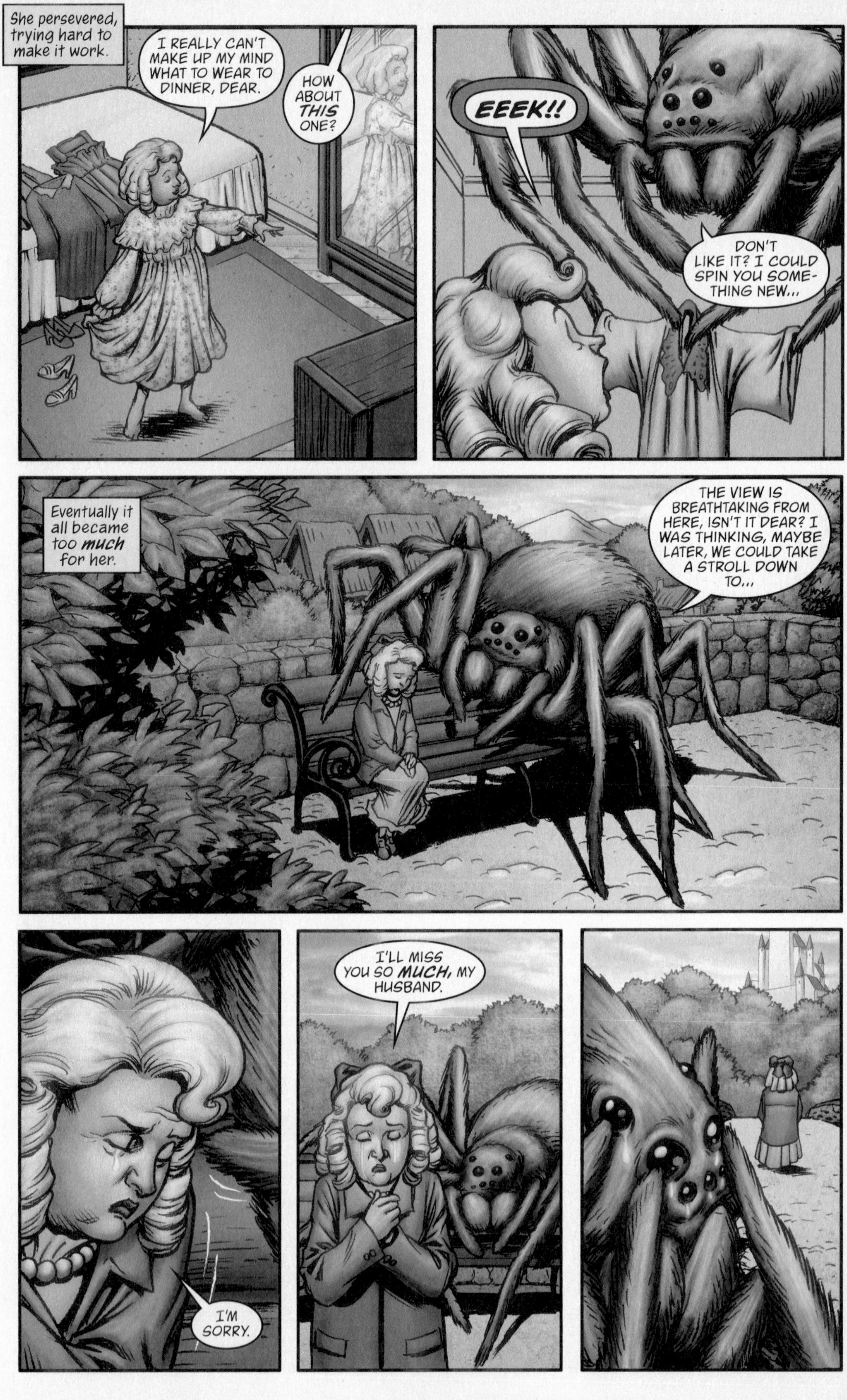
She persevered, trying hard to make it work.
I REALLY CAN'T MAKE UP MY MIND WHAT TO WEAR TO DINNER, DEAR.
HOW ABOUT THIS ONE?
EEEK!!
DON'T LIKE IT? I COULD SPIN YOU SOME-THING NEW...
Eventually it all became too much for her.
THE VIEW IS BREATHTAKING FROM HERE, ISN'T IT DEAR? I WAS THINKING, MAYBE LATER, WE COULD TAKE A STROLL DOWN TO...
I'M SORRY.
I'LL MISS YOU SO MUCH, MY HUSBAND.

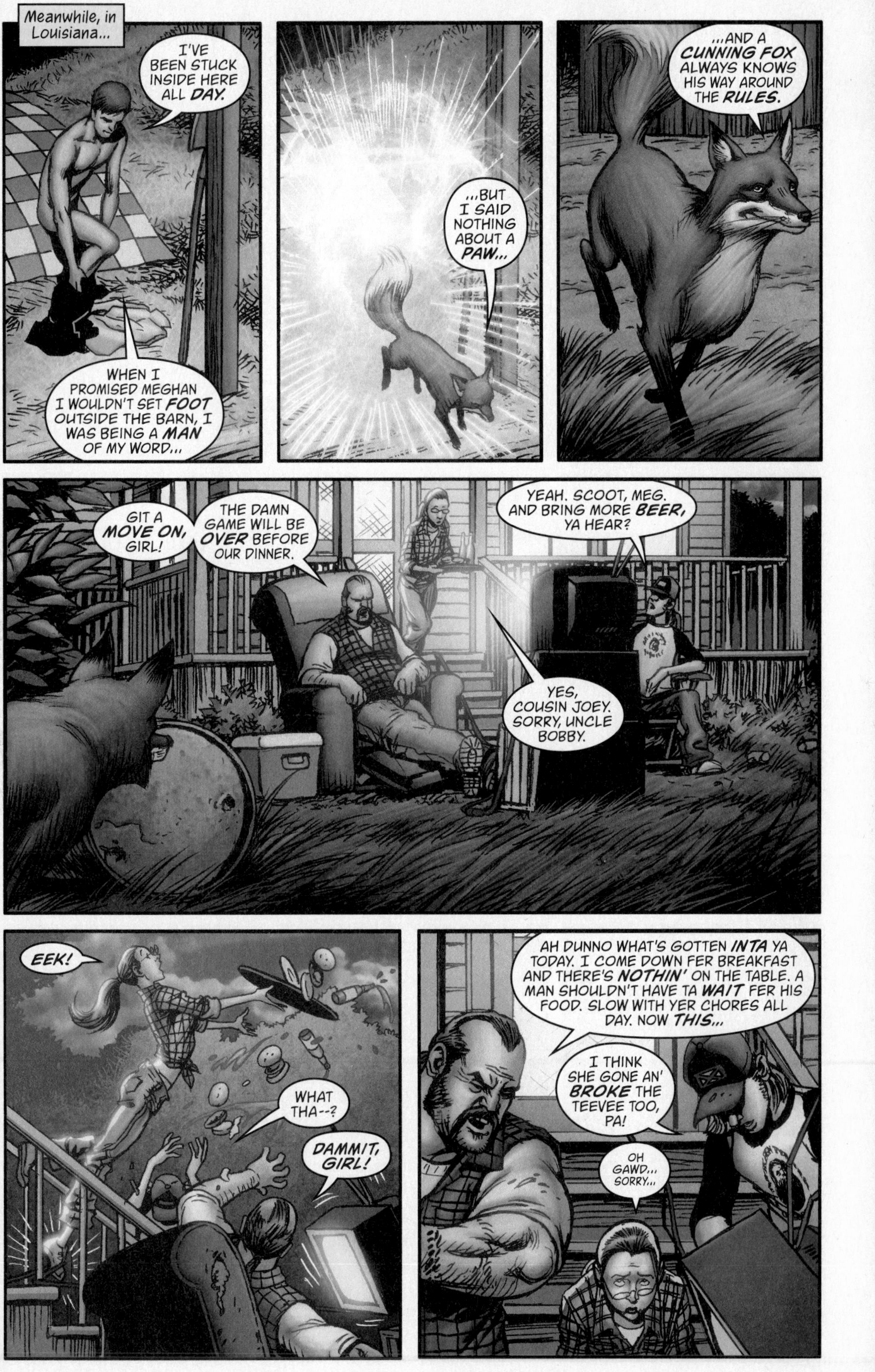
Meanwhile, in Louisiana...
I'VE BEEN STUCK INSIDE HERE ALL DAY.
WHEN I PROMISED MEGHAN I WOULDN'T SET FOOT OUTSIDE THE BARN, I WAS BEING A MAN OF MY WORD...
...BUT I SAID NOTHING ABOUT A PAW...
...AND A CUNNING FOX ALWAYS KNOWS HIS WAY AROUND THE RULES.
GIT A MOVE ON, GIRL!
THE DAMN GAME WILL BE OVER BEFORE OUR DINNER.
YEAH. SCOOT, MEG. AND BRING MORE BEER, YA HEAR?
YES, COUSIN JOEY. SORRY, UNCLE BOBBY.
EEK!
WHAT THA--?
DAMMIT, GIRL!
AH DUNNO WHAT'S GOTTEN INTA YA TODAY. I COME DOWN FER BREAKFAST AND THERE'S NOTHIN' ON THE TABLE. A MAN SHOULDN'T HAVE TA WAIT FER HIS FOOD. SLOW WITH YER CHORES ALL DAY. NOW THIS...
I THINK SHE GONE AN' BROKE THE TEEVEE TOO, PA!
OH GAWD... SORRY...

IT AIN'T GOOD ENOUGH, GIRL. YA HEAR? *DISRESPECTFUL.*

IT'S ALL'A THAT *READIN'*, AIN'T IT, PA? PUTS THEM FUNNY NOTIONS IN HER HEAD.

COULD BE, SON. RECKON AH BEEN TOO *GENEROUS.*

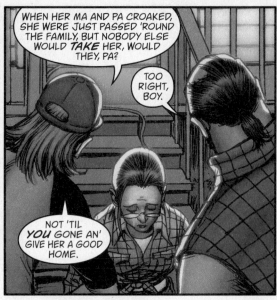

WHEN HER MA AND PA CROAKED, SHE WERE JUST PASSED 'ROUND THE FAMILY, BUT NOBODY ELSE WOULD *TAKE* HER, WOULD THEY, PA?

TOO RIGHT, BOY.

NOT 'TIL *YOU* GONE AN' GIVE HER A GOOD HOME.

NEED TA TEACH YA A LESSON. MAKE YA SHOW SOME DAMN *GRATITUDE!*

YEAH, PA. WHUP HER GOOD!

CLANG!

WHA--? *LOOK,* PA! A *FOX!*

YIKES!

DAMN. CLEAR YER MESS UP, MEG, YA HEAR? KITCHEN. FRESH SUPPER. *NOW.*

WHATCHA WAITIN' FER, BOY? FETCH THE *GUN!* DON'T WANT NO VERMIN GETTIN' IN THE HEN HOUSE.

AH'LL *GET* HIM, PA!

THE POOR GIRL SHOULDN'T HAVE TO ENDURE THIS.

BUT RIGHT NOW I THNK *DISCRETION* IS THE BETTER PART OF VALOR.

I'LL DO AS I'M TOLD. STAY PUT IN THE BARN.

WHERE IT'S SAFE AND--

THWACK!

OOGH...!

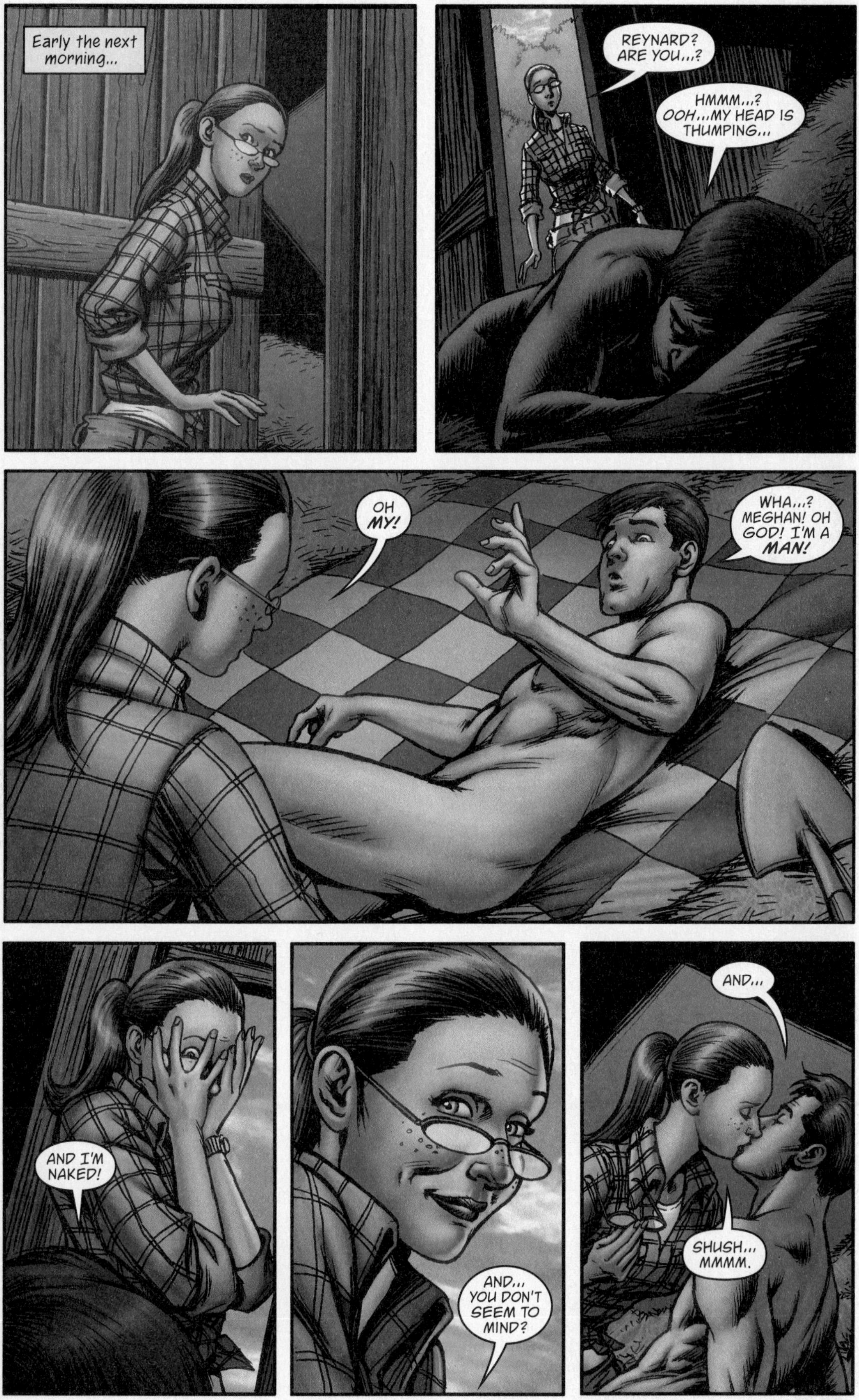
Early the next morning...
REYNARD? ARE YOU...?
HMMM...? OOH...MY HEAD IS THUMPING...
OH MY!
WHA...? MEGHAN! OH GOD! I'M A MAN!
AND I'M NAKED!
AND... YOU DON'T SEEM TO MIND?
AND...
SHUSH... MMMM.

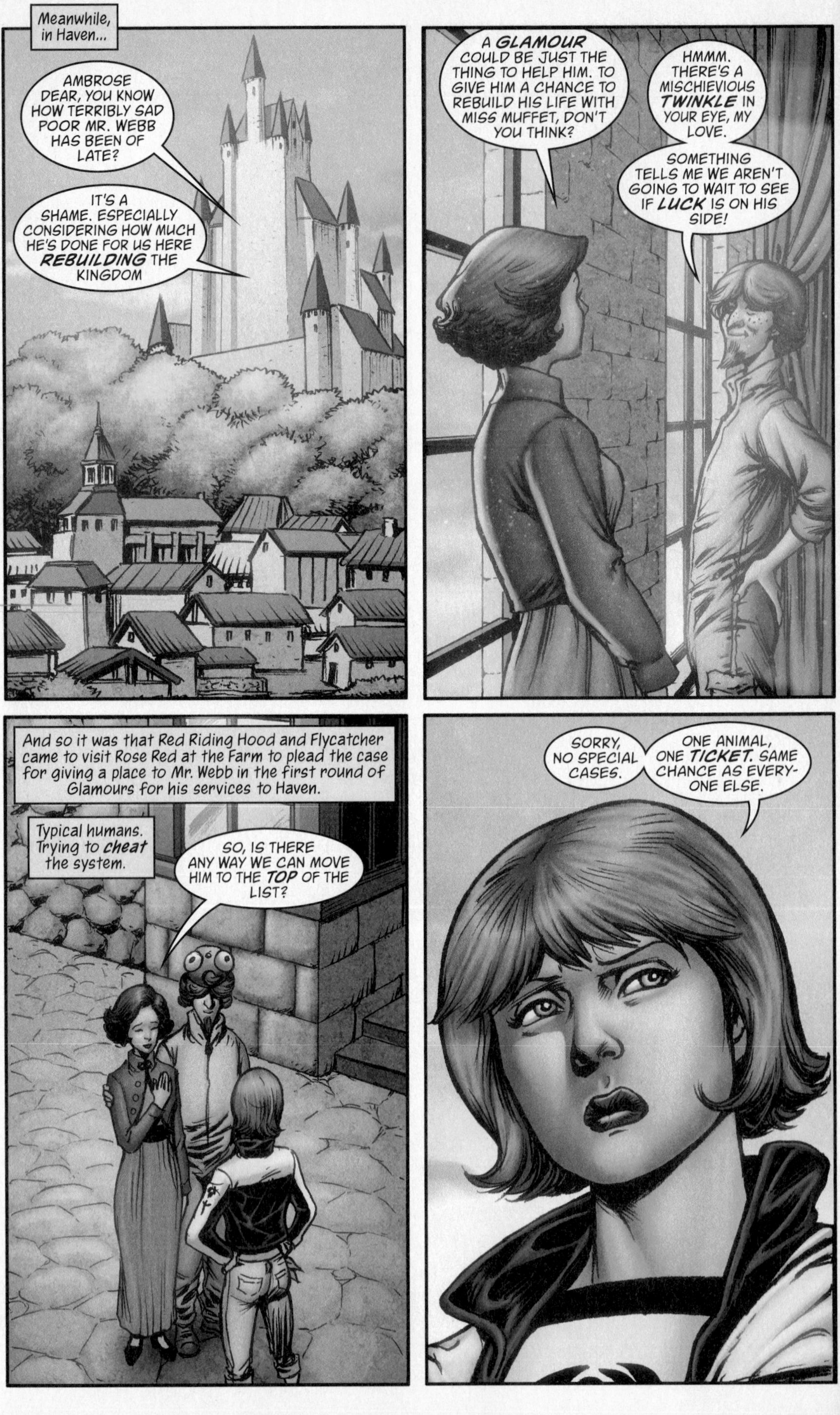
Meanwhile, in Haven...
AMBROSE DEAR, YOU KNOW HOW TERRIBLY SAD POOR MR. WEBB HAS BEEN OF LATE?
IT'S A SHAME. ESPECIALLY CONSIDERING HOW MUCH HE'S DONE FOR US HERE REBUILDING THE KINGDOM
A GLAMOUR COULD BE JUST THE THING TO HELP HIM. TO GIVE HIM A CHANCE TO REBUILD HIS LIFE WITH MISS MUFFET, DON'T YOU THINK?
HMMM. THERE'S A MISCHIEVIOUS TWINKLE IN YOUR EYE, MY LOVE.
SOMETHING TELLS ME WE AREN'T GOING TO WAIT TO SEE IF LUCK IS ON HIS SIDE!
And so it was that Red Riding Hood and Flycatcher came to visit Rose Red at the Farm to plead the case for giving a place to Mr. Webb in the first round of Glamours for his services to Haven.
Typical humans. Trying to cheat the system.
SO, IS THERE ANY WAY WE CAN MOVE HIM TO THE TOP OF THE LIST?
SORRY, NO SPECIAL CASES.
ONE ANIMAL, ONE TICKET. SAME CHANCE AS EVERY-ONE ELSE.

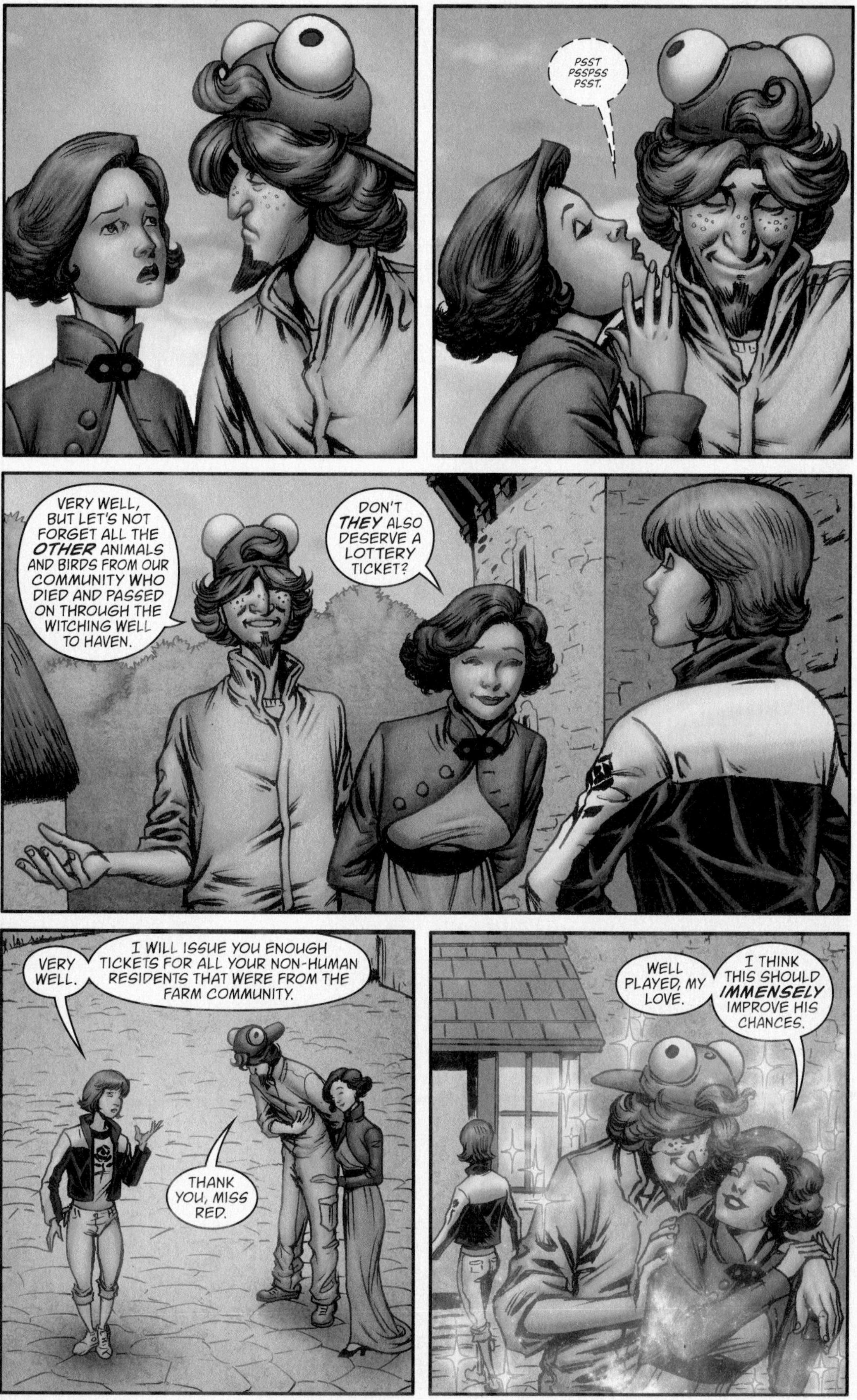
PSST PSSPSS PSST.
VERY WELL, BUT LET'S NOT FORGET ALL THE OTHER ANIMALS AND BIRDS FROM OUR COMMUNITY WHO DIED AND PASSED ON THROUGH THE WITCHING WELL TO HAVEN.
DON'T THEY ALSO DESERVE A LOTTERY TICKET?
VERY WELL.
I WILL ISSUE YOU ENOUGH TICKETS FOR ALL YOUR NON-HUMAN RESIDENTS THAT WERE FROM THE FARM COMMUNITY.
THANK YOU, MISS RED.
WELL PLAYED, MY LOVE.
I THINK THIS SHOULD IMMENSELY IMPROVE HIS CHANCES.

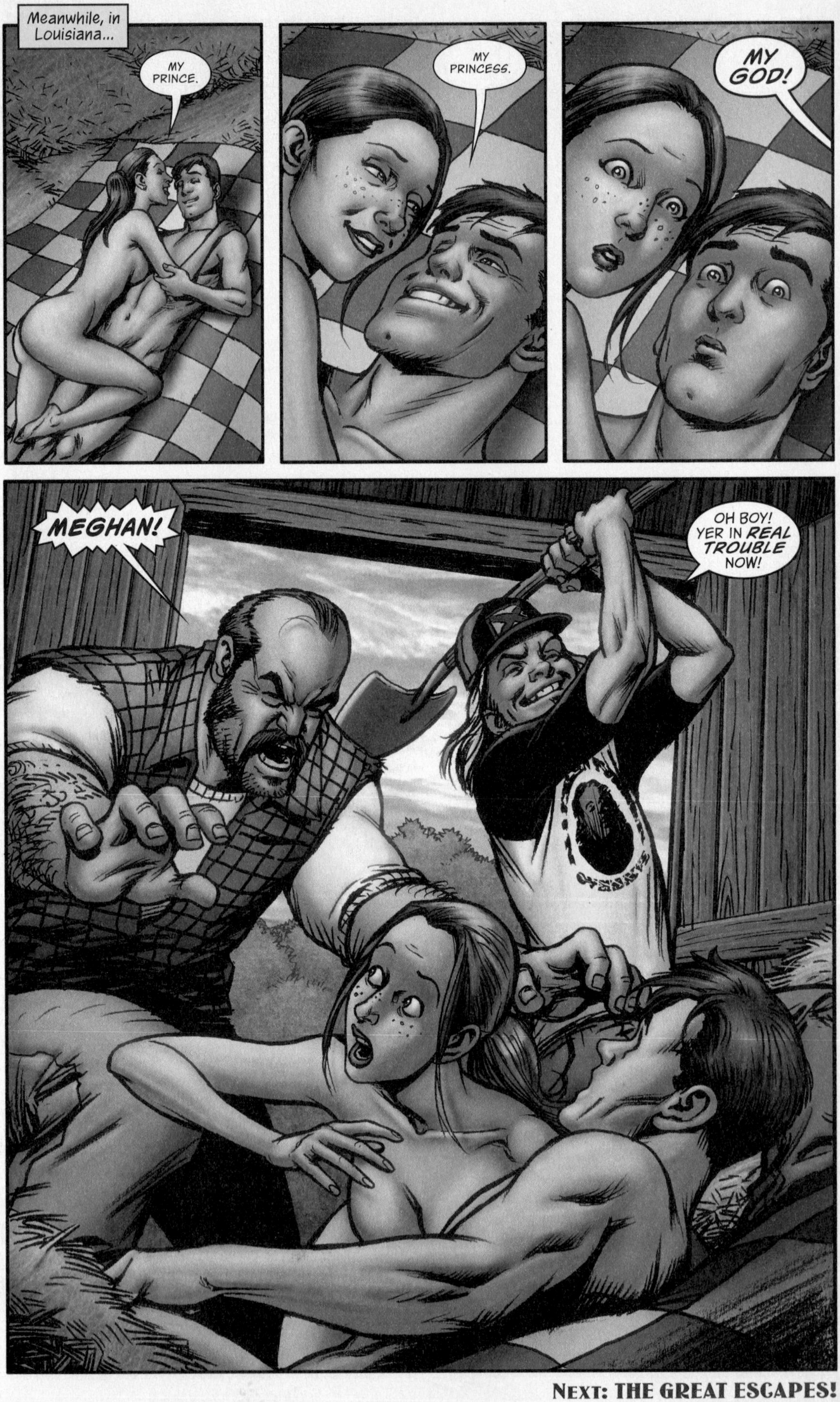
Meanwhile, in Louisiana...
MY PRINCE.
MY PRINCESS.
MY GOD!
MEGHAN!
OH BOY! YER IN REAL TROUBLE NOW!

Next: THE GREAT ESCAPES!

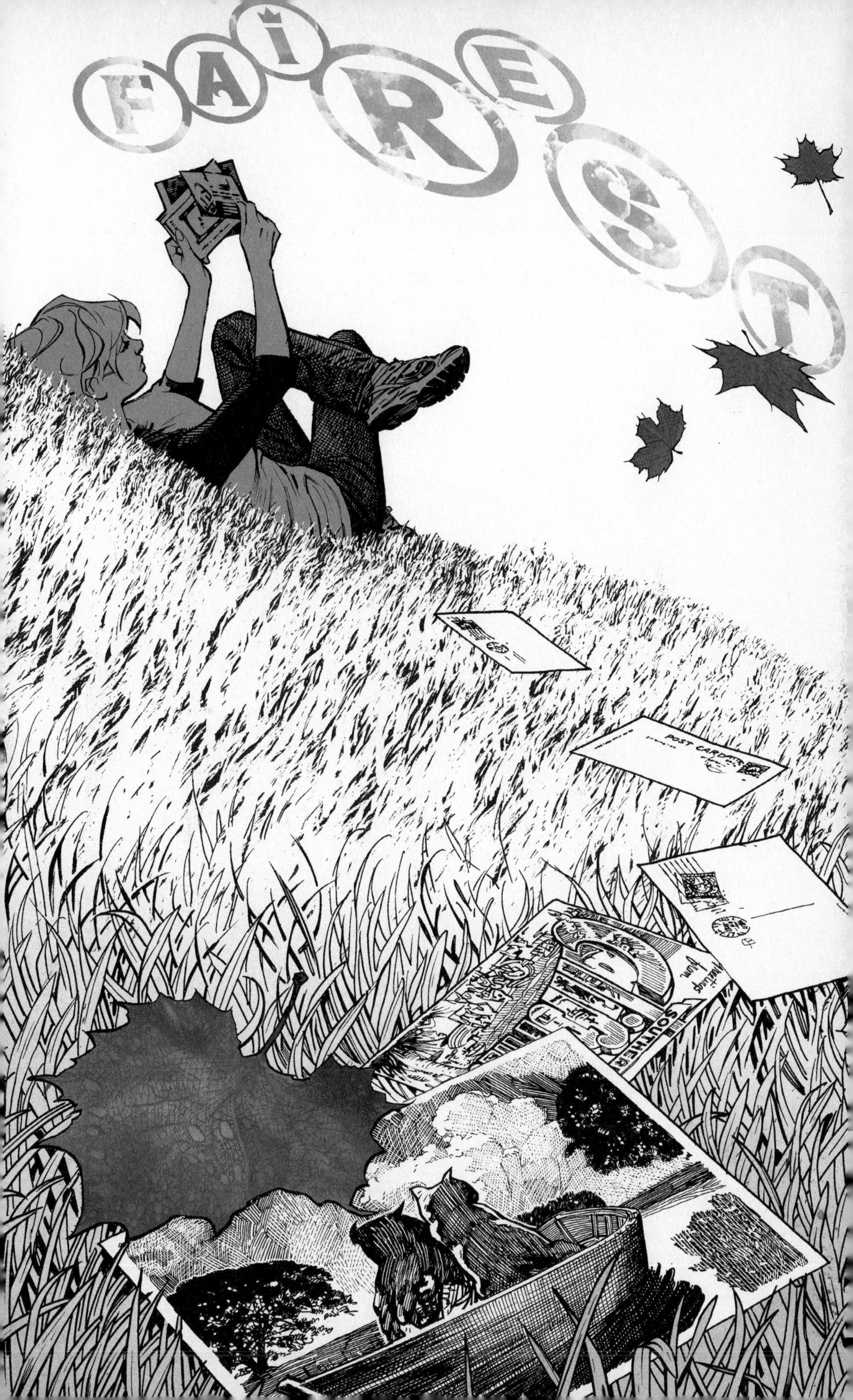
FAIREST
POST CARD

"I suspect it won't be long before we citizens of paw and wing will be returning to our Homelands."

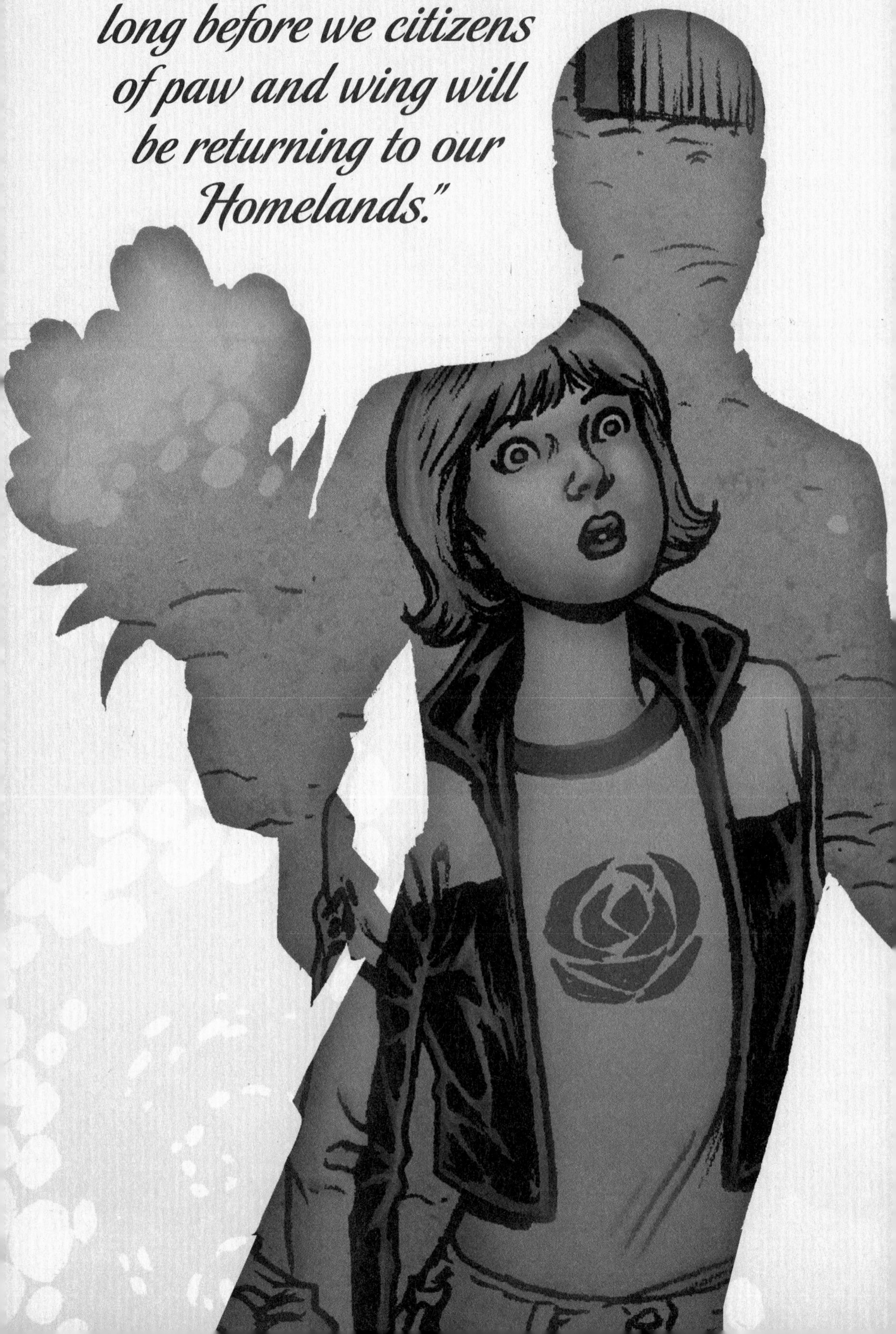

Reynard was incarcerated, somewhere deep in the heart of Louisiana, an arrogant Fable fox *adrift* in the world of mundane men.

...BLAH BLAH... PLEASE STOP... BLAH BLAH MY FAULT...

Head swimming.

Drowning.

...BLAH BLAH... TROUBLE... BLAH BLAH BLAH...BIG WHUPPING...

He found himself washed up on a most unforgiving shore.

...BLAH BLAH... DIGGING ME A BIG HOLE... BLAH BLAH BLAH...

...BLAH BLAH... UNGRATEFUL LITTLE BLAH...DON'T HURT... BLAH BLAH...

...REYNARD!!

Reynard must have been praying to be on the first boat *out* of there.

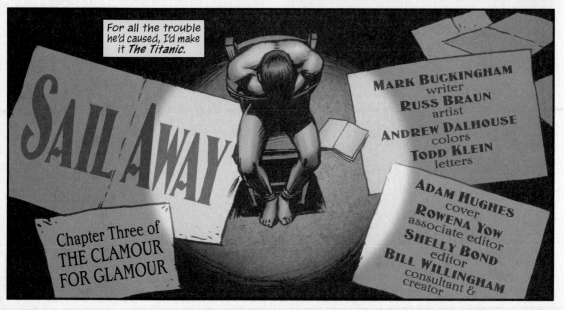

For all the trouble he'd caused, I'd make it *The Titanic*.

SAIL AWAY

Chapter Three of
THE CLAMOUR
FOR GLAMOUR

MARK BUCKINGHAM
writer
RUSS BRAUN
artist
ANDREW DALHOUSE
colors
TODD KLEIN
letters

ADAM HUGHES
cover
ROWENA YOW
associate editor
SHELLY BOND
editor
BILL WILLINGHAM
consultant &
creator

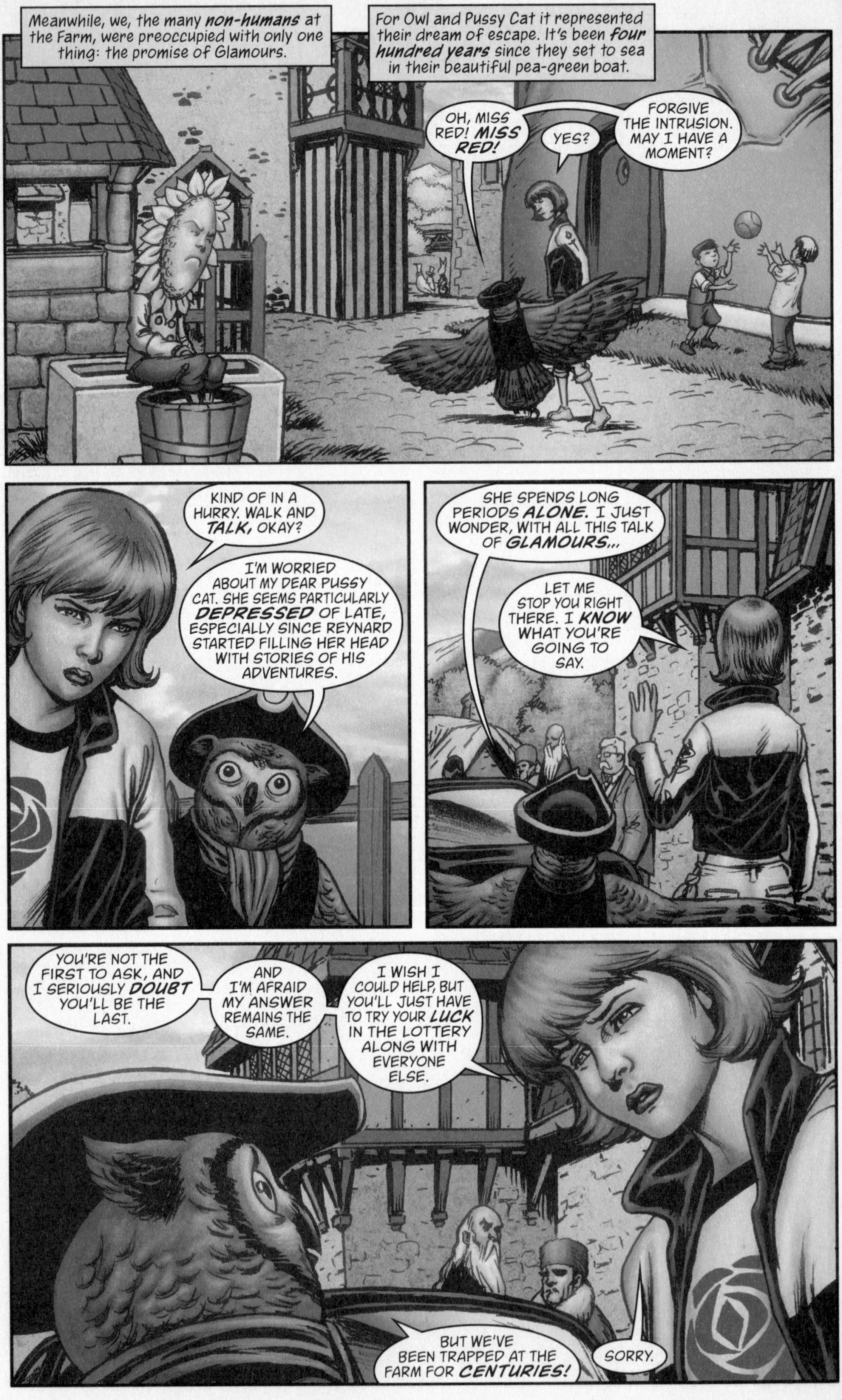
Meanwhile, we, the many non-humans at the Farm, were preoccupied with only one thing: the promise of Glamours.
For Owl and Pussy Cat it represented their dream of escape. It's been four hundred years since they set to sea in their beautiful pea-green boat.
OH, MISS RED! MISS RED!
YES?
FORGIVE THE INTRUSION. MAY I HAVE A MOMENT?
KIND OF IN A HURRY. WALK AND TALK, OKAY?
I'M WORRIED ABOUT MY DEAR PUSSY CAT. SHE SEEMS PARTICULARLY DEPRESSED OF LATE, ESPECIALLY SINCE REYNARD STARTED FILLING HER HEAD WITH STORIES OF HIS ADVENTURES.
SHE SPENDS LONG PERIODS ALONE. I JUST WONDER, WITH ALL THIS TALK OF GLAMOURS...
LET ME STOP YOU RIGHT THERE. I KNOW WHAT YOU'RE GOING TO SAY.
YOU'RE NOT THE FIRST TO ASK, AND I SERIOUSLY DOUBT YOU'LL BE THE LAST.
AND I'M AFRAID MY ANSWER REMAINS THE SAME.
I WISH I COULD HELP, BUT YOU'LL JUST HAVE TO TRY YOUR LUCK IN THE LOTTERY ALONG WITH EVERYONE ELSE.
BUT WE'VE BEEN TRAPPED AT THE FARM FOR CENTURIES!
SORRY.

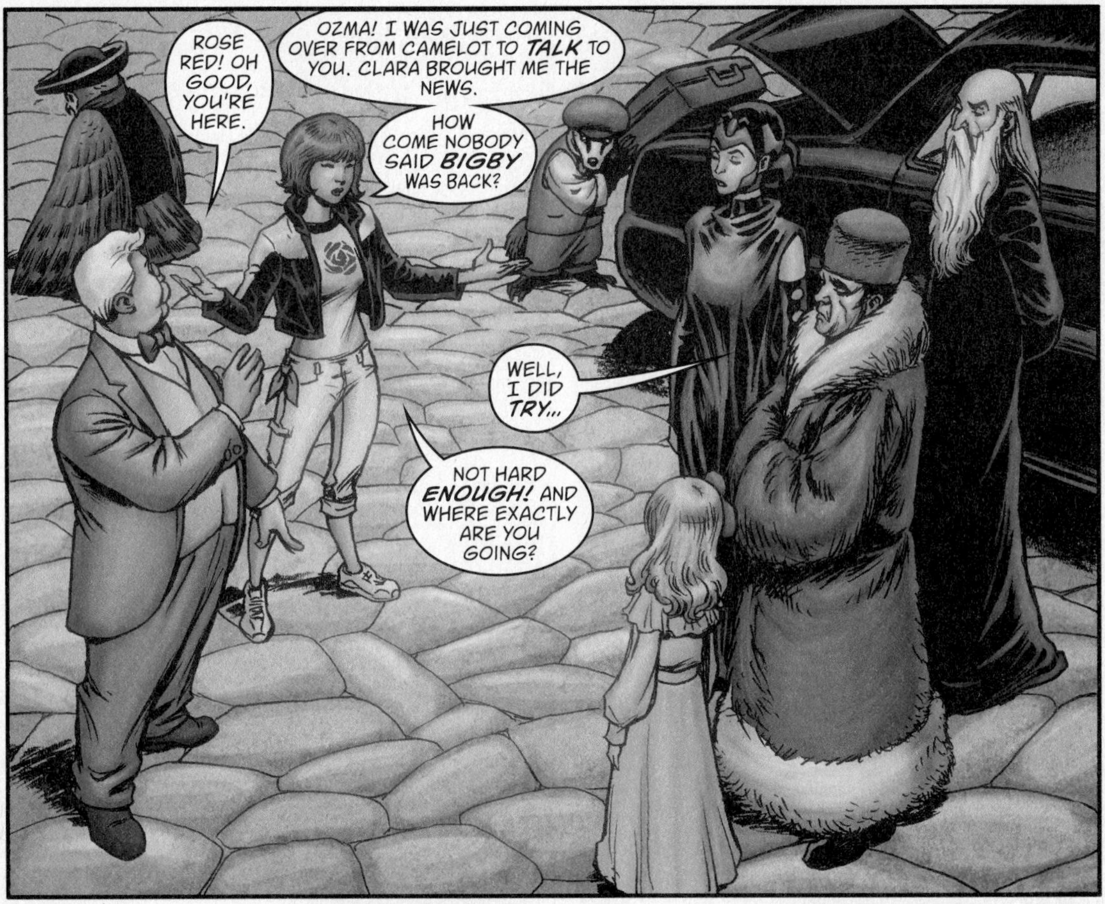
ROSE RED! OH GOOD, YOU'RE HERE.
OZMA! I WAS JUST COMING OVER FROM CAMELOT TO TALK TO YOU. CLARA BROUGHT ME THE NEWS.
HOW COME NOBODY SAID BIGBY WAS BACK?
WELL, I DID TRY...
NOT HARD ENOUGH! AND WHERE EXACTLY ARE YOU GOING?

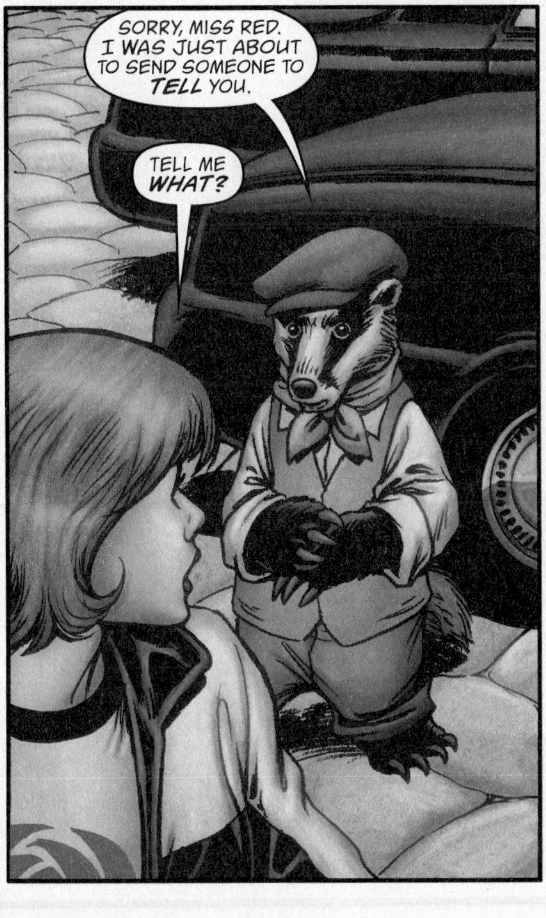
SORRY, MISS RED. I WAS JUST ABOUT TO SEND SOMEONE TO TELL YOU.
TELL ME WHAT?

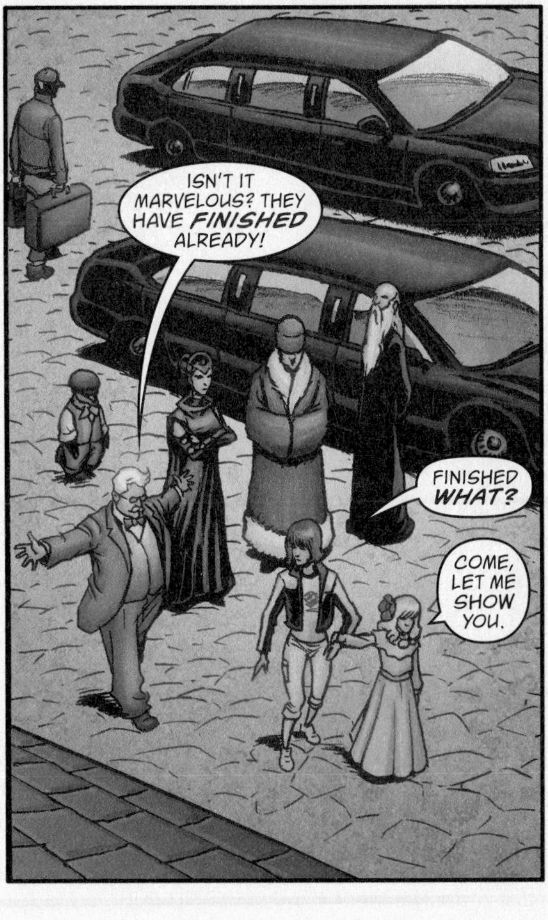
ISN'T IT MARVELOUS? THEY HAVE FINISHED ALREADY!
FINISHED WHAT?
COME, LET ME SHOW YOU.

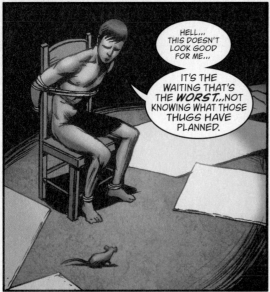

HELL... THIS DOESN'T LOOK GOOD FOR ME...

IT'S THE WAITING THAT'S THE *WORST*...NOT KNOWING WHAT THOSE THUGS HAVE PLANNED.

I REMEMBER SO LITTLE...SOMETHING ABOUT DIGGING HOLES... SHOTGUNS...VERMIN...

NOT *YOU*, LITTLE GUY.

FOR ONE MOMENT THERE I WAS FEELING PRETTY DAMN SPECIAL. MISTER *SMUG*. CENTER OF ATTENTION.

LOST IN THE ARMS OF...

OH GOD! *MEGHAN!*

ALL THIS TIME I'VE BEEN WONDERING WHAT THEY HAD PLANNED FOR *ME*...!

THAT BRIEF GLIMPSE OF THE *LIFE* SHE ENDURES HERE...

WHO *KNOWS* WHAT UNSPEAKABLE THINGS THOSE *MONSTERS* MIGHT BE DOING TO HER?

THAT POOR, SWEET GIRL.

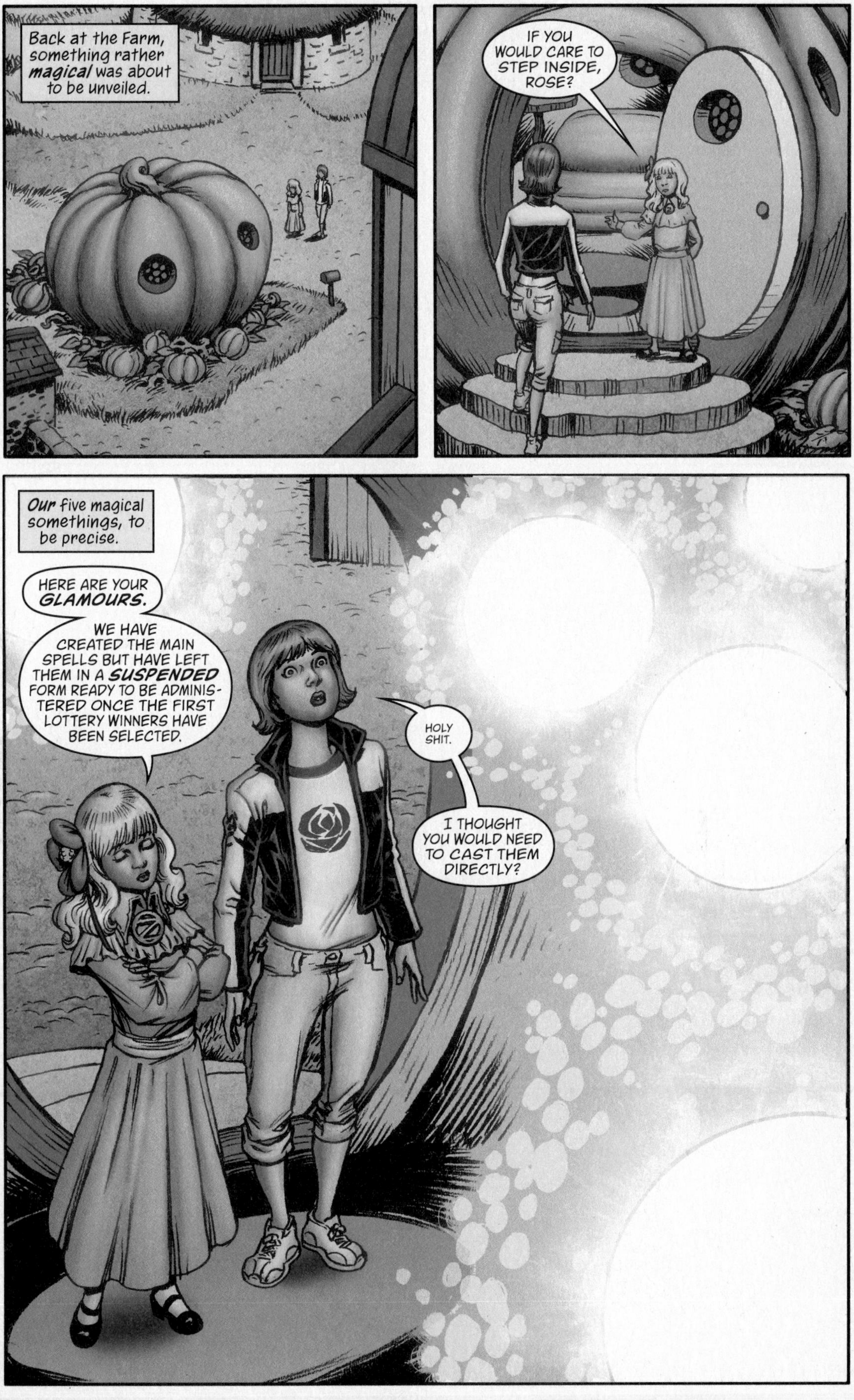
Back at the Farm, something rather magical was about to be unveiled.
IF YOU WOULD CARE TO STEP INSIDE, ROSE?
Our five magical somethings, to be precise.
HERE ARE YOUR GLAMOURS.
WE HAVE CREATED THE MAIN SPELLS BUT HAVE LEFT THEM IN A SUSPENDED FORM READY TO BE ADMINISTERED ONCE THE FIRST LOTTERY WINNERS HAVE BEEN SELECTED.
HOLY SHIT.
I THOUGHT YOU WOULD NEED TO CAST THEM DIRECTLY?

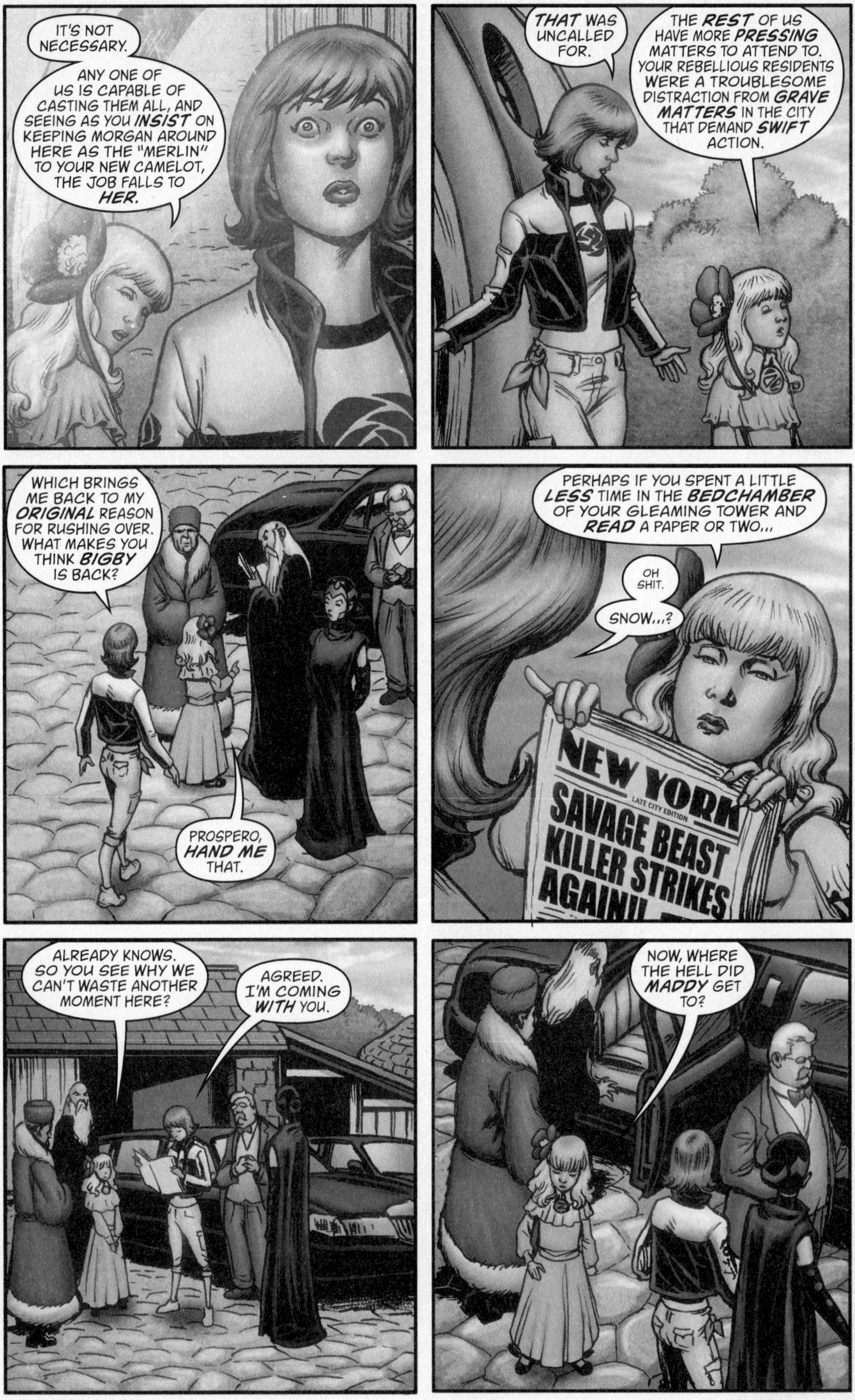
IT'S NOT NECESSARY.
ANY ONE OF US IS CAPABLE OF CASTING THEM ALL, AND SEEING AS YOU INSIST ON KEEPING MORGAN AROUND HERE AS THE "MERLIN" TO YOUR NEW CAMELOT, THE JOB FALLS TO HER.
THAT WAS UNCALLED FOR.
THE REST OF US HAVE MORE PRESSING MATTERS TO ATTEND TO. YOUR REBELLIOUS RESIDENTS WERE A TROUBLESOME DISTRACTION FROM GRAVE MATTERS IN THE CITY THAT DEMAND SWIFT ACTION.
WHICH BRINGS ME BACK TO MY ORIGINAL REASON FOR RUSHING OVER. WHAT MAKES YOU THINK BIGBY IS BACK?
PROSPERO, HAND ME THAT.
PERHAPS IF YOU SPENT A LITTLE LESS TIME IN THE BEDCHAMBER OF YOUR GLEAMING TOWER AND READ A PAPER OR TWO...
OH SHIT.
SNOW...?
NEW YORK
LATE CITY EDITION
SAVAGE BEAST KILLER STRIKES AGAIN!
ALREADY KNOWS. SO YOU SEE WHY WE CAN'T WASTE ANOTHER MOMENT HERE?
AGREED. I'M COMING WITH YOU.
NOW, WHERE THE HELL DID MADDY GET TO?

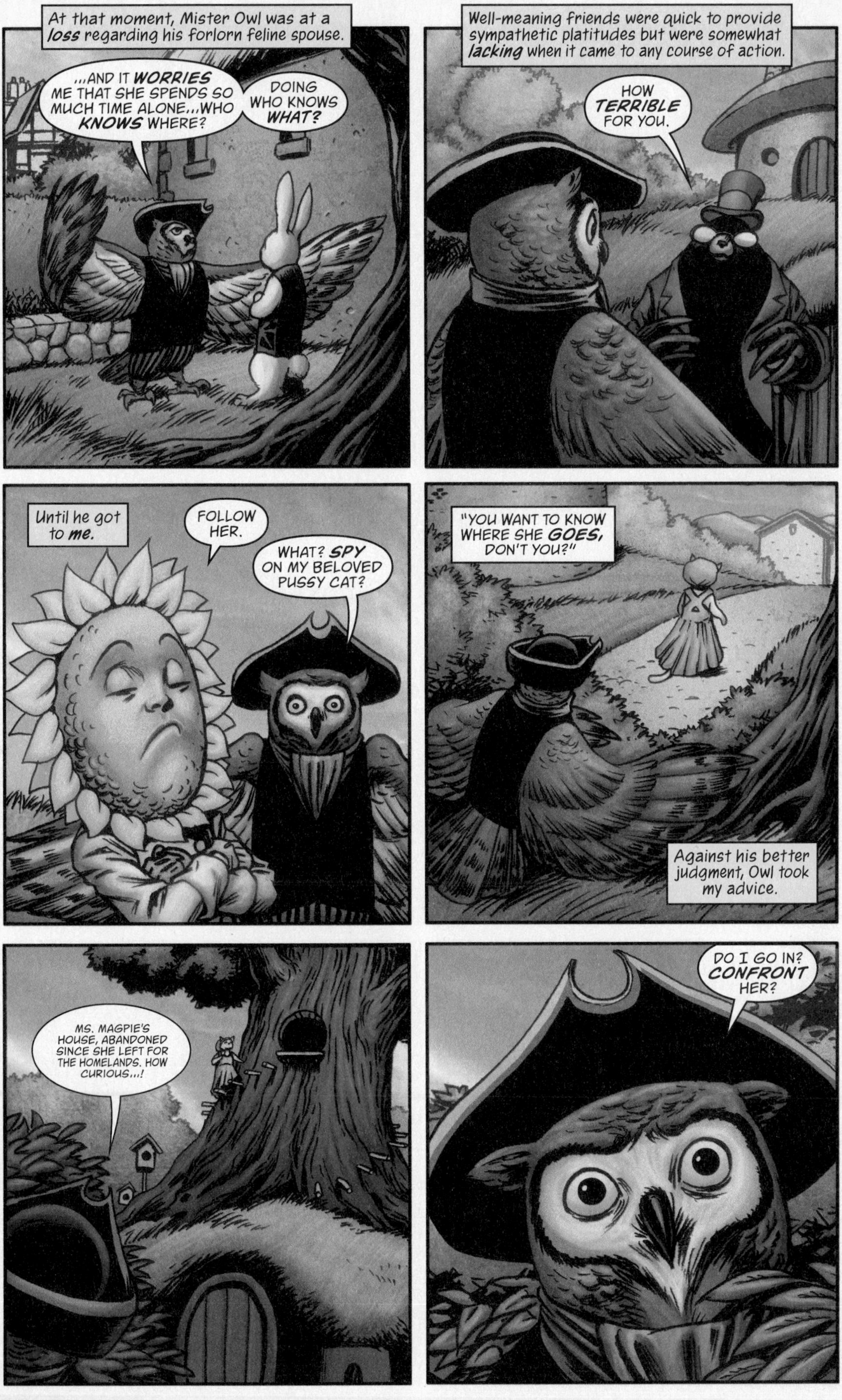
At that moment, Mister Owl was at a loss regarding his forlorn feline spouse.
...AND IT WORRIES ME THAT SHE SPENDS SO MUCH TIME ALONE...WHO KNOWS WHERE?
DOING WHO KNOWS WHAT?
Well-meaning friends were quick to provide sympathetic platitudes but were somewhat lacking when it came to any course of action.
HOW TERRIBLE FOR YOU.
Until he got to me.
FOLLOW HER.
WHAT? SPY ON MY BELOVED PUSSY CAT?
"YOU WANT TO KNOW WHERE SHE GOES, DON'T YOU?"
Against his better judgment, Owl took my advice.
MS. MAGPIE'S HOUSE, ABANDONED SINCE SHE LEFT FOR THE HOMELANDS. HOW CURIOUS...!
DO I GO IN? CONFRONT HER?

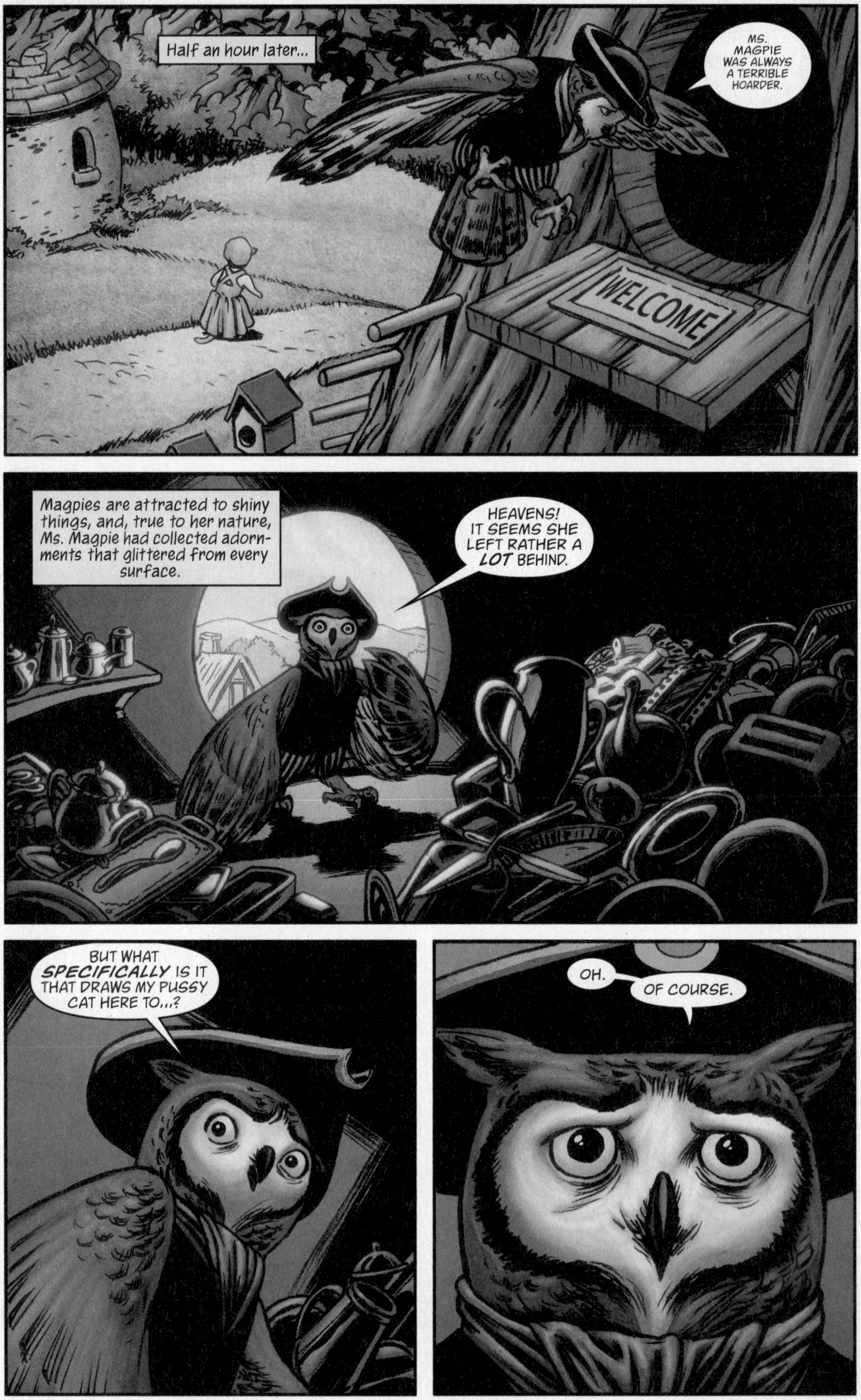
Half an hour later...
MS. MAGPIE WAS ALWAYS A TERRIBLE HOARDER.
WELCOME
Magpies are attracted to shiny things, and, true to her nature, Ms. Magpie had collected adornments that glittered from every surface.
HEAVENS! IT SEEMS SHE LEFT RATHER A *LOT* BEHIND.
BUT WHAT *SPECIFICALLY* IS IT THAT DRAWS MY PUSSY CAT HERE TO...?
OH.
OF COURSE.

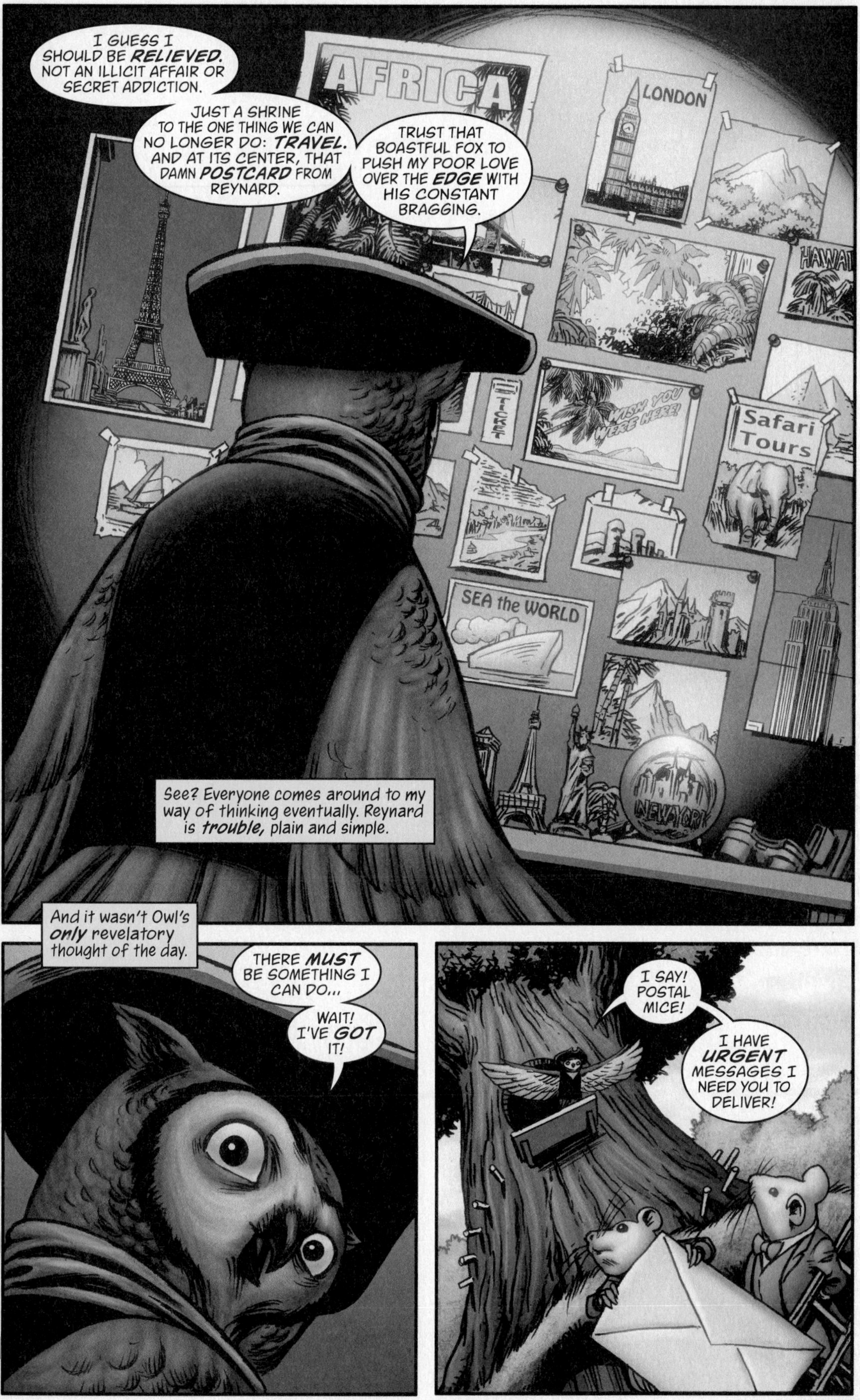

I GUESS I SHOULD BE *RELIEVED.* NOT AN ILLICIT AFFAIR OR SECRET ADDICTION.
JUST A SHRINE TO THE ONE THING WE CAN NO LONGER DO: *TRAVEL.* AND AT ITS CENTER, THAT DAMN *POSTCARD* FROM REYNARD.
TRUST THAT BOASTFUL FOX TO PUSH MY POOR LOVE OVER THE *EDGE* WITH HIS CONSTANT BRAGGING.
AFRICA
LONDON
TICKET
WISH YOU WERE HERE!
Safari Tours
SEA the WORLD
See? Everyone comes around to my way of thinking eventually. Reynard is *trouble,* plain and simple.
And it wasn't Owl's *only* revelatory thought of the day.
THERE *MUST* BE SOMETHING I CAN DO...
WAIT! I'VE *GOT* IT!
I SAY! POSTAL MICE!
I HAVE *URGENT* MESSAGES I NEED YOU TO DELIVER!

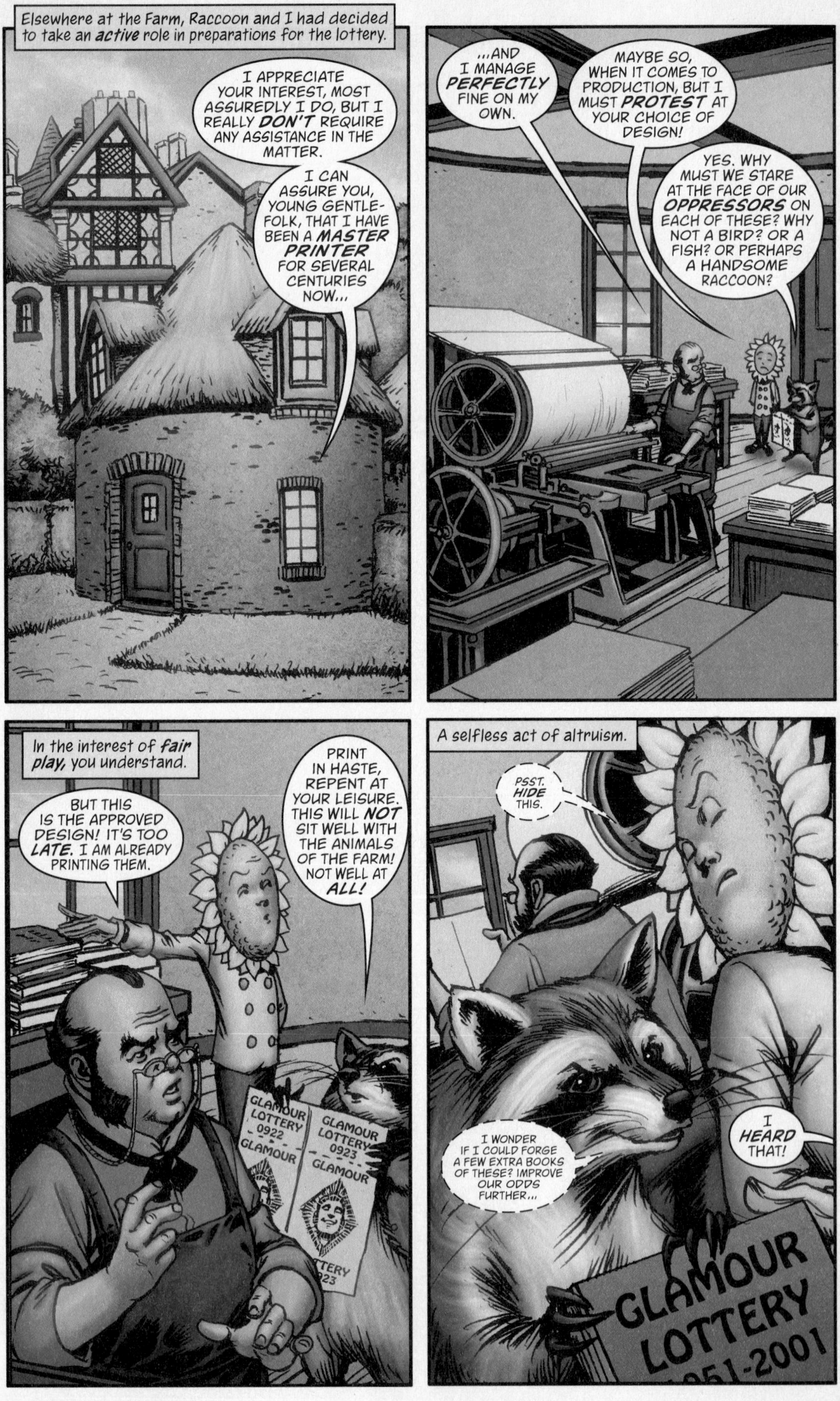
Elsewhere at the Farm, Raccoon and I had decided to take an *active* role in preparations for the lottery.
I APPRECIATE YOUR INTEREST, MOST ASSUREDLY I DO, BUT I REALLY **DON'T** REQUIRE ANY ASSISTANCE IN THE MATTER.
I CAN ASSURE YOU, YOUNG GENTLE-FOLK, THAT I HAVE BEEN A **MASTER PRINTER** FOR SEVERAL CENTURIES NOW...
...AND I MANAGE **PERFECTLY** FINE ON MY OWN.
MAYBE SO, WHEN IT COMES TO PRODUCTION, BUT I MUST **PROTEST** AT YOUR CHOICE OF DESIGN!
YES. WHY MUST WE STARE AT THE FACE OF OUR **OPPRESSORS** ON EACH OF THESE? WHY NOT A BIRD? OR A FISH? OR PERHAPS A HANDSOME RACCOON?
In the interest of *fair play,* you understand.
BUT THIS IS THE APPROVED DESIGN! IT'S TOO **LATE.** I AM ALREADY PRINTING THEM.
PRINT IN HASTE, REPENT AT YOUR LEISURE. THIS WILL **NOT** SIT WELL WITH THE ANIMALS OF THE FARM! NOT WELL AT **ALL!**
GLAMOUR LOTTERY 0922 GLAMOUR
GLAMOUR LOTTERY 0923 GLAMOUR
A selfless act of altruism.
PSST. **HIDE** THIS.
I WONDER IF I COULD FORGE A FEW EXTRA BOOKS OF THESE? IMPROVE OUR ODDS FURTHER...
I **HEARD** THAT!
GLAMOUR LOTTERY

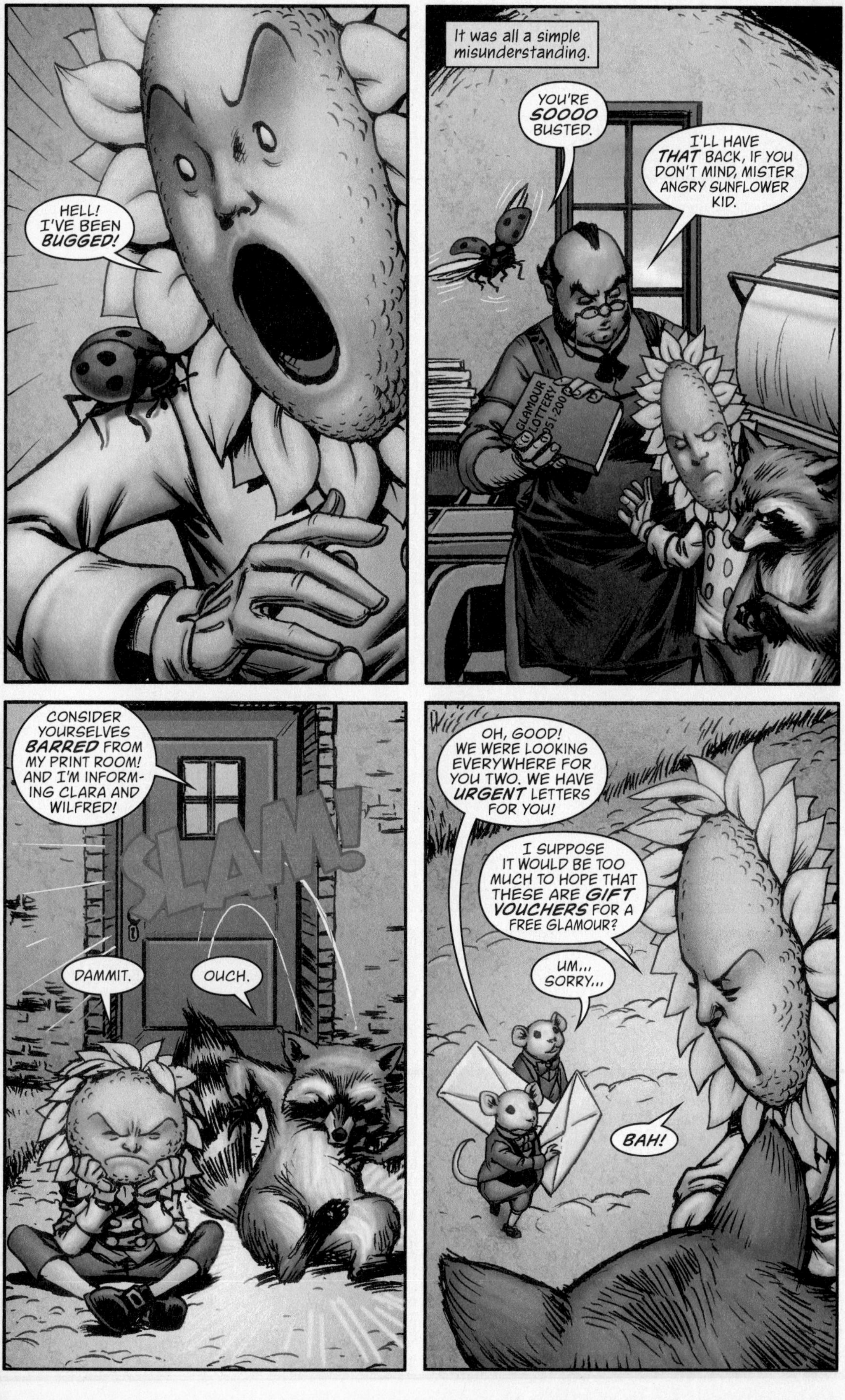
HELL! I'VE BEEN BUGGED!
It was all a simple misunderstanding.
YOU'RE SOOOO BUSTED.
I'LL HAVE THAT BACK, IF YOU DON'T MIND, MISTER ANGRY SUNFLOWER KID.
GLAMOUR LOTTERY
CONSIDER YOURSELVES BARRED FROM MY PRINT ROOM! AND I'M INFORMING CLARA AND WILFRED!
SLAM!
DAMMIT.
OUCH.
OH, GOOD! WE WERE LOOKING EVERYWHERE FOR YOU TWO. WE HAVE URGENT LETTERS FOR YOU!
I SUPPOSE IT WOULD BE TOO MUCH TO HOPE THAT THESE ARE GIFT VOUCHERS FOR A FREE GLAMOUR?
UM... SORRY...
BAH!

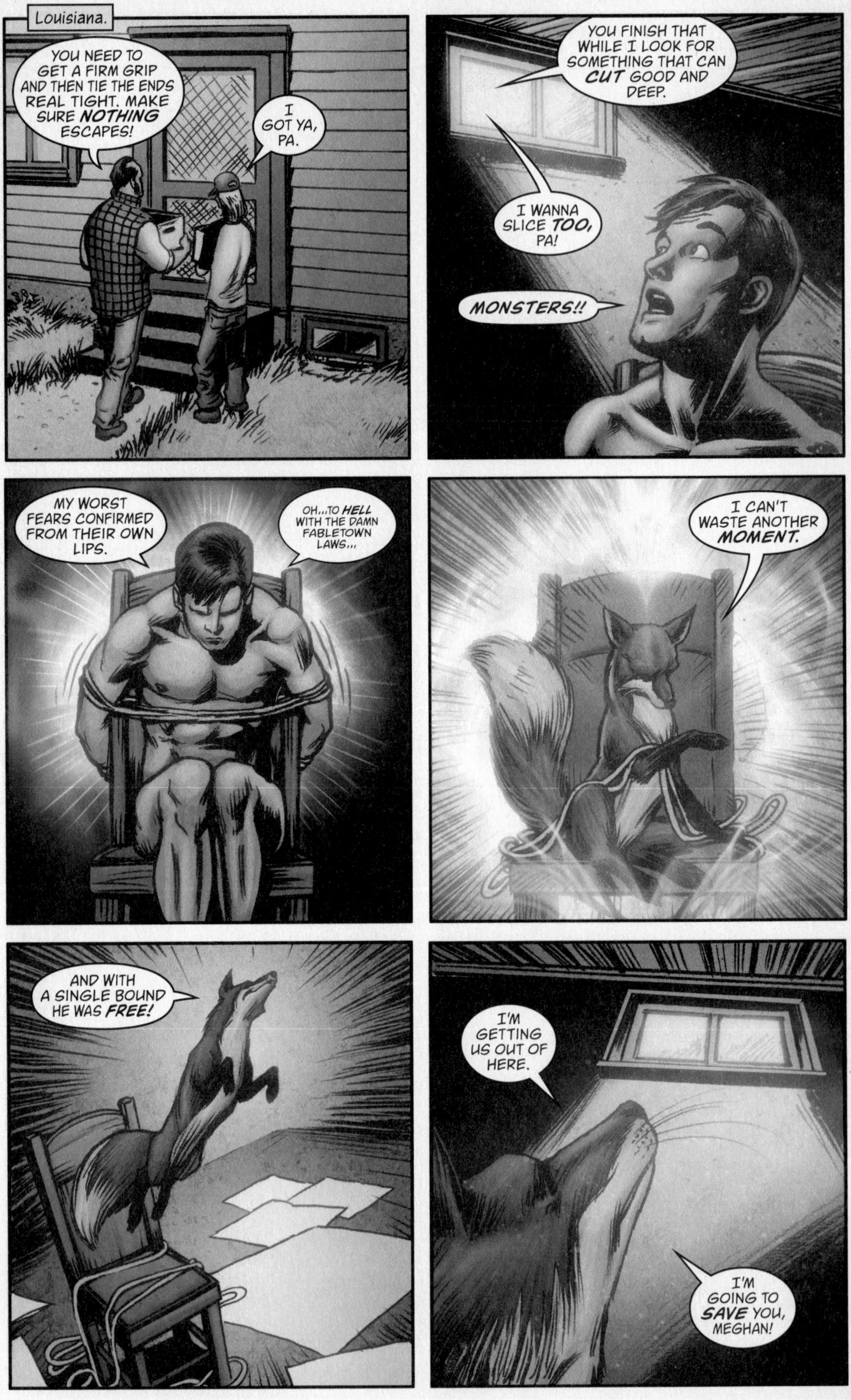
Louisiana.
YOU NEED TO GET A FIRM GRIP AND THEN TIE THE ENDS REAL TIGHT. MAKE SURE NOTHING ESCAPES!
I GOT YA, PA.
YOU FINISH THAT WHILE I LOOK FOR SOMETHING THAT CAN CUT GOOD AND DEEP.
I WANNA SLICE TOO, PA!
MONSTERS!!
MY WORST FEARS CONFIRMED FROM THEIR OWN LIPS.
OH...TO HELL WITH THE DAMN FABLETOWN LAWS...
I CAN'T WASTE ANOTHER MOMENT.
AND WITH A SINGLE BOUND HE WAS FREE!
I'M GETTING US OUT OF HERE.
I'M GOING TO SAVE YOU, MEGHAN!

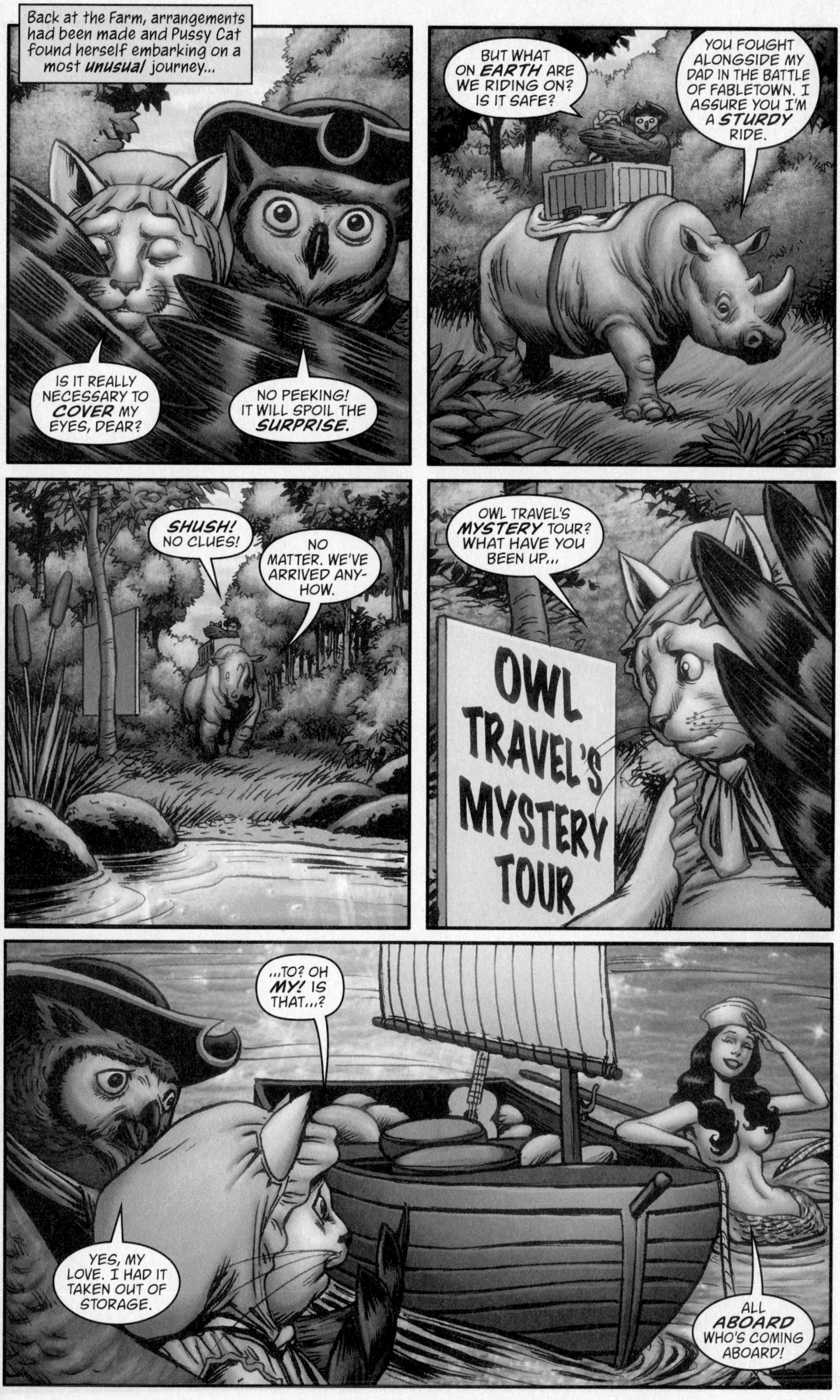

Back at the Farm, arrangements had been made and Pussy Cat found herself embarking on a most *unusual* journey...
IS IT REALLY NECESSARY TO **COVER** MY EYES, DEAR?
NO PEEKING! IT WILL SPOIL THE **SURPRISE.**
BUT WHAT ON **EARTH** ARE WE RIDING ON? IS IT SAFE?
YOU FOUGHT ALONGSIDE MY DAD IN THE BATTLE OF FABLETOWN. I ASSURE YOU I'M A **STURDY** RIDE.
SHUSH! NO CLUES!
NO MATTER. WE'VE ARRIVED ANY-HOW.
OWL TRAVEL'S **MYSTERY** TOUR? WHAT HAVE YOU BEEN UP...
OWL TRAVEL'S MYSTERY TOUR
...TO? OH **MY!** IS THAT...?
YES, MY LOVE. I HAD IT TAKEN OUT OF STORAGE.
ALL **ABOARD** WHO'S COMING ABOARD!

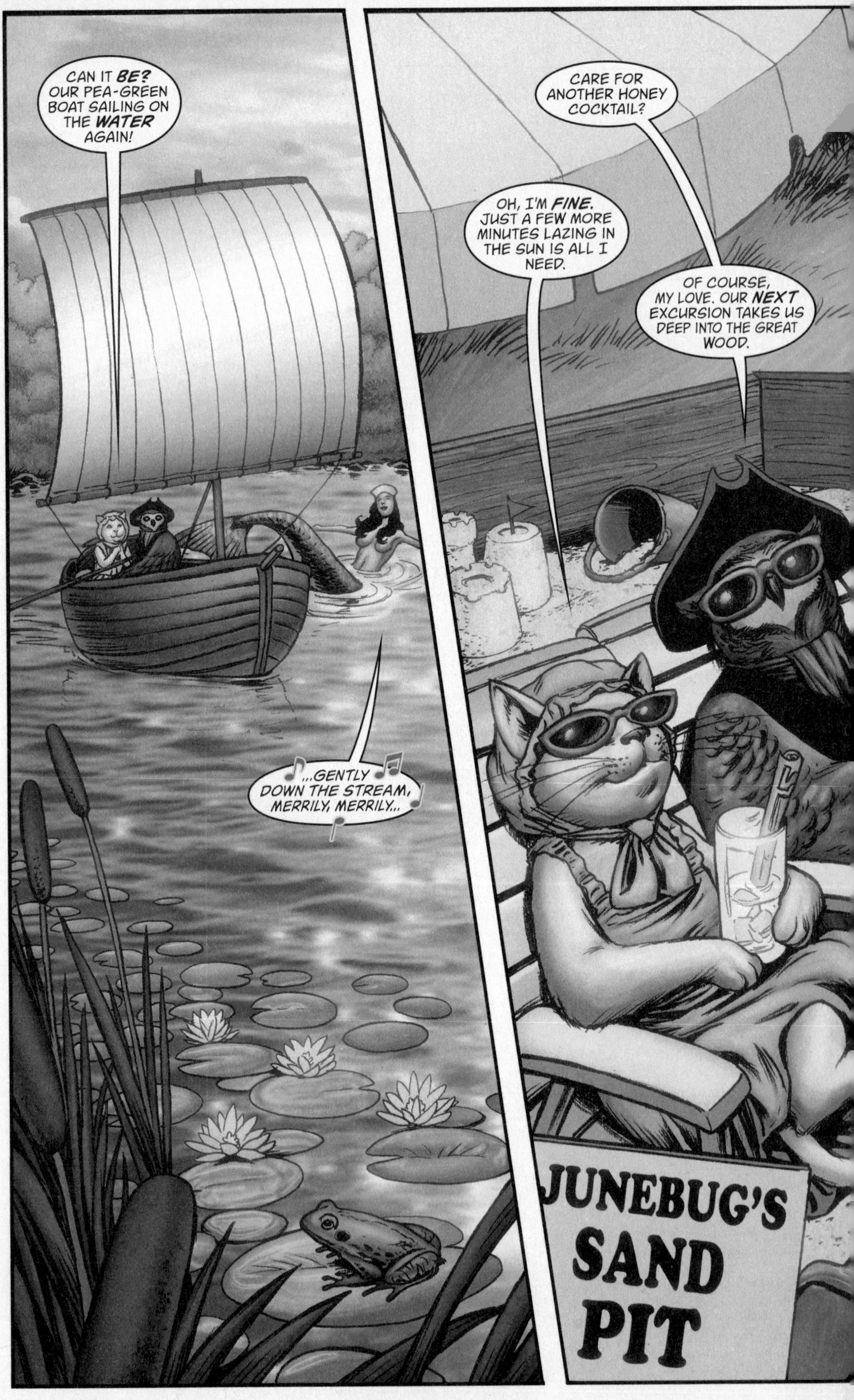
CAN IT BE? OUR PEA-GREEN BOAT SAILING ON THE WATER AGAIN!
...GENTLY DOWN THE STREAM, MERRILY, MERRILY...
CARE FOR ANOTHER HONEY COCKTAIL?
OH, I'M FINE. JUST A FEW MORE MINUTES LAZING IN THE SUN IS ALL I NEED.
OF COURSE, MY LOVE. OUR NEXT EXCURSION TAKES US DEEP INTO THE GREAT WOOD.
JUNEBUG'S SAND PIT

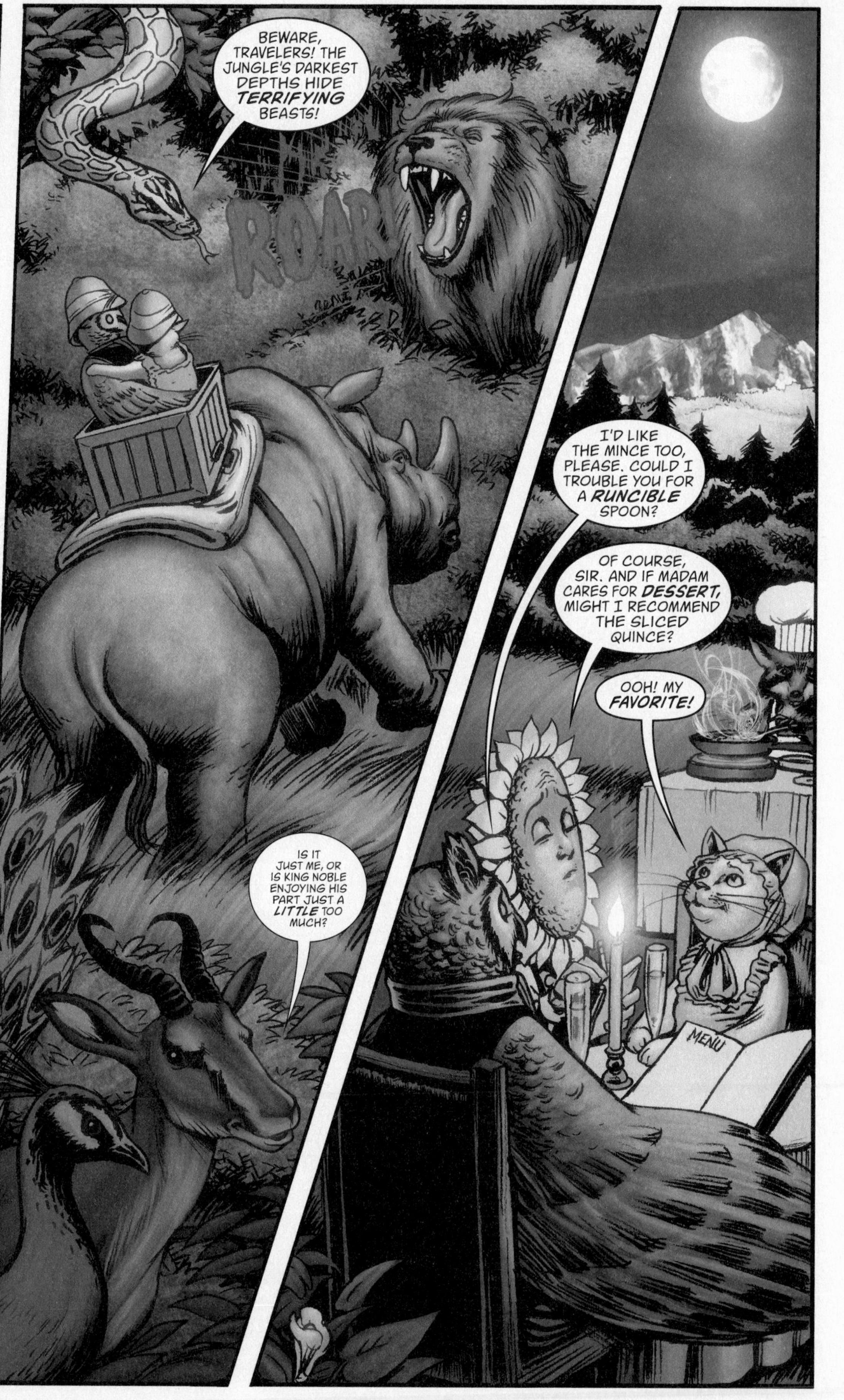
BEWARE, TRAVELERS! THE JUNGLE'S DARKEST DEPTHS HIDE *TERRIFYING* BEASTS!
ROAR!
IS IT JUST ME, OR IS KING NOBLE ENJOYING HIS PART JUST A *LITTLE* TOO MUCH?
I'D LIKE THE MINCE TOO, PLEASE. COULD I TROUBLE YOU FOR A *RUNCIBLE* SPOON?
OF COURSE, SIR. AND IF MADAM CARES FOR *DESSERT,* MIGHT I RECOMMEND THE SLICED QUINCE?
OOH! MY *FAVORITE!*
MENU

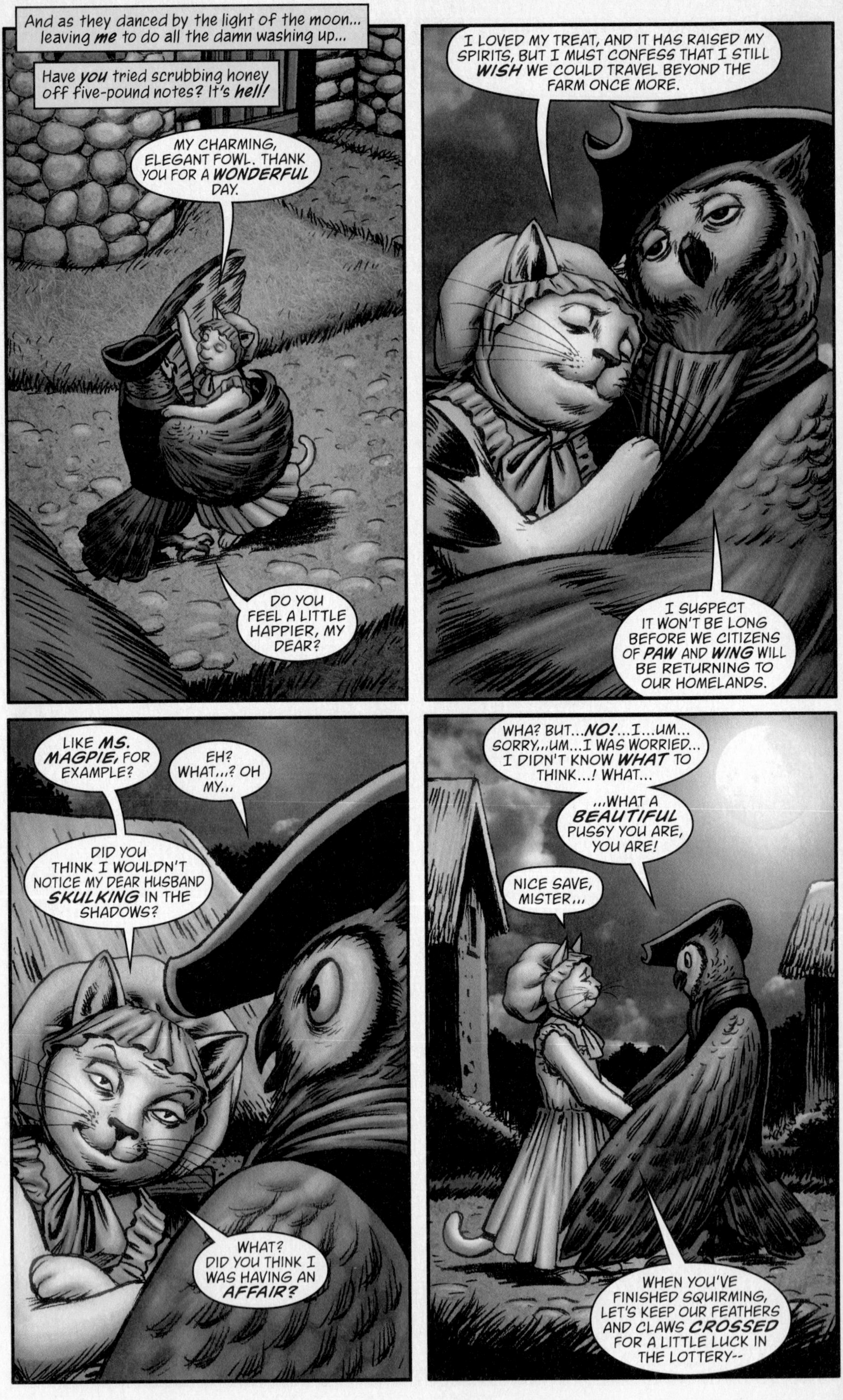

And as they danced by the light of the moon... leaving me to do all the damn washing up...
Have you tried scrubbing honey off five-pound notes? It's hell!
MY CHARMING, ELEGANT FOWL. THANK YOU FOR A WONDERFUL DAY.
DO YOU FEEL A LITTLE HAPPIER, MY DEAR?
I LOVED MY TREAT, AND IT HAS RAISED MY SPIRITS, BUT I MUST CONFESS THAT I STILL WISH WE COULD TRAVEL BEYOND THE FARM ONCE MORE.
I SUSPECT IT WON'T BE LONG BEFORE WE CITIZENS OF PAW AND WING WILL BE RETURNING TO OUR HOMELANDS.
LIKE MS. MAGPIE, FOR EXAMPLE?
EH? WHAT...? OH MY...
DID YOU THINK I WOULDN'T NOTICE MY DEAR HUSBAND SKULKING IN THE SHADOWS?
WHAT? DID YOU THINK I WAS HAVING AN AFFAIR?
WHA? BUT...NO!...I...UM... SORRY...UM...I WAS WORRIED... I DIDN'T KNOW WHAT TO THINK...! WHAT...
...WHAT A BEAUTIFUL PUSSY YOU ARE, YOU ARE!
NICE SAVE, MISTER...
WHEN YOU'VE FINISHED SQUIRMING, LET'S KEEP OUR FEATHERS AND CLAWS CROSSED FOR A LITTLE LUCK IN THE LOTTERY--

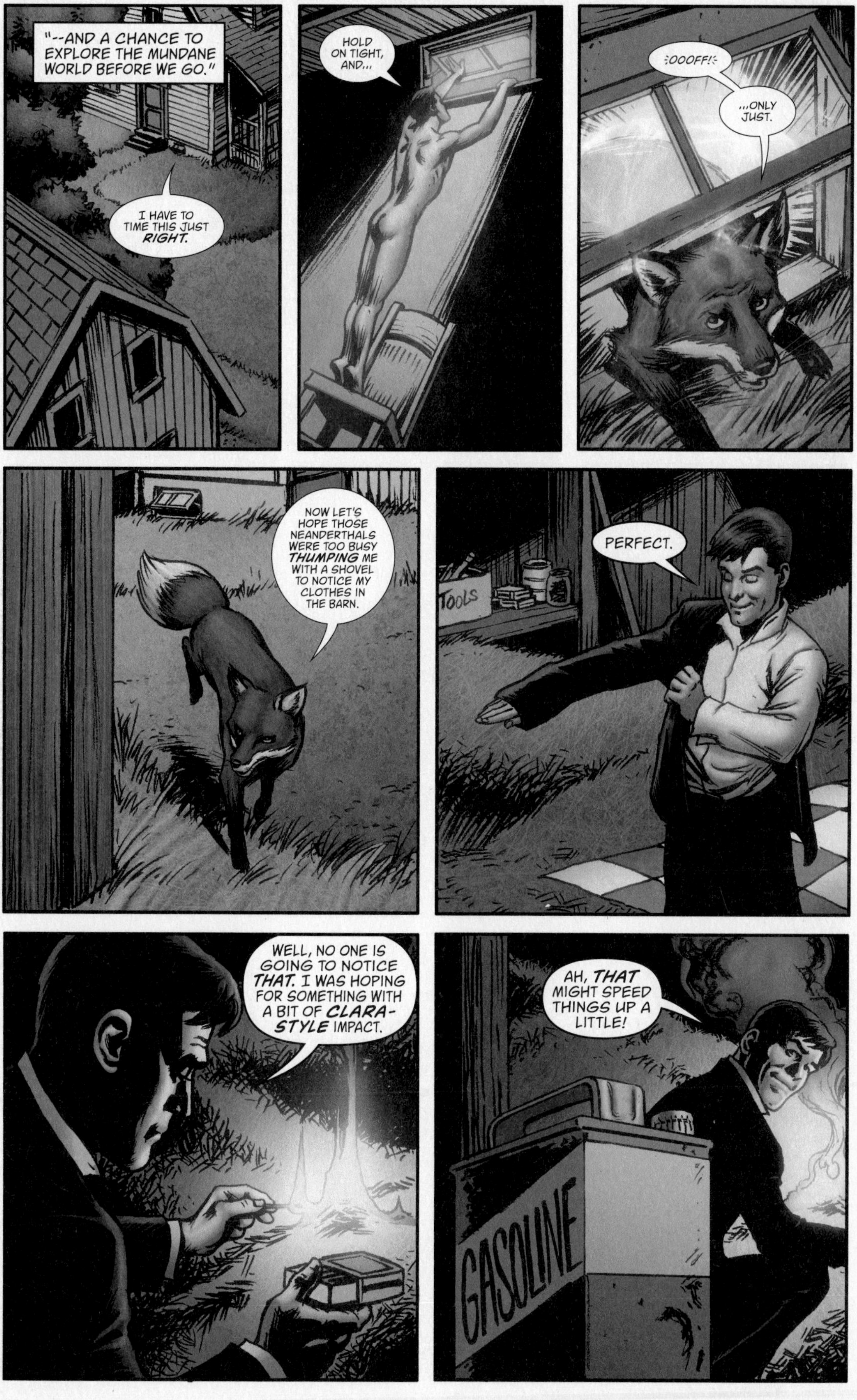
"--AND A CHANCE TO EXPLORE THE MUNDANE WORLD BEFORE WE GO."
I HAVE TO TIME THIS JUST RIGHT.
HOLD ON TIGHT, AND...
OOOFF!
...ONLY JUST.
NOW LET'S HOPE THOSE NEANDERTHALS WERE TOO BUSY THUMPING ME WITH A SHOVEL TO NOTICE MY CLOTHES IN THE BARN.
TOOLS
PERFECT.
WELL, NO ONE IS GOING TO NOTICE THAT. I WAS HOPING FOR SOMETHING WITH A BIT OF CLARA-STYLE IMPACT.
AH, THAT MIGHT SPEED THINGS UP A LITTLE!
GASOLINE

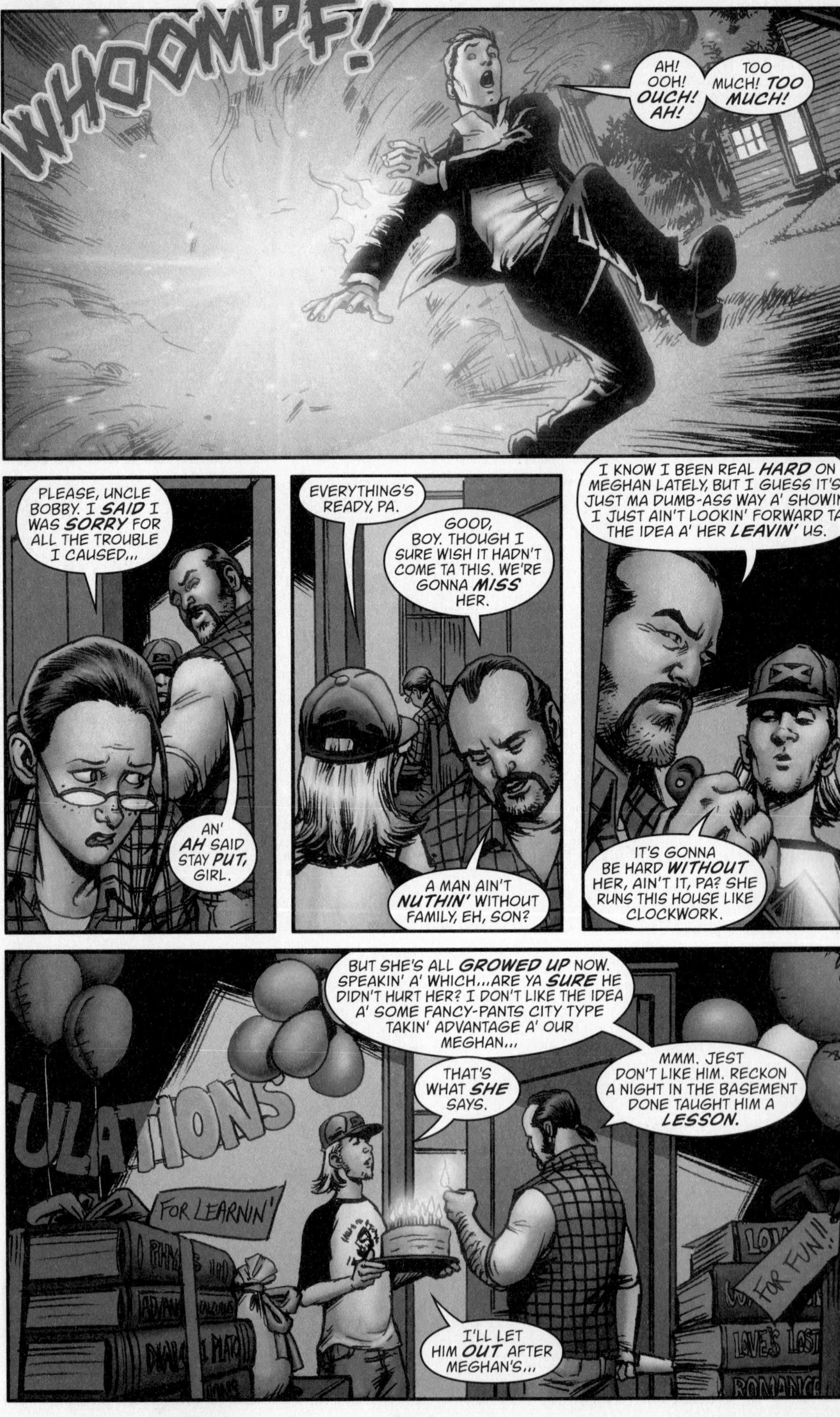
WHOOMPF!
AH! OOH! OUCH! AH!
TOO MUCH! TOO MUCH!
PLEASE, UNCLE BOBBY. I SAID I WAS SORRY FOR ALL THE TROUBLE I CAUSED...
AN' AH SAID STAY PUT, GIRL.
EVERYTHING'S READY, PA.
GOOD, BOY. THOUGH I SURE WISH IT HADN'T COME TA THIS. WE'RE GONNA MISS HER.
A MAN AIN'T NUTHIN' WITHOUT FAMILY, EH, SON?
I KNOW I BEEN REAL HARD ON MEGHAN LATELY, BUT I GUESS IT'S JUST MA DUMB-ASS WAY A' SHOWIN' I JUST AIN'T LOOKIN' FORWARD TA THE IDEA A' HER LEAVIN' US.
IT'S GONNA BE HARD WITHOUT HER, AIN'T IT, PA? SHE RUNS THIS HOUSE LIKE CLOCKWORK.
BUT SHE'S ALL GROWED UP NOW. SPEAKIN' A' WHICH...ARE YA SURE HE DIDN'T HURT HER? I DON'T LIKE THE IDEA A' SOME FANCY-PANTS CITY TYPE TAKIN' ADVANTAGE A' OUR MEGHAN...
THAT'S WHAT SHE SAYS.
MMM. JEST DON'T LIKE HIM. RECKON A NIGHT IN THE BASEMENT DONE TAUGHT HIM A LESSON.
I'LL LET HIM OUT AFTER MEGHAN'S...
ULATIONS
FOR LEARNIN'
FOR FUN!!
LOVE'S LOST
ROMANCE

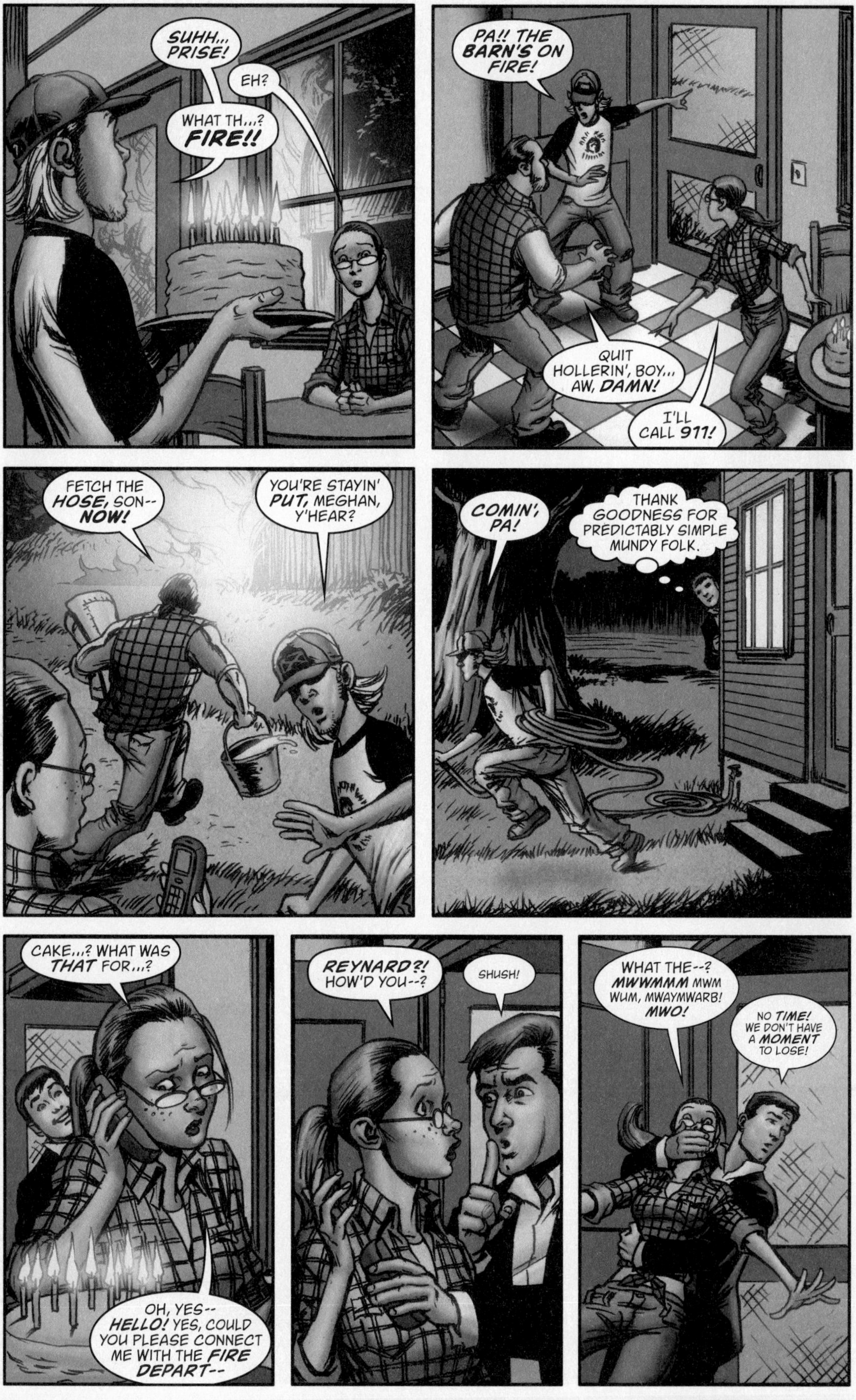
SUHH... PRISE!
EH?
WHAT TH...? FIRE!!
PA!! THE BARN'S ON FIRE!
QUIT HOLLERIN', BOY... AW, DAMN!
I'LL CALL 911!
FETCH THE HOSE, SON-- NOW!
YOU'RE STAYIN' PUT, MEGHAN, Y'HEAR?
COMIN', PA!
THANK GOODNESS FOR PREDICTABLY SIMPLE MUNDY FOLK.
CAKE...? WHAT WAS THAT FOR...?
OH, YES-- HELLO! YES, COULD YOU PLEASE CONNECT ME WITH THE FIRE DEPART--
REYNARD?! HOW'D YOU--?
SHUSH!
WHAT THE--? MWWMMM MWM WUM, MWAYMWARB! MWO!
NO TIME! WE DON'T HAVE A MOMENT TO LOSE!

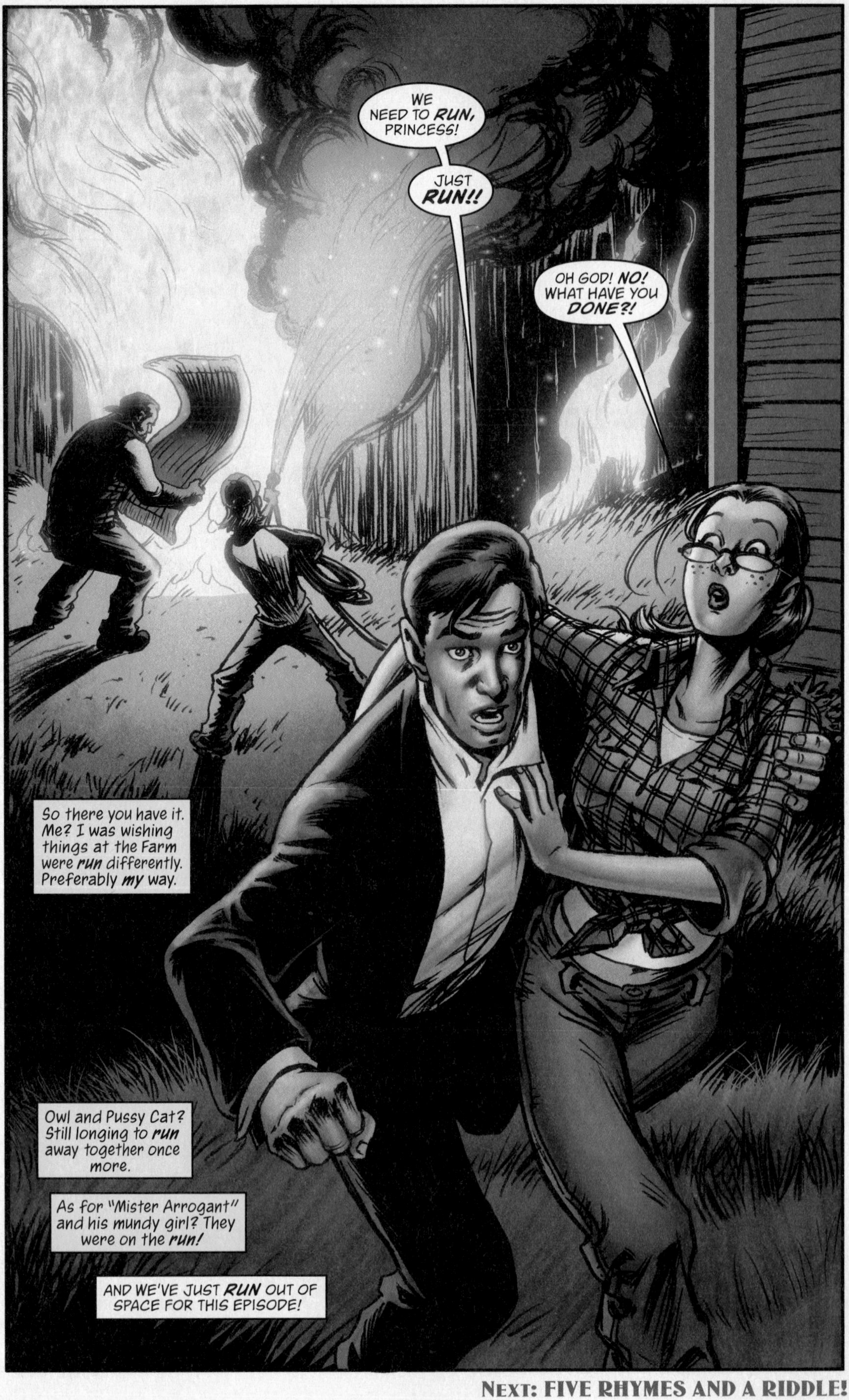
WE NEED TO RUN, PRINCESS!
JUST RUN!!
OH GOD! NO! WHAT HAVE YOU DONE?!
So there you have it. Me? I was wishing things at the Farm were run differently. Preferably my way.
Owl and Pussy Cat? Still longing to run away together once more.
As for "Mister Arrogant" and his mundy girl? They were on the run!
AND WE'VE JUST RUN OUT OF SPACE FOR THIS EPISODE!

Next: FIVE RHYMES AND A RIDDLE!

THERE'S A MUNDY SONG THAT'S STUCK IN MY HEAD.

EYES FORWARD, MISTER!

HONEY, CAN YA *BLAME* ME?

WOW.

DAMN HOT.

FAiREST

STRUGGLE TO RECALL THE BAND'S NAME--*THE WINDOWS* MAYBE? SOMETHING TO DO WITH PORTALS INTO HUMAN DWELLINGS, ANYWAY.

I ESPECIALLY LIKED THE CHORUS, AS THE SINGER SCREAMED ABOUT SETTING THE NIGHT ON *FIRE*.

WHICH RESONATES WITH ME, FOR OBVIOUS REASONS.

I AM THE EGGMAN DINER

MY LOVE...

CLARA? OH MY...

AS *DRAGONS* BY NATURE ARE *FIRE-STARTERS*.

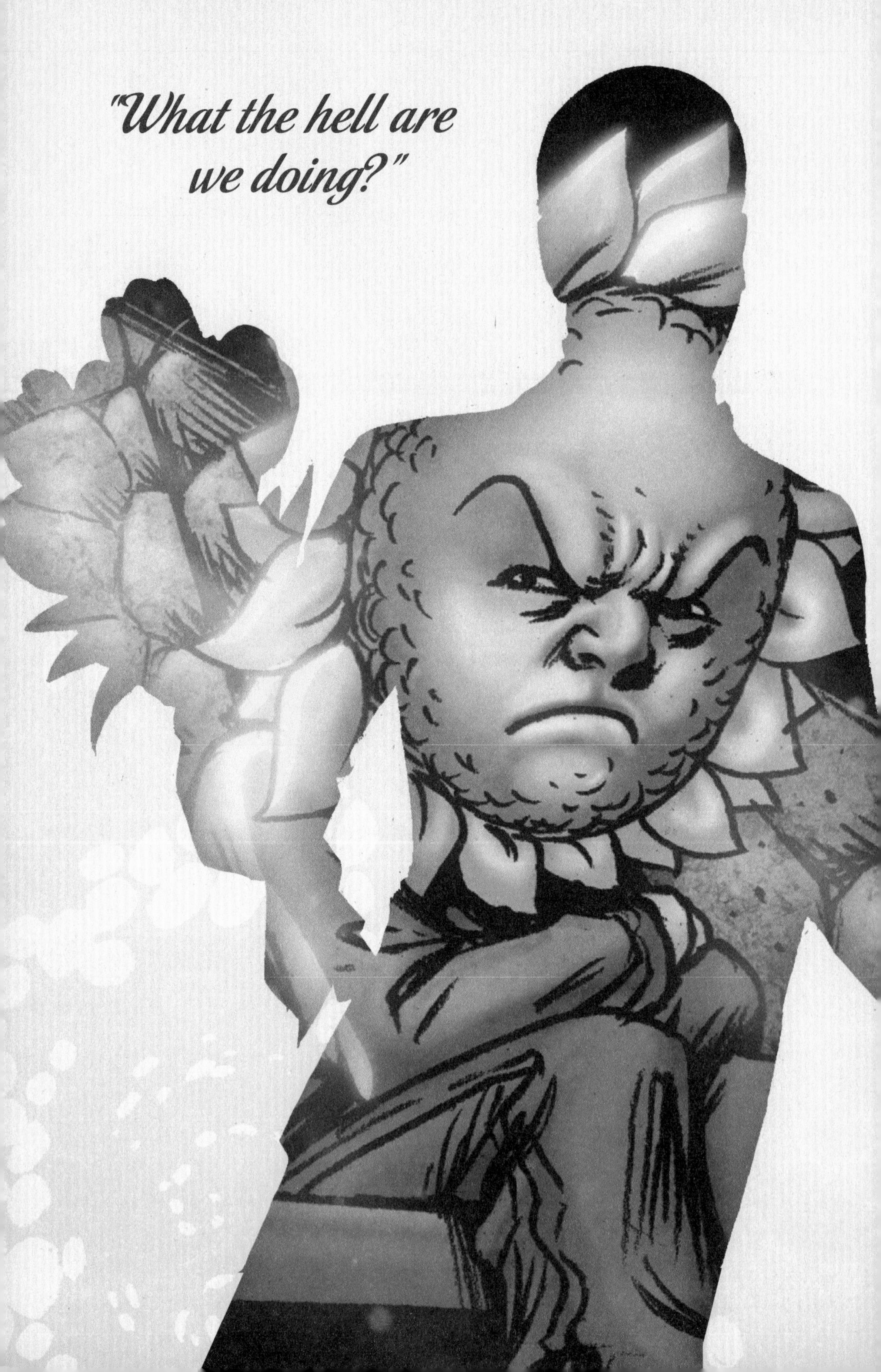
"What the hell are we doing?"

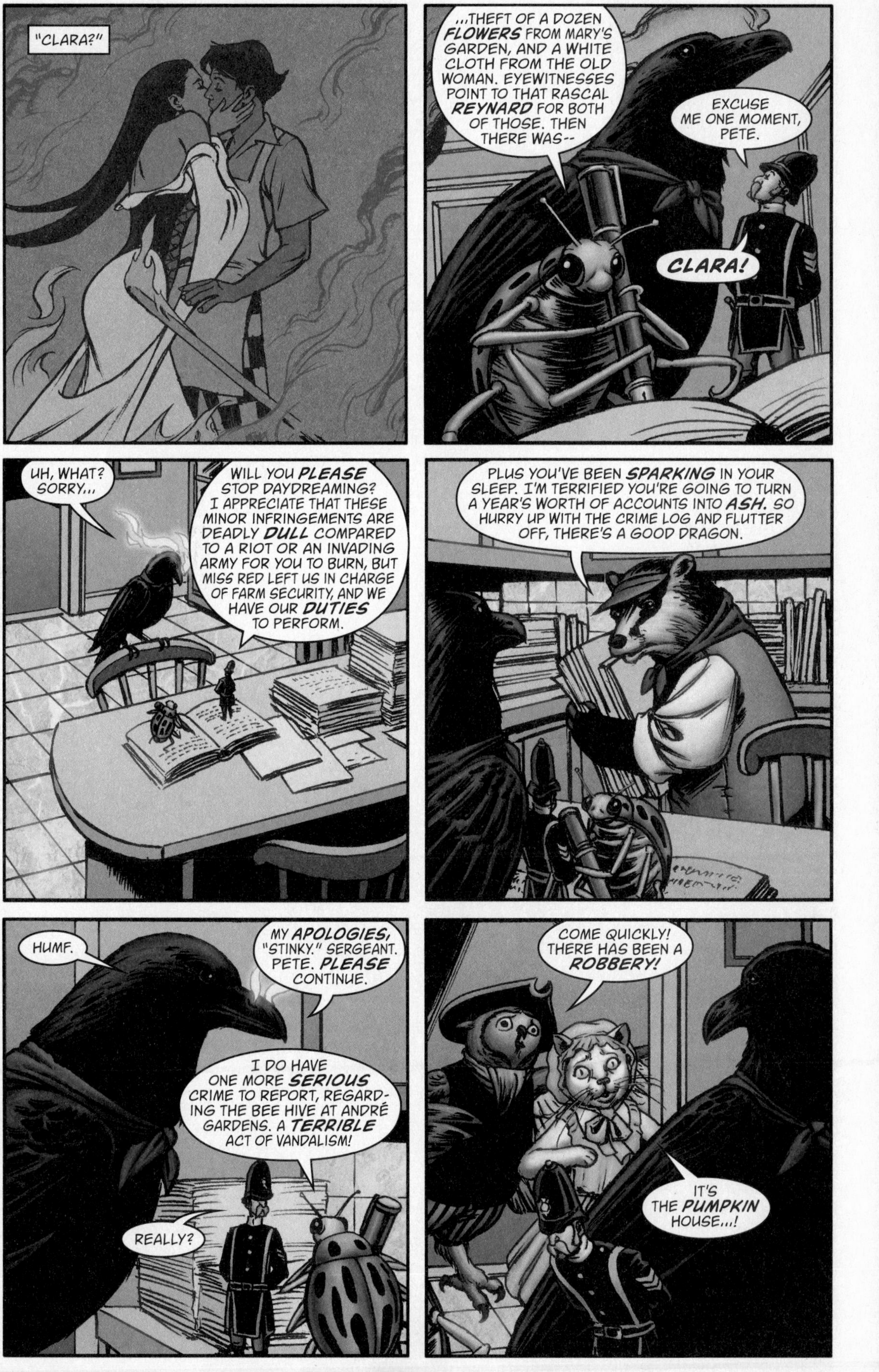
"CLARA?"
...THEFT OF A DOZEN FLOWERS FROM MARY'S GARDEN, AND A WHITE CLOTH FROM THE OLD WOMAN. EYEWITNESSES POINT TO THAT RASCAL REYNARD FOR BOTH OF THOSE. THEN THERE WAS--
EXCUSE ME ONE MOMENT, PETE.
CLARA!
UH, WHAT? SORRY...
WILL YOU PLEASE STOP DAYDREAMING? I APPRECIATE THAT THESE MINOR INFRINGEMENTS ARE DEADLY DULL COMPARED TO A RIOT OR AN INVADING ARMY FOR YOU TO BURN, BUT MISS RED LEFT US IN CHARGE OF FARM SECURITY, AND WE HAVE OUR DUTIES TO PERFORM.
PLUS YOU'VE BEEN SPARKING IN YOUR SLEEP. I'M TERRIFIED YOU'RE GOING TO TURN A YEAR'S WORTH OF ACCOUNTS INTO ASH. SO HURRY UP WITH THE CRIME LOG AND FLUTTER OFF, THERE'S A GOOD DRAGON.
HUMF.
MY APOLOGIES, "STINKY." SERGEANT. PETE. PLEASE CONTINUE.
I DO HAVE ONE MORE SERIOUS CRIME TO REPORT, REGARDING THE BEE HIVE AT ANDRÉ GARDENS. A TERRIBLE ACT OF VANDALISM!
REALLY?
COME QUICKLY! THERE HAS BEEN A ROBBERY!
IT'S THE PUMPKIN HOUSE...!

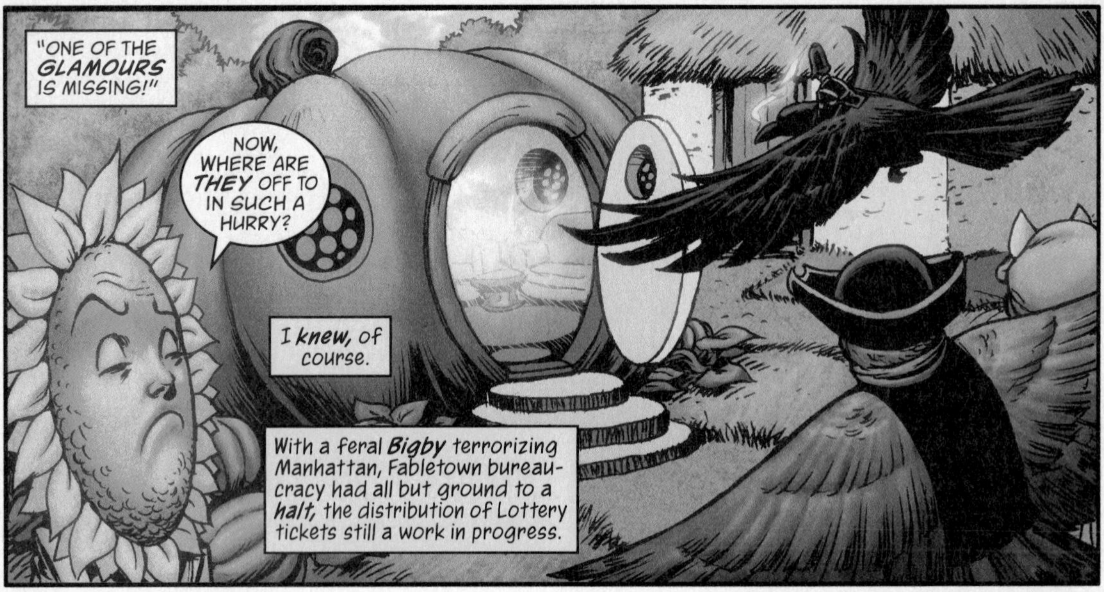
"ONE OF THE GLAMOURS IS MISSING!"
NOW, WHERE ARE THEY OFF TO IN SUCH A HURRY?
I knew, of course.
With a feral Bigby terrorizing Manhattan, Fabletown bureaucracy had all but ground to a halt, the distribution of Lottery tickets still a work in progress.

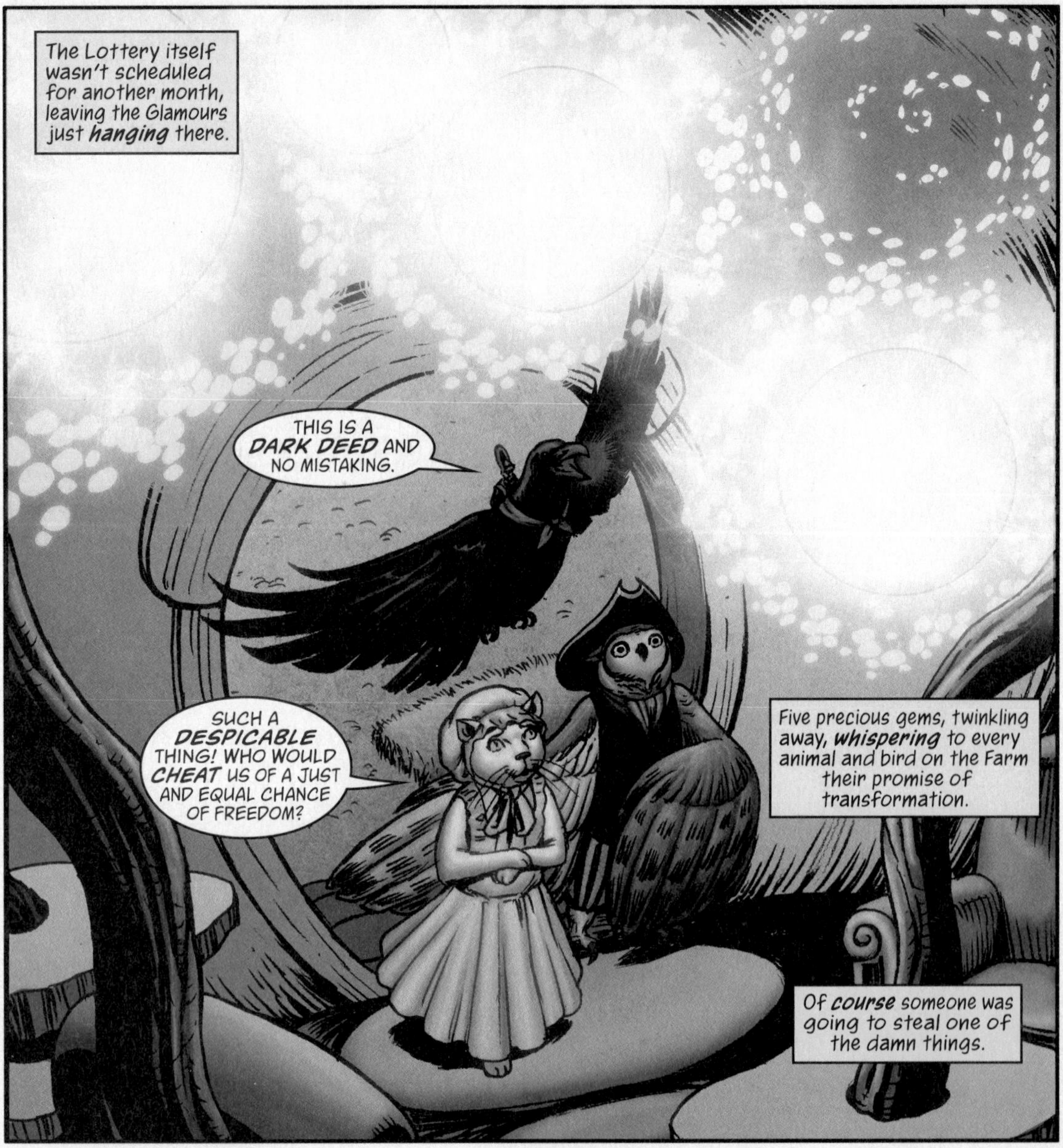
The Lottery itself wasn't scheduled for another month, leaving the Glamours just hanging there.
THIS IS A DARK DEED AND NO MISTAKING.
SUCH A DESPICABLE THING! WHO WOULD CHEAT US OF A JUST AND EQUAL CHANCE OF FREEDOM?
Five precious gems, twinkling away, whispering to every animal and bird on the Farm their promise of transformation.
Of course someone was going to steal one of the damn things.

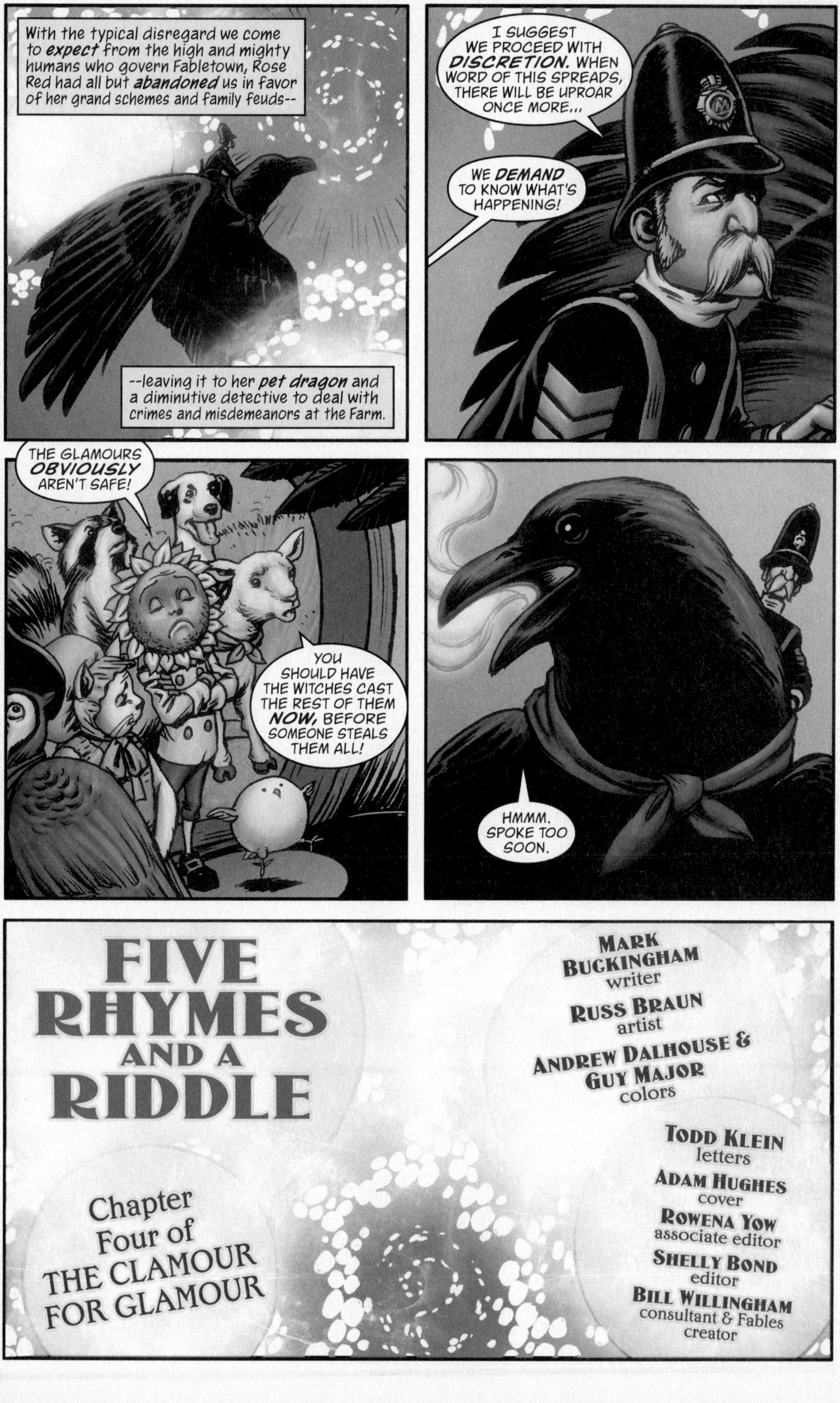
With the typical disregard we come to *expect* from the high and mighty humans who govern Fabletown, Rose Red had all but *abandoned* us in favor of her grand schemes and family feuds--
--leaving it to her *pet dragon* and a diminutive detective to deal with crimes and misdemeanors at the Farm.
I SUGGEST WE PROCEED WITH *DISCRETION.* WHEN WORD OF THIS SPREADS, THERE WILL BE UPROAR ONCE MORE...
WE *DEMAND* TO KNOW WHAT'S HAPPENING!
THE GLAMOURS *OBVIOUSLY* AREN'T SAFE!
YOU SHOULD HAVE THE WITCHES CAST THE REST OF THEM *NOW,* BEFORE SOMEONE STEALS THEM ALL!
HMMM. SPOKE TOO SOON.
FIVE RHYMES AND A RIDDLE
Chapter Four of THE CLAMOUR FOR GLAMOUR
MARK BUCKINGHAM writer
RUSS BRAUN artist
ANDREW DALHOUSE & GUY MAJOR colors
TODD KLEIN letters
ADAM HUGHES cover
ROWENA YOW associate editor
SHELLY BOND editor
BILL WILLINGHAM consultant & Fables creator

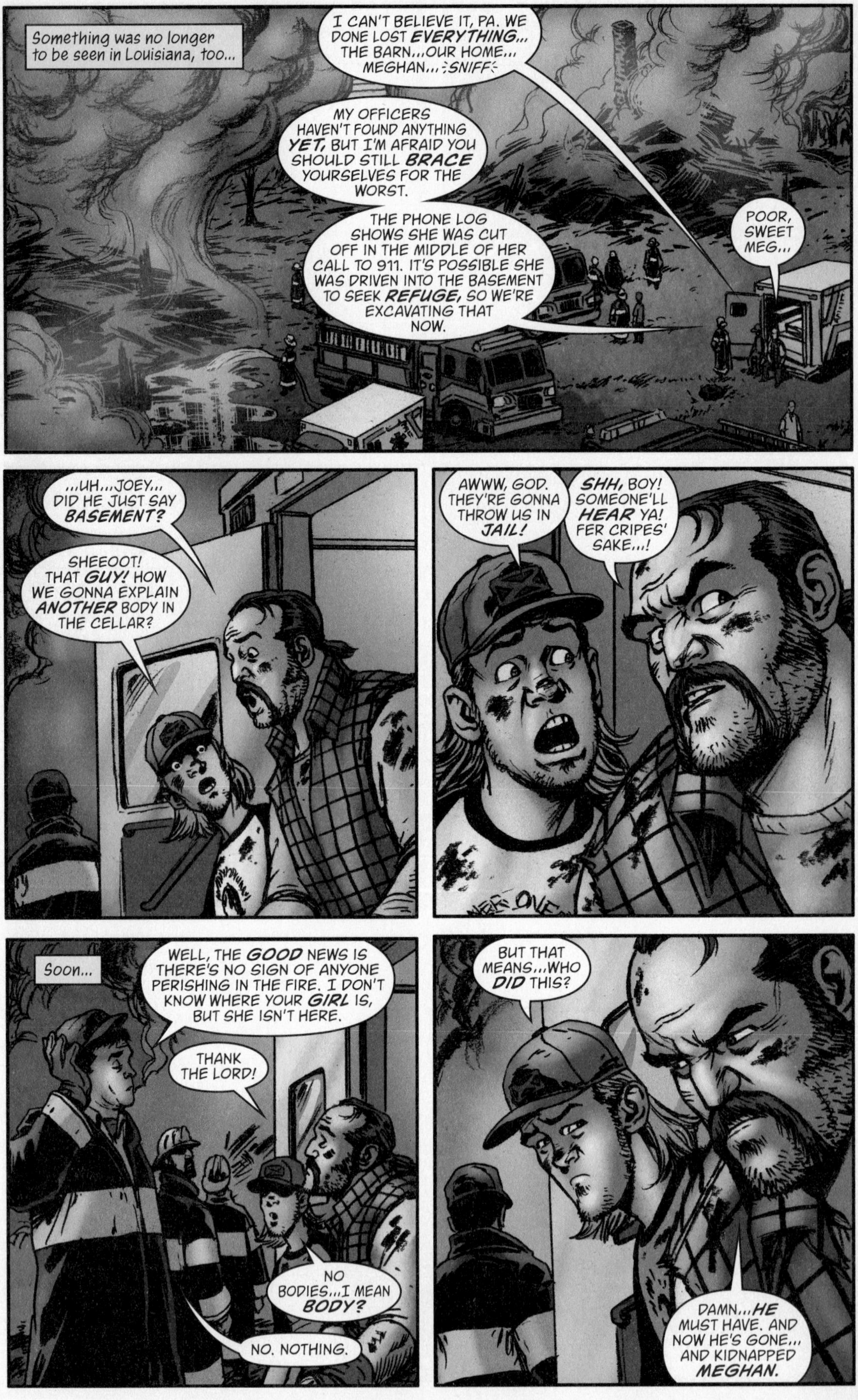
Something was no longer to be seen in Louisiana, too...
I CAN'T BELIEVE IT, PA. WE DONE LOST EVERYTHING... THE BARN...OUR HOME... MEGHAN... SNIFF
MY OFFICERS HAVEN'T FOUND ANYTHING YET, BUT I'M AFRAID YOU SHOULD STILL BRACE YOURSELVES FOR THE WORST.
THE PHONE LOG SHOWS SHE WAS CUT OFF IN THE MIDDLE OF HER CALL TO 911. IT'S POSSIBLE SHE WAS DRIVEN INTO THE BASEMENT TO SEEK REFUGE, SO WE'RE EXCAVATING THAT NOW.
POOR, SWEET MEG...
...UH...JOEY... DID HE JUST SAY BASEMENT?
SHEEOOT! THAT GUY! HOW WE GONNA EXPLAIN ANOTHER BODY IN THE CELLAR?
AWWW, GOD. THEY'RE GONNA THROW US IN JAIL!
SHH, BOY! SOMEONE'LL HEAR YA! FER CRIPES' SAKE...!
Soon...
WELL, THE GOOD NEWS IS THERE'S NO SIGN OF ANYONE PERISHING IN THE FIRE. I DON'T KNOW WHERE YOUR GIRL IS, BUT SHE ISN'T HERE.
THANK THE LORD!
NO BODIES...I MEAN BODY?
NO. NOTHING.
BUT THAT MEANS...WHO DID THIS?
DAMN...HE MUST HAVE. AND NOW HE'S GONE... AND KIDNAPPED MEGHAN.

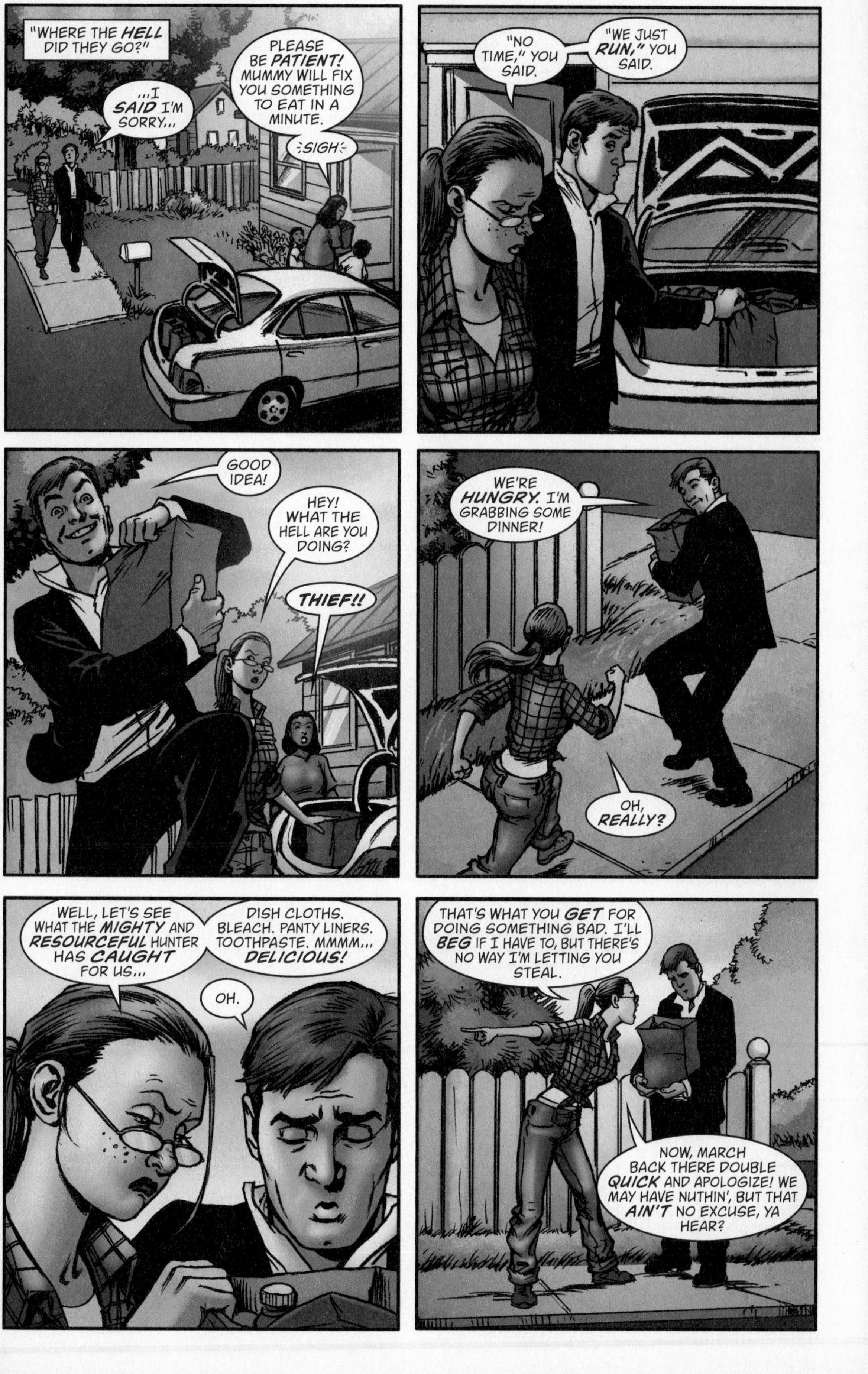
"WHERE THE HELL DID THEY GO?"
...I SAID I'M SORRY...
PLEASE BE PATIENT! MUMMY WILL FIX YOU SOMETHING TO EAT IN A MINUTE.
SIGH
"NO TIME," YOU SAID.
"WE JUST RUN," YOU SAID.
GOOD IDEA!
HEY! WHAT THE HELL ARE YOU DOING?
THIEF!!
WE'RE HUNGRY. I'M GRABBING SOME DINNER!
OH, REALLY?
WELL, LET'S SEE WHAT THE MIGHTY AND RESOURCEFUL HUNTER HAS CAUGHT FOR US...
DISH CLOTHS. BLEACH. PANTY LINERS. TOOTHPASTE. MMMM... DELICIOUS!
OH.
THAT'S WHAT YOU GET FOR DOING SOMETHING BAD. I'LL BEG IF I HAVE TO, BUT THERE'S NO WAY I'M LETTING YOU STEAL.
NOW, MARCH BACK THERE DOUBLE QUICK AND APOLOGIZE! WE MAY HAVE NUTHIN', BUT THAT AIN'T NO EXCUSE, YA HEAR?

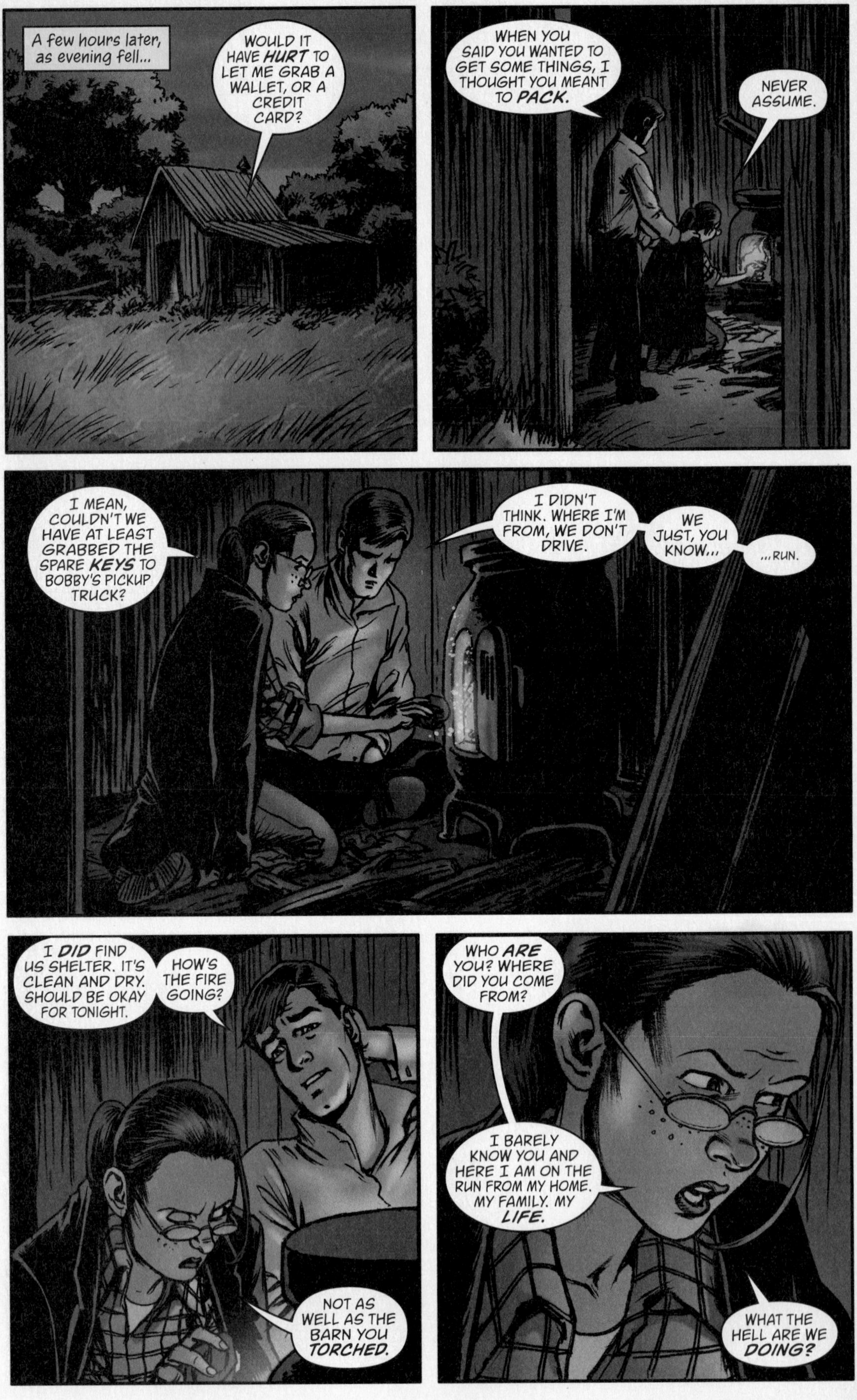
A few hours later, as evening fell...
WOULD IT HAVE HURT TO LET ME GRAB A WALLET, OR A CREDIT CARD?
WHEN YOU SAID YOU WANTED TO GET SOME THINGS, I THOUGHT YOU MEANT TO PACK.
NEVER ASSUME.
I MEAN, COULDN'T WE HAVE AT LEAST GRABBED THE SPARE KEYS TO BOBBY'S PICKUP TRUCK?
I DIDN'T THINK. WHERE I'M FROM, WE DON'T DRIVE.
WE JUST, YOU KNOW...
...RUN.
I DID FIND US SHELTER. IT'S CLEAN AND DRY. SHOULD BE OKAY FOR TONIGHT.
HOW'S THE FIRE GOING?
NOT AS WELL AS THE BARN YOU TORCHED.
WHO ARE YOU? WHERE DID YOU COME FROM?
I BARELY KNOW YOU AND HERE I AM ON THE RUN FROM MY HOME. MY FAMILY. MY LIFE.
WHAT THE HELL ARE WE DOING?

I'M **SAVING** YOU.

I TOLD YOU, PRINCESS. THE THINGS I HEARD. THE **TERRIBLE** THINGS THEY WERE PLANNING...

I **REFUSE** TO BELIEVE IT. BOBBY AND JOEY-- NEITHER OF THEM EVER LAID A **FINGER** ON ME.

NONE OF THIS MAKES SENSE.

I SHOULD GO BACK...

...HOME?

NOOOO!!

WHAT IS IT?

OH NO.

Farm destroyed in late night blaze

...ched for comme ...rd said, "No comment.

Fire crews are searchi... the debris for victi...

IT... IT **CAN'T** BE...

OH, GOD... **NO!**

MEGHAN...I...

I C-CAN'T GO BACK...

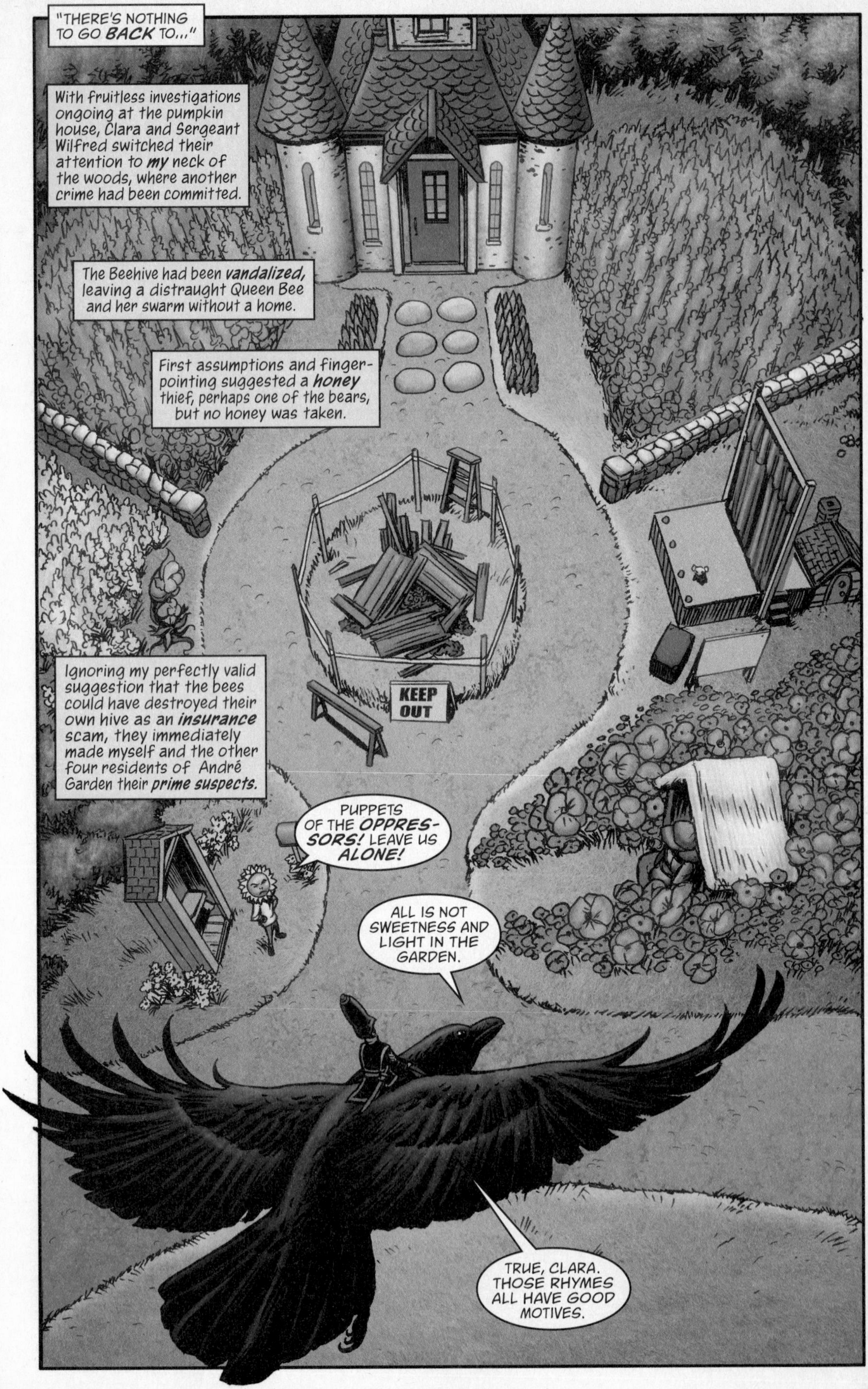
"THERE'S NOTHING TO GO BACK TO..."
With fruitless investigations ongoing at the pumpkin house, Clara and Sergeant Wilfred switched their attention to my neck of the woods, where another crime had been committed.
The Beehive had been vandalized, leaving a distraught Queen Bee and her swarm without a home.
First assumptions and finger-pointing suggested a honey thief, perhaps one of the bears, but no honey was taken.
KEEP OUT
Ignoring my perfectly valid suggestion that the bees could have destroyed their own hive as an insurance scam, they immediately made myself and the other four residents of André Garden their prime suspects.
PUPPETS OF THE OPPRES-SORS! LEAVE US ALONE!
ALL IS NOT SWEETNESS AND LIGHT IN THE GARDEN.
TRUE, CLARA. THOSE RHYMES ALL HAVE GOOD MOTIVES.

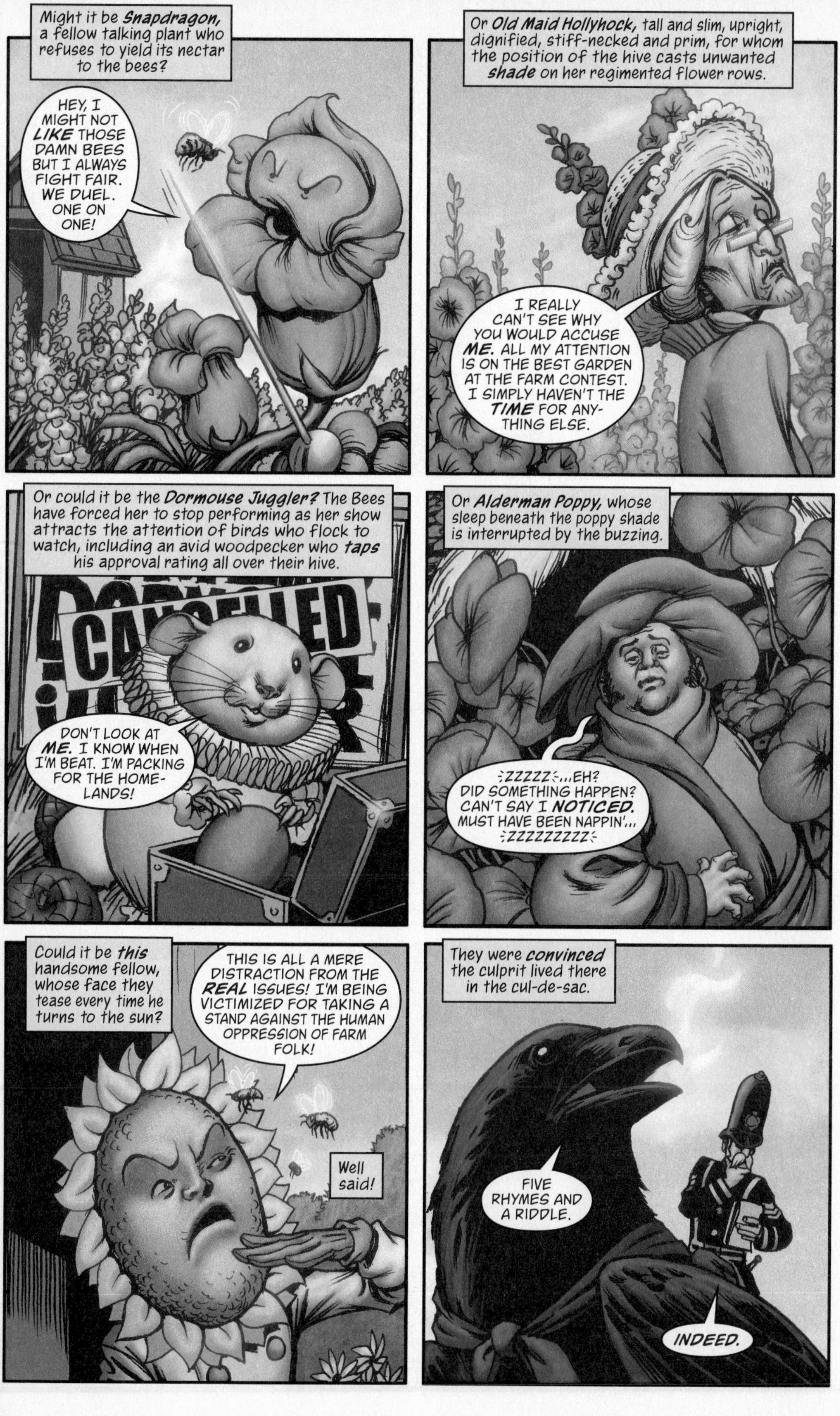

Might it be Snapdragon, a fellow talking plant who refuses to yield its nectar to the bees?
HEY, I MIGHT NOT LIKE THOSE DAMN BEES BUT I ALWAYS FIGHT FAIR. WE DUEL. ONE ON ONE!
Or Old Maid Hollyhock, tall and slim, upright, dignified, stiff-necked and prim, for whom the position of the hive casts unwanted shade on her regimented flower rows.
I REALLY CAN'T SEE WHY YOU WOULD ACCUSE ME. ALL MY ATTENTION IS ON THE BEST GARDEN AT THE FARM CONTEST. I SIMPLY HAVEN'T THE TIME FOR ANY-THING ELSE.
Or could it be the Dormouse Juggler? The Bees have forced her to stop performing as her show attracts the attention of birds who flock to watch, including an avid woodpecker who taps his approval rating all over their hive.
DON'T LOOK AT ME. I KNOW WHEN I'M BEAT. I'M PACKING FOR THE HOME-LANDS!
Or Alderman Poppy, whose sleep beneath the poppy shade is interrupted by the buzzing.
ZZZZZ...EH? DID SOMETHING HAPPEN? CAN'T SAY I NOTICED. MUST HAVE BEEN NAPPIN'... ZZZZZZZZZ
Could it be this handsome fellow, whose face they tease every time he turns to the sun?
THIS IS ALL A MERE DISTRACTION FROM THE REAL ISSUES! I'M BEING VICTIMIZED FOR TAKING A STAND AGAINST THE HUMAN OPPRESSION OF FARM FOLK!
Well said!
They were convinced the culprit lived there in the cul-de-sac.
FIVE RHYMES AND A RIDDLE.
INDEED.

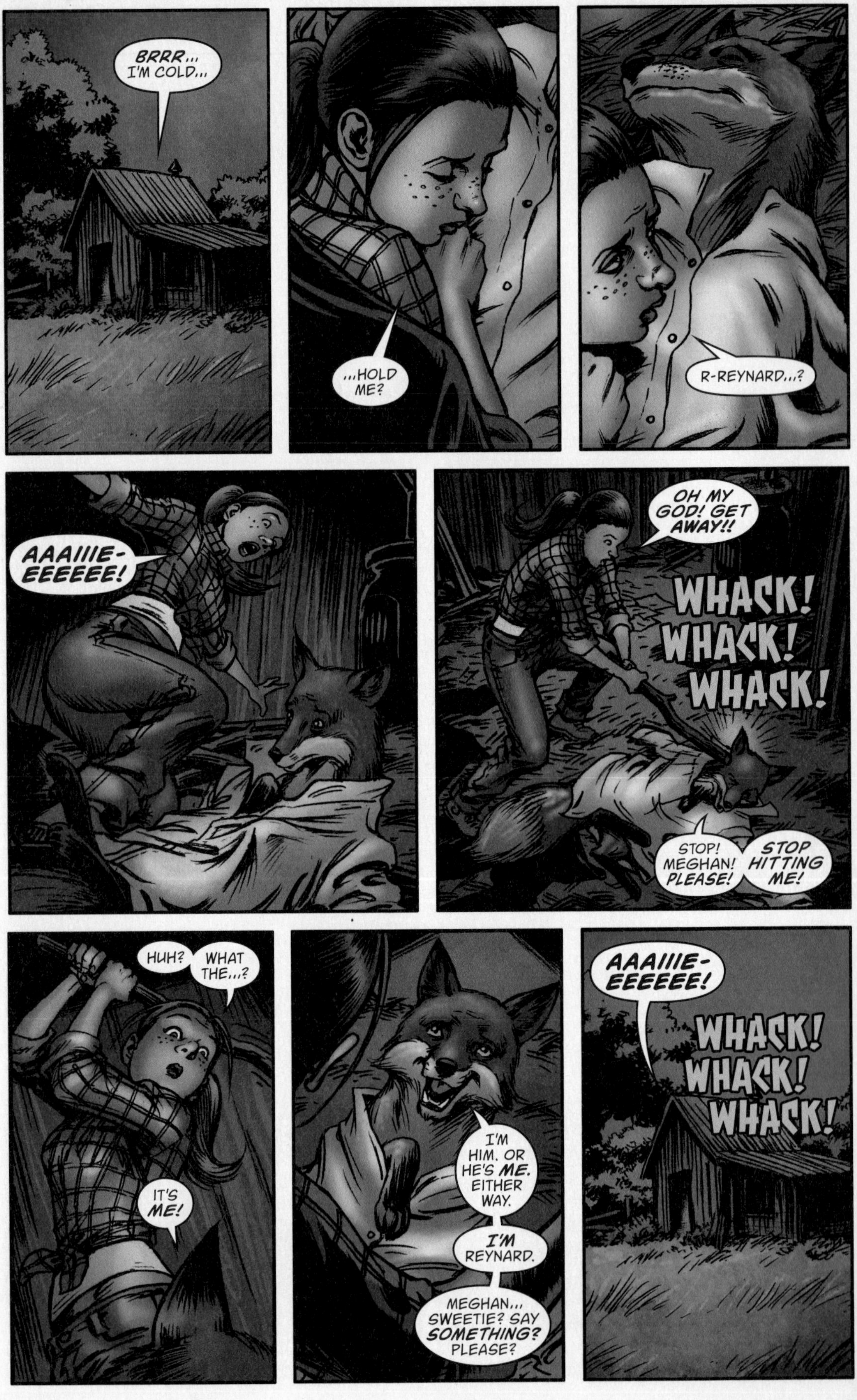
BRRR... I'M COLD...
...HOLD ME?
R-REYNARD...?
AAAIIIE-EEEEEE!
OH MY GOD! GET AWAY!!
WHACK! WHACK! WHACK!
STOP! MEGHAN! PLEASE!
STOP HITTING ME!
HUH?
WHAT THE...?
IT'S ME!
I'M HIM. OR HE'S ME. EITHER WAY.
I'M REYNARD.
MEGHAN... SWEETIE? SAY SOMETHING? PLEASE?
AAAIIIE-EEEEEE!
WHACK! WHACK! WHACK!

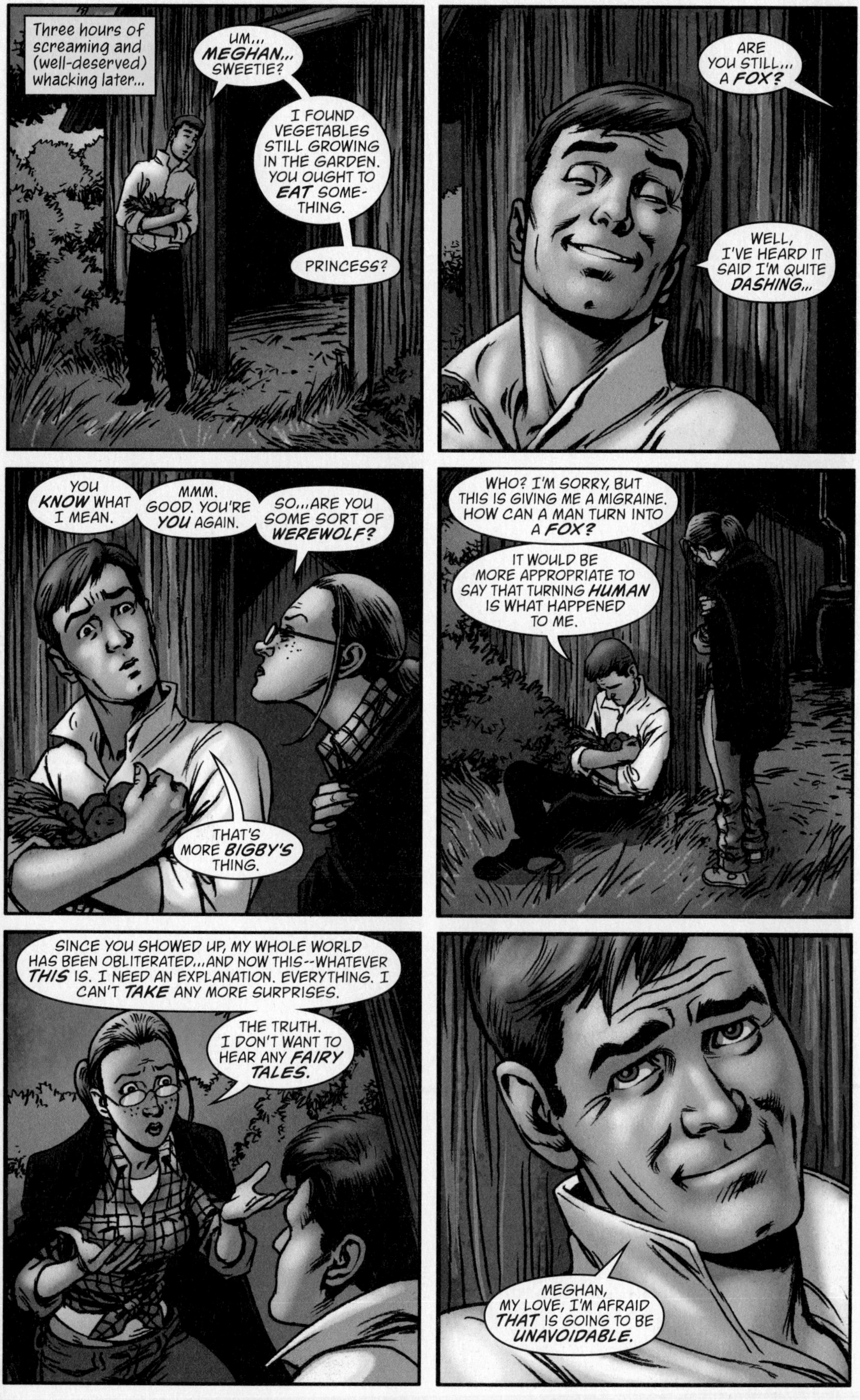
Three hours of screaming and (well-deserved) whacking later...
UM... MEGHAN... SWEETIE?
I FOUND VEGETABLES STILL GROWING IN THE GARDEN. YOU OUGHT TO EAT SOME-THING.
PRINCESS?
ARE YOU STILL... A FOX?
WELL, I'VE HEARD IT SAID I'M QUITE DASHING...
YOU KNOW WHAT I MEAN.
MMM. GOOD. YOU'RE YOU AGAIN.
SO...ARE YOU SOME SORT OF WEREWOLF?
THAT'S MORE BIGBY'S THING.
WHO? I'M SORRY, BUT THIS IS GIVING ME A MIGRAINE. HOW CAN A MAN TURN INTO A FOX?
IT WOULD BE MORE APPROPRIATE TO SAY THAT TURNING HUMAN IS WHAT HAPPENED TO ME.
SINCE YOU SHOWED UP, MY WHOLE WORLD HAS BEEN OBLITERATED...AND NOW THIS--WHATEVER THIS IS. I NEED AN EXPLANATION. EVERYTHING. I CAN'T TAKE ANY MORE SURPRISES.
THE TRUTH. I DON'T WANT TO HEAR ANY FAIRY TALES.
MEGHAN, MY LOVE, I'M AFRAID THAT IS GOING TO BE UNAVOIDABLE.

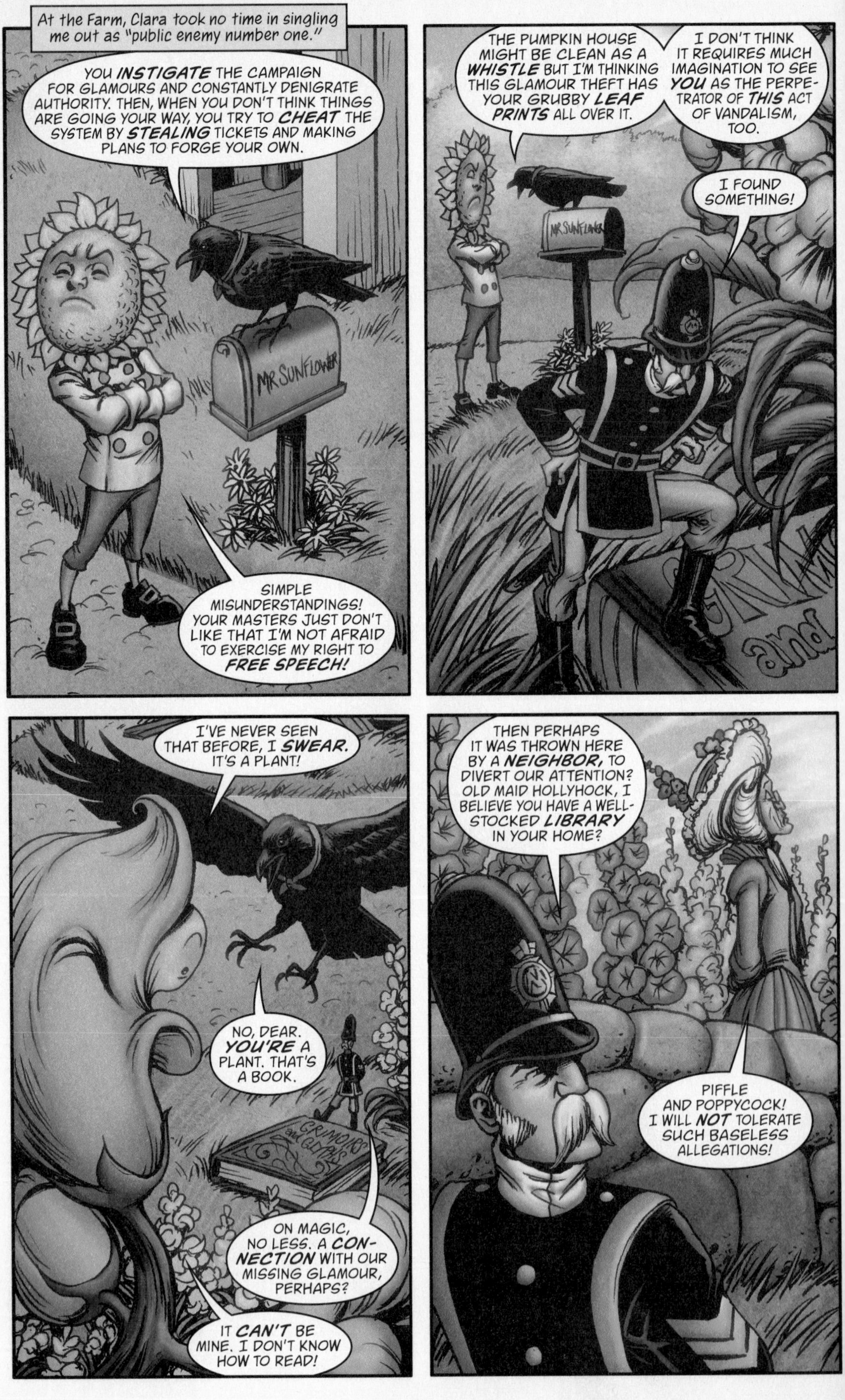
At the Farm, Clara took no time in singling me out as "public enemy number one."
YOU INSTIGATE THE CAMPAIGN FOR GLAMOURS AND CONSTANTLY DENIGRATE AUTHORITY. THEN, WHEN YOU DON'T THINK THINGS ARE GOING YOUR WAY, YOU TRY TO CHEAT THE SYSTEM BY STEALING TICKETS AND MAKING PLANS TO FORGE YOUR OWN.
MR SUNFLOWER
SIMPLE MISUNDERSTANDINGS! YOUR MASTERS JUST DON'T LIKE THAT I'M NOT AFRAID TO EXERCISE MY RIGHT TO FREE SPEECH!
THE PUMPKIN HOUSE MIGHT BE CLEAN AS A WHISTLE BUT I'M THINKING THIS GLAMOUR THEFT HAS YOUR GRUBBY LEAF PRINTS ALL OVER IT.
I DON'T THINK IT REQUIRES MUCH IMAGINATION TO SEE YOU AS THE PERPETRATOR OF THIS ACT OF VANDALISM, TOO.
I FOUND SOMETHING!
I'VE NEVER SEEN THAT BEFORE, I SWEAR. IT'S A PLANT!
NO, DEAR. YOU'RE A PLANT. THAT'S A BOOK.
ON MAGIC, NO LESS. A CONNECTION WITH OUR MISSING GLAMOUR, PERHAPS?
IT CAN'T BE MINE. I DON'T KNOW HOW TO READ!
THEN PERHAPS IT WAS THROWN HERE BY A NEIGHBOR, TO DIVERT OUR ATTENTION? OLD MAID HOLLYHOCK, I BELIEVE YOU HAVE A WELL-STOCKED LIBRARY IN YOUR HOME?
PIFFLE AND POPPYCOCK! I WILL NOT TOLERATE SUCH BASELESS ALLEGATIONS!

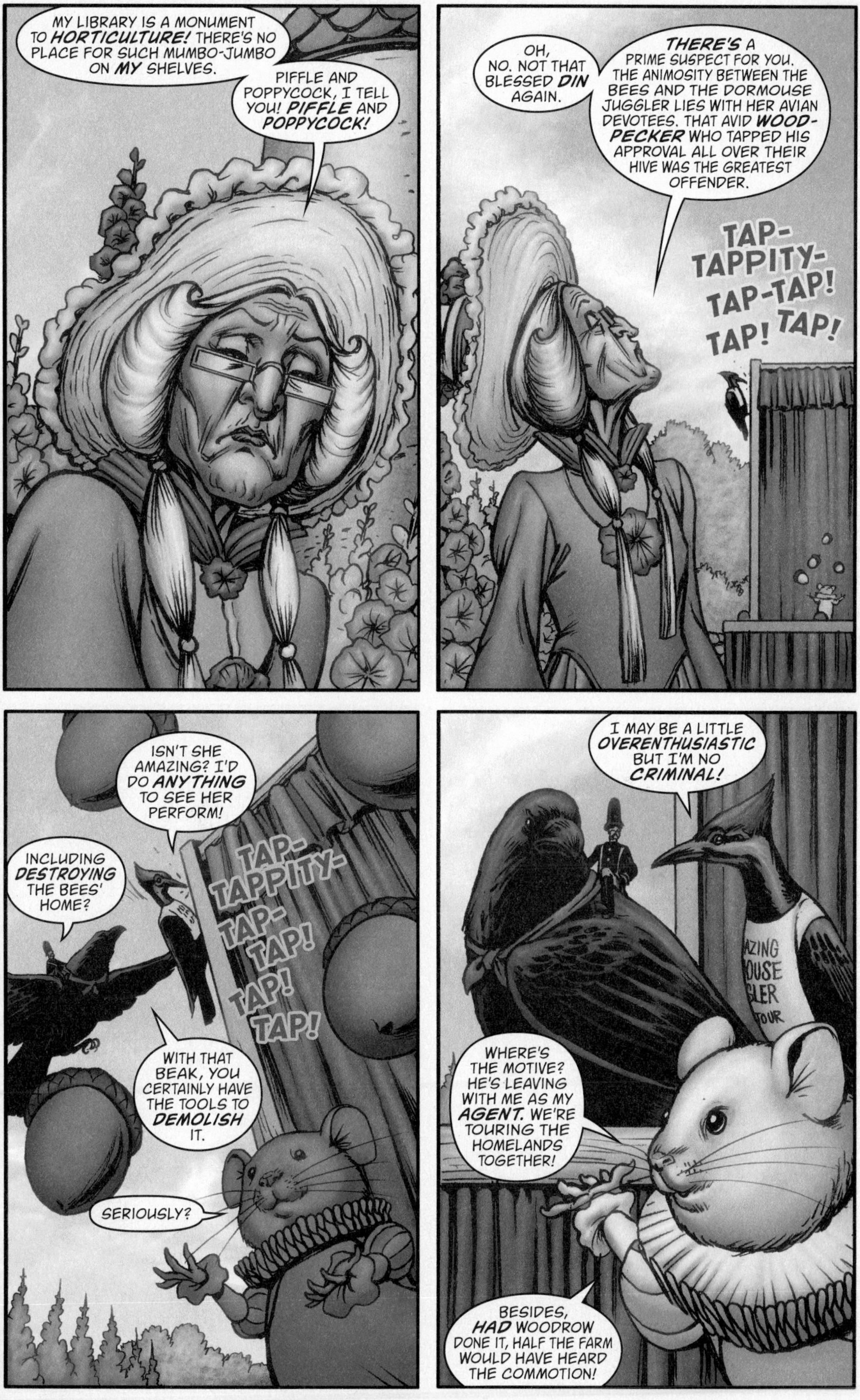
MY LIBRARY IS A MONUMENT TO HORTICULTURE! THERE'S NO PLACE FOR SUCH MUMBO-JUMBO ON MY SHELVES.
PIFFLE AND POPPYCOCK, I TELL YOU! PIFFLE AND POPPYCOCK!
OH, NO. NOT THAT BLESSED DIN AGAIN.
THERE'S A PRIME SUSPECT FOR YOU. THE ANIMOSITY BETWEEN THE BEES AND THE DORMOUSE JUGGLER LIES WITH HER AVIAN DEVOTEES. THAT AVID WOODPECKER WHO TAPPED HIS APPROVAL ALL OVER THEIR HIVE WAS THE GREATEST OFFENDER.
TAP-TAPPITY-TAP-TAP! TAP! TAP!
ISN'T SHE AMAZING? I'D DO ANYTHING TO SEE HER PERFORM!
INCLUDING DESTROYING THE BEES' HOME?
TAP-TAPPITY-TAP-TAP! TAP! TAP!
WITH THAT BEAK, YOU CERTAINLY HAVE THE TOOLS TO DEMOLISH IT.
SERIOUSLY?
I MAY BE A LITTLE OVERENTHUSIASTIC BUT I'M NO CRIMINAL!
WHERE'S THE MOTIVE? HE'S LEAVING WITH ME AS MY AGENT. WE'RE TOURING THE HOMELANDS TOGETHER!
BESIDES, HAD WOODROW DONE IT, HALF THE FARM WOULD HAVE HEARD THE COMMOTION!

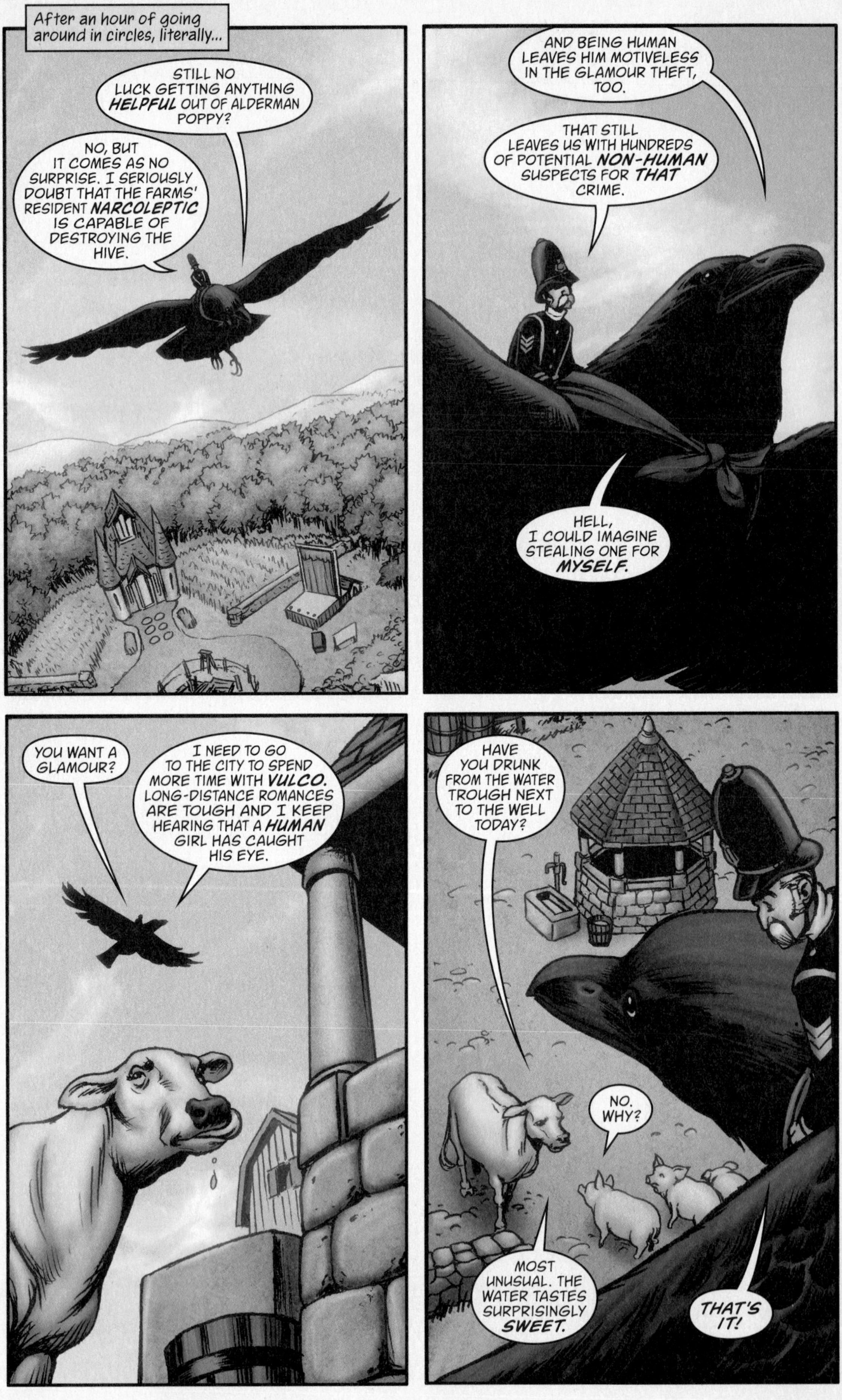
After an hour of going around in circles, literally...
STILL NO LUCK GETTING ANYTHING HELPFUL OUT OF ALDERMAN POPPY?
NO, BUT IT COMES AS NO SURPRISE. I SERIOUSLY DOUBT THAT THE FARMS' RESIDENT NARCOLEPTIC IS CAPABLE OF DESTROYING THE HIVE.
AND BEING HUMAN LEAVES HIM MOTIVELESS IN THE GLAMOUR THEFT, TOO.
THAT STILL LEAVES US WITH HUNDREDS OF POTENTIAL NON-HUMAN SUSPECTS FOR THAT CRIME.
HELL, I COULD IMAGINE STEALING ONE FOR MYSELF.
YOU WANT A GLAMOUR?
I NEED TO GO TO THE CITY TO SPEND MORE TIME WITH VULCO. LONG-DISTANCE ROMANCES ARE TOUGH AND I KEEP HEARING THAT A HUMAN GIRL HAS CAUGHT HIS EYE.
HAVE YOU DRUNK FROM THE WATER TROUGH NEXT TO THE WELL TODAY?
NO. WHY?
MOST UNUSUAL. THE WATER TASTES SURPRISINGLY SWEET.
THAT'S IT!

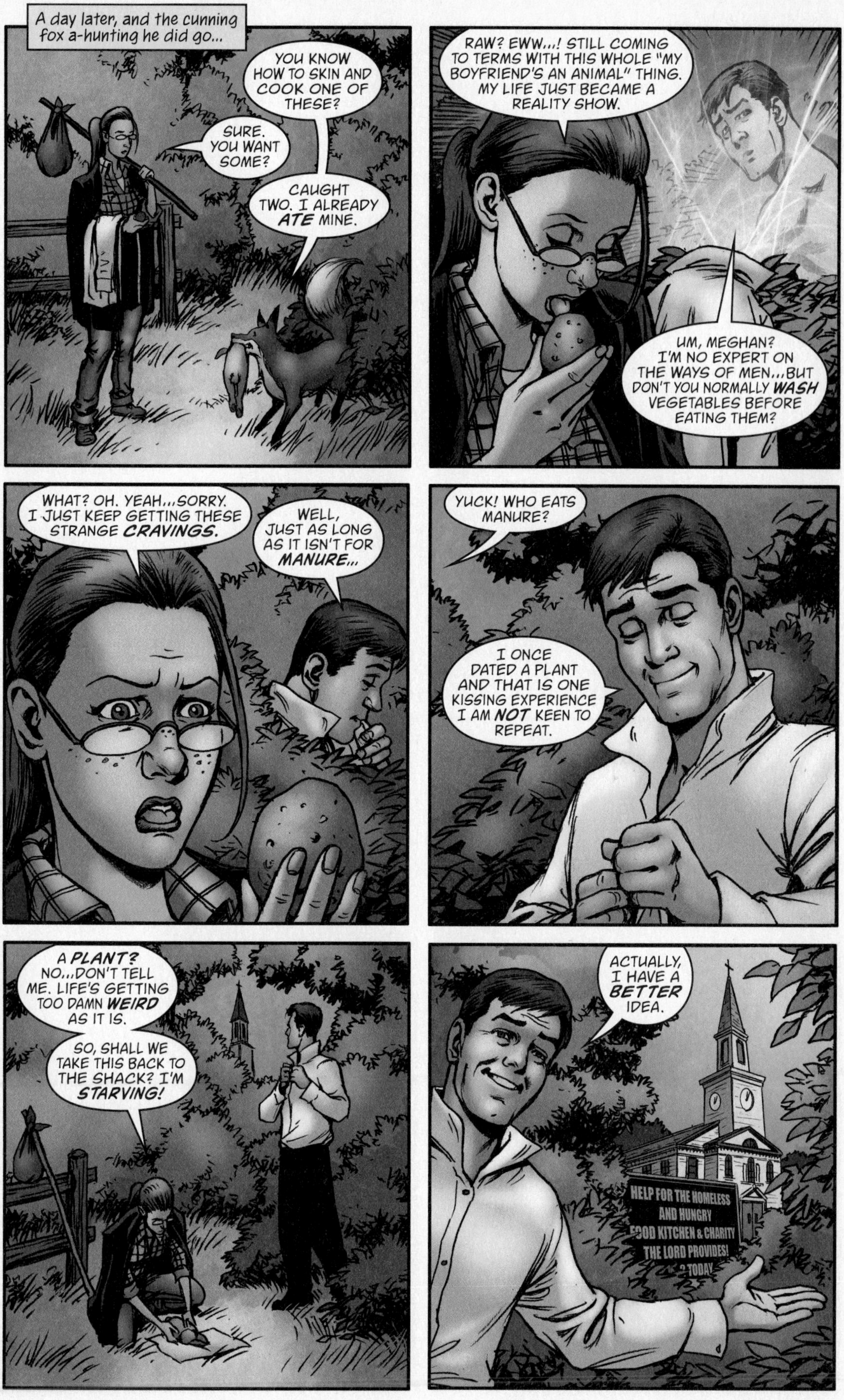

A day later, and the cunning fox a-hunting he did go...
YOU KNOW HOW TO SKIN AND COOK ONE OF THESE?
SURE. YOU WANT SOME?
CAUGHT TWO. I ALREADY ATE MINE.
RAW? EWW...! STILL COMING TO TERMS WITH THIS WHOLE "MY BOYFRIEND'S AN ANIMAL" THING. MY LIFE JUST BECAME A REALITY SHOW.
UM, MEGHAN? I'M NO EXPERT ON THE WAYS OF MEN...BUT DON'T YOU NORMALLY WASH VEGETABLES BEFORE EATING THEM?
WHAT? OH. YEAH...SORRY. I JUST KEEP GETTING THESE STRANGE CRAVINGS.
WELL, JUST AS LONG AS IT ISN'T FOR MANURE...
YUCK! WHO EATS MANURE?
I ONCE DATED A PLANT AND THAT IS ONE KISSING EXPERIENCE I AM NOT KEEN TO REPEAT.
A PLANT? NO...DON'T TELL ME. LIFE'S GETTING TOO DAMN WEIRD AS IT IS.
SO, SHALL WE TAKE THIS BACK TO THE SHACK? I'M STARVING!
ACTUALLY, I HAVE A BETTER IDEA.
HELP FOR THE HOMELESS
AND HUNGRY
OOD KITCHEN & CHARITY
THE LORD PROVIDES!
TODAY

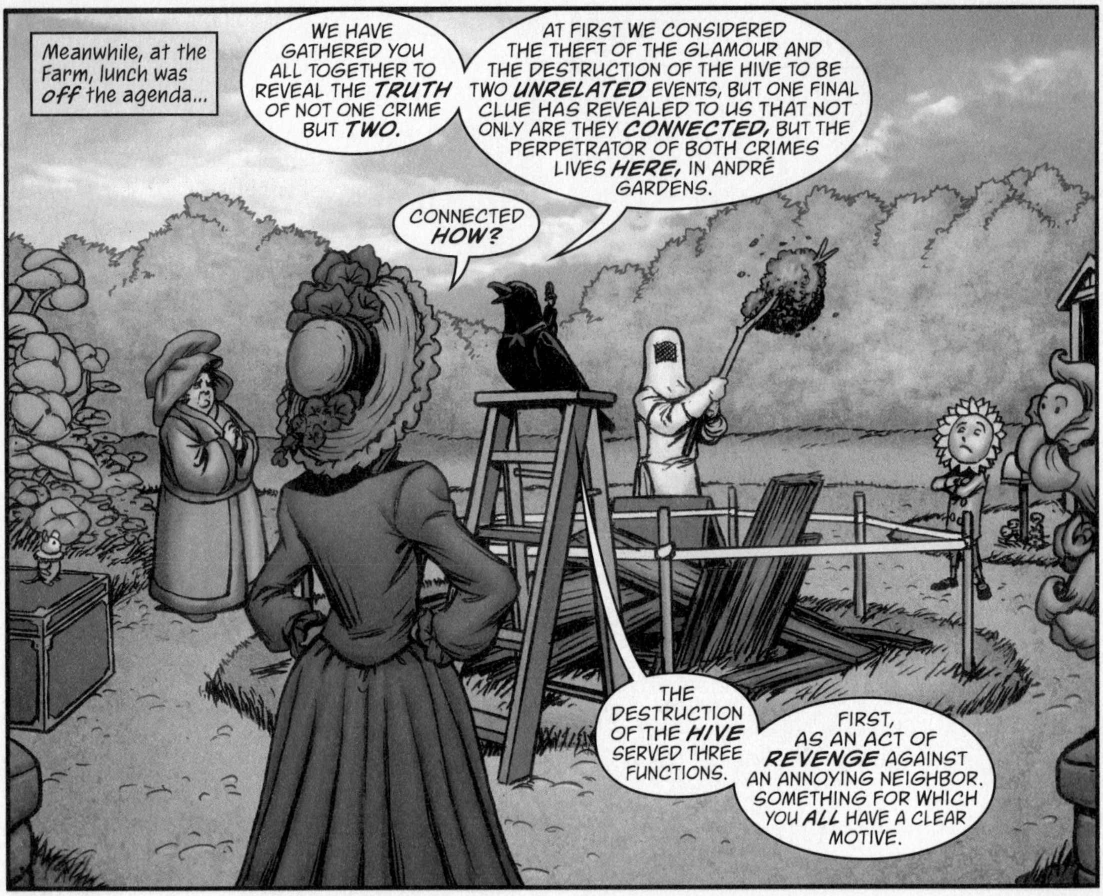
Meanwhile, at the Farm, lunch was *off* the agenda...
WE HAVE GATHERED YOU ALL TOGETHER TO REVEAL THE **TRUTH** OF NOT ONE CRIME BUT **TWO.**
AT FIRST WE CONSIDERED THE THEFT OF THE GLAMOUR AND THE DESTRUCTION OF THE HIVE TO BE TWO **UNRELATED** EVENTS, BUT ONE FINAL CLUE HAS REVEALED TO US THAT NOT ONLY ARE THEY **CONNECTED,** BUT THE PERPETRATOR OF BOTH CRIMES LIVES **HERE,** IN ANDRÉ GARDENS.
CONNECTED **HOW?**
THE DESTRUCTION OF THE **HIVE** SERVED THREE FUNCTIONS.
FIRST, AS AN ACT OF **REVENGE** AGAINST AN ANNOYING NEIGHBOR. SOMETHING FOR WHICH YOU **ALL** HAVE A CLEAR MOTIVE.

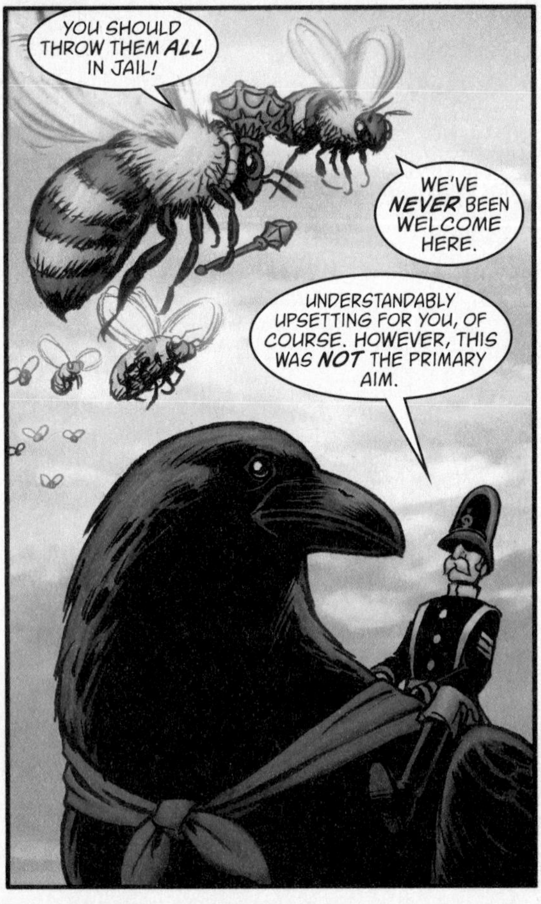
YOU SHOULD THROW THEM **ALL** IN JAIL!
WE'VE **NEVER** BEEN WELCOME HERE.
UNDERSTANDABLY UPSETTING FOR YOU, OF COURSE. HOWEVER, THIS WAS **NOT** THE PRIMARY AIM.

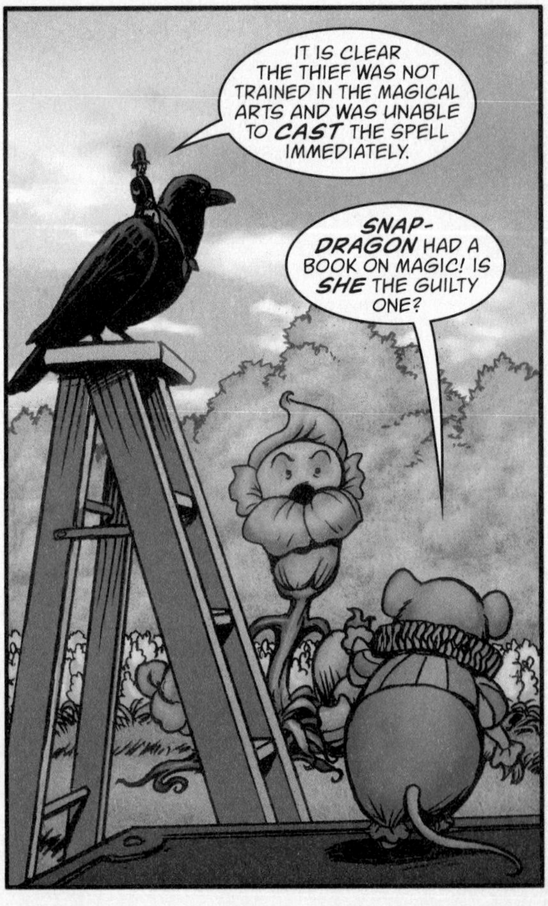
IT IS CLEAR THE THIEF WAS NOT TRAINED IN THE MAGICAL ARTS AND WAS UNABLE TO **CAST** THE SPELL IMMEDIATELY.
SNAP-DRAGON HAD A BOOK ON MAGIC! IS **SHE** THE GUILTY ONE?

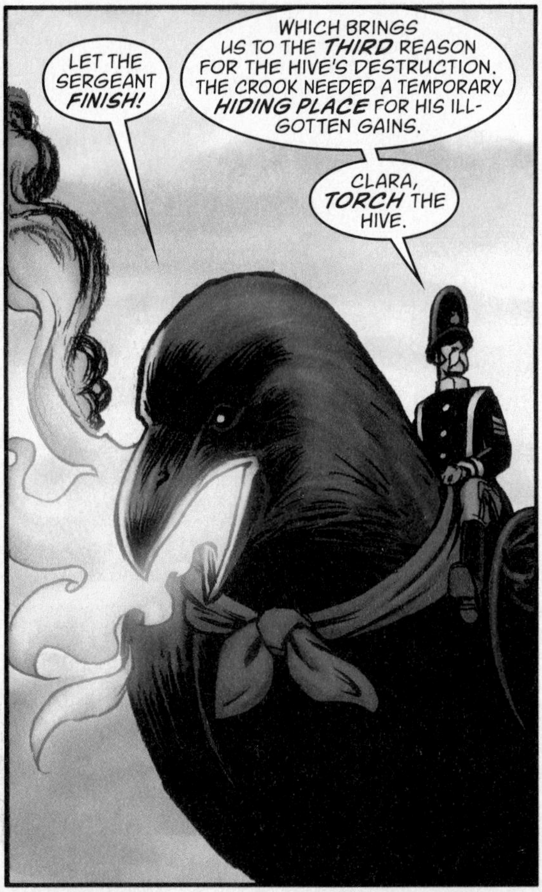
WHICH BRINGS US TO THE ***THIRD*** REASON FOR THE HIVE'S DESTRUCTION. THE CROOK NEEDED A TEMPORARY ***HIDING PLACE*** FOR HIS ILL-GOTTEN GAINS.
LET THE SERGEANT ***FINISH!***
CLARA, ***TORCH*** THE HIVE.

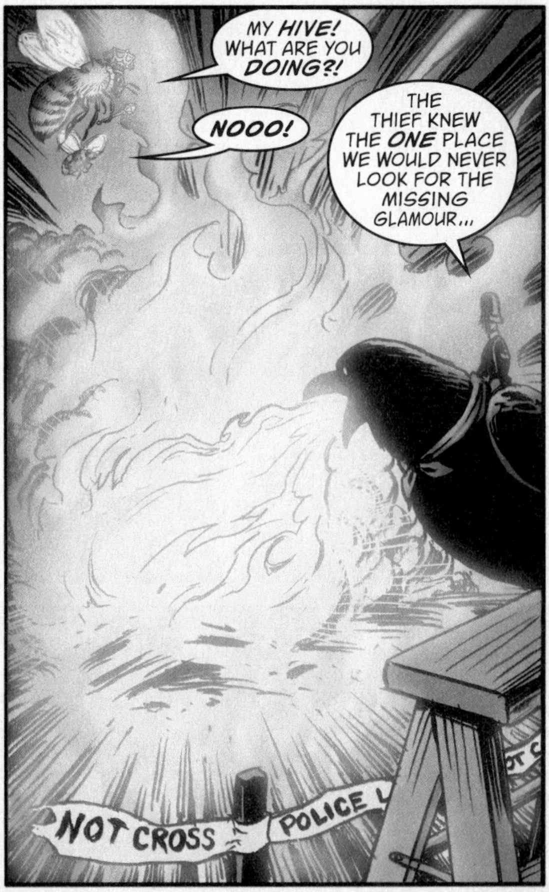
MY ***HIVE!*** WHAT ARE YOU ***DOING?!***
NOOO!
THE THIEF KNEW THE ***ONE*** PLACE WE WOULD NEVER LOOK FOR THE MISSING GLAMOUR...
NOT CROSS
POLICE L

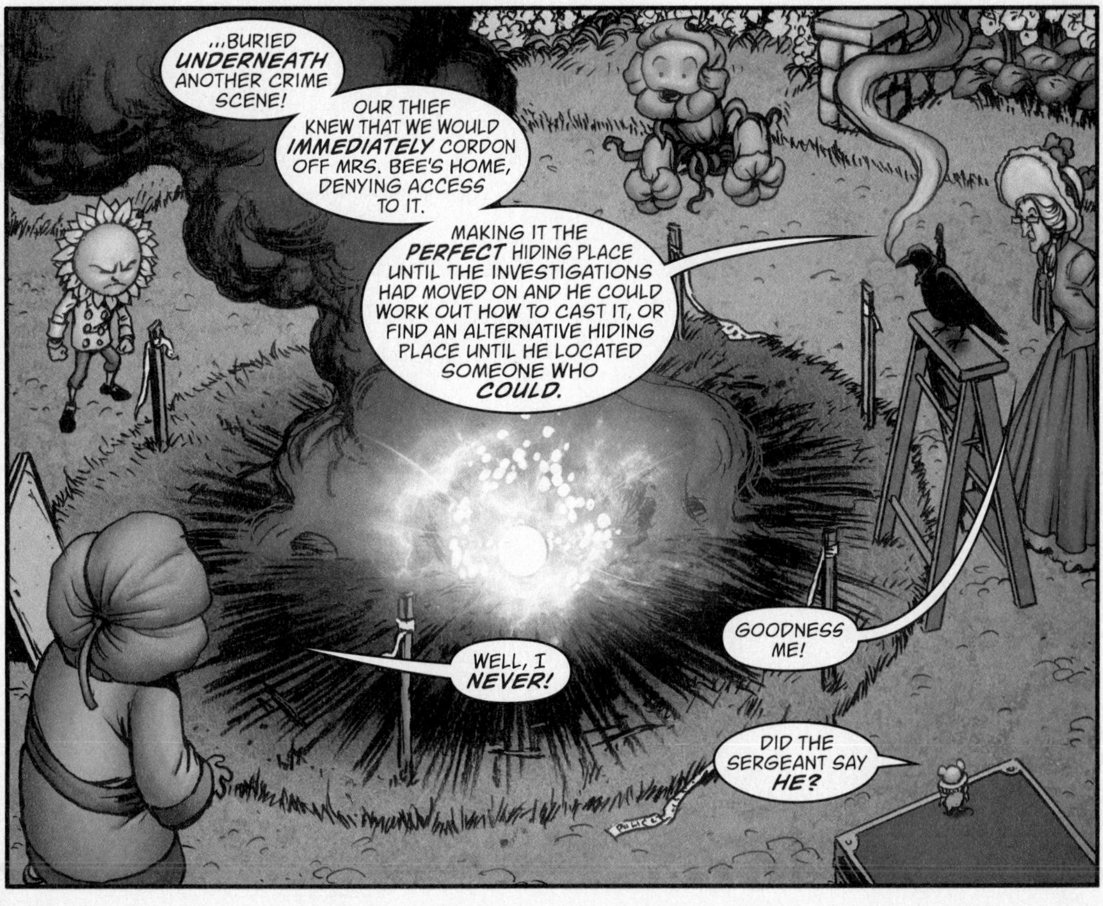
...BURIED ***UNDERNEATH*** ANOTHER CRIME SCENE!
OUR THIEF KNEW THAT WE WOULD ***IMMEDIATELY*** CORDON OFF MRS. BEE'S HOME, DENYING ACCESS TO IT.
MAKING IT THE ***PERFECT*** HIDING PLACE UNTIL THE INVESTIGATIONS HAD MOVED ON AND HE COULD WORK OUT HOW TO CAST IT, OR FIND AN ALTERNATIVE HIDING PLACE UNTIL HE LOCATED SOMEONE WHO ***COULD.***
GOODNESS ME!
WELL, I ***NEVER!***
DID THE SERGEANT SAY ***HE?***

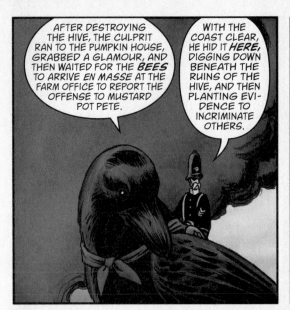

AFTER DESTROYING THE HIVE, THE CULPRIT RAN TO THE PUMPKIN HOUSE, GRABBED A GLAMOUR, AND THEN WAITED FOR THE **BEES** TO ARRIVE *EN MASSE* AT THE FARM OFFICE TO REPORT THE OFFENSE TO MUSTARD POT PETE.

WITH THE COAST CLEAR, HE HID IT **HERE**, DIGGING DOWN BENEATH THE RUINS OF THE HIVE, AND THEN PLANTING EVIDENCE TO INCRIMINATE OTHERS.

FINALLY, HE SCRUPULOUSLY CLEANED THE SCENE *AND* HIMSELF AT THE WATER TROUGH IN THE FARM SQUARE.

AND **WHO** DO WE KNOW AMONG THOSE GATHERED WHO HAS RECENTLY TAKEN TO WASHING HIMSELF IN THE TROUGH?

Oh, did I forget to mention?

MISTER SUNFLOWER.

DRAT AND **BLAST!**

It was me.

Judgment was swift and severe.

IT SAYS HERE YOU ARE SENTENCED TO TWO WEEKS IMPRISONMENT IN THE CAMELOT DUNGEON TO CONTEMPLATE THE ERROR OF YOUR WAYS, FOLLOWED BY A *YEAR* OF COMMUNITY SERVICE...

...STARTING WITH THE BUILDING OF A BRAND NEW BEE HIVE.

"MISTER SUNFLOWER MUST *ALSO* FORFEIT HIS RIGHT TO A GLAMOUR IN THE *LOTTERY*."

My bitterness just *grew*.

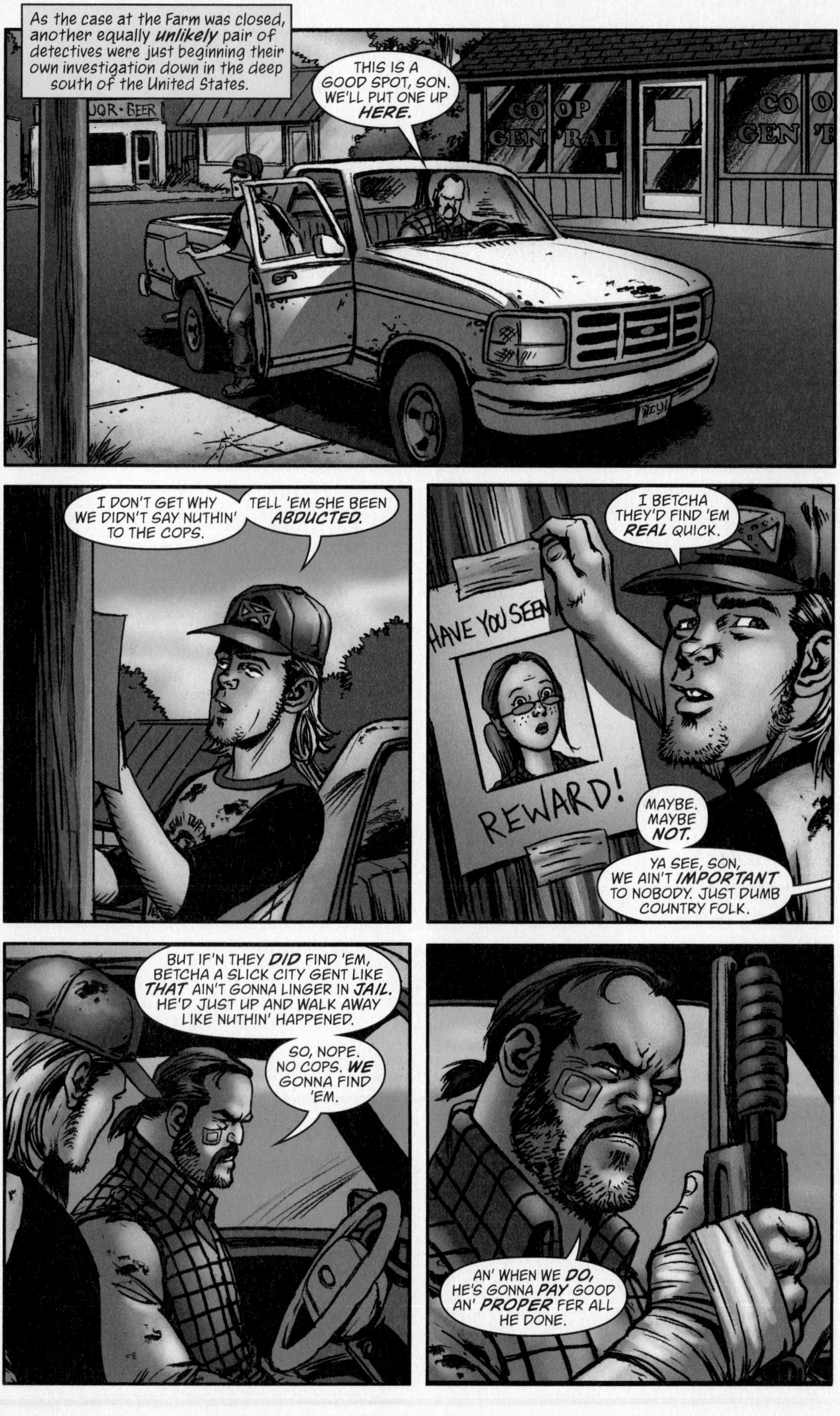
As the case at the Farm was closed, another equally unlikely pair of detectives were just beginning their own investigation down in the deep south of the United States.
THIS IS A GOOD SPOT, SON. WE'LL PUT ONE UP HERE.
CO OP GEN'RAL
I DON'T GET WHY WE DIDN'T SAY NUTHIN' TO THE COPS.
TELL 'EM SHE BEEN ABDUCTED.
I BETCHA THEY'D FIND 'EM REAL QUICK.
HAVE YOU SEEN
REWARD!
MAYBE. MAYBE NOT.
YA SEE, SON, WE AIN'T IMPORTANT TO NOBODY. JUST DUMB COUNTRY FOLK.
BUT IF'N THEY DID FIND 'EM, BETCHA A SLICK CITY GENT LIKE THAT AIN'T GONNA LINGER IN JAIL. HE'D JUST UP AND WALK AWAY LIKE NUTHIN' HAPPENED.
SO, NOPE. NO COPS. WE GONNA FIND 'EM.
AN' WHEN WE DO, HE'S GONNA PAY GOOD AN' PROPER FER ALL HE DONE.

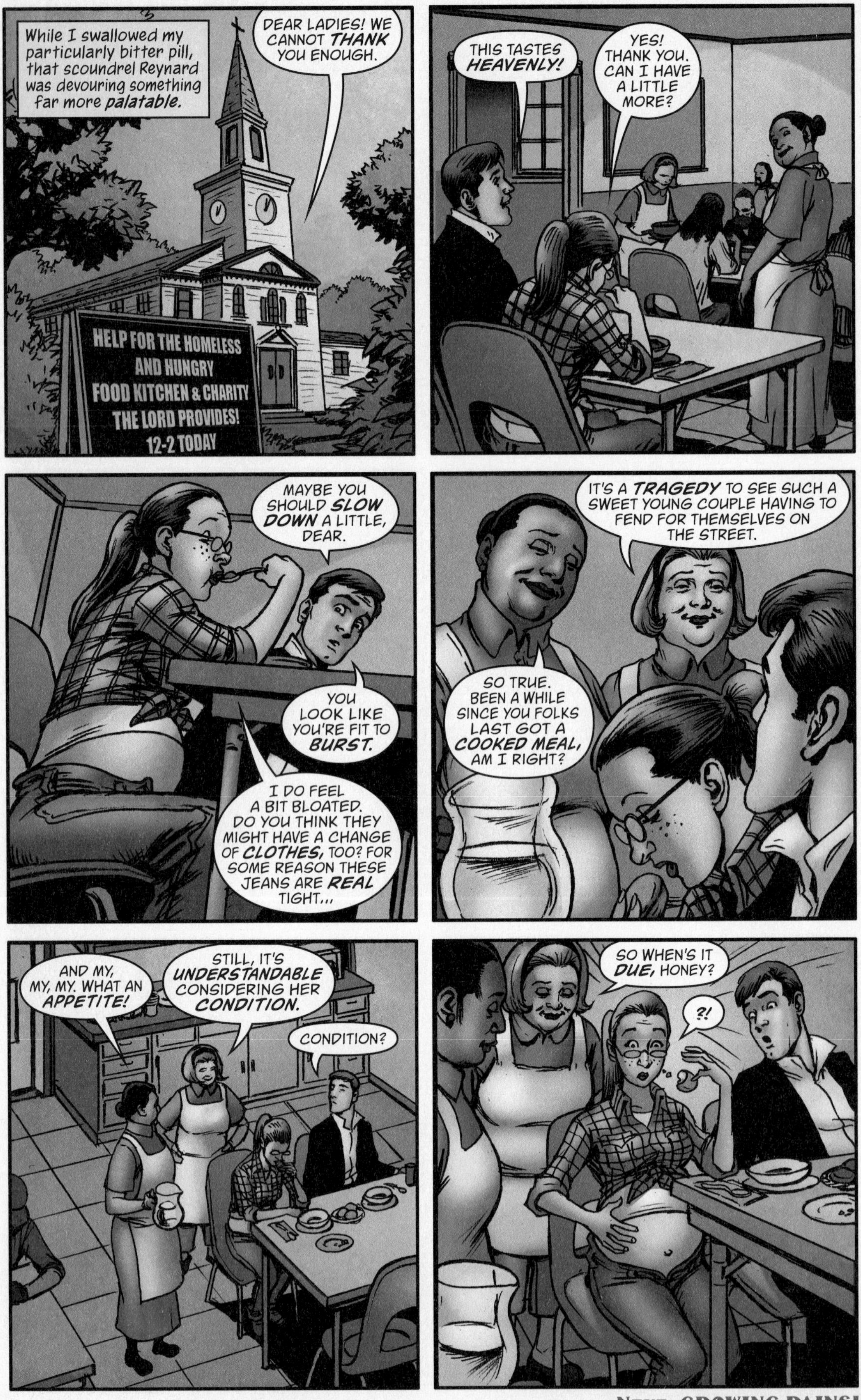
While I swallowed my particularly bitter pill, that scoundrel Reynard was devouring something far more *palatable.*
DEAR LADIES! WE CANNOT **THANK** YOU ENOUGH.
HELP FOR THE HOMELESS AND HUNGRY
FOOD KITCHEN & CHARITY
THE LORD PROVIDES!
12-2 TODAY
THIS TASTES **HEAVENLY!**
YES! THANK YOU. CAN I HAVE A LITTLE MORE?
MAYBE YOU SHOULD **SLOW DOWN** A LITTLE, DEAR.
YOU LOOK LIKE YOU'RE FIT TO **BURST.**
I DO FEEL A BIT BLOATED. DO YOU THINK THEY MIGHT HAVE A CHANGE OF **CLOTHES,** TOO? FOR SOME REASON THESE JEANS ARE **REAL** TIGHT...
IT'S A **TRAGEDY** TO SEE SUCH A SWEET YOUNG COUPLE HAVING TO FEND FOR THEMSELVES ON THE STREET.
SO TRUE. BEEN A WHILE SINCE YOU FOLKS LAST GOT A **COOKED MEAL,** AM I RIGHT?
AND MY, MY, MY. WHAT AN **APPETITE!**
STILL, IT'S **UNDERSTANDABLE** CONSIDERING HER **CONDITION.**
CONDITION?
SO WHEN'S IT **DUE,** HONEY?
?!

NEXT: GROWING PAINS!

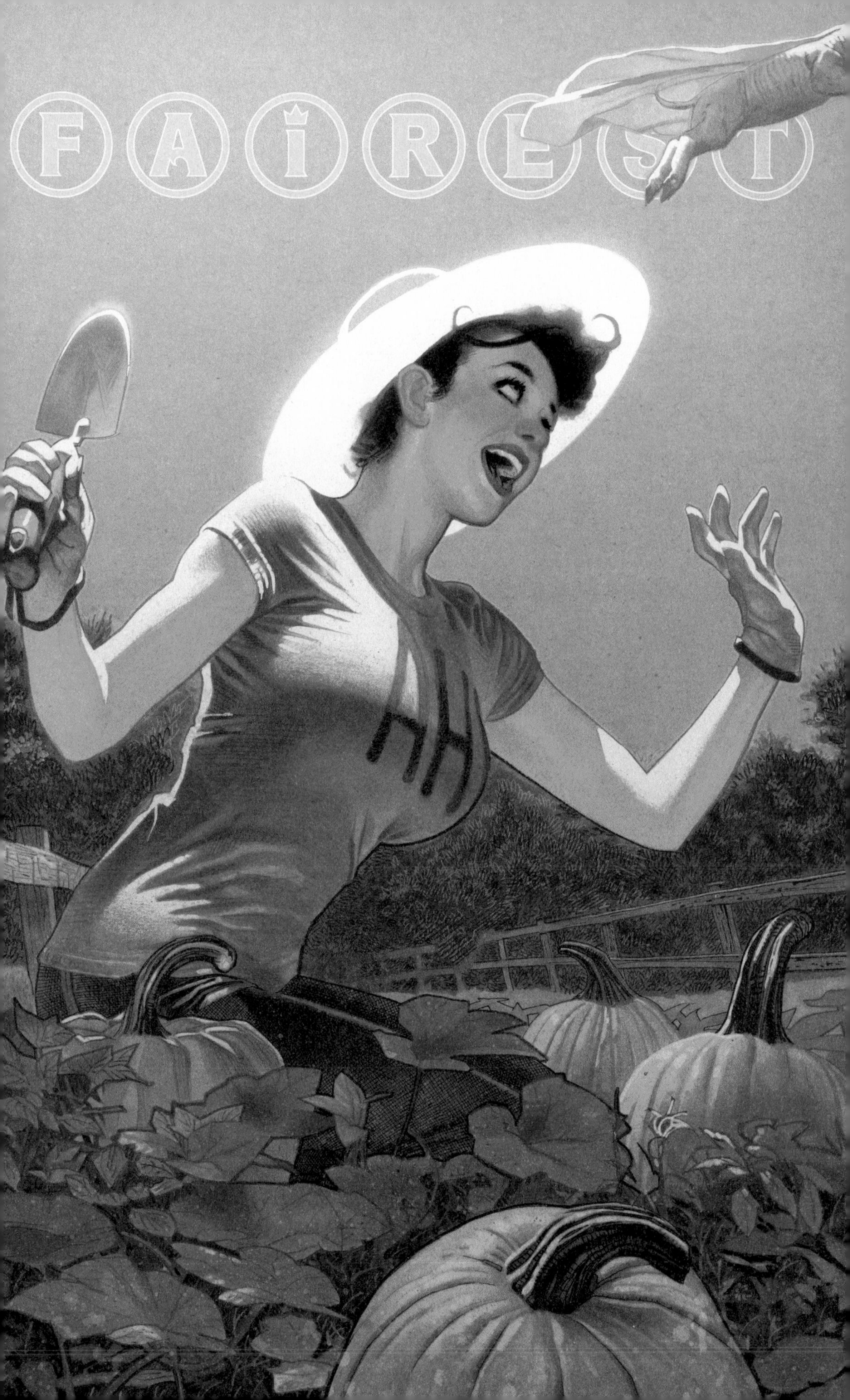
FAIREST

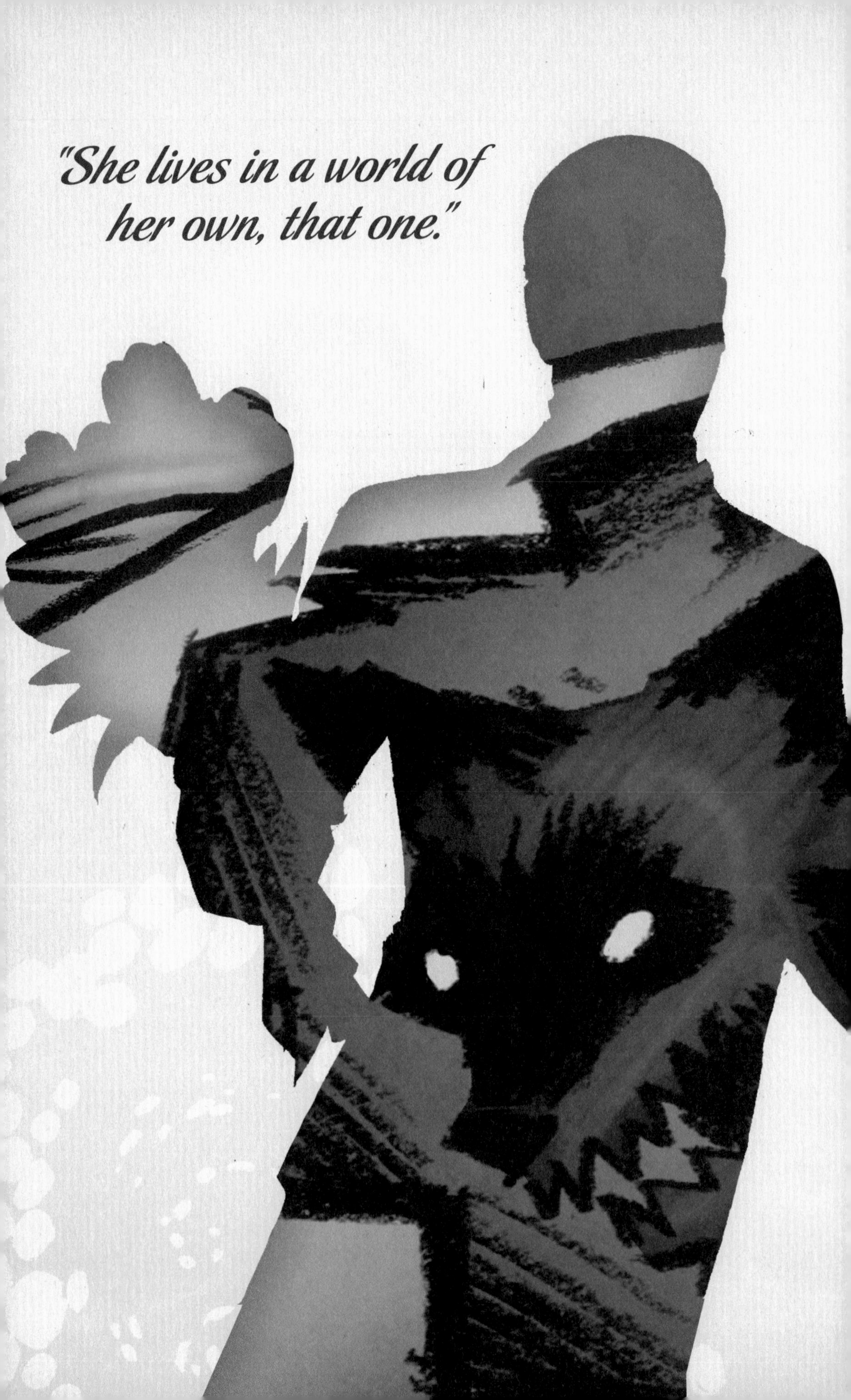
"She lives in a world of her own, that one."

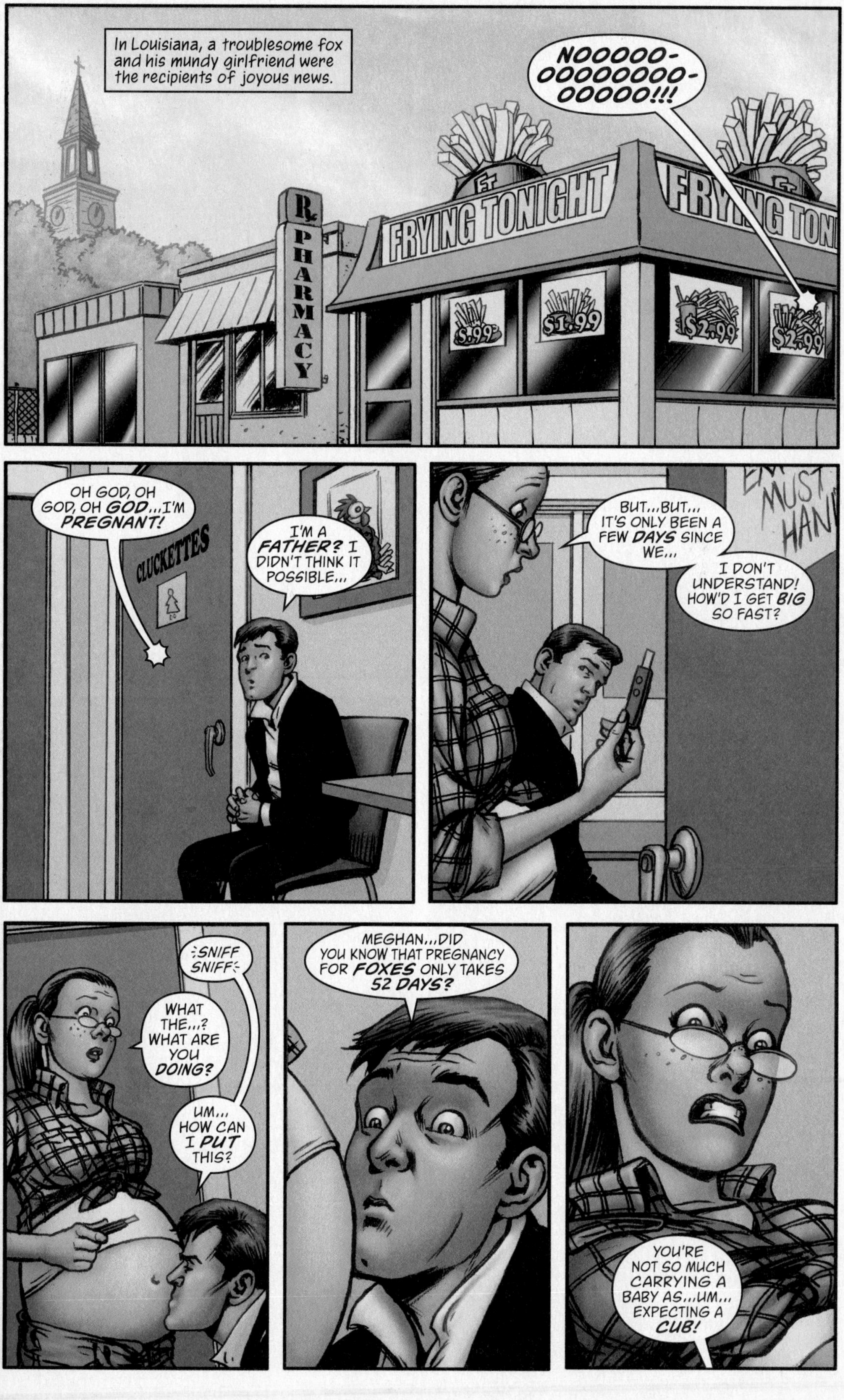

In Louisiana, a troublesome fox and his mundy girlfriend were the recipients of joyous news.
NOOOOO-OOOOOOOOO-OOOOO!!!
FRYING TONIGHT
R PHARMACY
$.99
$1.99
$2.99
$2.99
OH GOD, OH GOD, OH GOD...I'M PREGNANT!
CLUCKETTES
I'M A FATHER? I DIDN'T THINK IT POSSIBLE...
BUT...BUT... IT'S ONLY BEEN A FEW DAYS SINCE WE...
I DON'T UNDERSTAND! HOW'D I GET BIG SO FAST?
SNIFF SNIFF
WHAT THE...? WHAT ARE YOU DOING?
UM... HOW CAN I PUT THIS?
MEGHAN...DID YOU KNOW THAT PREGNANCY FOR FOXES ONLY TAKES 52 DAYS?
YOU'RE NOT SO MUCH CARRYING A BABY AS...UM... EXPECTING A CUB!

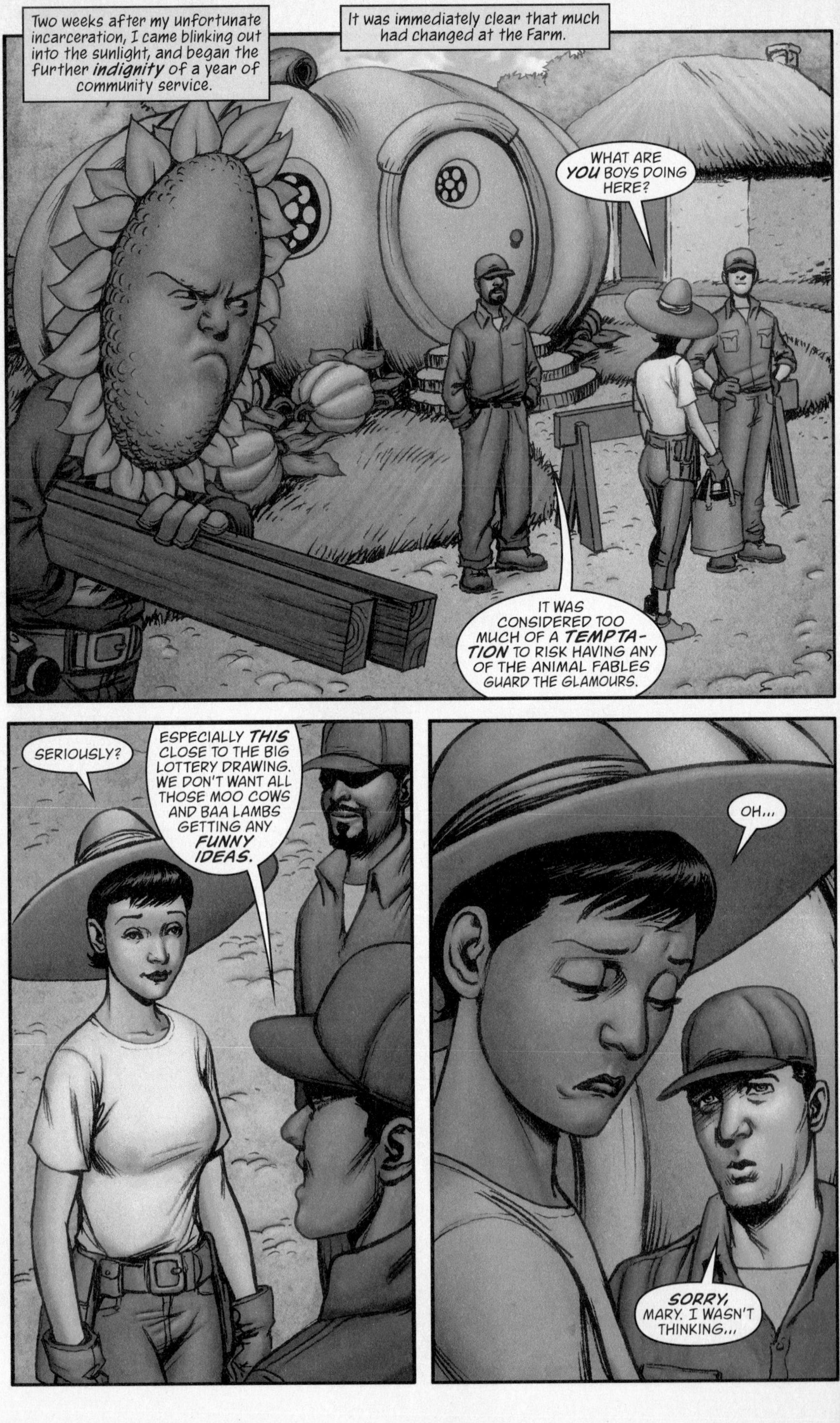
Two weeks after my unfortunate incarceration, I came blinking out into the sunlight, and began the further *indignity* of a year of community service.
It was immediately clear that much had changed at the Farm.
WHAT ARE *YOU* BOYS DOING HERE?
IT WAS CONSIDERED TOO MUCH OF A *TEMPTATION* TO RISK HAVING ANY OF THE ANIMAL FABLES GUARD THE GLAMOURS.
SERIOUSLY?
ESPECIALLY *THIS* CLOSE TO THE BIG LOTTERY DRAWING. WE DON'T WANT ALL THOSE MOO COWS AND BAA LAMBS GETTING ANY *FUNNY IDEAS.*
OH...
SORRY, MARY. I WASN'T THINKING...

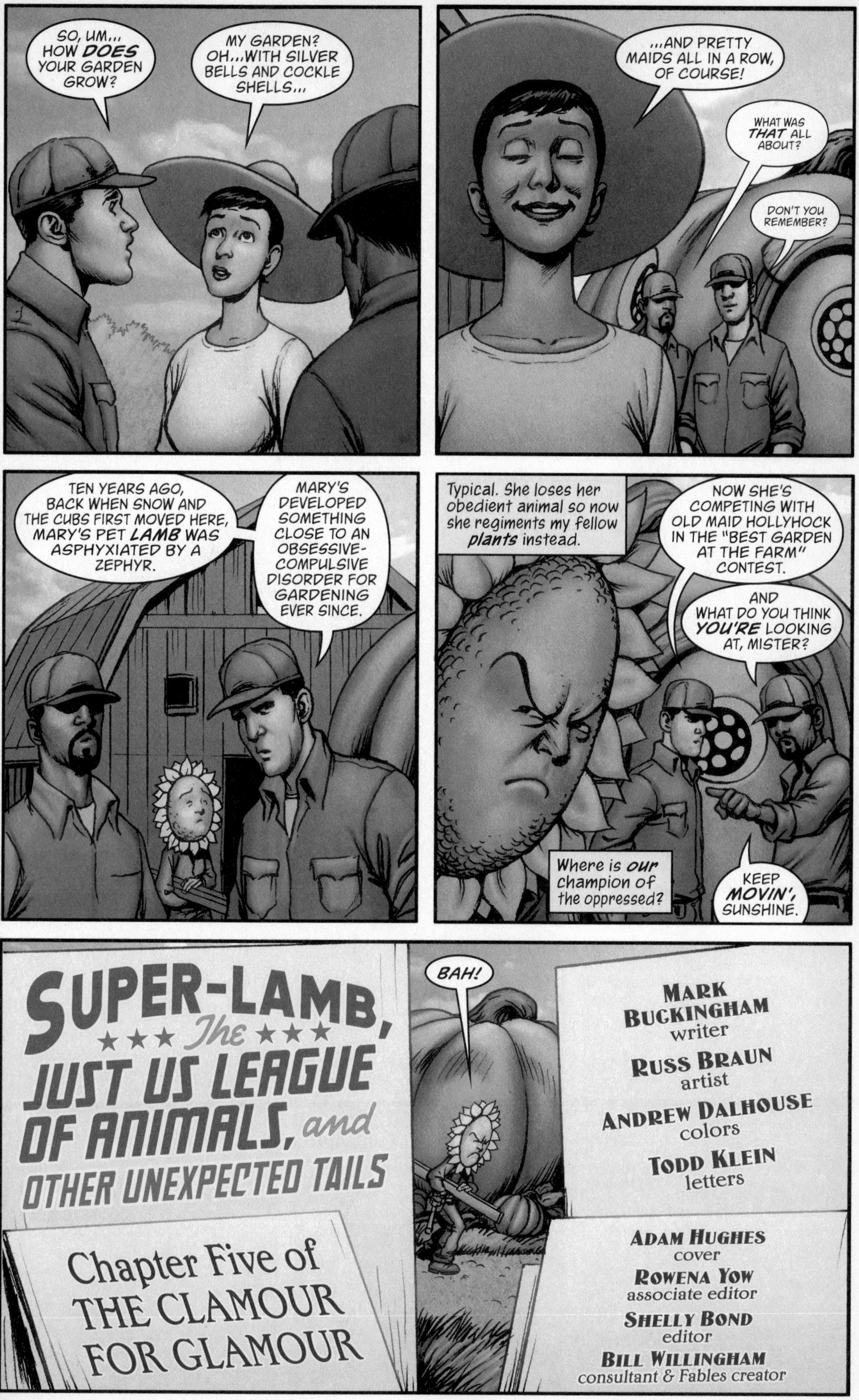

SO, UM... HOW DOES YOUR GARDEN GROW?
MY GARDEN? OH...WITH SILVER BELLS AND COCKLE SHELLS...
...AND PRETTY MAIDS ALL IN A ROW, OF COURSE!
WHAT WAS THAT ALL ABOUT?
DON'T YOU REMEMBER?
TEN YEARS AGO, BACK WHEN SNOW AND THE CUBS FIRST MOVED HERE, MARY'S PET LAMB WAS ASPHYXIATED BY A ZEPHYR.
MARY'S DEVELOPED SOMETHING CLOSE TO AN OBSESSIVE-COMPULSIVE DISORDER FOR GARDENING EVER SINCE.
Typical. She loses her obedient animal so now she regiments my fellow plants instead.
NOW SHE'S COMPETING WITH OLD MAID HOLLYHOCK IN THE "BEST GARDEN AT THE FARM" CONTEST.
AND WHAT DO YOU THINK YOU'RE LOOKING AT, MISTER?
Where is our champion of the oppressed?
KEEP MOVIN', SUNSHINE.
SUPER-LAMB, The JUST US LEAGUE OF ANIMALS, and OTHER UNEXPECTED TAILS
Chapter Five of THE CLAMOUR FOR GLAMOUR
BAH!
MARK BUCKINGHAM writer
RUSS BRAUN artist
ANDREW DALHOUSE colors
TODD KLEIN letters
ADAM HUGHES cover
ROWENA YOW associate editor
SHELLY BOND editor
BILL WILLINGHAM consultant & Fables creator

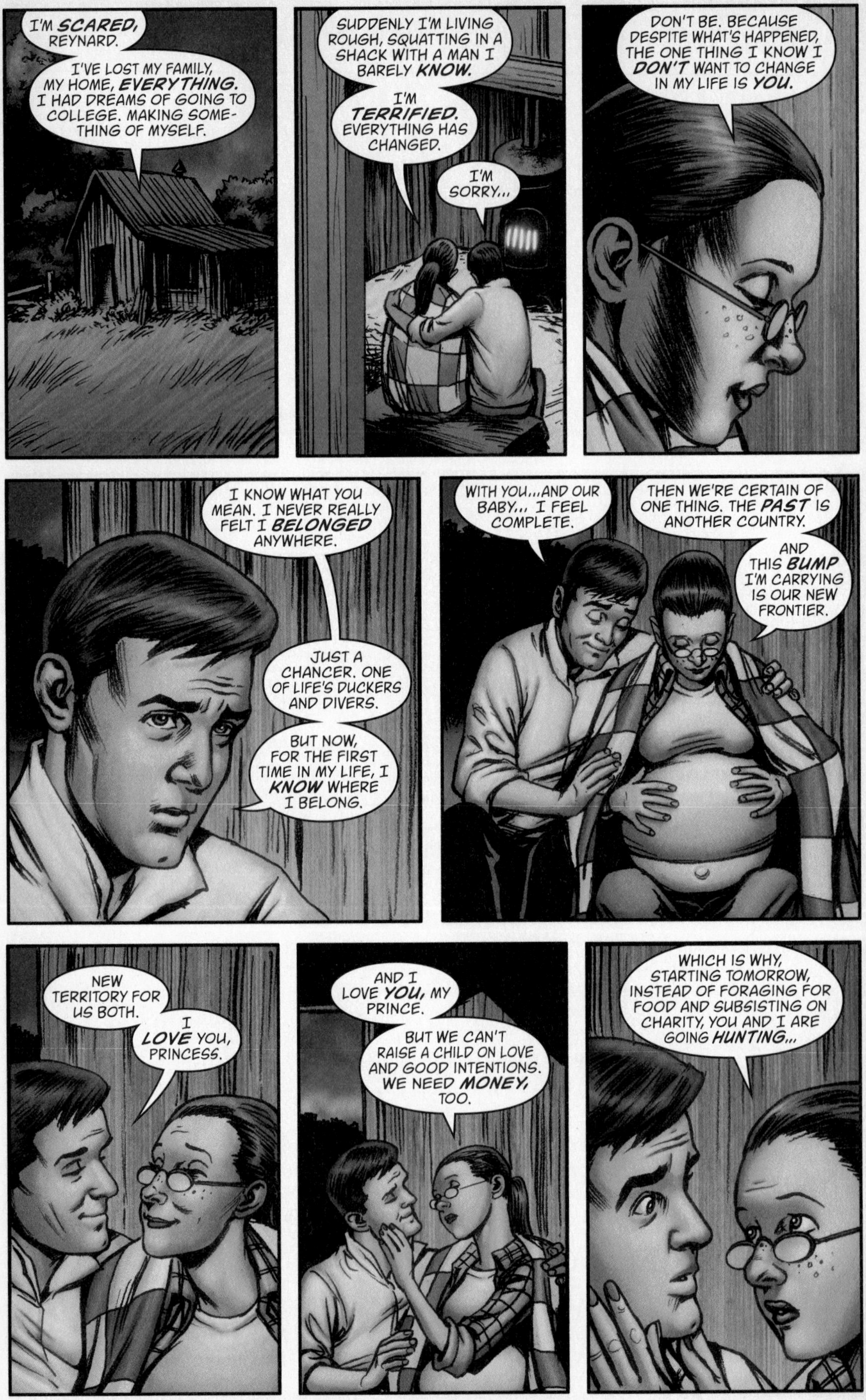
I'M SCARED, REYNARD.
I'VE LOST MY FAMILY, MY HOME, EVERYTHING. I HAD DREAMS OF GOING TO COLLEGE. MAKING SOME-THING OF MYSELF.
SUDDENLY I'M LIVING ROUGH, SQUATTING IN A SHACK WITH A MAN I BARELY KNOW.
I'M TERRIFIED. EVERYTHING HAS CHANGED.
I'M SORRY...
DON'T BE. BECAUSE DESPITE WHAT'S HAPPENED, THE ONE THING I KNOW I DON'T WANT TO CHANGE IN MY LIFE IS YOU.
I KNOW WHAT YOU MEAN. I NEVER REALLY FELT I BELONGED ANYWHERE.
JUST A CHANCER. ONE OF LIFE'S DUCKERS AND DIVERS.
BUT NOW, FOR THE FIRST TIME IN MY LIFE, I KNOW WHERE I BELONG.
WITH YOU...AND OUR BABY... I FEEL COMPLETE.
THEN WE'RE CERTAIN OF ONE THING. THE PAST IS ANOTHER COUNTRY.
AND THIS BUMP I'M CARRYING IS OUR NEW FRONTIER.
NEW TERRITORY FOR US BOTH.
I LOVE YOU, PRINCESS.
AND I LOVE YOU, MY PRINCE.
BUT WE CAN'T RAISE A CHILD ON LOVE AND GOOD INTENTIONS. WE NEED MONEY, TOO.
WHICH IS WHY, STARTING TOMORROW, INSTEAD OF FORAGING FOR FOOD AND SUBSISTING ON CHARITY, YOU AND I ARE GOING HUNTING...

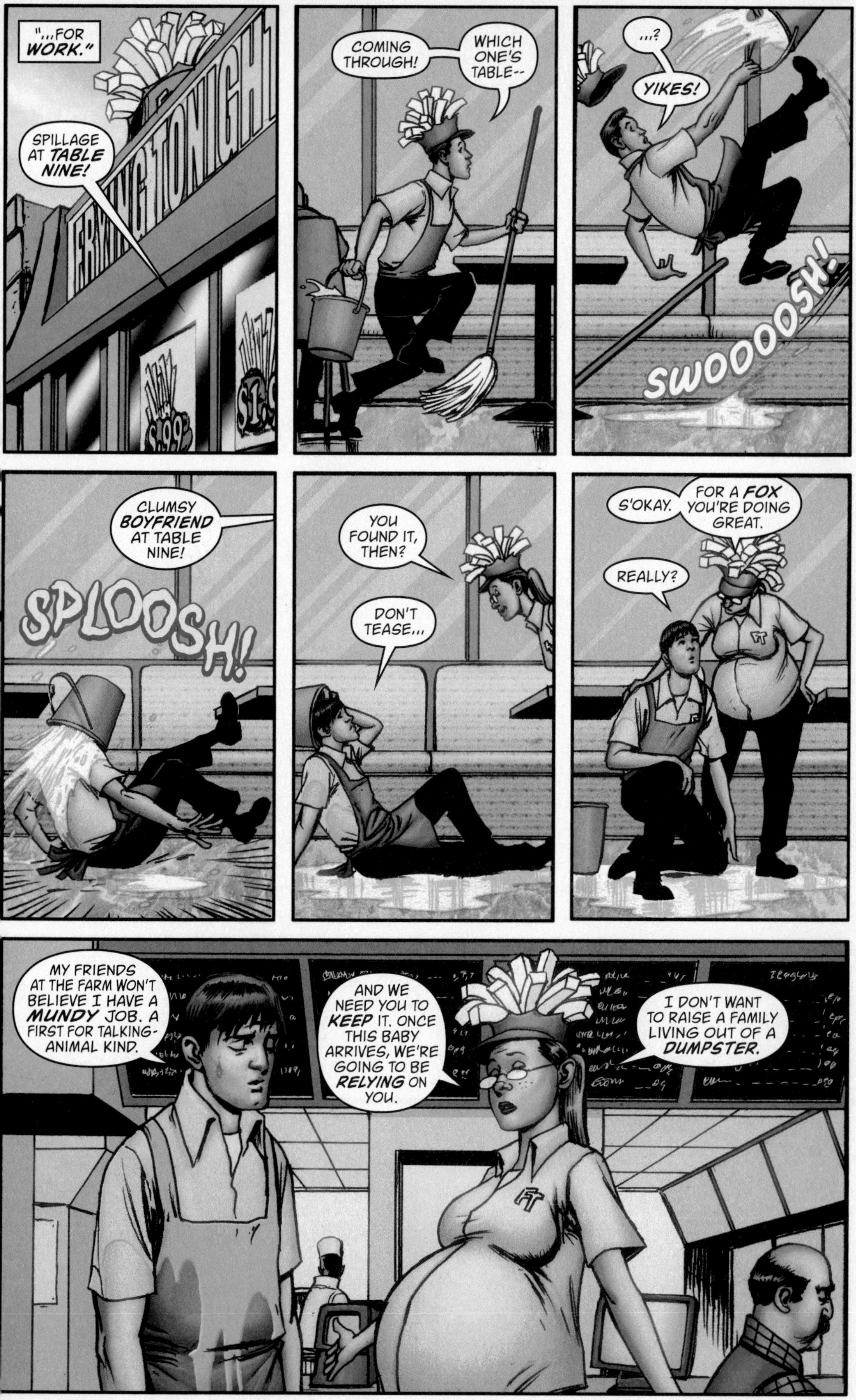
"...FOR WORK."
SPILLAGE AT TABLE NINE!
COMING THROUGH!
WHICH ONE'S TABLE--
...?
YIKES!
SWOOOOSH!
CLUMSY BOYFRIEND AT TABLE NINE!
SPLOOSH!
YOU FOUND IT, THEN?
DON'T TEASE...
S'OKAY.
FOR A FOX YOU'RE DOING GREAT.
REALLY?
MY FRIENDS AT THE FARM WON'T BELIEVE I HAVE A MUNDY JOB. A FIRST FOR TALKING-ANIMAL KIND.
AND WE NEED YOU TO KEEP IT. ONCE THIS BABY ARRIVES, WE'RE GOING TO BE RELYING ON YOU.
I DON'T WANT TO RAISE A FAMILY LIVING OUT OF A DUMPSTER.

After two *interminably* long weeks of waiting, the day of the lottery was almost upon us.

STOP *FIDGETING*, LUNA.

CAN'T HELP IT WITH THAT HYPERACTIVE BALL OF *WOOL* RUNNING AROUND MY *HOOVES*.

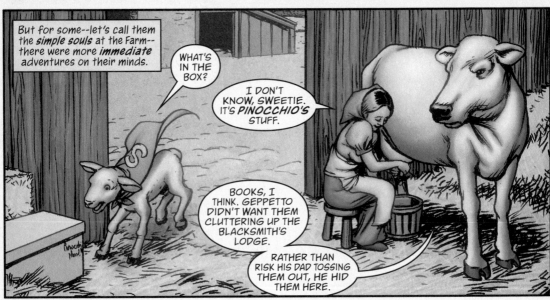

But for some--let's call them the *simple souls* at the Farm-- there were more *immediate* adventures on their minds.

WHAT'S IN THE BOX?

I DON'T KNOW, SWEETIE. IT'S *PINOCCHIO'S* STUFF.

BOOKS, I THINK. GEPPETTO DIDN'T WANT THEM CLUTTERING UP THE BLACKSMITH'S LODGE.

RATHER THAN RISK HIS DAD TOSSING THEM OUT, HE HID THEM HERE.

OH *BOY!* COMIC BOOKS!

HEY! THAT'S OTHER PEOPLE'S *PROPERTY,* YOUNG LADY!

Pinocchio's! Hands off!!!

SAVE YOUR BREATH. SHE LIVES IN A WORLD OF HER *OWN,* THAT ONE.

WOW! THIS STUFF IS *AMAZING!*

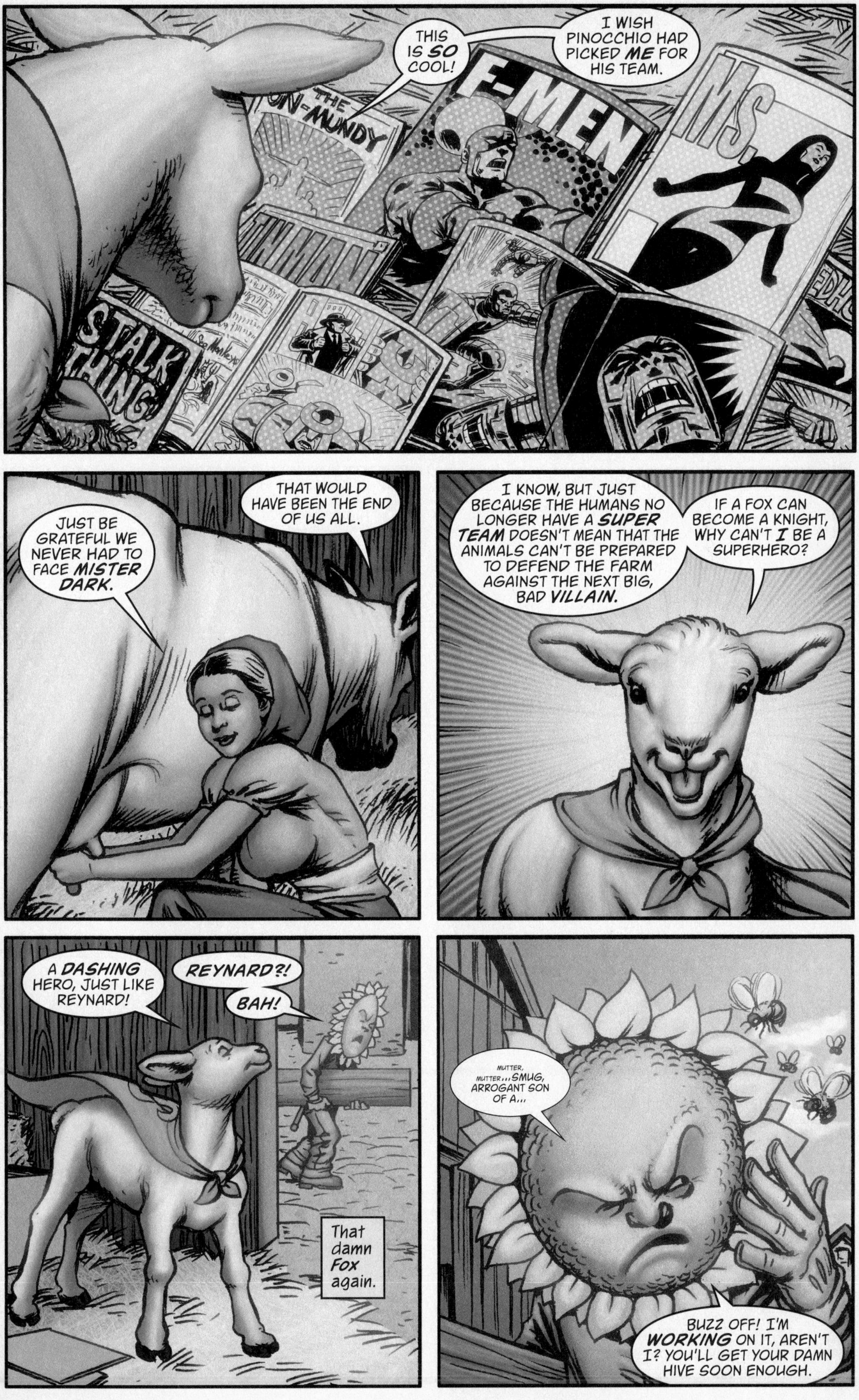
THIS IS SO COOL!
I WISH PINOCCHIO HAD PICKED ME FOR HIS TEAM.
THE UN-MUNDY
F-MEN
MS.
STALK THING
JUST BE GRATEFUL WE NEVER HAD TO FACE MISTER DARK.
THAT WOULD HAVE BEEN THE END OF US ALL.
I KNOW, BUT JUST BECAUSE THE HUMANS NO LONGER HAVE A SUPER TEAM DOESN'T MEAN THAT THE ANIMALS CAN'T BE PREPARED TO DEFEND THE FARM AGAINST THE NEXT BIG, BAD VILLAIN.
IF A FOX CAN BECOME A KNIGHT, WHY CAN'T I BE A SUPERHERO?
A DASHING HERO, JUST LIKE REYNARD!
REYNARD?!
BAH!
That damn Fox again.
MUTTER, MUTTER... SMUG, ARROGANT SON OF A...
BUZZ OFF! I'M WORKING ON IT, AREN'T I? YOU'LL GET YOUR DAMN HIVE SOON ENOUGH.

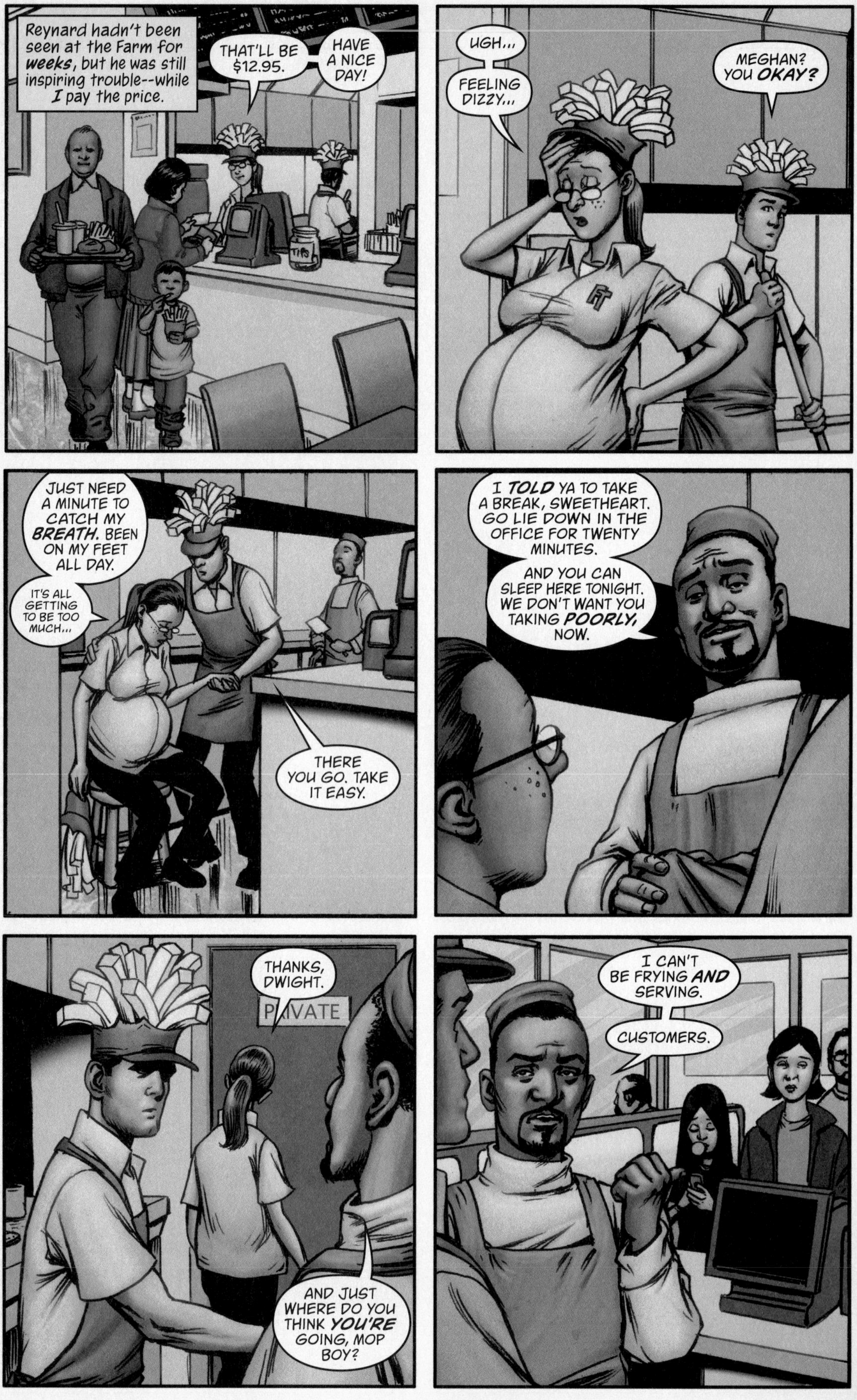

Reynard hadn't been seen at the Farm for *weeks*, but he was still inspiring trouble--while *I* pay the price.
THAT'LL BE $12.95.
HAVE A NICE DAY!
TIPS
UGH...
FEELING DIZZY...
MEGHAN? YOU *OKAY?*
JUST NEED A MINUTE TO CATCH MY *BREATH.* BEEN ON MY FEET ALL DAY.
IT'S ALL GETTING TO BE TOO MUCH...
THERE YOU GO. TAKE IT EASY.
I *TOLD* YA TO TAKE A BREAK, SWEETHEART. GO LIE DOWN IN THE OFFICE FOR TWENTY MINUTES.
AND YOU CAN SLEEP HERE TONIGHT. WE DON'T WANT YOU TAKING *POORLY,* NOW.
THANKS, DWIGHT.
PRIVATE
AND JUST WHERE DO YOU THINK *YOU'RE* GOING, MOP BOY?
I CAN'T BE FRYING *AND* SERVING.
CUSTOMERS.

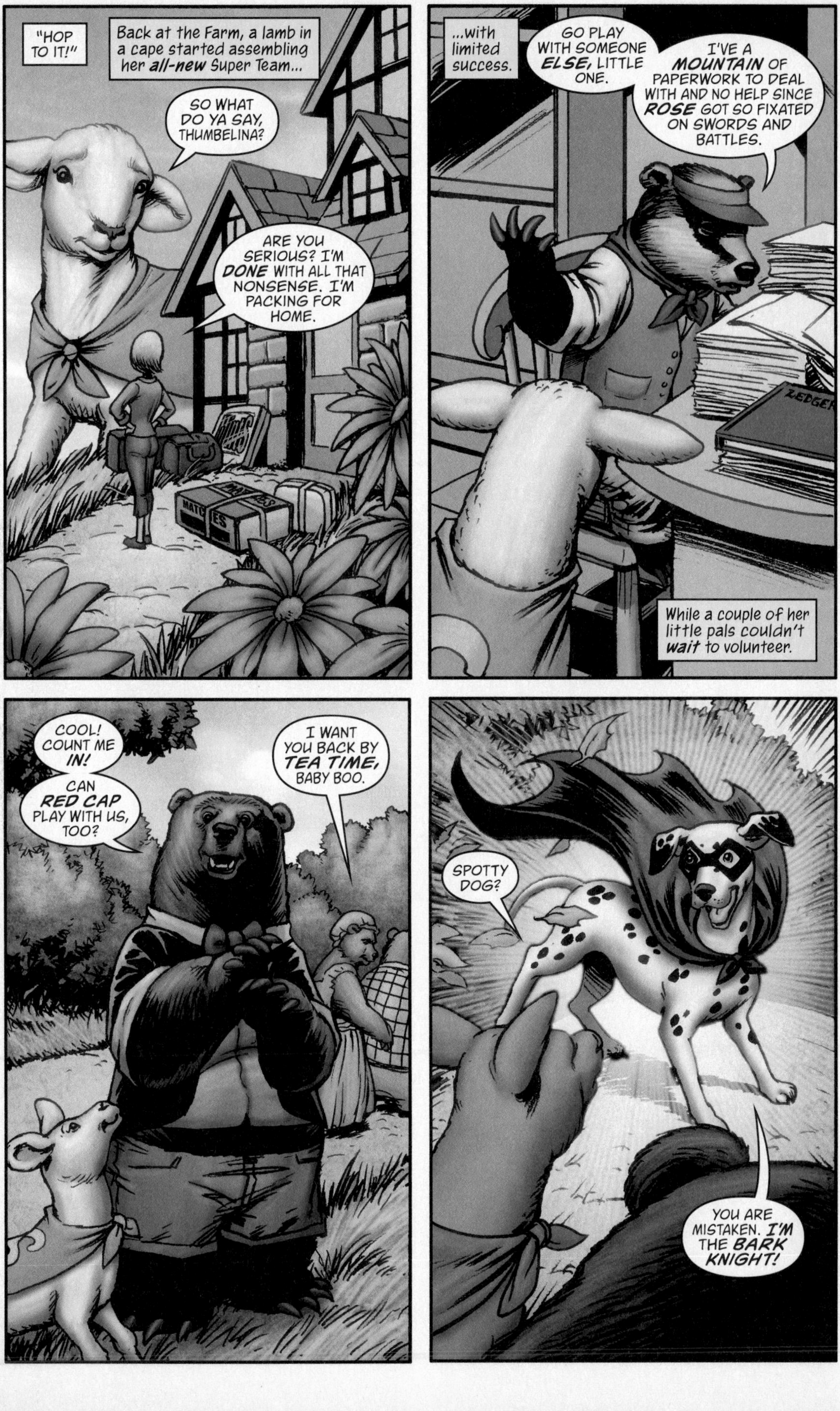
"HOP TO IT!"
Back at the Farm, a lamb in a cape started assembling her ***all-new*** Super Team...
SO WHAT DO YA SAY, THUMBELINA?
ARE YOU SERIOUS? I'M ***DONE*** WITH ALL THAT NONSENSE. I'M PACKING FOR HOME.
...with limited success.
GO PLAY WITH SOMEONE ***ELSE,*** LITTLE ONE.
I'VE A ***MOUNTAIN*** OF PAPERWORK TO DEAL WITH AND NO HELP SINCE ***ROSE*** GOT SO FIXATED ON SWORDS AND BATTLES.
While a couple of her little pals couldn't ***wait*** to volunteer.
COOL! COUNT ME ***IN!***
CAN ***RED CAP*** PLAY WITH US, TOO?
I WANT YOU BACK BY ***TEA TIME,*** BABY BOO.
SPOTTY DOG?
YOU ARE MISTAKEN. ***I'M*** THE ***BARK KNIGHT!***

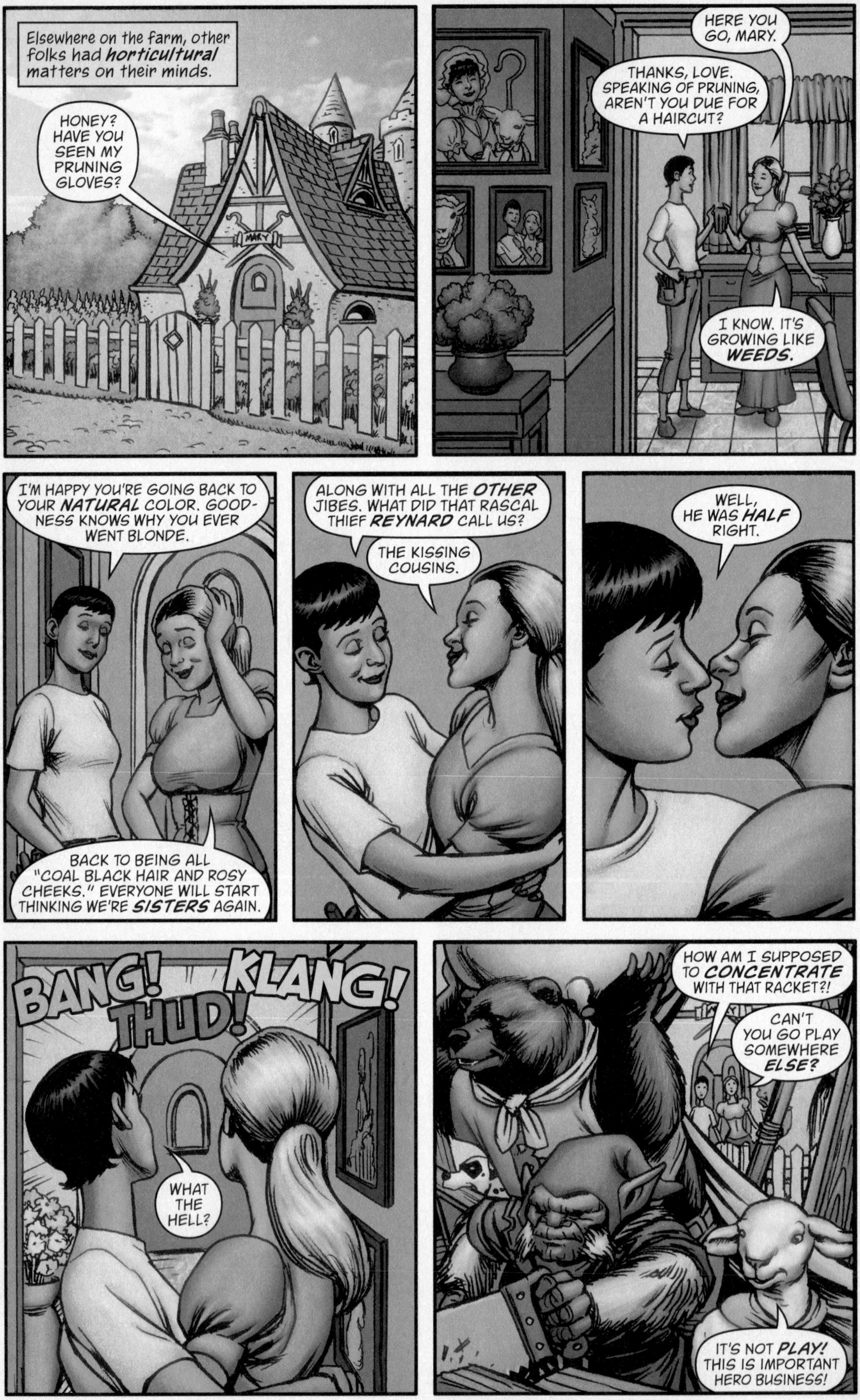
Elsewhere on the farm, other folks had horticultural matters on their minds.
HONEY? HAVE YOU SEEN MY PRUNING GLOVES?
MARY
HERE YOU GO, MARY.
THANKS, LOVE. SPEAKING OF PRUNING, AREN'T YOU DUE FOR A HAIRCUT?
I KNOW. IT'S GROWING LIKE WEEDS.
I'M HAPPY YOU'RE GOING BACK TO YOUR NATURAL COLOR. GOODNESS KNOWS WHY YOU EVER WENT BLONDE.
BACK TO BEING ALL "COAL BLACK HAIR AND ROSY CHEEKS." EVERYONE WILL START THINKING WE'RE SISTERS AGAIN.
ALONG WITH ALL THE OTHER JIBES. WHAT DID THAT RASCAL THIEF REYNARD CALL US?
THE KISSING COUSINS.
WELL, HE WAS HALF RIGHT.
BANG! THUD! KLANG!
WHAT THE HELL?
HOW AM I SUPPOSED TO CONCENTRATE WITH THAT RACKET?!
CAN'T YOU GO PLAY SOMEWHERE ELSE?
IT'S NOT PLAY! THIS IS IMPORTANT HERO BUSINESS!

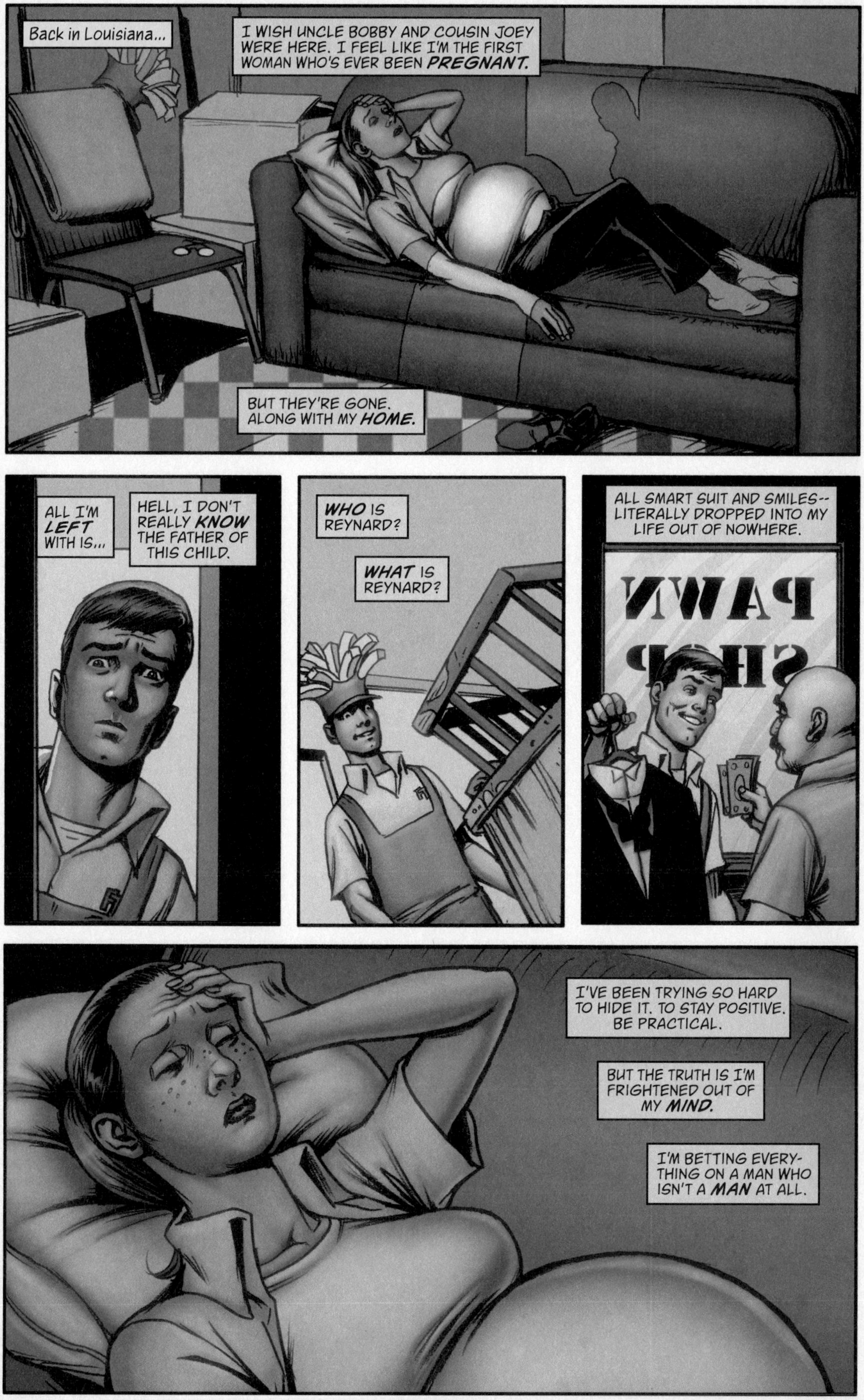
Back in Louisiana...
I WISH UNCLE BOBBY AND COUSIN JOEY WERE HERE. I FEEL LIKE I'M THE FIRST WOMAN WHO'S EVER BEEN PREGNANT.
BUT THEY'RE GONE. ALONG WITH MY HOME.
ALL I'M LEFT WITH IS...
HELL, I DON'T REALLY KNOW THE FATHER OF THIS CHILD.
WHO IS REYNARD?
WHAT IS REYNARD?
ALL SMART SUIT AND SMILES-- LITERALLY DROPPED INTO MY LIFE OUT OF NOWHERE.
PAWN SHOP
I'VE BEEN TRYING SO HARD TO HIDE IT. TO STAY POSITIVE. BE PRACTICAL.
BUT THE TRUTH IS I'M FRIGHTENED OUT OF MY MIND.
I'M BETTING EVERY-THING ON A MAN WHO ISN'T A MAN AT ALL.

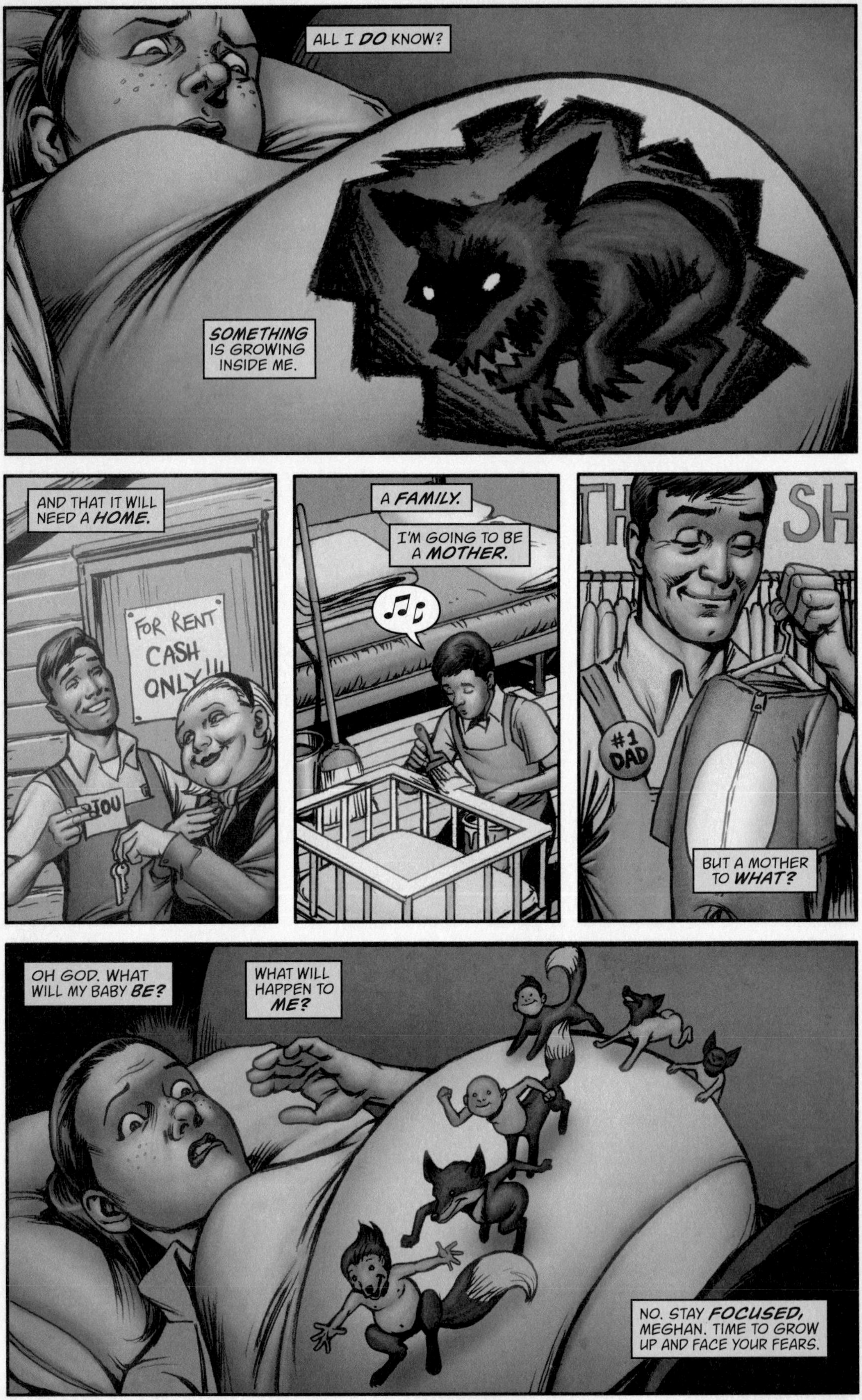
ALL I DO KNOW?
SOMETHING IS GROWING INSIDE ME.
AND THAT IT WILL NEED A HOME.
FOR RENT CASH ONLY!!!
IOU
A FAMILY.
I'M GOING TO BE A MOTHER.
♫♪
#1 DAD
BUT A MOTHER TO WHAT?
OH GOD. WHAT WILL MY BABY BE?
WHAT WILL HAPPEN TO ME?
NO. STAY FOCUSED, MEGHAN. TIME TO GROW UP AND FACE YOUR FEARS.

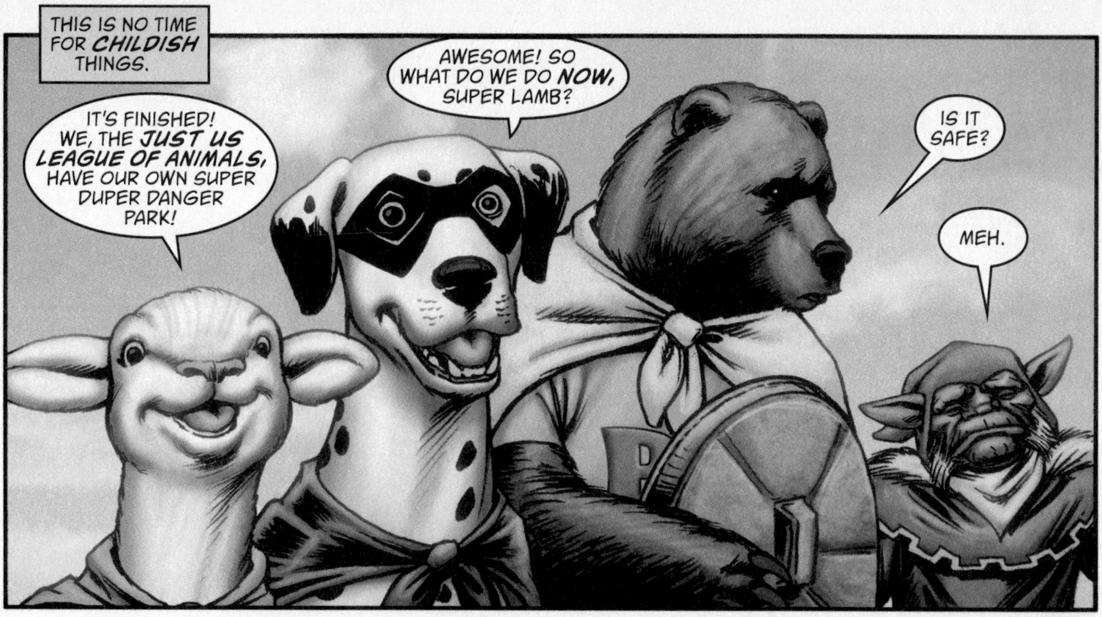
THIS IS NO TIME FOR CHILDISH THINGS.
IT'S FINISHED! WE, THE JUST US LEAGUE OF ANIMALS, HAVE OUR OWN SUPER DUPER DANGER PARK!
AWESOME! SO WHAT DO WE DO NOW, SUPER LAMB?
IS IT SAFE?
MEH.

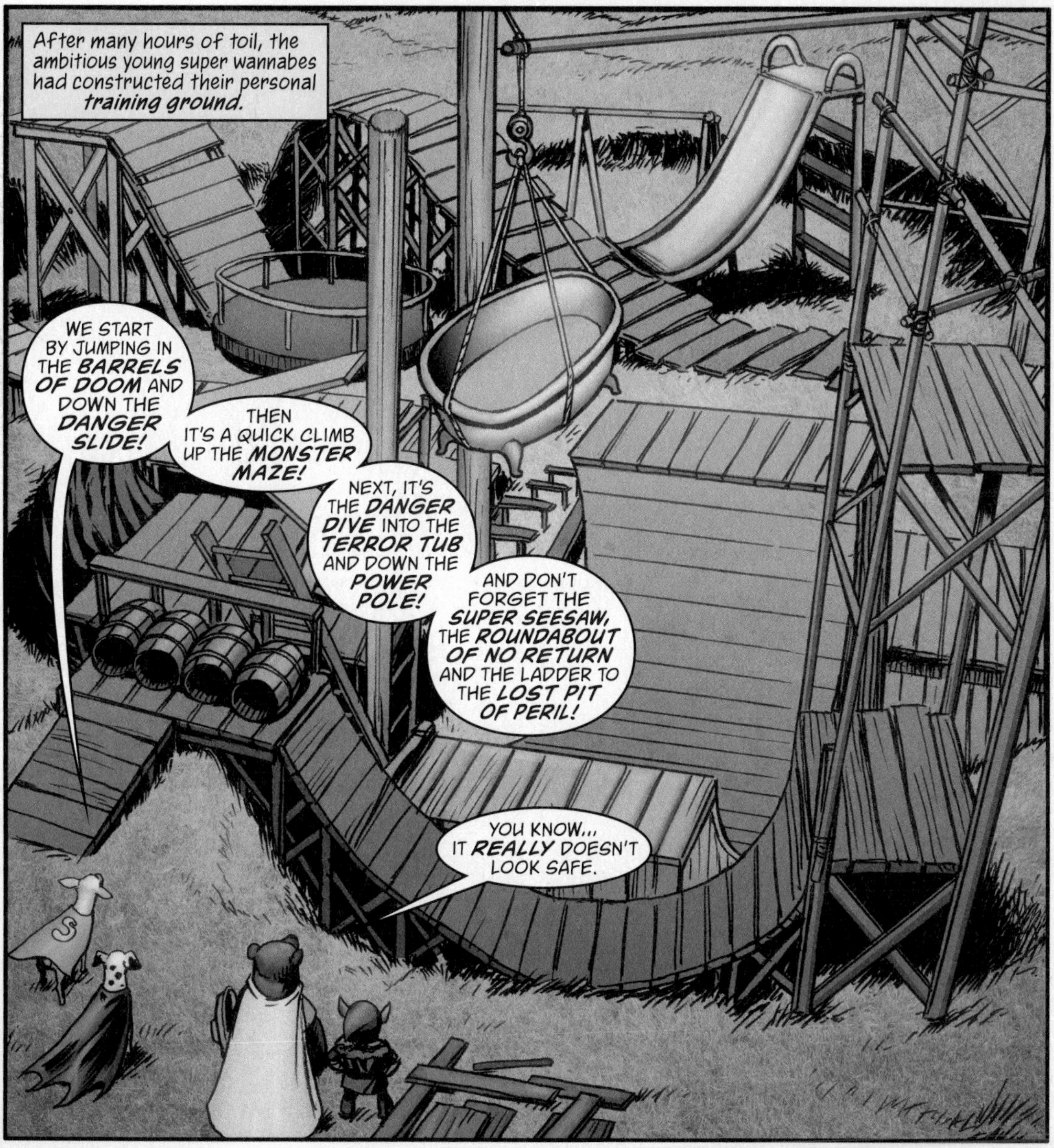
After many hours of toil, the ambitious young super wannabes had constructed their personal training ground.
WE START BY JUMPING IN THE BARRELS OF DOOM AND DOWN THE DANGER SLIDE!
THEN IT'S A QUICK CLIMB UP THE MONSTER MAZE!
NEXT, IT'S THE DANGER DIVE INTO THE TERROR TUB AND DOWN THE POWER POLE!
AND DON'T FORGET THE SUPER SEESAW, THE ROUNDABOUT OF NO RETURN AND THE LADDER TO THE LOST PIT OF PERIL!
YOU KNOW... IT REALLY DOESN'T LOOK SAFE.

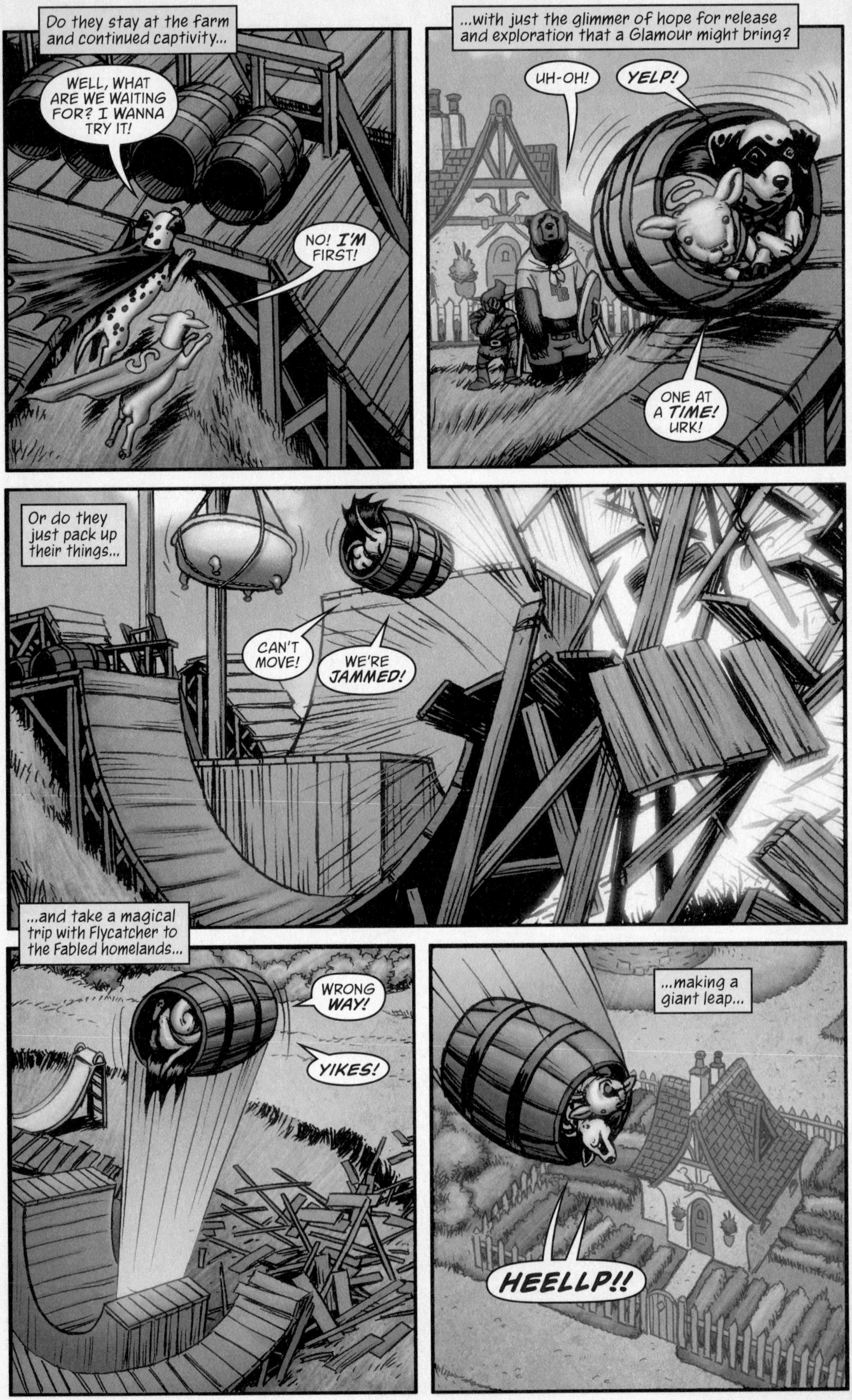
Do they stay at the farm and continued captivity...
WELL, WHAT ARE WE WAITING FOR? I WANNA TRY IT!
NO! I'M FIRST!
...with just the glimmer of hope for release and exploration that a Glamour might bring?
UH-OH!
YELP!
ONE AT A TIME! URK!
Or do they just pack up their things...
CAN'T MOVE!
WE'RE JAMMED!
...and take a magical trip with Flycatcher to the Fabled homelands...
WRONG WAY!
YIKES!
...making a giant leap...
HEELLP!!

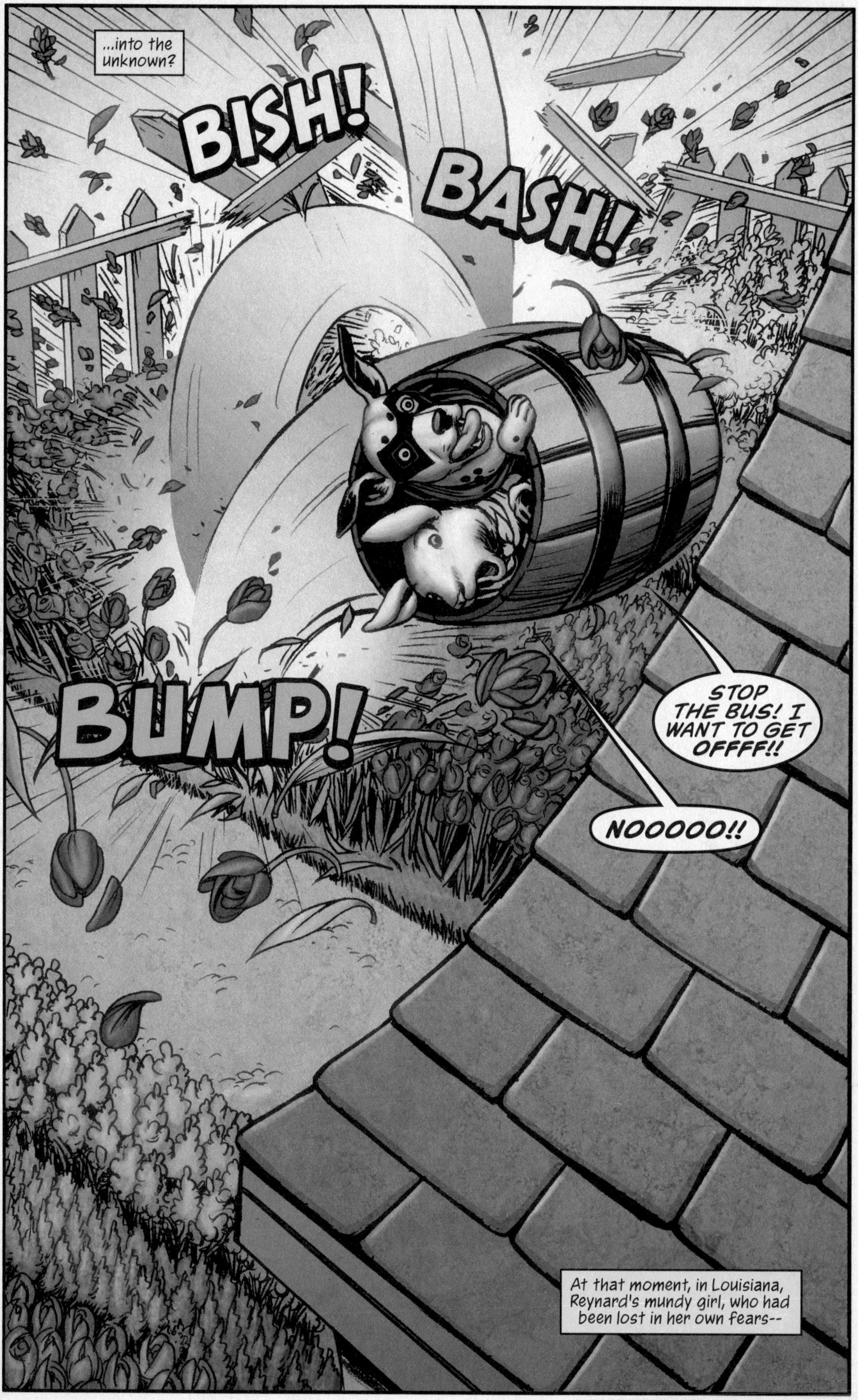
...into the unknown?
BISH!
BASH!
BUMP!
STOP THE BUS! I WANT TO GET OFFFF!!
NOOOOO!!
At that moment, in Louisiana, Reynard's mundy girl, who had been lost in her own fears--

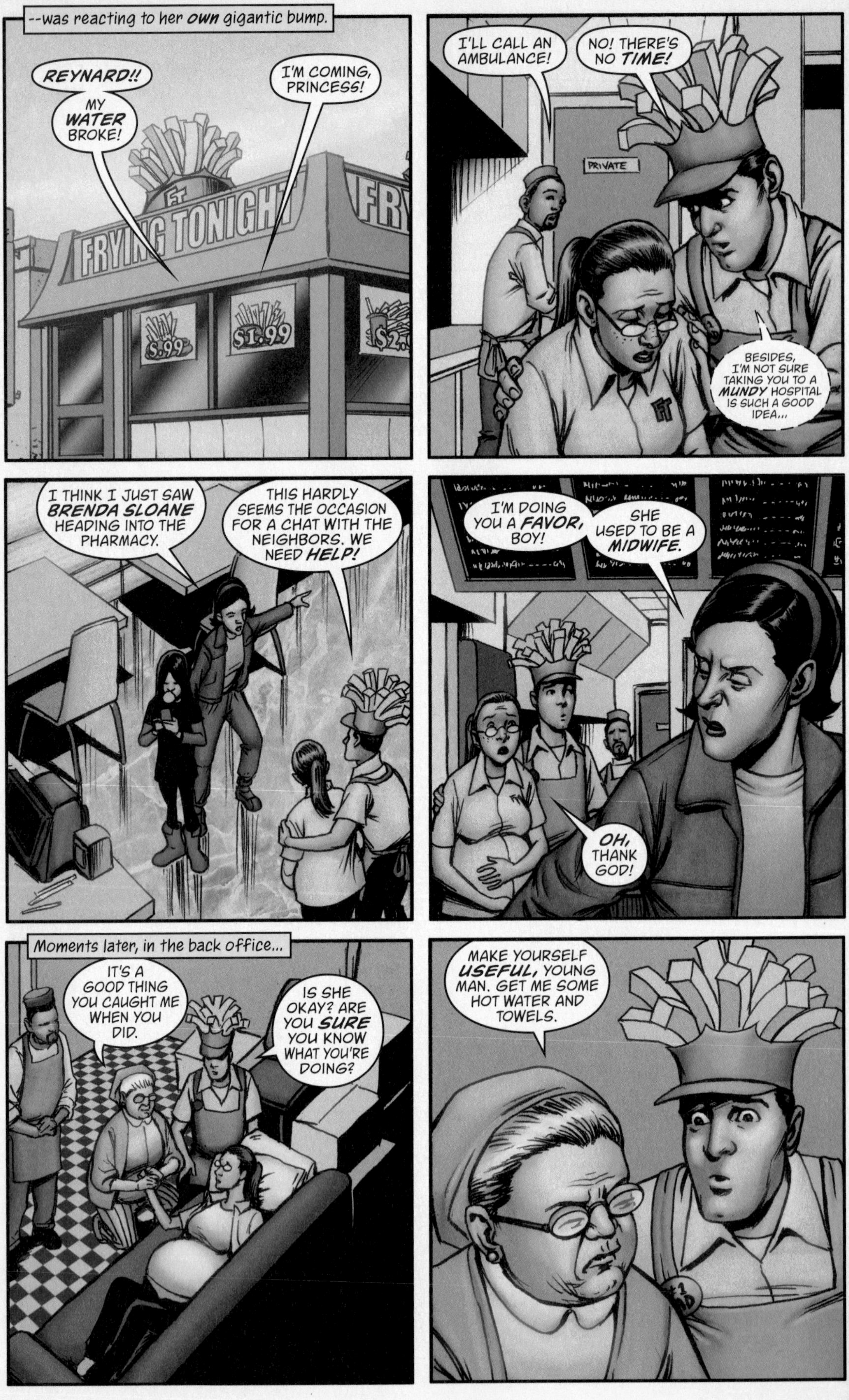
--was reacting to her own gigantic bump.
REYNARD!!
MY WATER BROKE!
I'M COMING, PRINCESS!
FRYING TONIGHT
FRY
$.99
$1.99
I'LL CALL AN AMBULANCE!
NO! THERE'S NO TIME!
PRIVATE
BESIDES, I'M NOT SURE TAKING YOU TO A MUNDY HOSPITAL IS SUCH A GOOD IDEA...
I THINK I JUST SAW BRENDA SLOANE HEADING INTO THE PHARMACY.
THIS HARDLY SEEMS THE OCCASION FOR A CHAT WITH THE NEIGHBORS. WE NEED HELP!
I'M DOING YOU A FAVOR, BOY!
SHE USED TO BE A MIDWIFE.
OH, THANK GOD!
Moments later, in the back office...
IT'S A GOOD THING YOU CAUGHT ME WHEN YOU DID.
IS SHE OKAY? ARE YOU SURE YOU KNOW WHAT YOU'RE DOING?
MAKE YOURSELF USEFUL, YOUNG MAN. GET ME SOME HOT WATER AND TOWELS.

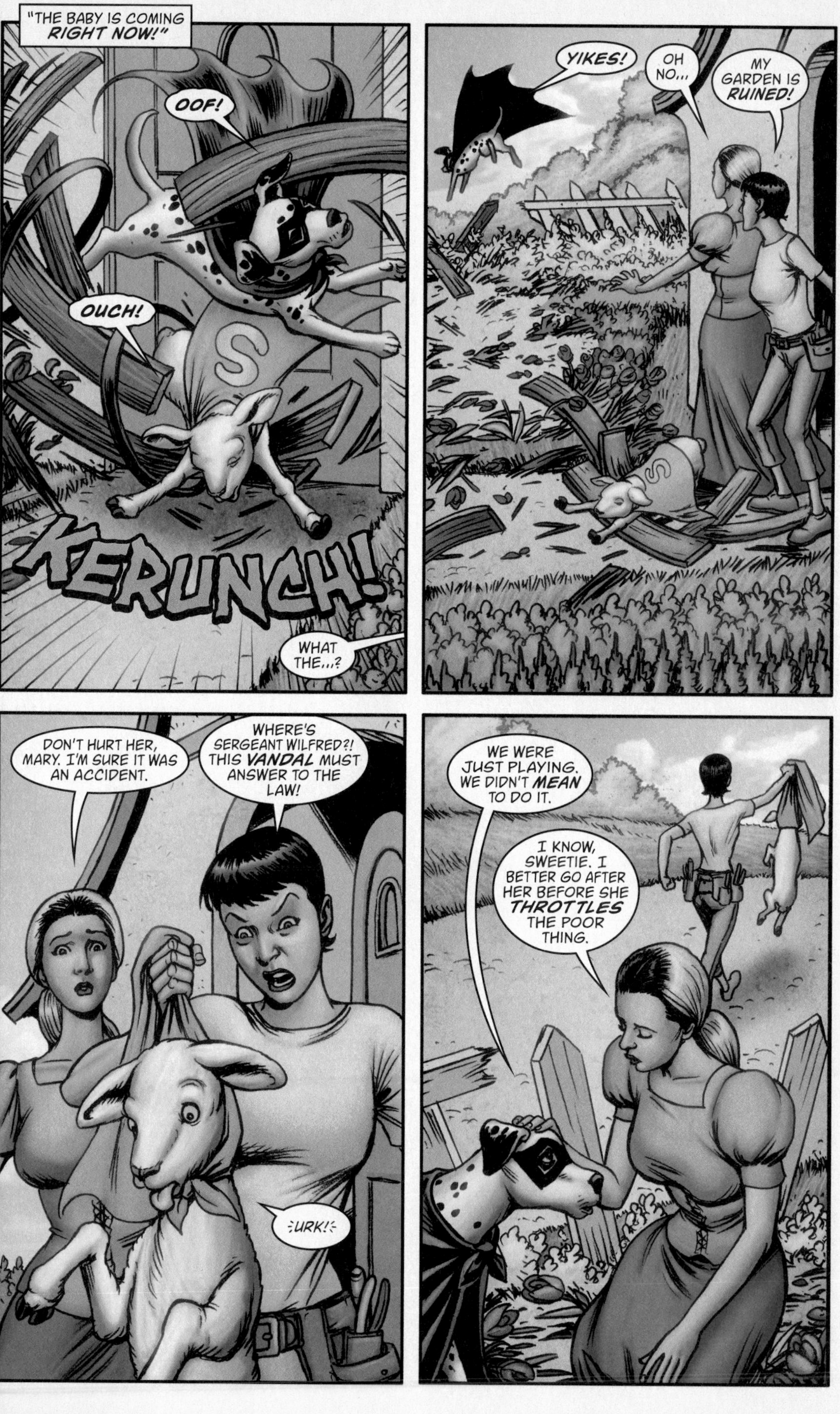
"THE BABY IS COMING RIGHT NOW!"
OOF!
OUCH!
KERUNCH!
WHAT THE...?
YIKES!
OH NO...
MY GARDEN IS RUINED!
DON'T HURT HER, MARY. I'M SURE IT WAS AN ACCIDENT.
WHERE'S SERGEANT WILFRED?! THIS VANDAL MUST ANSWER TO THE LAW!
URK!
WE WERE JUST PLAYING. WE DIDN'T MEAN TO DO IT.
I KNOW, SWEETIE. I BETTER GO AFTER HER BEFORE SHE THROTTLES THE POOR THING.

I **DEMAND** YOU HAVE THIS HOOLIGAN **JAILED** IMMEDIATELY!

SOLIDARITY, NON-HUMAN SISTER!

GOOD TO SEE SOMEONE **ELSE** TAKE A STAND AGAINST OUR OPPRESSORS!

IT'S BEEN HARD **ENOUGH** COPING, WITHOUT MY **OWN** DEAR, DECEASED LITTLE LAMB, BUT NOW TO LOSE MY GARDEN, TOO!

ALL THOSE **FLOWERS** CRUSHED!

¡GASP!¡

MURDERER!!

MMM.

FOR A FIRST OFFENSE BY A **JUVENILE** I'D SUGGEST A WARNING.

TRUE, BUT I THINK SOME SORT OF **COMMUNITY SERVICE** TO COMPENSATE THE VICTIM MIGHT BE APPROPRIATE?

VERY WELL. I SENTENCE YOU TO **TWO MONTHS** IN SERVICE TO MARY AS HER NEW LITTLE LAMB.

YOU MUST HELP RESTORE HER GARDEN, AND DO ANYTHING **ELSE** SHE ASKS OF YOU.

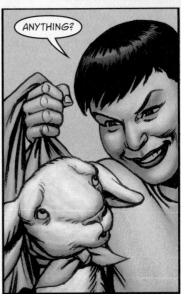

ANYTHING?

COME ON, LITTLE LAMB. YOU KNOW THE RULES.

EVERYWHERE THAT **MARY** GOES, HER LAMB IS **SURE** TO GO.

BIG DRAW TODAY! WILL YOU BE A WINNER?

THIS IS SO HUMILIATING...

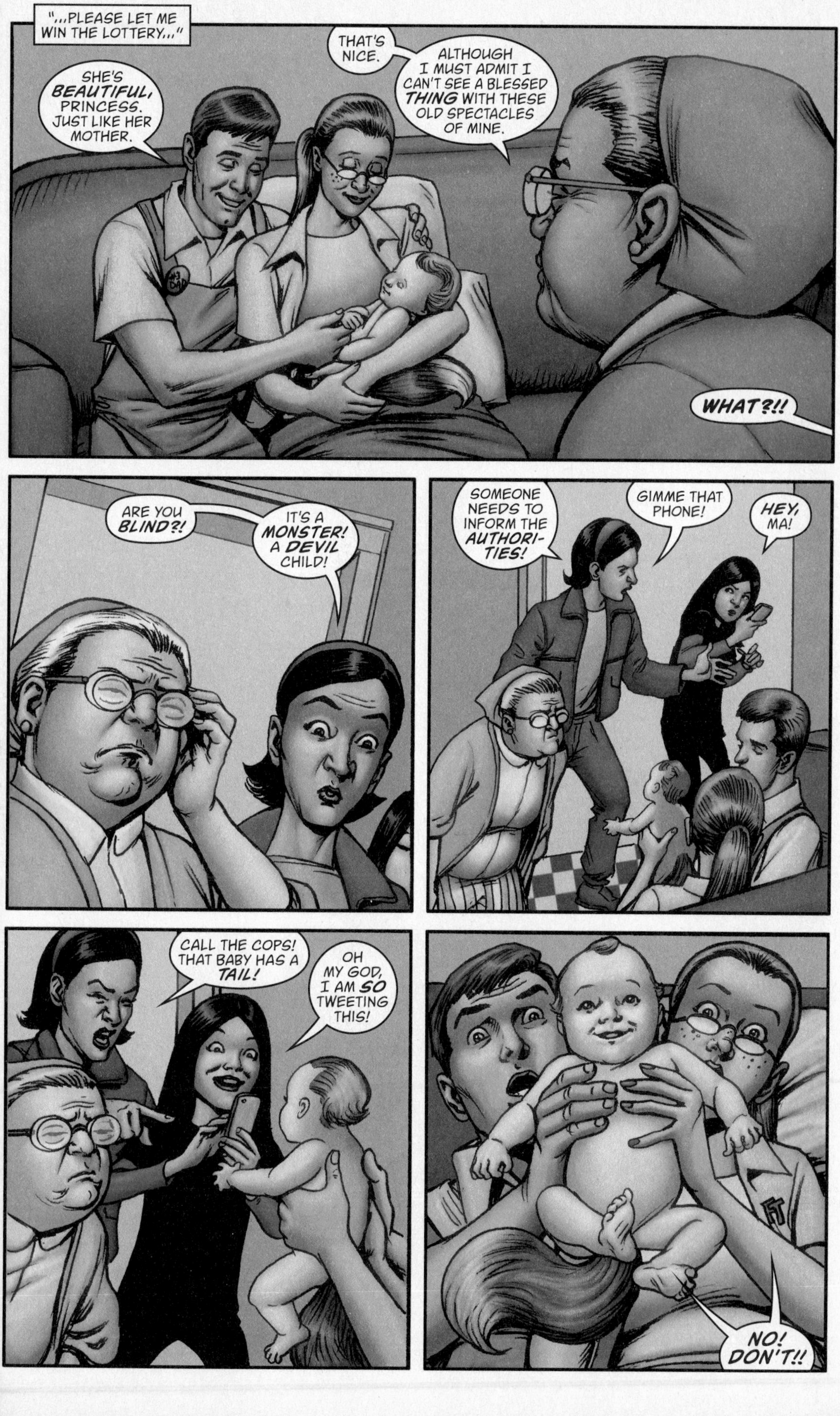
"...PLEASE LET ME WIN THE LOTTERY..."
SHE'S BEAUTIFUL, PRINCESS. JUST LIKE HER MOTHER.
THAT'S NICE.
ALTHOUGH I MUST ADMIT I CAN'T SEE A BLESSED THING WITH THESE OLD SPECTACLES OF MINE.
WHAT?!!
ARE YOU BLIND?!
IT'S A MONSTER! A DEVIL CHILD!
SOMEONE NEEDS TO INFORM THE AUTHORI-TIES!
GIMME THAT PHONE!
HEY, MA!
CALL THE COPS! THAT BABY HAS A TAIL!
OH MY GOD, I AM SO TWEETING THIS!
NO! DON'T!!

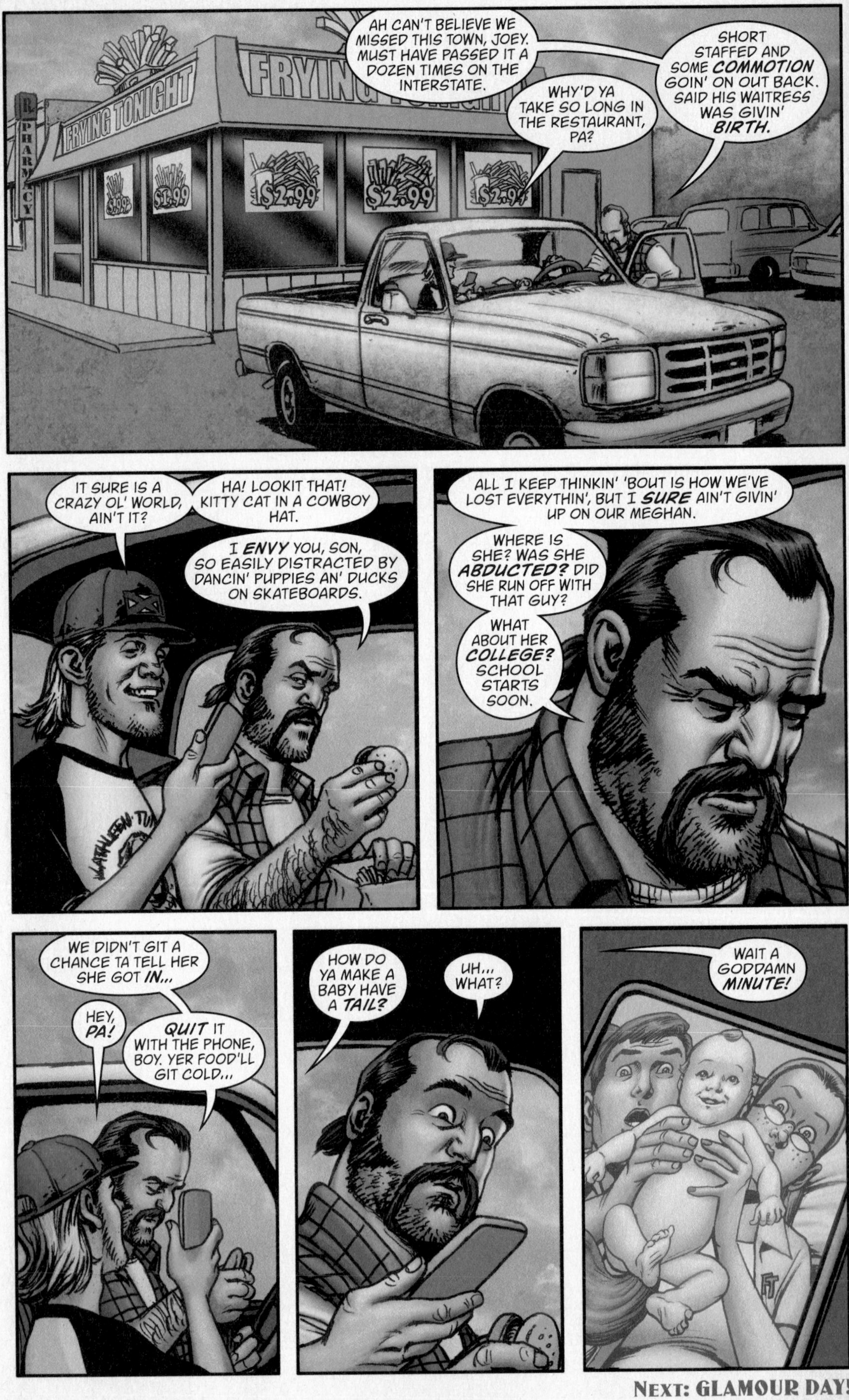
FRYING TONIGHT
FRYING TONIGHT
PHARMACY
$2.99
$2.99
AH CAN'T BELIEVE WE MISSED THIS TOWN, JOEY. MUST HAVE PASSED IT A DOZEN TIMES ON THE INTERSTATE.
WHY'D YA TAKE SO LONG IN THE RESTAURANT, PA?
SHORT STAFFED AND SOME COMMOTION GOIN' ON OUT BACK. SAID HIS WAITRESS WAS GIVIN' BIRTH.
IT SURE IS A CRAZY OL' WORLD, AIN'T IT?
HA! LOOKIT THAT! KITTY CAT IN A COWBOY HAT.
I ENVY YOU, SON, SO EASILY DISTRACTED BY DANCIN' PUPPIES AN' DUCKS ON SKATEBOARDS.
ALL I KEEP THINKIN' 'BOUT IS HOW WE'VE LOST EVERYTHIN', BUT I SURE AIN'T GIVIN' UP ON OUR MEGHAN.
WHERE IS SHE? WAS SHE ABDUCTED? DID SHE RUN OFF WITH THAT GUY?
WHAT ABOUT HER COLLEGE? SCHOOL STARTS SOON.
WE DIDN'T GIT A CHANCE TA TELL HER SHE GOT IN...
HEY, PA!
QUIT IT WITH THE PHONE, BOY. YER FOOD'LL GIT COLD...
HOW DO YA MAKE A BABY HAVE A TAIL?
UH... WHAT?
WAIT A GODDAMN MINUTE!

NEXT: GLAMOUR DAY!

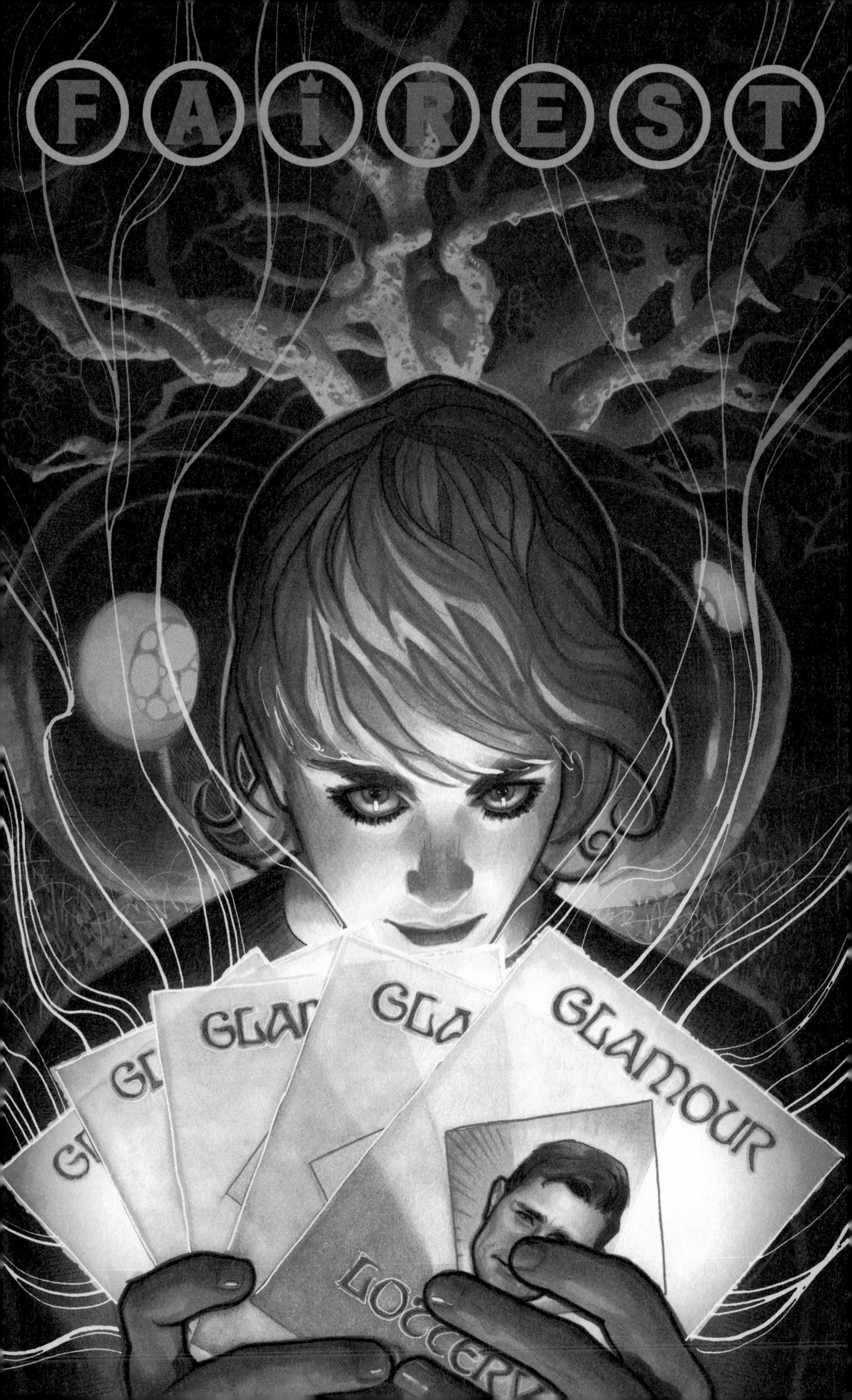
FAIREST
GLAMOUR

"How would you like to have your very own fairy tale kingdom?"

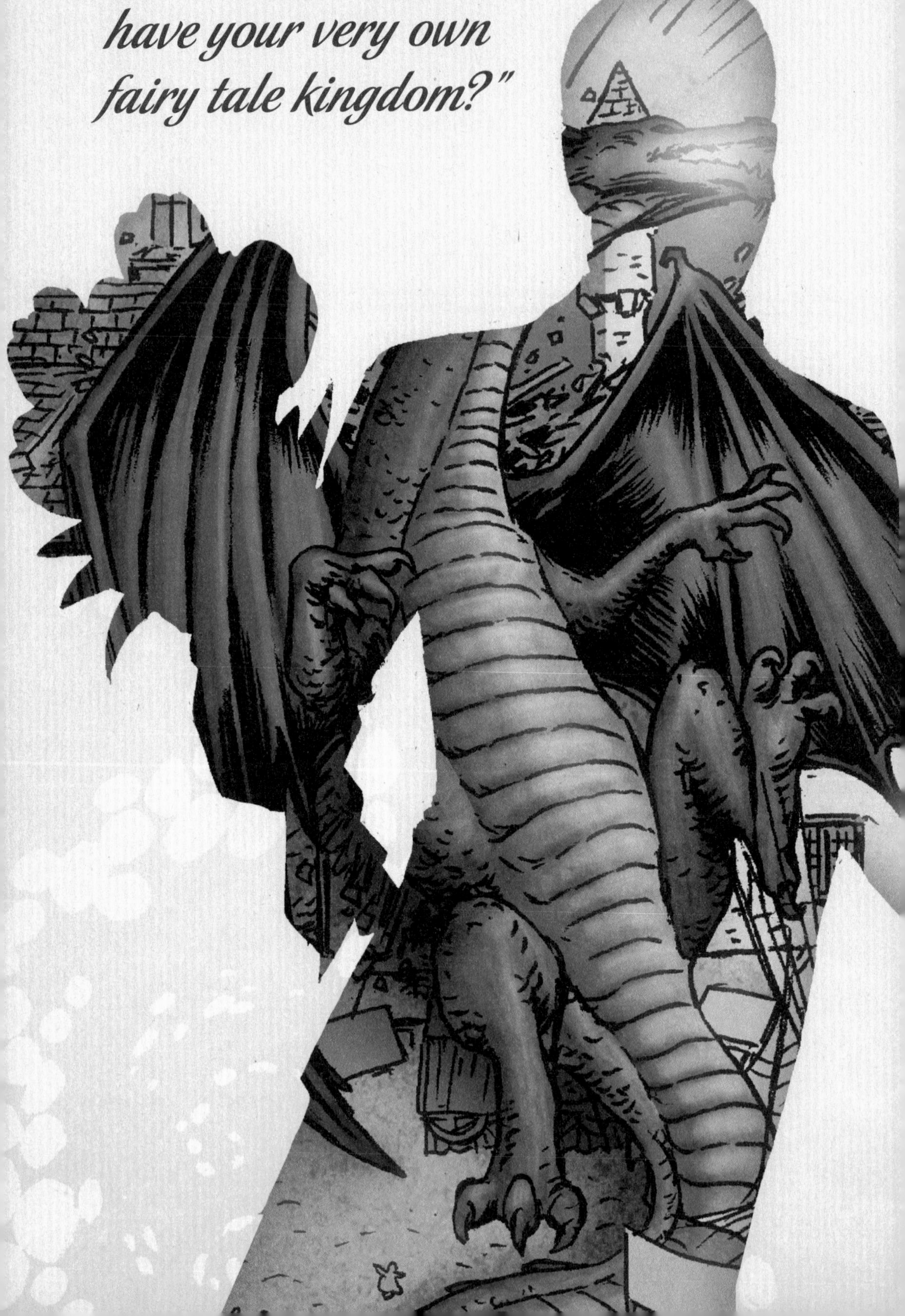

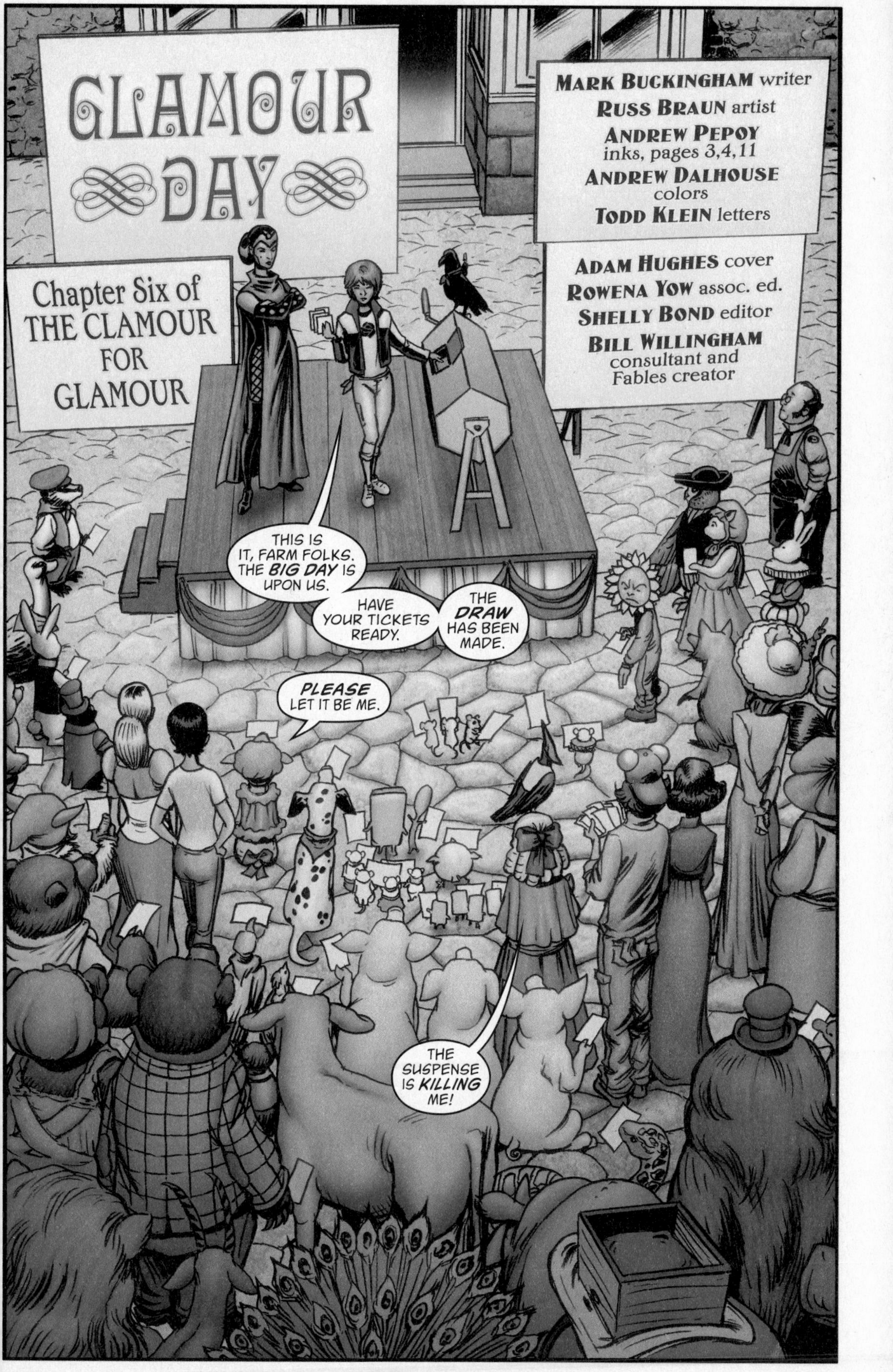
GLAMOUR DAY
Chapter Six of THE CLAMOUR FOR GLAMOUR
MARK BUCKINGHAM writer
RUSS BRAUN artist
ANDREW PEPOY inks, pages 3,4,11
ANDREW DALHOUSE colors
TODD KLEIN letters
ADAM HUGHES cover
ROWENA YOW assoc. ed.
SHELLY BOND editor
BILL WILLINGHAM consultant and Fables creator
THIS IS IT, FARM FOLKS. THE BIG DAY IS UPON US.
HAVE YOUR TICKETS READY.
THE DRAW HAS BEEN MADE.
PLEASE LET IT BE ME.
THE SUSPENSE IS KILLING ME!

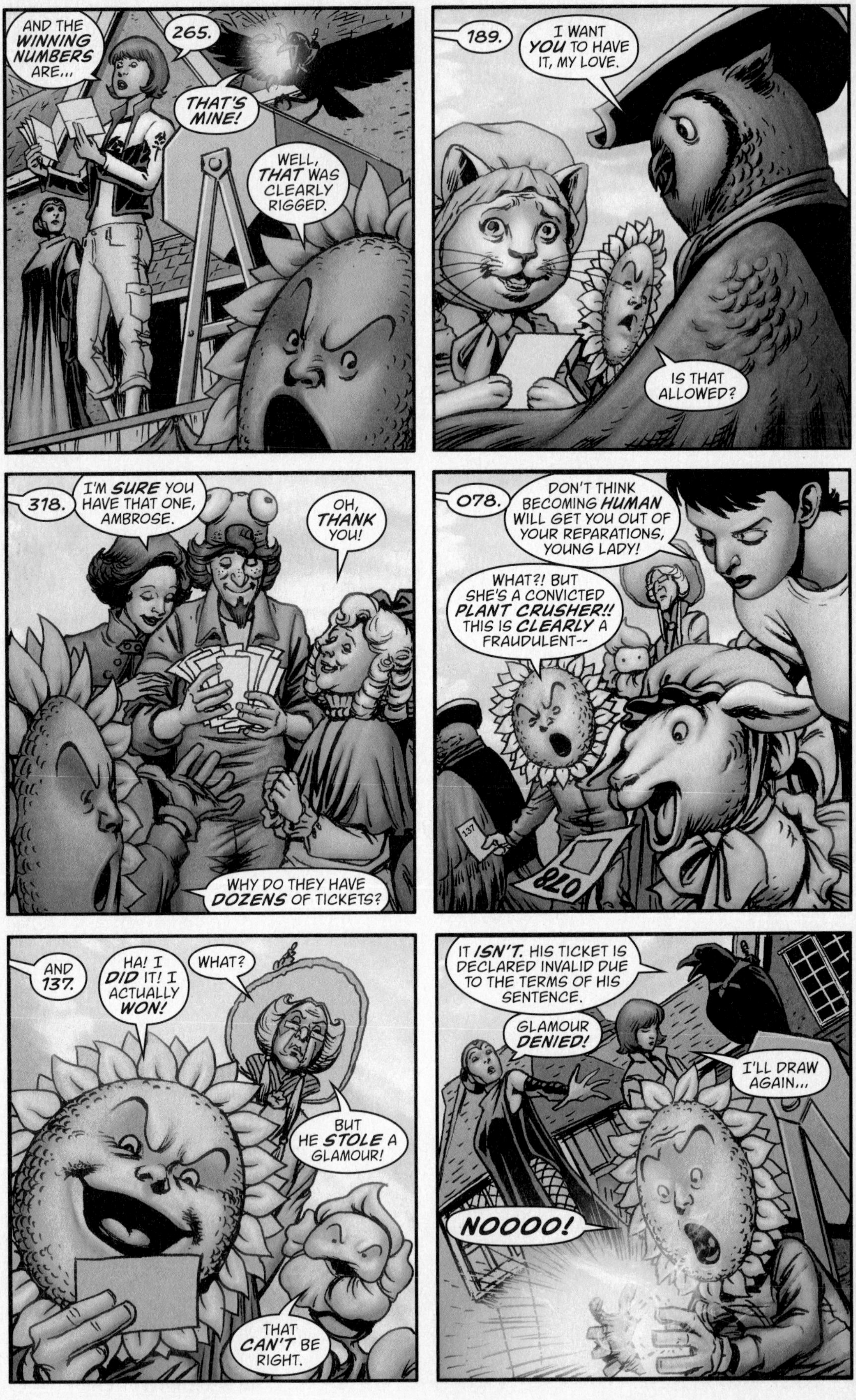
AND THE WINNING NUMBERS ARE...
265.
THAT'S MINE!
WELL, THAT WAS CLEARLY RIGGED.
189.
I WANT YOU TO HAVE IT, MY LOVE.
IS THAT ALLOWED?
318.
I'M SURE YOU HAVE THAT ONE, AMBROSE.
OH, THANK YOU!
WHY DO THEY HAVE DOZENS OF TICKETS?
078.
DON'T THINK BECOMING HUMAN WILL GET YOU OUT OF YOUR REPARATIONS, YOUNG LADY!
WHAT?! BUT SHE'S A CONVICTED PLANT CRUSHER!! THIS IS CLEARLY A FRAUDULENT--
AND 137.
HA! I DID IT! I ACTUALLY WON!
WHAT?
BUT HE STOLE A GLAMOUR!
THAT CAN'T BE RIGHT.
IT ISN'T. HIS TICKET IS DECLARED INVALID DUE TO THE TERMS OF HIS SENTENCE.
GLAMOUR DENIED!
I'LL DRAW AGAIN...
NOOOO!

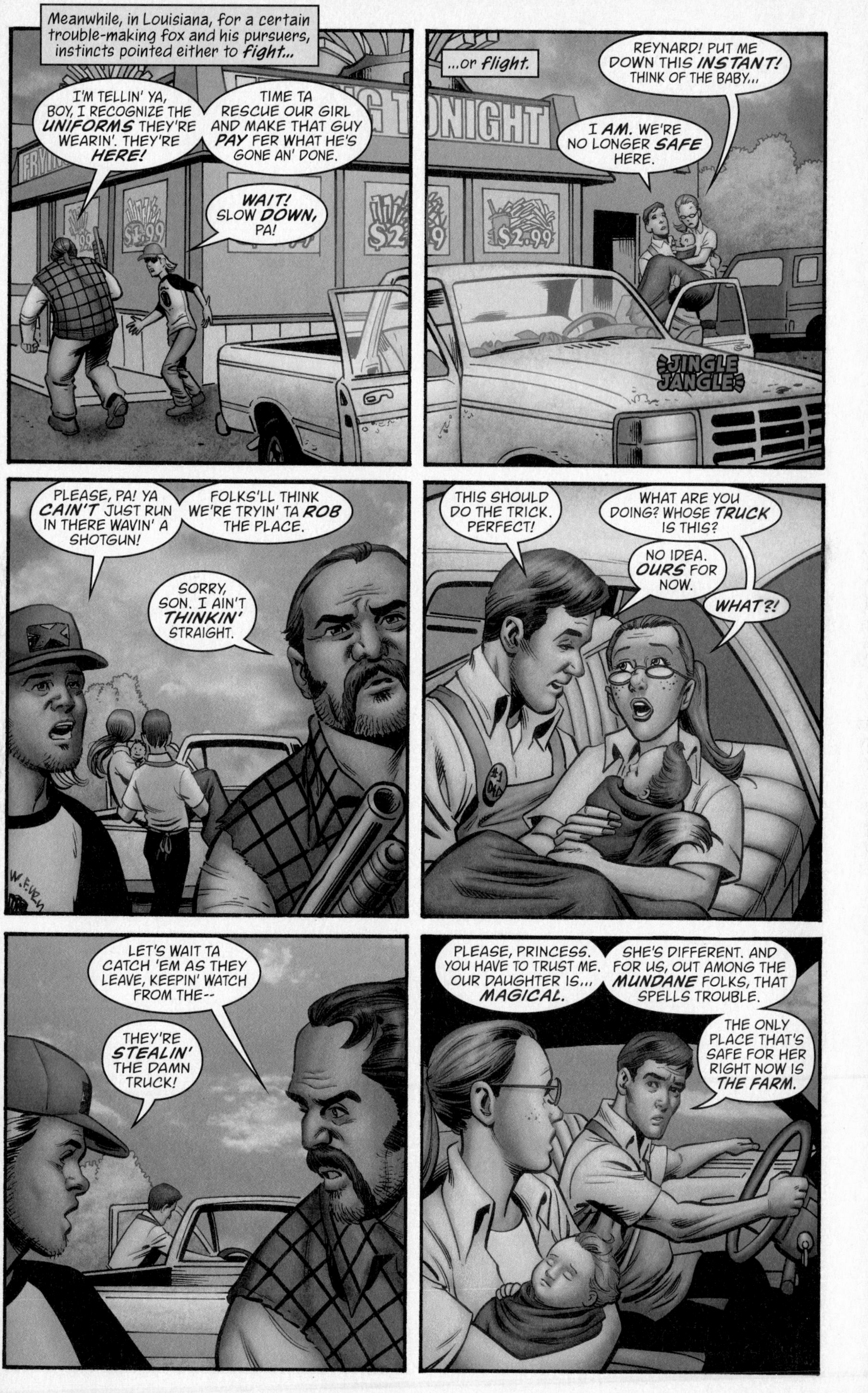
Meanwhile, in Louisiana, for a certain trouble-making fox and his pursuers, instincts pointed either to fight...
I'M TELLIN' YA, BOY, I RECOGNIZE THE UNIFORMS THEY'RE WEARIN'. THEY'RE HERE!
TIME TA RESCUE OUR GIRL AND MAKE THAT GUY PAY FER WHAT HE'S GONE AN' DONE.
WAIT! SLOW DOWN, PA!
...or flight.
REYNARD! PUT ME DOWN THIS INSTANT! THINK OF THE BABY...
I AM. WE'RE NO LONGER SAFE HERE.
JINGLE JANGLE
PLEASE, PA! YA CAIN'T JUST RUN IN THERE WAVIN' A SHOTGUN!
FOLKS'LL THINK WE'RE TRYIN' TA ROB THE PLACE.
SORRY, SON. I AIN'T THINKIN' STRAIGHT.
THIS SHOULD DO THE TRICK. PERFECT!
WHAT ARE YOU DOING? WHOSE TRUCK IS THIS?
NO IDEA. OURS FOR NOW.
WHAT?!
LET'S WAIT TA CATCH 'EM AS THEY LEAVE, KEEPIN' WATCH FROM THE--
THEY'RE STEALIN' THE DAMN TRUCK!
PLEASE, PRINCESS. YOU HAVE TO TRUST ME. OUR DAUGHTER IS... MAGICAL.
SHE'S DIFFERENT. AND FOR US, OUT AMONG THE MUNDANE FOLKS, THAT SPELLS TROUBLE.
THE ONLY PLACE THAT'S SAFE FOR HER RIGHT NOW IS THE FARM.

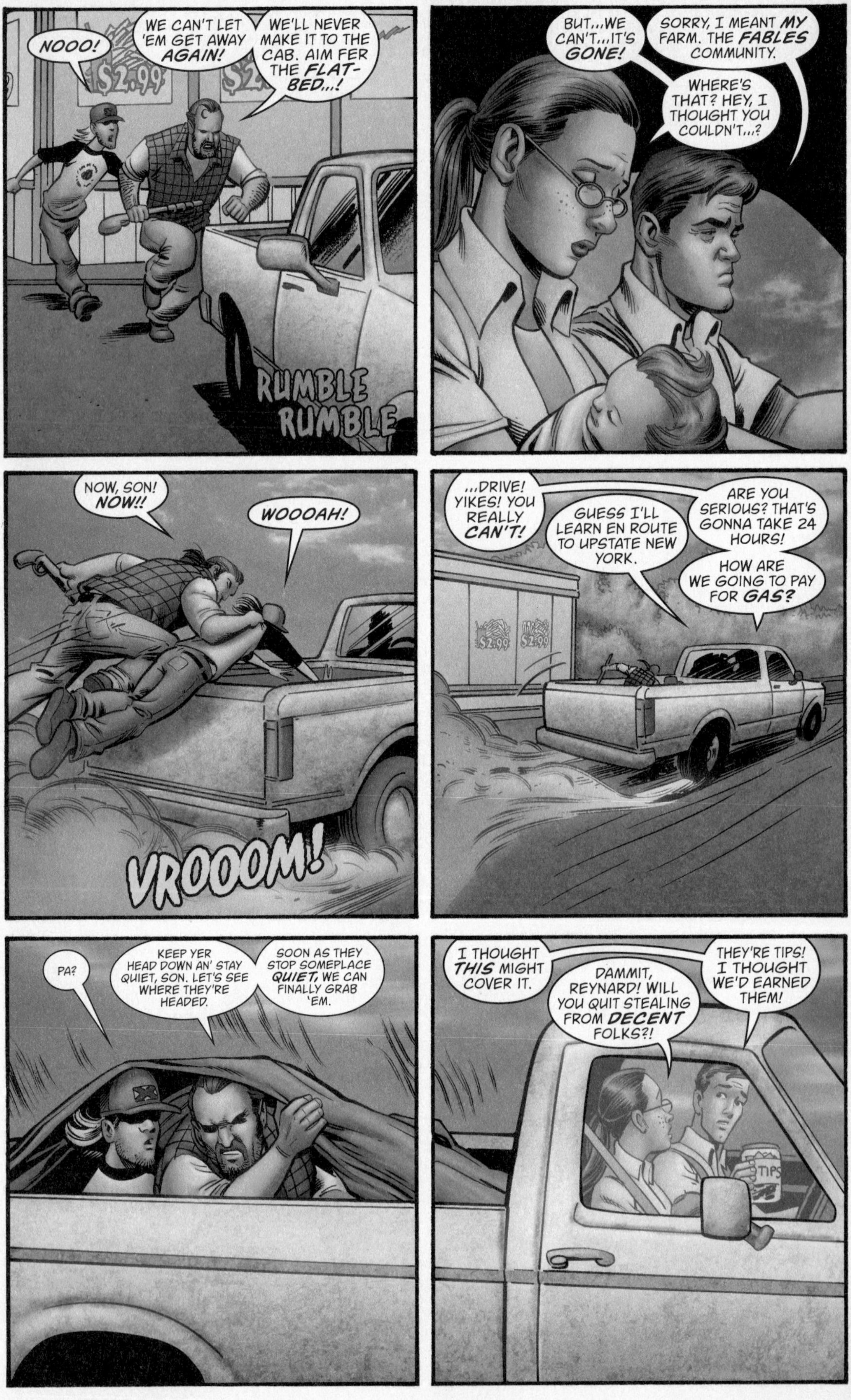
NOOO!
WE CAN'T LET 'EM GET AWAY AGAIN!
WE'LL NEVER MAKE IT TO THE CAB. AIM FER THE FLAT-BED...!
$2.99
RUMBLE RUMBLE
BUT...WE CAN'T...IT'S GONE!
SORRY, I MEANT MY FARM. THE FABLES COMMUNITY.
WHERE'S THAT? HEY, I THOUGHT YOU COULDN'T...?
NOW, SON! NOW!!
WOOOAH!
VROOOM!
...DRIVE! YIKES! YOU REALLY CAN'T!
GUESS I'LL LEARN EN ROUTE TO UPSTATE NEW YORK.
ARE YOU SERIOUS? THAT'S GONNA TAKE 24 HOURS!
HOW ARE WE GOING TO PAY FOR GAS?
$2.99
$2.99
PA?
KEEP YER HEAD DOWN AN' STAY QUIET, SON. LET'S SEE WHERE THEY'RE HEADED.
SOON AS THEY STOP SOMEPLACE QUIET, WE CAN FINALLY GRAB 'EM.
I THOUGHT THIS MIGHT COVER IT.
DAMMIT, REYNARD! WILL YOU QUIT STEALING FROM DECENT FOLKS?!
THEY'RE TIPS! I THOUGHT WE'D EARNED THEM!
TIPS

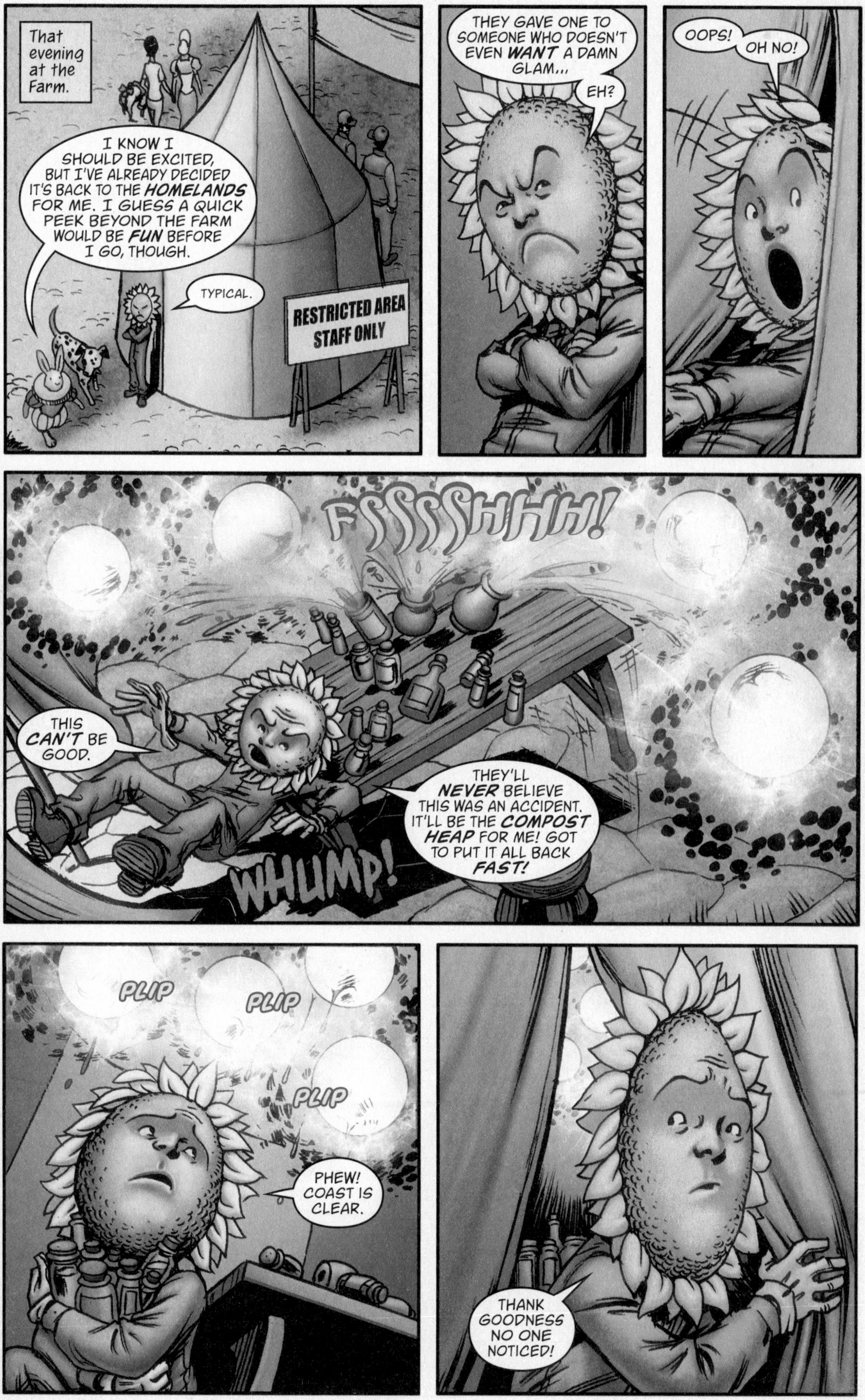
That evening at the Farm.
I KNOW I SHOULD BE EXCITED, BUT I'VE ALREADY DECIDED IT'S BACK TO THE HOMELANDS FOR ME. I GUESS A QUICK PEEK BEYOND THE FARM WOULD BE FUN BEFORE I GO, THOUGH.
TYPICAL.
RESTRICTED AREA STAFF ONLY
THEY GAVE ONE TO SOMEONE WHO DOESN'T EVEN WANT A DAMN GLAM...
EH?
OOPS!
OH NO!
FSSSSHHHH!
THIS CAN'T BE GOOD.
THEY'LL NEVER BELIEVE THIS WAS AN ACCIDENT. IT'LL BE THE COMPOST HEAP FOR ME! GOT TO PUT IT ALL BACK FAST!
WHUMP!
PLIP
PLIP
PLIP
PHEW! COAST IS CLEAR.
THANK GOODNESS NO ONE NOTICED!

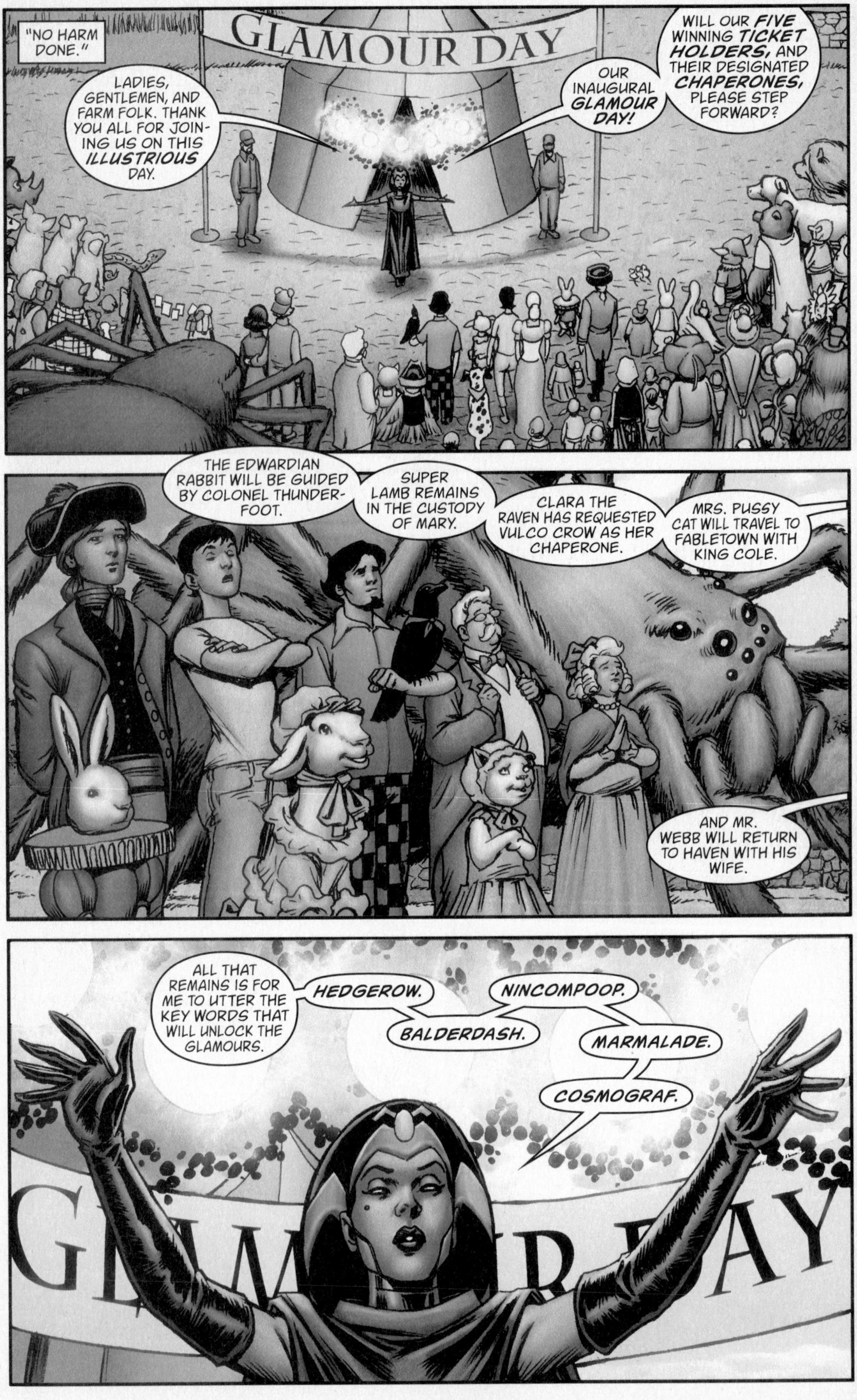
"NO HARM DONE."
GLAMOUR DAY
LADIES, GENTLEMEN, AND FARM FOLK. THANK YOU ALL FOR JOINING US ON THIS ILLUSTRIOUS DAY.
OUR INAUGURAL GLAMOUR DAY!
WILL OUR FIVE WINNING TICKET HOLDERS, AND THEIR DESIGNATED CHAPERONES, PLEASE STEP FORWARD?
THE EDWARDIAN RABBIT WILL BE GUIDED BY COLONEL THUNDERFOOT.
SUPER LAMB REMAINS IN THE CUSTODY OF MARY.
CLARA THE RAVEN HAS REQUESTED VULCO CROW AS HER CHAPERONE.
MRS. PUSSY CAT WILL TRAVEL TO FABLETOWN WITH KING COLE.
AND MR. WEBB WILL RETURN TO HAVEN WITH HIS WIFE.
ALL THAT REMAINS IS FOR ME TO UTTER THE KEY WORDS THAT WILL UNLOCK THE GLAMOURS.
HEDGEROW.
BALDERDASH.
NINCOMPOOP.
MARMALADE.
COSMOGRAF.

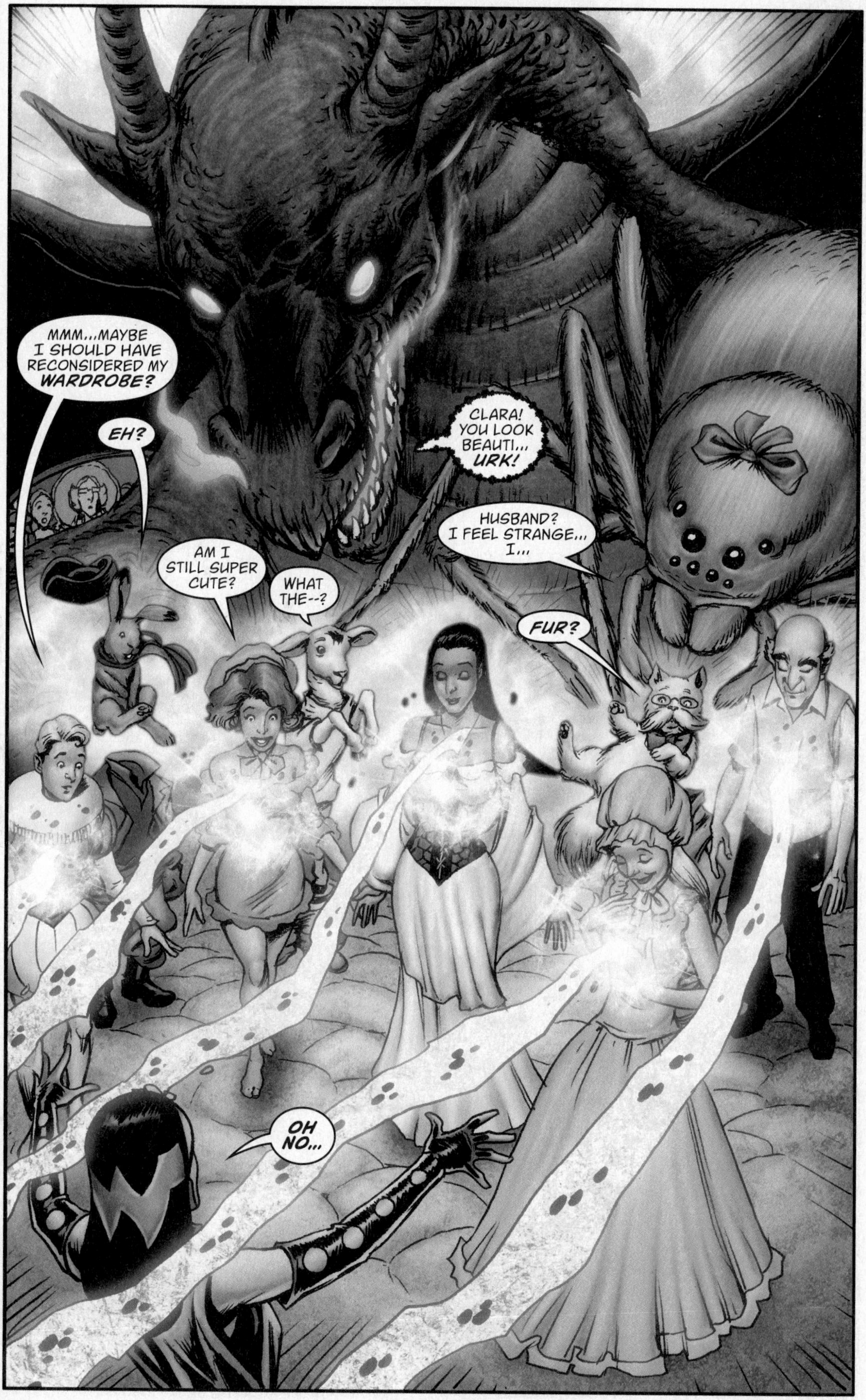
MMM...MAYBE I SHOULD HAVE RECONSIDERED MY WARDROBE?
EH?
CLARA! YOU LOOK BEAUTI... URK!
HUSBAND? I FEEL STRANGE... I...
AM I STILL SUPER CUTE?
WHAT THE--?
FUR?
OH NO...

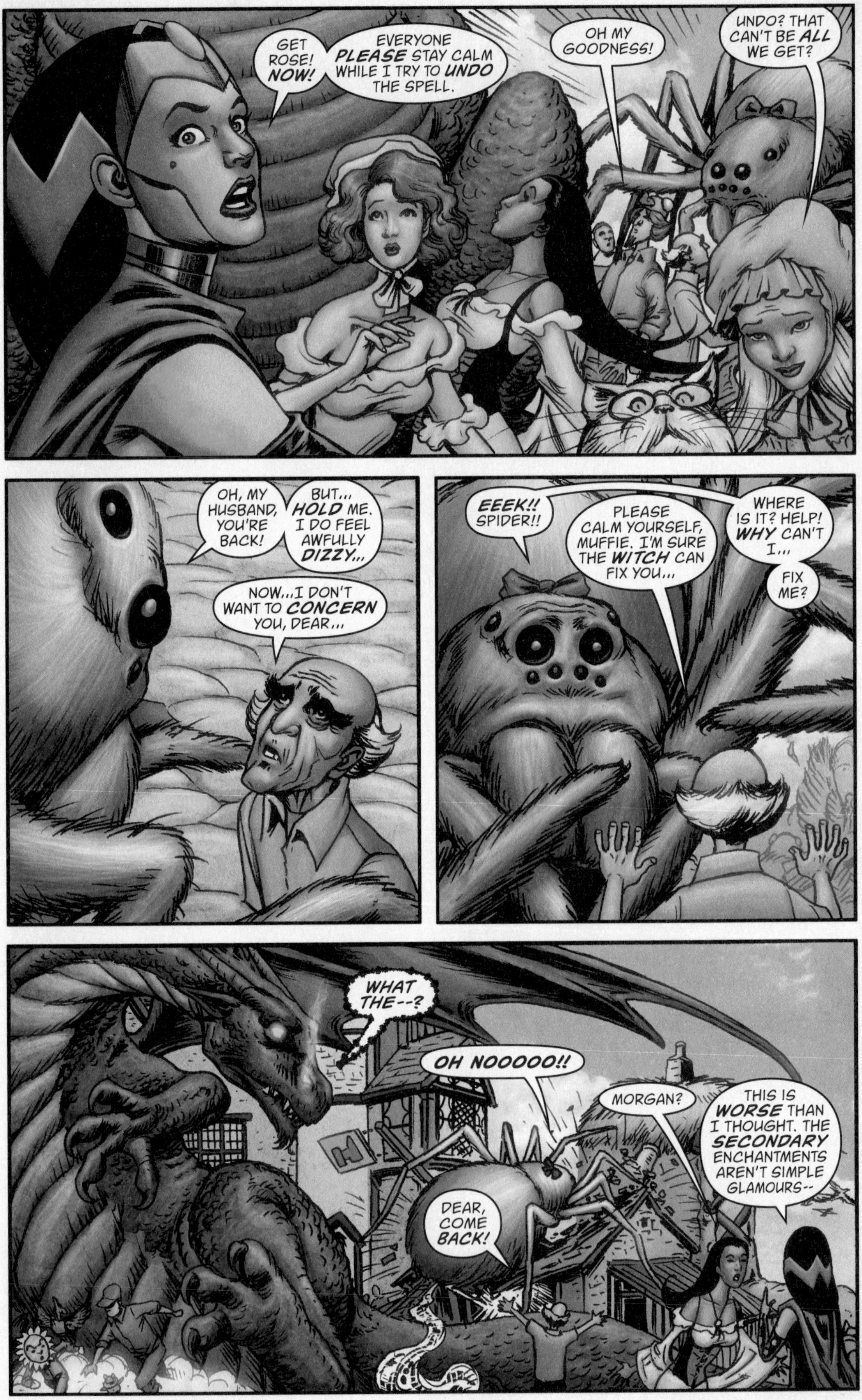
GET ROSE! NOW!
EVERYONE PLEASE STAY CALM WHILE I TRY TO UNDO THE SPELL.
OH MY GOODNESS!
UNDO? THAT CAN'T BE ALL WE GET?
OH, MY HUSBAND, YOU'RE BACK!
BUT... HOLD ME. I DO FEEL AWFULLY DIZZY...
NOW...I DON'T WANT TO CONCERN YOU, DEAR...
EEEK!! SPIDER!!
PLEASE CALM YOURSELF, MUFFIE. I'M SURE THE WITCH CAN FIX YOU...
WHERE IS IT? HELP! WHY CAN'T I...
FIX ME?
WHAT THE--?
OH NOOOOO!!
MORGAN?
THIS IS WORSE THAN I THOUGHT. THE SECONDARY ENCHANTMENTS AREN'T SIMPLE GLAMOURS--
DEAR, COME BACK!

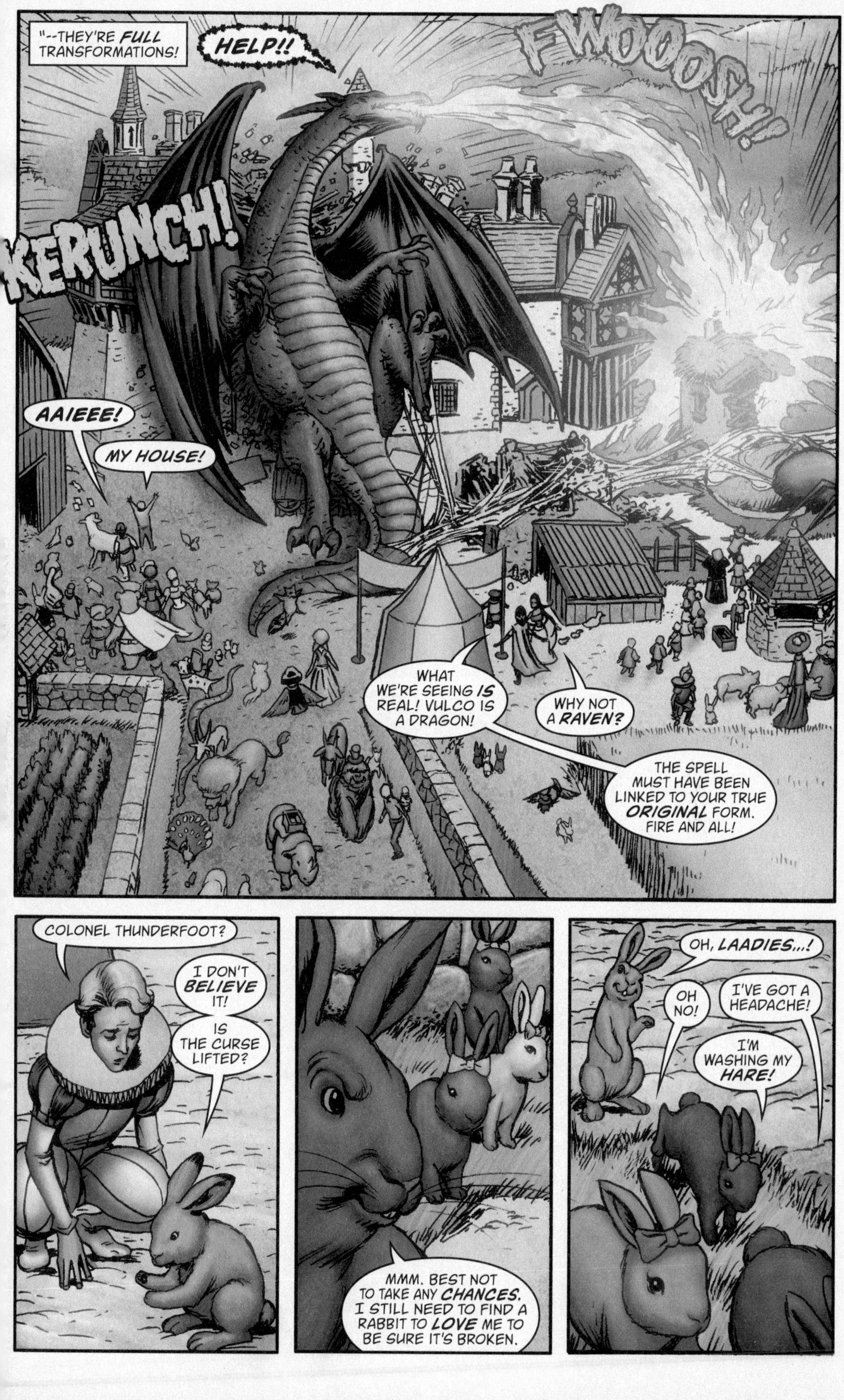
"--THEY'RE FULL TRANSFORMATIONS!
HELP!!
FWOOOSH!!
KERUNCH!
AAIEEE!
MY HOUSE!
WHAT WE'RE SEEING IS REAL! VULCO IS A DRAGON!
WHY NOT A RAVEN?
THE SPELL MUST HAVE BEEN LINKED TO YOUR TRUE ORIGINAL FORM. FIRE AND ALL!
COLONEL THUNDERFOOT?
I DON'T BELIEVE IT!
IS THE CURSE LIFTED?
MMM. BEST NOT TO TAKE ANY CHANCES. I STILL NEED TO FIND A RABBIT TO LOVE ME TO BE SURE IT'S BROKEN.
OH, LAADIES...!
OH NO!
I'VE GOT A HEADACHE!
I'M WASHING MY HARE!

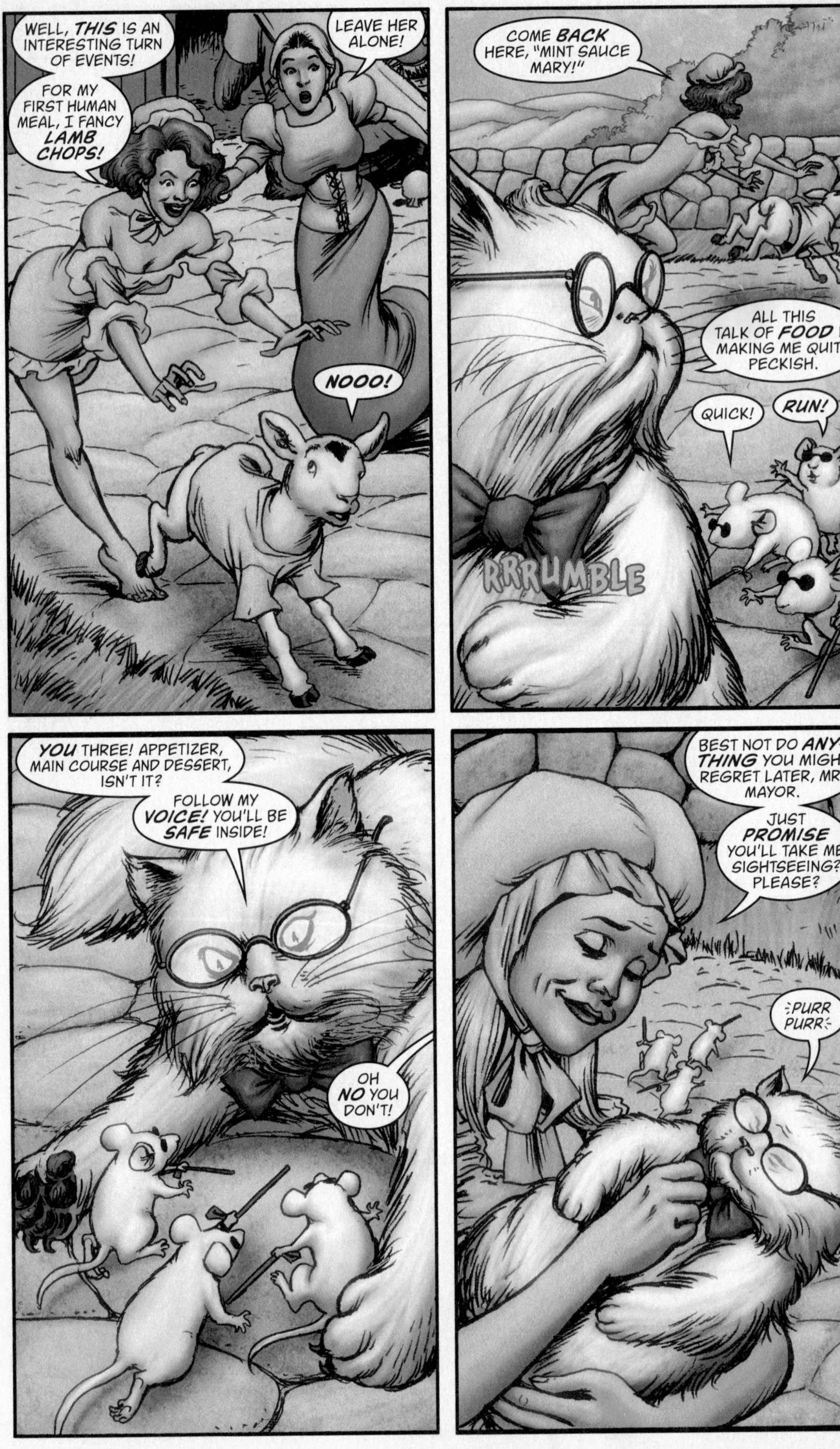
WELL, THIS IS AN INTERESTING TURN OF EVENTS!
FOR MY FIRST HUMAN MEAL, I FANCY LAMB CHOPS!
LEAVE HER ALONE!
NOOO!
COME BACK HERE, "MINT SAUCE MARY!"
ALL THIS TALK OF FOOD IS MAKING ME QUITE PECKISH.
QUICK!
RUN!
RRRUMBLE
YOU THREE! APPETIZER, MAIN COURSE AND DESSERT, ISN'T IT?
FOLLOW MY VOICE! YOU'LL BE SAFE INSIDE!
OH NO YOU DON'T!
BEST NOT DO ANY-THING YOU MIGHT REGRET LATER, MR. MAYOR.
JUST PROMISE YOU'LL TAKE ME SIGHTSEEING? PLEASE?
PURR PURR

I CAN'T BELIEVE THEY JUST DROVE ALL THE WAY TO UPSTATE NEW YORK.

THIS IS GOOD, SON. REMOTE. NO PRYIN' EYES. SOON AS THEY STOP, I'M FINALLY GOIN' TO *GET* HIM.

New York State Wine Country is for Lovers

WE'RE ENTERING THE FARM TERRITORY NOW SO WE SHOULD BE SAFE. THERE'S A *CONCEALMENT* SPELL THAT KEEPS MUNDYS FROM SEEING US.

WE CAN STILL SEE YOUR SILLY DADDY, CAN'T WE, *FAIR*?

FAIR?

WELL, HER HAIR AND SKIN ARE FAIR, AND SHE *IS* ABSOLUTELY BEAUTIFUL.

FAIREST IN ALL THE LAND.

FAIR FOX. I LIKE IT!

THANK GOD, WE'RE ALMOST THERE.

IS IT SUPPOSED TO BE ON *FIRE*?

I'M SENSING A THEME.

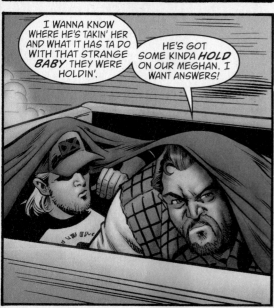

I WANNA KNOW WHERE HE'S TAKIN' HER AND WHAT IT HAS TA DO WITH THAT STRANGE *BABY* THEY WERE HOLDIN'.

HE'S GOT SOME KINDA *HOLD* ON OUR MEGHAN. I WANT ANSWERS!

AND YOU REALLY THINK YOUR FRIENDS CAN HELP US?

I'M SURE THEY CAN, SWEETIE.

IF THEY DON'T *LYNCH* ME FIRST.

#1 DAD

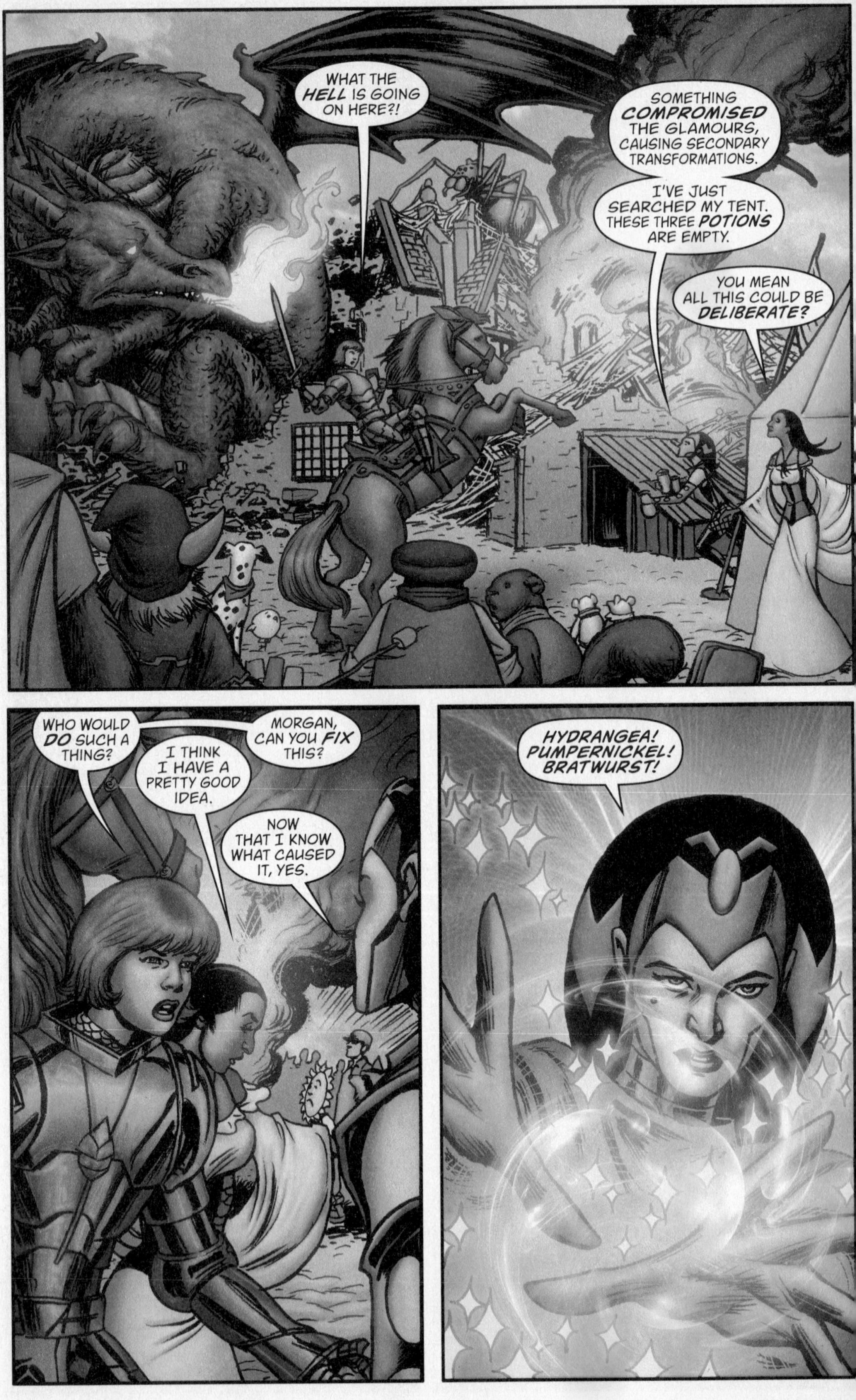
WHAT THE HELL IS GOING ON HERE?!
SOMETHING COMPROMISED THE GLAMOURS, CAUSING SECONDARY TRANSFORMATIONS.
I'VE JUST SEARCHED MY TENT. THESE THREE POTIONS ARE EMPTY.
YOU MEAN ALL THIS COULD BE DELIBERATE?
WHO WOULD DO SUCH A THING?
I THINK I HAVE A PRETTY GOOD IDEA.
MORGAN, CAN YOU FIX THIS?
NOW THAT I KNOW WHAT CAUSED IT, YES.
HYDRANGEA! PUMPERNICKEL! BRATWURST!

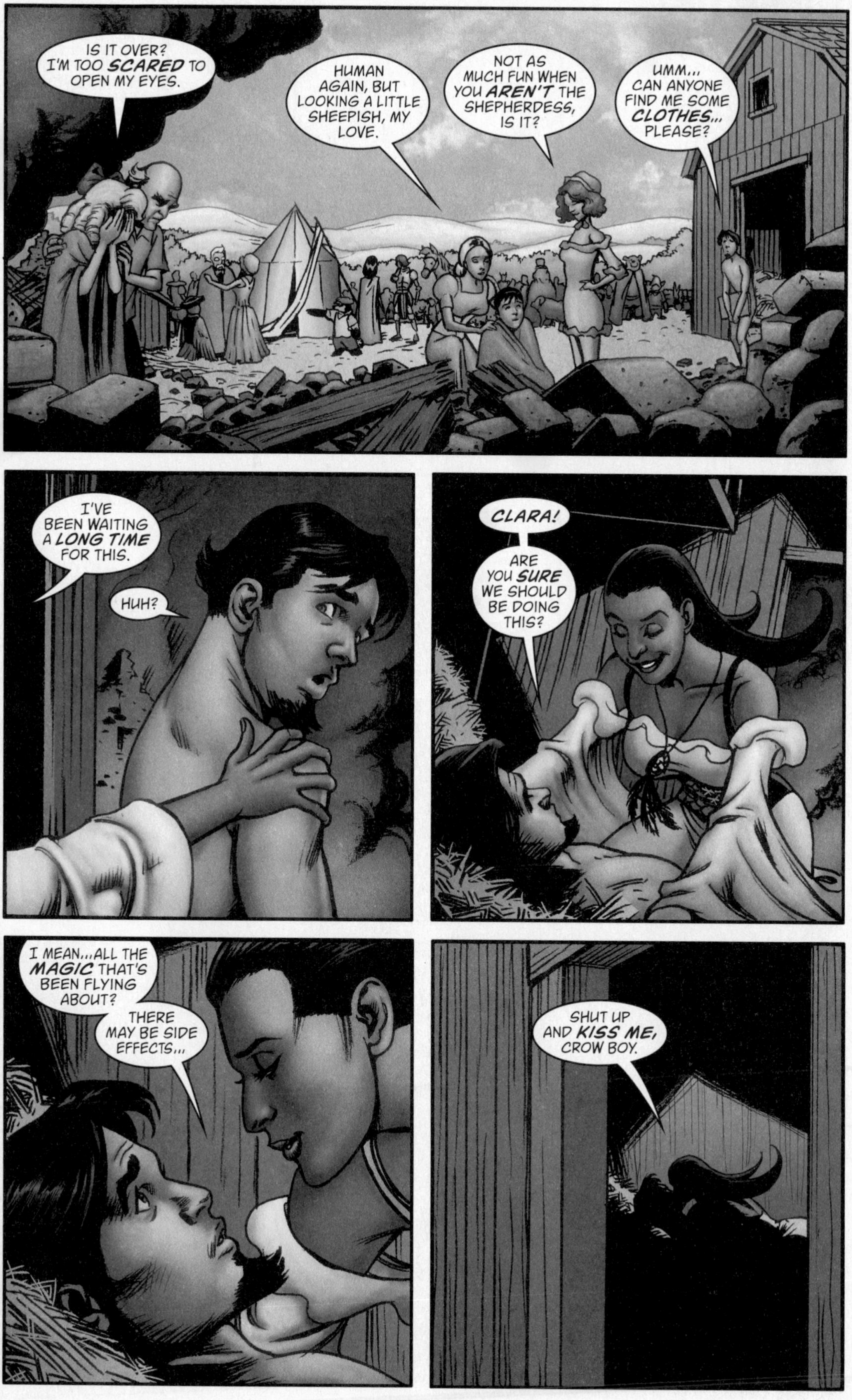
IS IT OVER? I'M TOO SCARED TO OPEN MY EYES.
HUMAN AGAIN, BUT LOOKING A LITTLE SHEEPISH, MY LOVE.
NOT AS MUCH FUN WHEN YOU AREN'T THE SHEPHERDESS, IS IT?
UMM... CAN ANYONE FIND ME SOME CLOTHES... PLEASE?
I'VE BEEN WAITING A LONG TIME FOR THIS.
HUH?
CLARA!
ARE YOU SURE WE SHOULD BE DOING THIS?
I MEAN...ALL THE MAGIC THAT'S BEEN FLYING ABOUT?
THERE MAY BE SIDE EFFECTS...
SHUT UP AND KISS ME, CROW BOY.

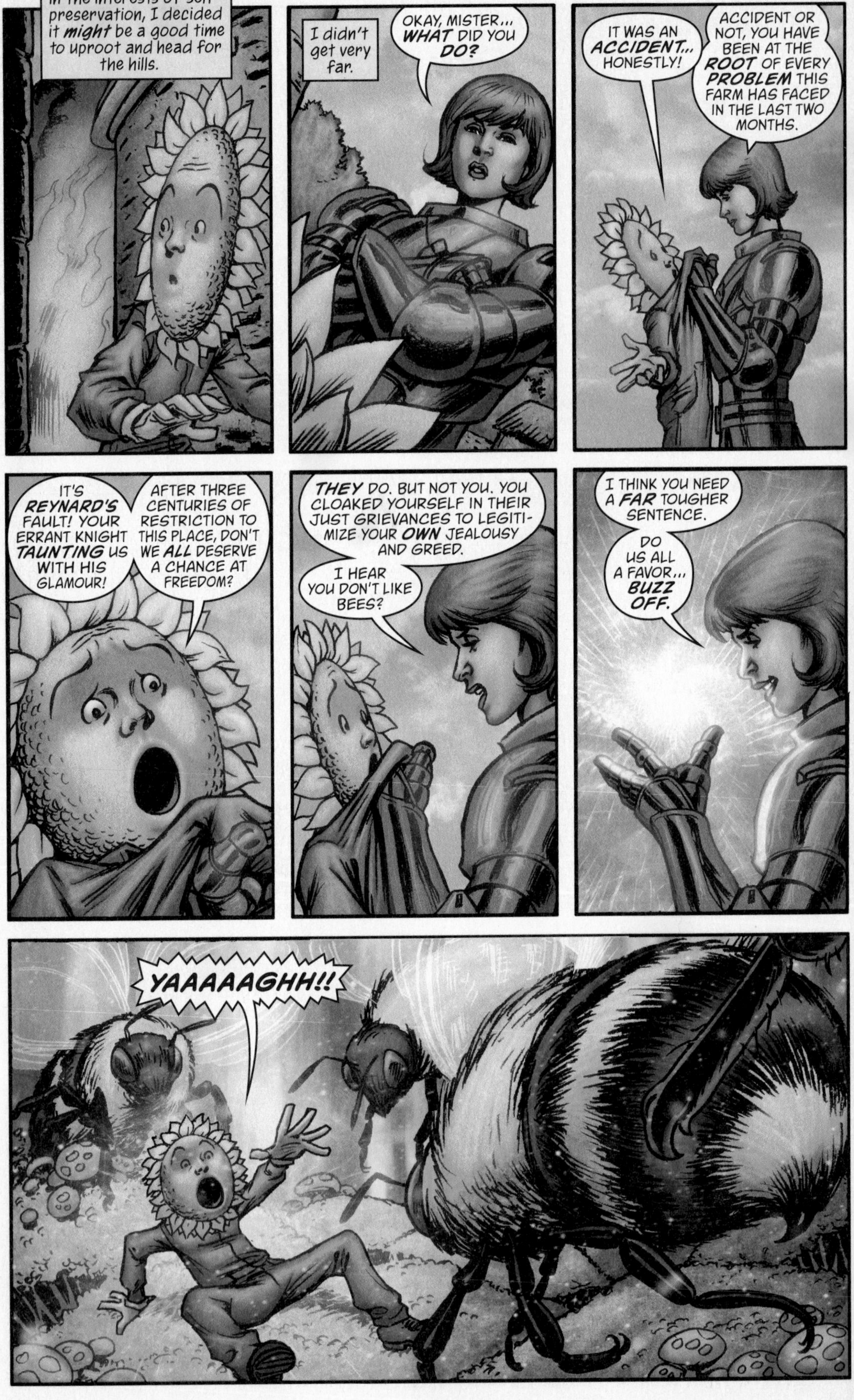
In the interests of self-preservation, I decided it *might* be a good time to uproot and head for the hills.
I didn't get very far.
OKAY, MISTER... **WHAT** DID YOU **DO?**
IT WAS AN **ACCIDENT...** HONESTLY!
ACCIDENT OR NOT, YOU HAVE BEEN AT THE **ROOT** OF EVERY **PROBLEM** THIS FARM HAS FACED IN THE LAST TWO MONTHS.
IT'S **REYNARD'S** FAULT! YOUR ERRANT KNIGHT **TAUNTING** US WITH HIS GLAMOUR!
AFTER THREE CENTURIES OF RESTRICTION TO THIS PLACE, DON'T WE **ALL** DESERVE A CHANCE AT FREEDOM?
THEY DO. BUT NOT YOU. YOU CLOAKED YOURSELF IN THEIR JUST GRIEVANCES TO LEGITIMIZE YOUR **OWN** JEALOUSY AND GREED.
I HEAR YOU DON'T LIKE BEES?
I THINK YOU NEED A **FAR** TOUGHER SENTENCE.
DO US ALL A FAVOR... **BUZZ OFF.**
YAAAAAGHH!!

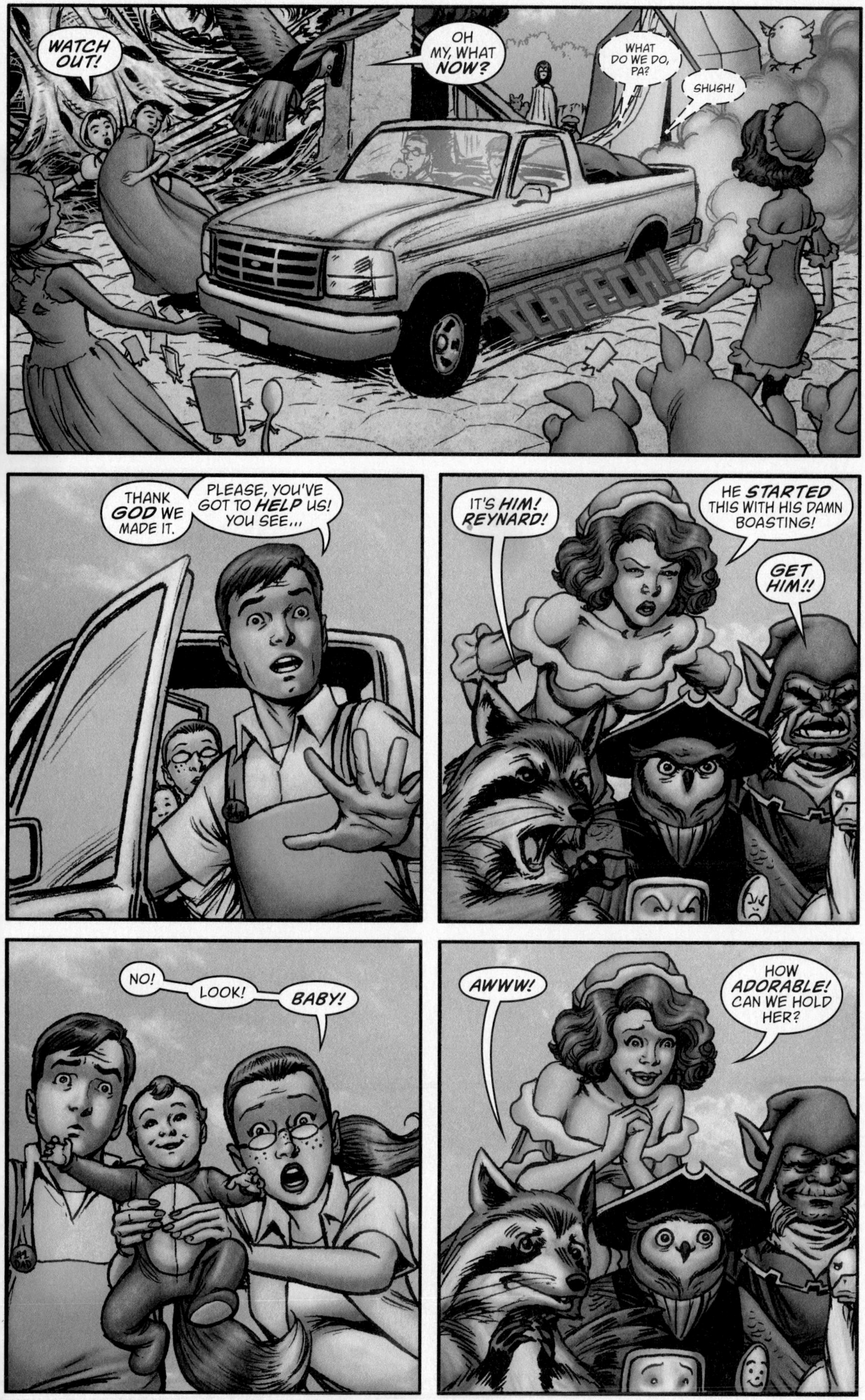

WATCH OUT!
OH MY, WHAT NOW?
WHAT DO WE DO, PA?
SHUSH!
SCREECH!
THANK GOD WE MADE IT.
PLEASE, YOU'VE GOT TO HELP US! YOU SEE...
IT'S HIM! REYNARD!
HE STARTED THIS WITH HIS DAMN BOASTING!
GET HIM!!
NO!
LOOK!
BABY!
AWWW!
HOW ADORABLE! CAN WE HOLD HER?

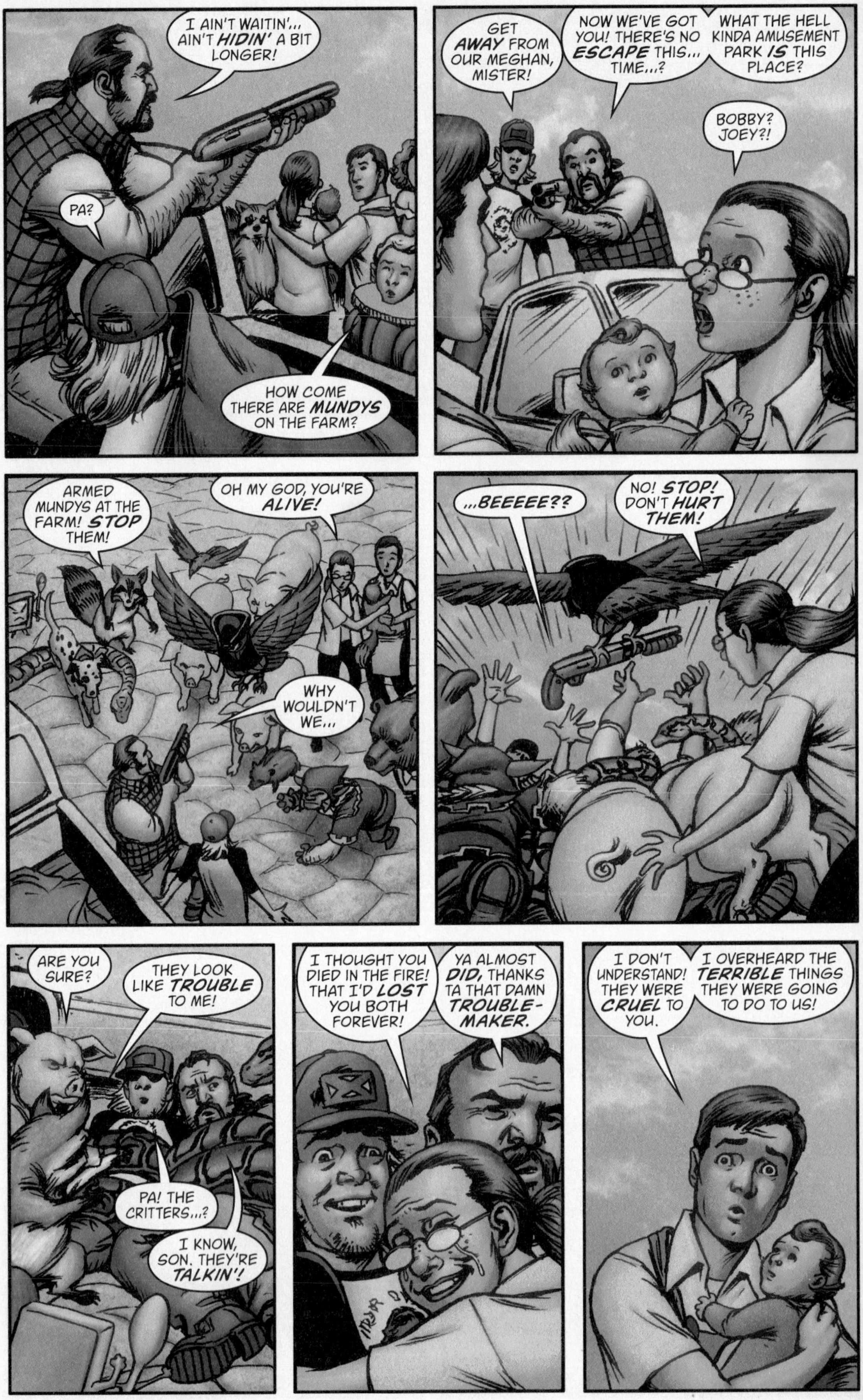

I AIN'T WAITIN'... AIN'T HIDIN' A BIT LONGER!
PA?
HOW COME THERE ARE MUNDYS ON THE FARM?
GET AWAY FROM OUR MEGHAN, MISTER!
NOW WE'VE GOT YOU! THERE'S NO ESCAPE THIS... TIME...?
WHAT THE HELL KINDA AMUSEMENT PARK IS THIS PLACE?
BOBBY? JOEY?!
ARMED MUNDYS AT THE FARM! STOP THEM!
OH MY GOD, YOU'RE ALIVE!
WHY WOULDN'T WE...
...BEEEEE??
NO! STOP! DON'T HURT THEM!
ARE YOU SURE?
THEY LOOK LIKE TROUBLE TO ME!
PA! THE CRITTERS...?
I KNOW, SON. THEY'RE TALKIN'!
I THOUGHT YOU DIED IN THE FIRE! THAT I'D LOST YOU BOTH FOREVER!
YA ALMOST DID, THANKS TA THAT DAMN TROUBLE-MAKER.
I DON'T UNDERSTAND! THEY WERE CRUEL TO YOU.
I OVERHEARD THE TERRIBLE THINGS THEY WERE GOING TO DO TO US!

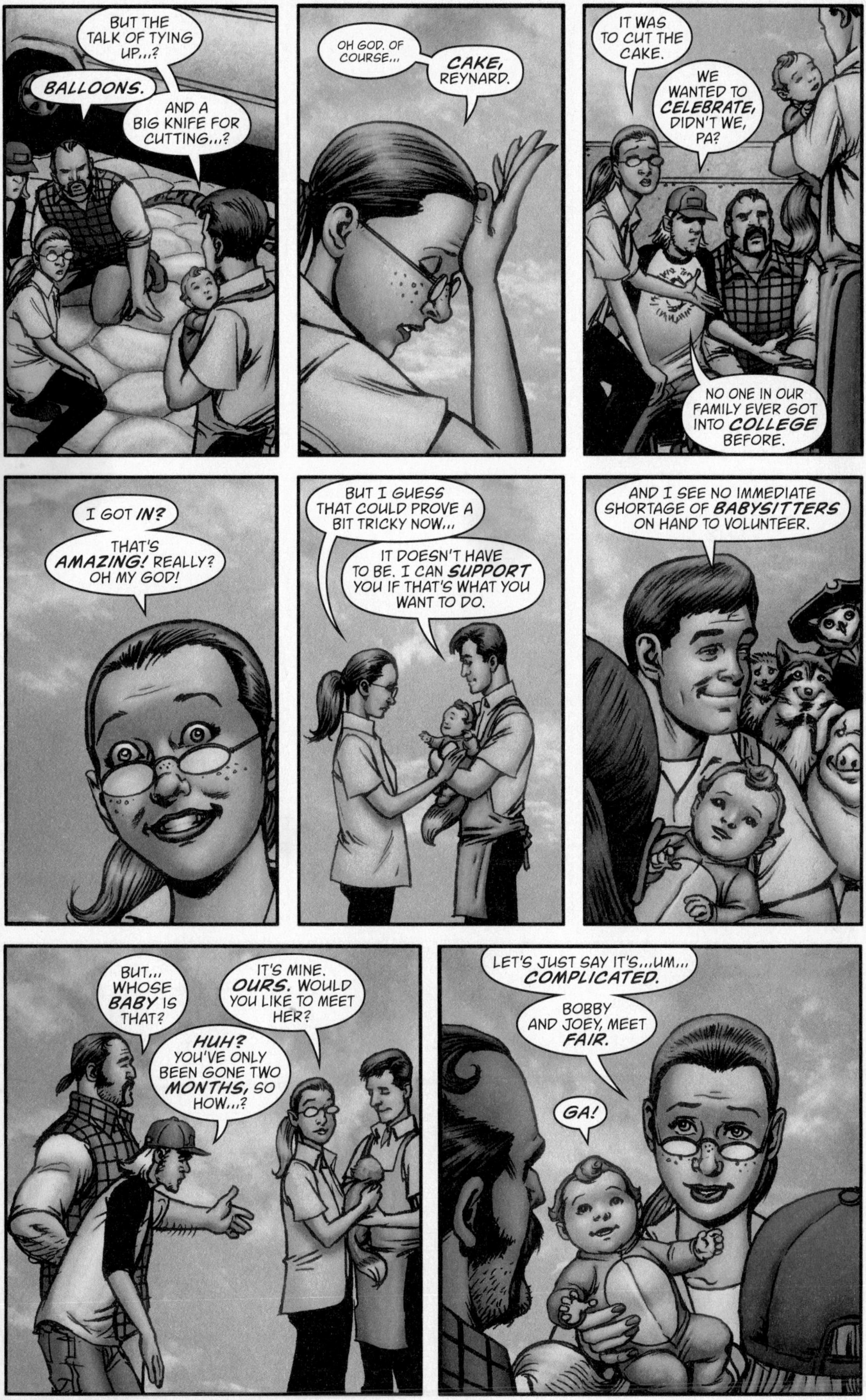
BUT THE TALK OF TYING UP...?
BALLOONS.
AND A BIG KNIFE FOR CUTTING...?
OH GOD. OF COURSE...
CAKE, REYNARD.
IT WAS TO CUT THE CAKE.
WE WANTED TO CELEBRATE, DIDN'T WE, PA?
NO ONE IN OUR FAMILY EVER GOT INTO COLLEGE BEFORE.
I GOT IN?
THAT'S AMAZING! REALLY? OH MY GOD!
BUT I GUESS THAT COULD PROVE A BIT TRICKY NOW...
IT DOESN'T HAVE TO BE. I CAN SUPPORT YOU IF THAT'S WHAT YOU WANT TO DO.
AND I SEE NO IMMEDIATE SHORTAGE OF BABYSITTERS ON HAND TO VOLUNTEER.
BUT... WHOSE BABY IS THAT?
IT'S MINE. OURS. WOULD YOU LIKE TO MEET HER?
HUH? YOU'VE ONLY BEEN GONE TWO MONTHS, SO HOW...?
LET'S JUST SAY IT'S...UM... COMPLICATED.
BOBBY AND JOEY, MEET FAIR.
GA!

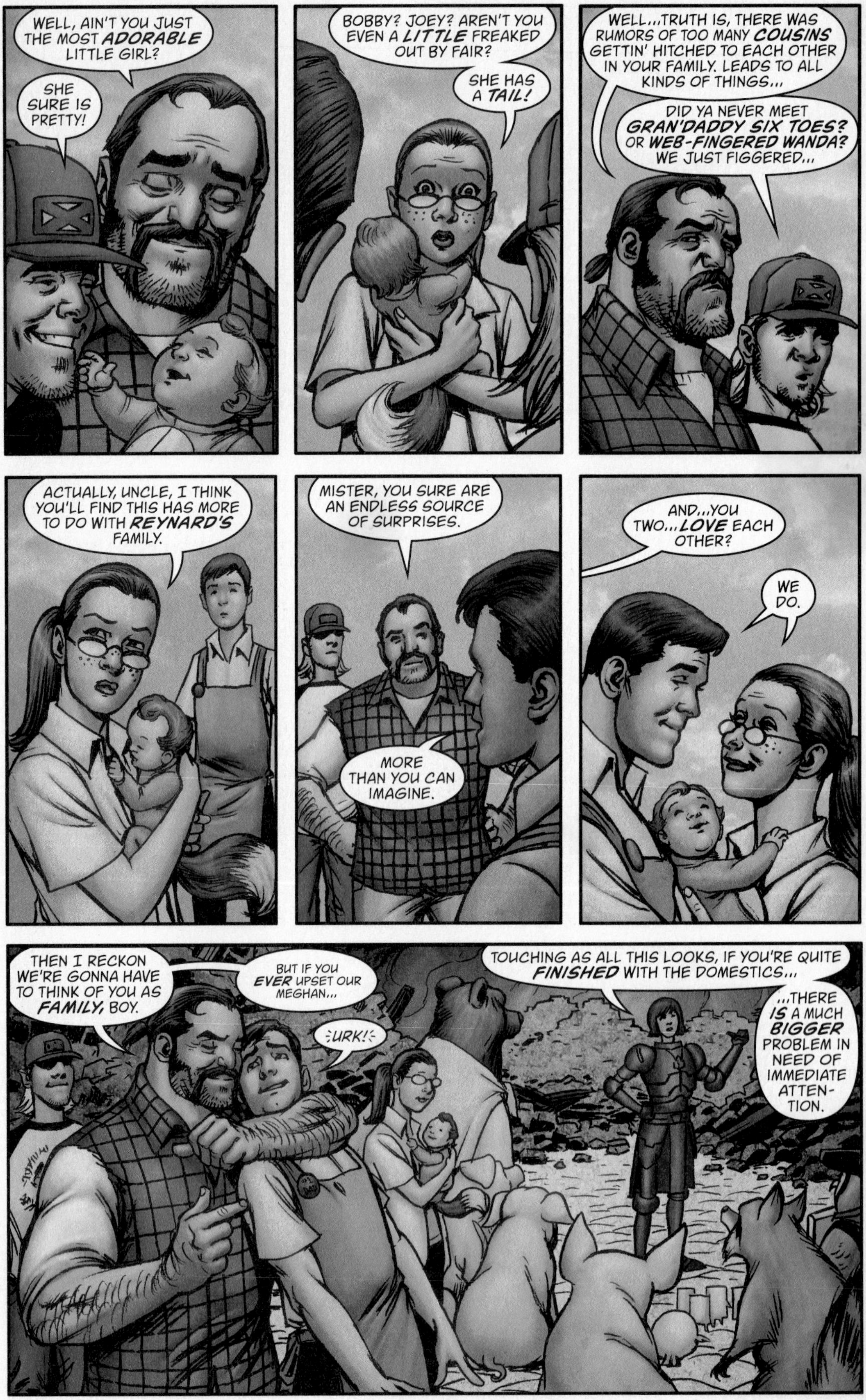

WELL, AIN'T YOU JUST THE MOST ADORABLE LITTLE GIRL?
SHE SURE IS PRETTY!
BOBBY? JOEY? AREN'T YOU EVEN A LITTLE FREAKED OUT BY FAIR?
SHE HAS A TAIL!
WELL...TRUTH IS, THERE WAS RUMORS OF TOO MANY COUSINS GETTIN' HITCHED TO EACH OTHER IN YOUR FAMILY. LEADS TO ALL KINDS OF THINGS...
DID YA NEVER MEET GRAN'DADDY SIX TOES? OR WEB-FINGERED WANDA? WE JUST FIGGERED...
ACTUALLY, UNCLE, I THINK YOU'LL FIND THIS HAS MORE TO DO WITH REYNARD'S FAMILY.
MISTER, YOU SURE ARE AN ENDLESS SOURCE OF SURPRISES.
MORE THAN YOU CAN IMAGINE.
AND...YOU TWO...LOVE EACH OTHER?
WE DO.
THEN I RECKON WE'RE GONNA HAVE TO THINK OF YOU AS FAMILY, BOY.
BUT IF YOU EVER UPSET OUR MEGHAN...
URK!
TOUCHING AS ALL THIS LOOKS, IF YOU'RE QUITE FINISHED WITH THE DOMESTICS...
...THERE IS A MUCH BIGGER PROBLEM IN NEED OF IMMEDIATE ATTENTION.

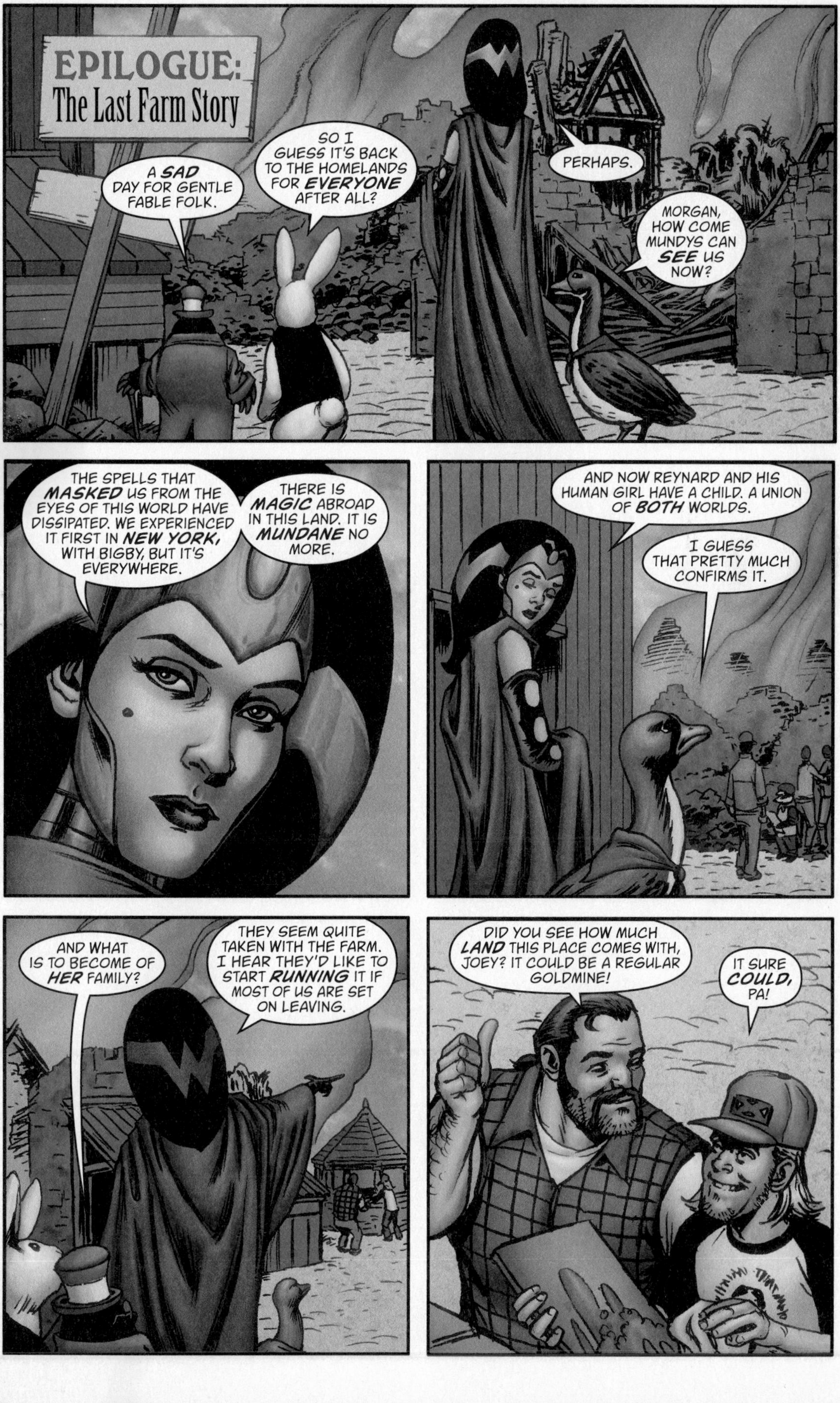
EPILOGUE:
The Last Farm Story
A SAD DAY FOR GENTLE FABLE FOLK.
SO I GUESS IT'S BACK TO THE HOMELANDS FOR EVERYONE AFTER ALL?
PERHAPS.
MORGAN, HOW COME MUNDYS CAN SEE US NOW?
THE SPELLS THAT MASKED US FROM THE EYES OF THIS WORLD HAVE DISSIPATED. WE EXPERIENCED IT FIRST IN NEW YORK, WITH BIGBY, BUT IT'S EVERYWHERE.
THERE IS MAGIC ABROAD IN THIS LAND. IT IS MUNDANE NO MORE.
AND NOW REYNARD AND HIS HUMAN GIRL HAVE A CHILD. A UNION OF BOTH WORLDS.
I GUESS THAT PRETTY MUCH CONFIRMS IT.
AND WHAT IS TO BECOME OF HER FAMILY?
THEY SEEM QUITE TAKEN WITH THE FARM. I HEAR THEY'D LIKE TO START RUNNING IT IF MOST OF US ARE SET ON LEAVING.
DID YOU SEE HOW MUCH LAND THIS PLACE COMES WITH, JOEY? IT COULD BE A REGULAR GOLDMINE!
IT SURE COULD, PA!

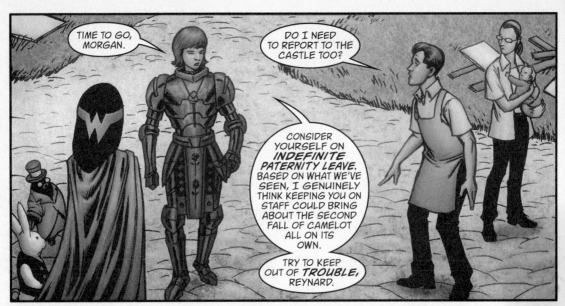

TIME TO GO, MORGAN.

DO I NEED TO REPORT TO THE CASTLE TOO?

CONSIDER YOURSELF ON *INDEFINITE PATERNITY LEAVE.* BASED ON WHAT WE'VE SEEN, I GENUINELY THINK KEEPING YOU ON STAFF COULD BRING ABOUT THE SECOND FALL OF CAMELOT ALL ON ITS OWN.

TRY TO KEEP OUT OF *TROUBLE,* REYNARD.

SO...UMM.... WHAT DO WE DO NOW?

DO WE ALL STAY HERE WITH *YOU?*

OH, I THINK WE CAN DO BETTER THAN THAT.

HOW WOULD YOU LIKE TO HAVE YOUR VERY OWN *FAIRY TALE KINGDOM?*

I'M SOMETHING OF A *HERO* TO THE FABLES COMMUNITY, YOU KNOW.

DID I MENTION I'M A *KNIGHT* OF NEW CAMELOT?

OH LORD, THERE HE GOES AGAIN...

THE END

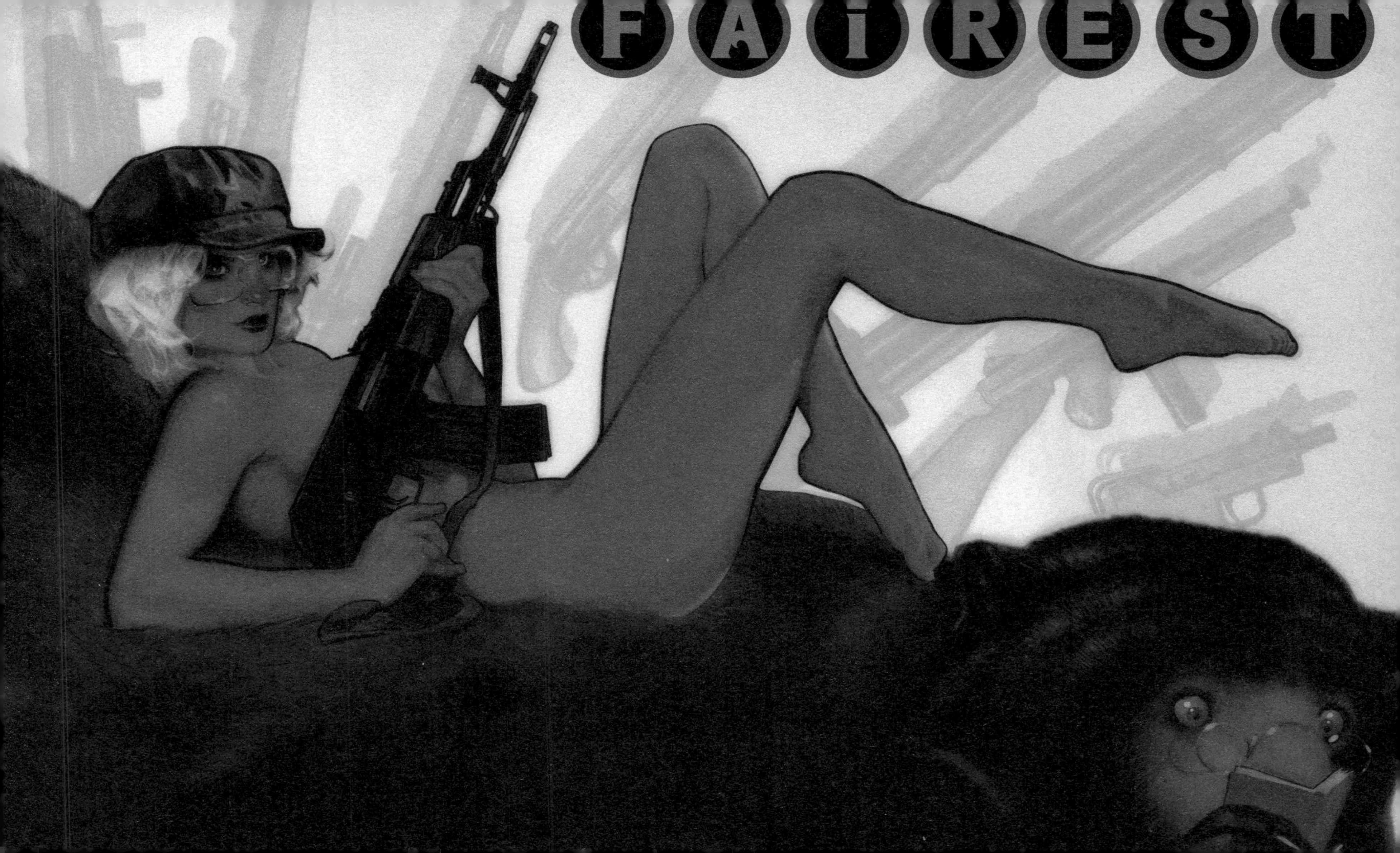
FAIREST

"Instead of the power and glory I deserve, I'm doomed to be a feast for wolf and worm."

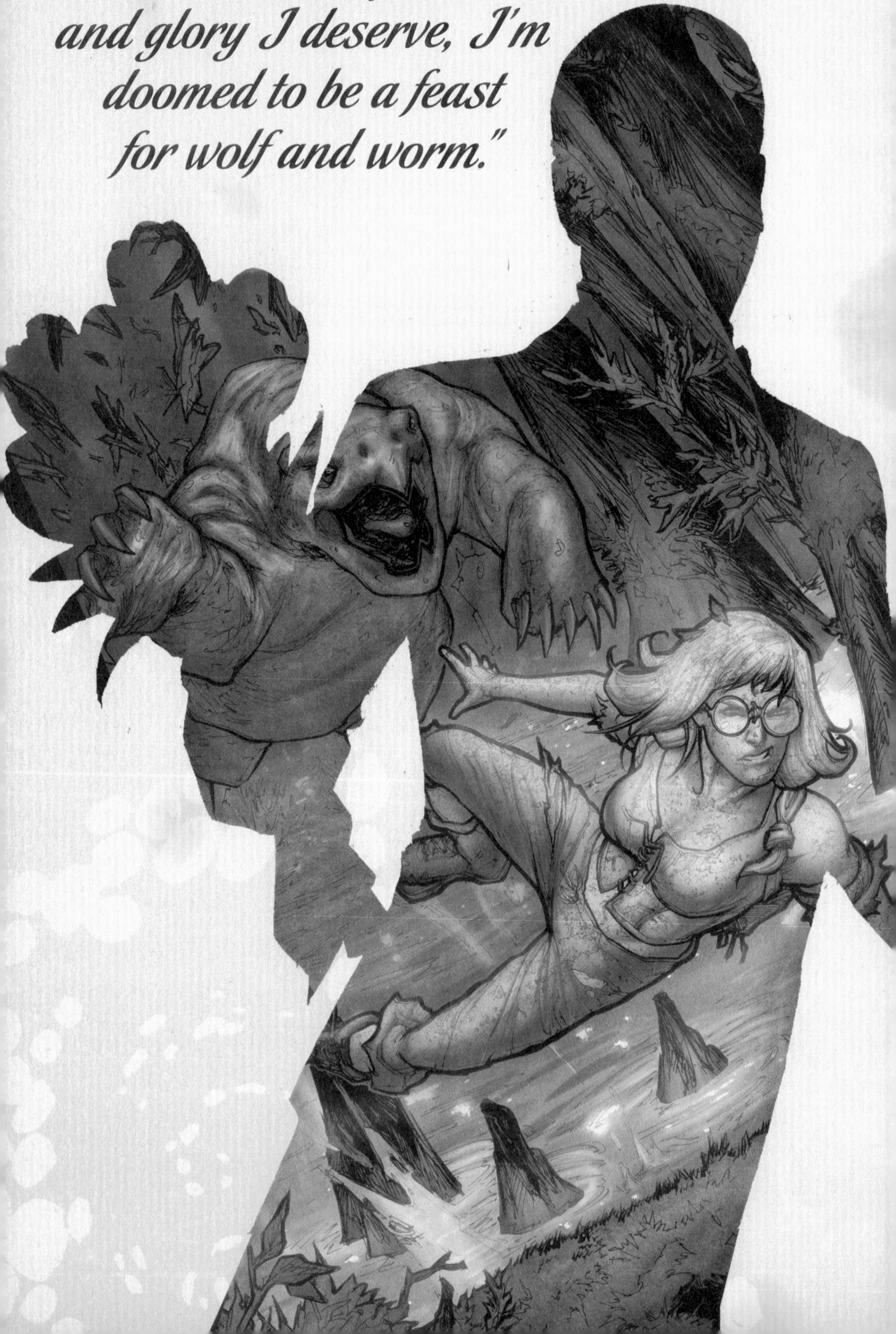

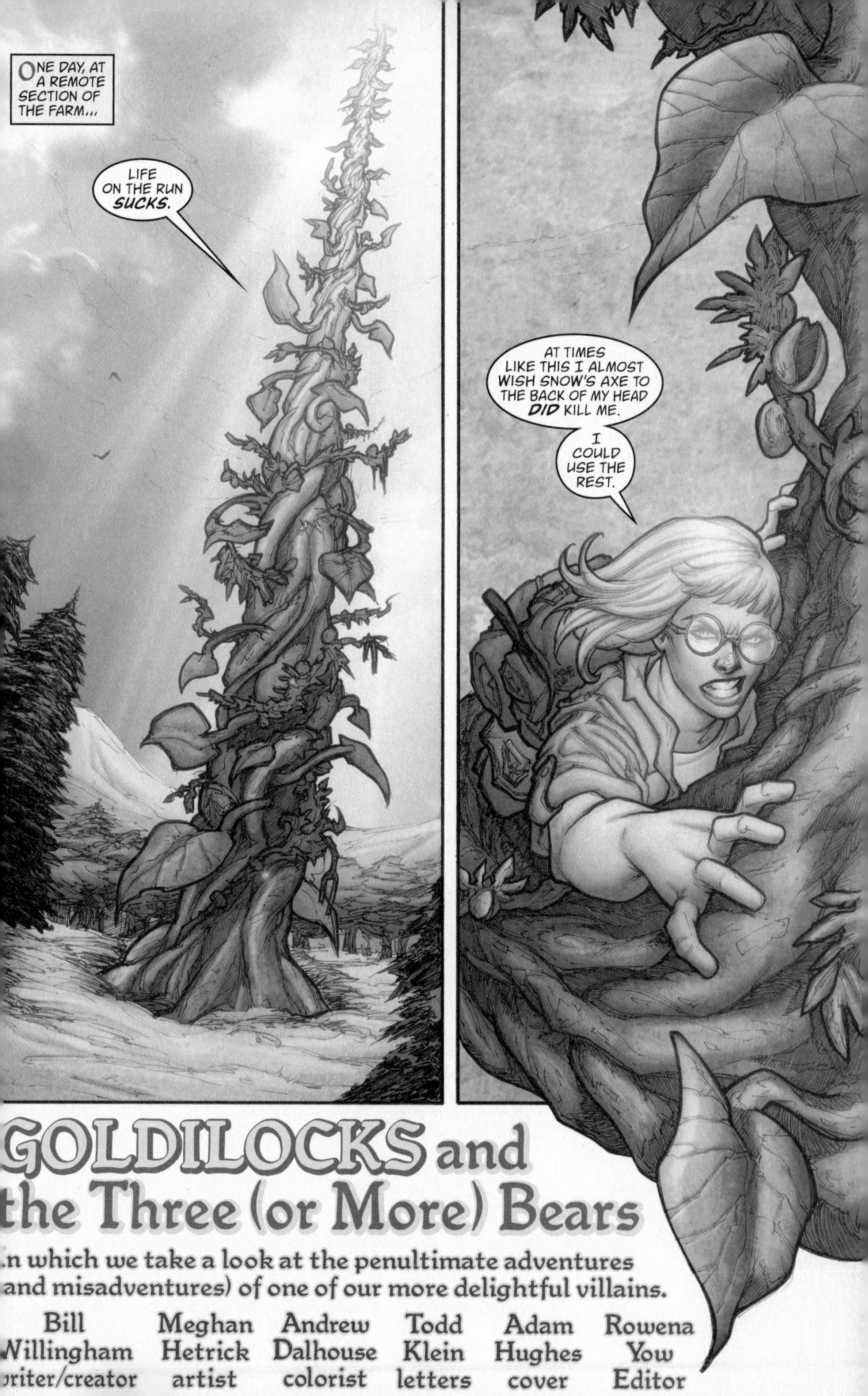
ONE DAY, AT A REMOTE SECTION OF THE FARM...
LIFE ON THE RUN SUCKS.
AT TIMES LIKE THIS I ALMOST WISH SNOW'S AXE TO THE BACK OF MY HEAD DID KILL ME.
I COULD USE THE REST.

GOLDILOCKS and the Three (or More) Bears

(In which we take a look at the penultimate adventures (and misadventures) of one of our more delightful villains.

Bill Willingham	Meghan Hetrick	Andrew Dalhouse	Todd Klein	Adam Hughes	Rowena Yow
writer/creator	artist	colorist	letters	cover	Editor

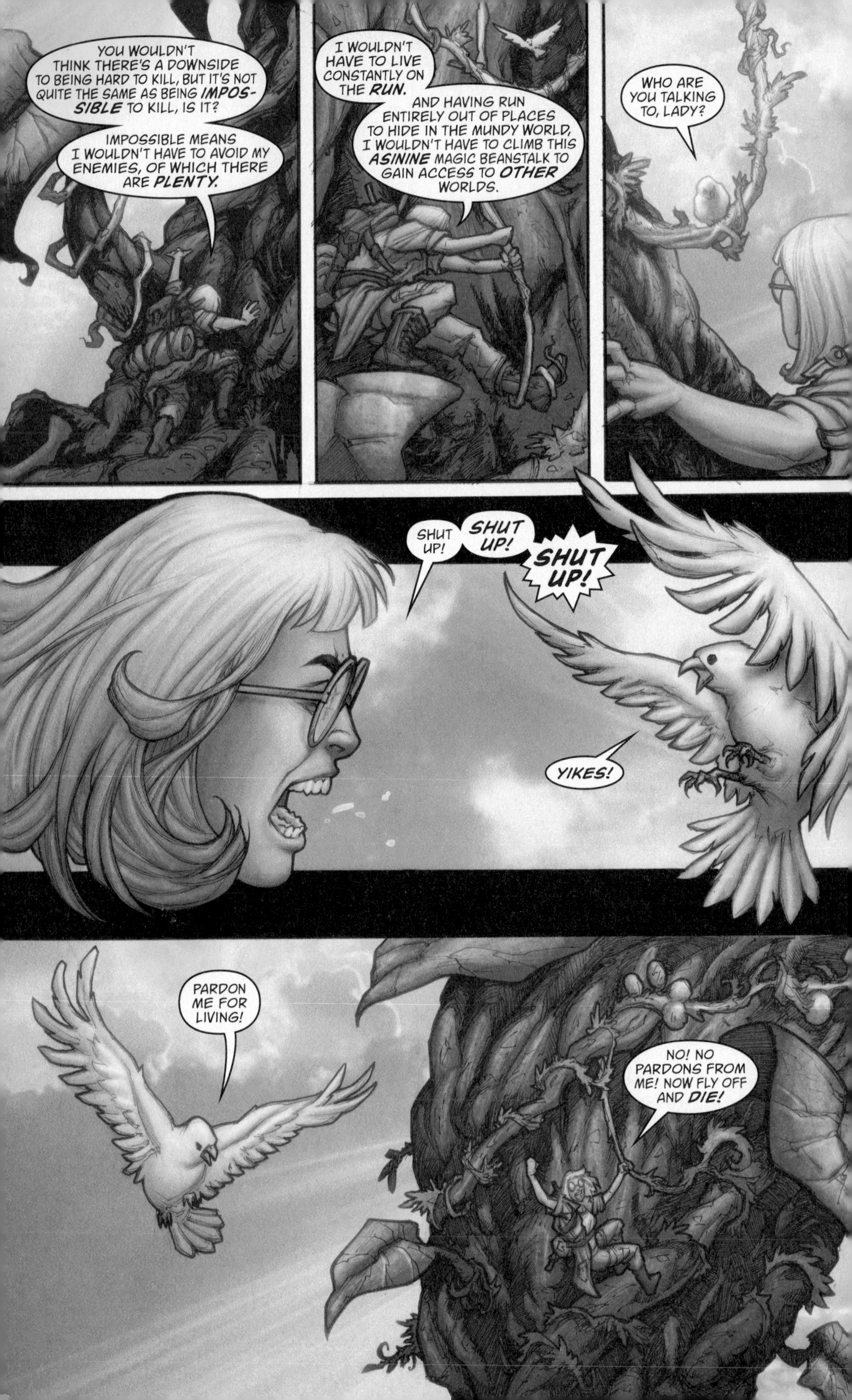
YOU WOULDN'T THINK THERE'S A DOWNSIDE TO BEING HARD TO KILL, BUT IT'S NOT QUITE THE SAME AS BEING IMPOSSIBLE TO KILL, IS IT?
IMPOSSIBLE MEANS I WOULDN'T HAVE TO AVOID MY ENEMIES, OF WHICH THERE ARE PLENTY.
I WOULDN'T HAVE TO LIVE CONSTANTLY ON THE RUN.
AND HAVING RUN ENTIRELY OUT OF PLACES TO HIDE IN THE MUNDY WORLD, I WOULDN'T HAVE TO CLIMB THIS ASININE MAGIC BEANSTALK TO GAIN ACCESS TO OTHER WORLDS.
WHO ARE YOU TALKING TO, LADY?
SHUT UP!
SHUT UP!
SHUT UP!
YIKES!
PARDON ME FOR LIVING!
NO! NO PARDONS FROM ME! NOW FLY OFF AND DIE!

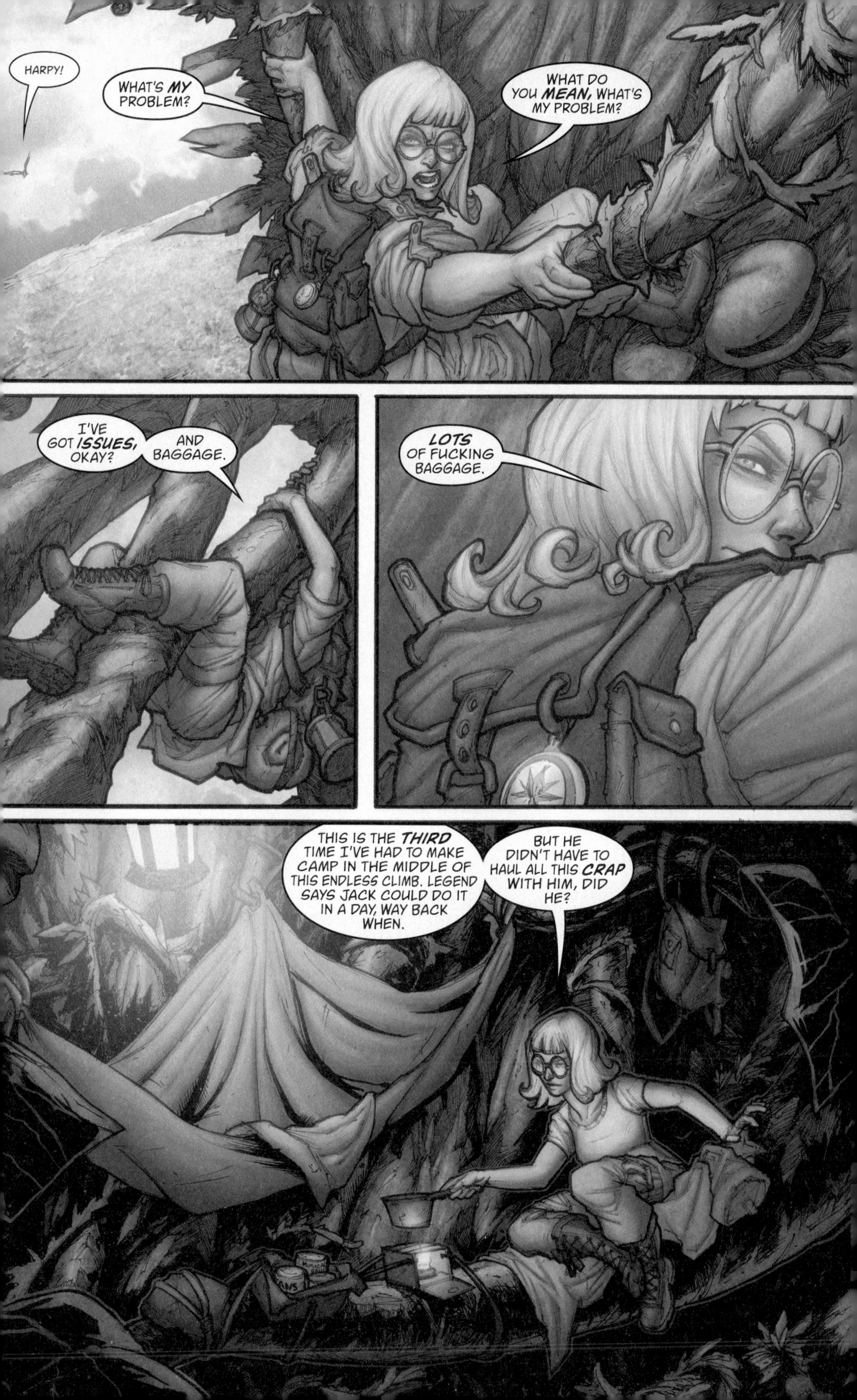
HARPY!
WHAT'S MY PROBLEM?
WHAT DO YOU MEAN, WHAT'S MY PROBLEM?
I'VE GOT ISSUES, OKAY?
AND BAGGAGE.
LOTS OF FUCKING BAGGAGE.
THIS IS THE THIRD TIME I'VE HAD TO MAKE CAMP IN THE MIDDLE OF THIS ENDLESS CLIMB. LEGEND SAYS JACK COULD DO IT IN A DAY, WAY BACK WHEN.
BUT HE DIDN'T HAVE TO HAUL ALL THIS CRAP WITH HIM, DID HE?

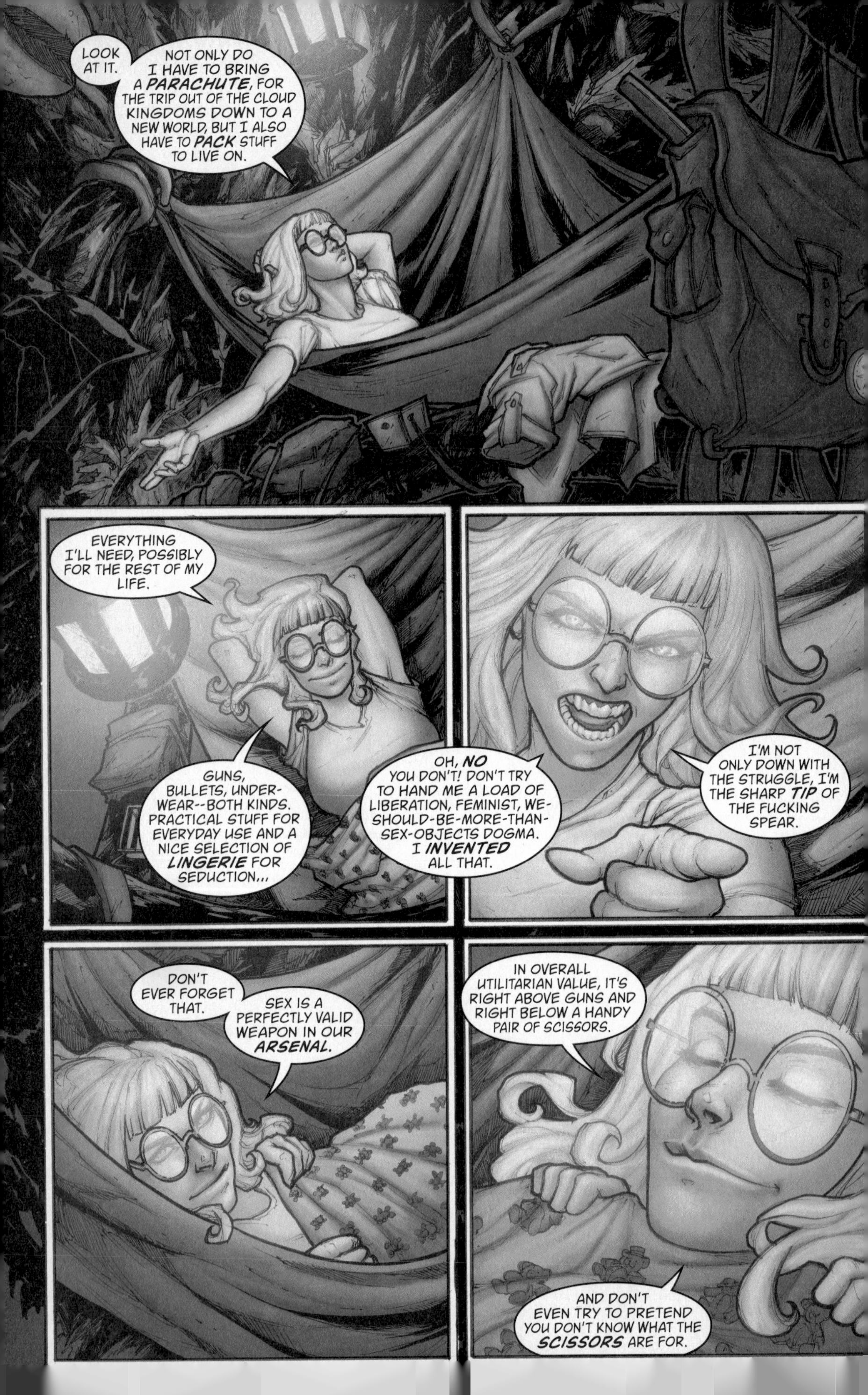
LOOK AT IT.
NOT ONLY DO I HAVE TO BRING A PARACHUTE, FOR THE TRIP OUT OF THE CLOUD KINGDOMS DOWN TO A NEW WORLD, BUT I ALSO HAVE TO PACK STUFF TO LIVE ON.
EVERYTHING I'LL NEED, POSSIBLY FOR THE REST OF MY LIFE.
GUNS, BULLETS, UNDER-WEAR--BOTH KINDS. PRACTICAL STUFF FOR EVERYDAY USE AND A NICE SELECTION OF LINGERIE FOR SEDUCTION...
OH, NO YOU DON'T! DON'T TRY TO HAND ME A LOAD OF LIBERATION, FEMINIST, WE-SHOULD-BE-MORE-THAN-SEX-OBJECTS DOGMA. I INVENTED ALL THAT.
I'M NOT ONLY DOWN WITH THE STRUGGLE, I'M THE SHARP TIP OF THE FUCKING SPEAR.
DON'T EVER FORGET THAT.
SEX IS A PERFECTLY VALID WEAPON IN OUR ARSENAL.
IN OVERALL UTILITARIAN VALUE, IT'S RIGHT ABOVE GUNS AND RIGHT BELOW A HANDY PAIR OF SCISSORS.
AND DON'T EVEN TRY TO PRETEND YOU DON'T KNOW WHAT THE SCISSORS ARE FOR.

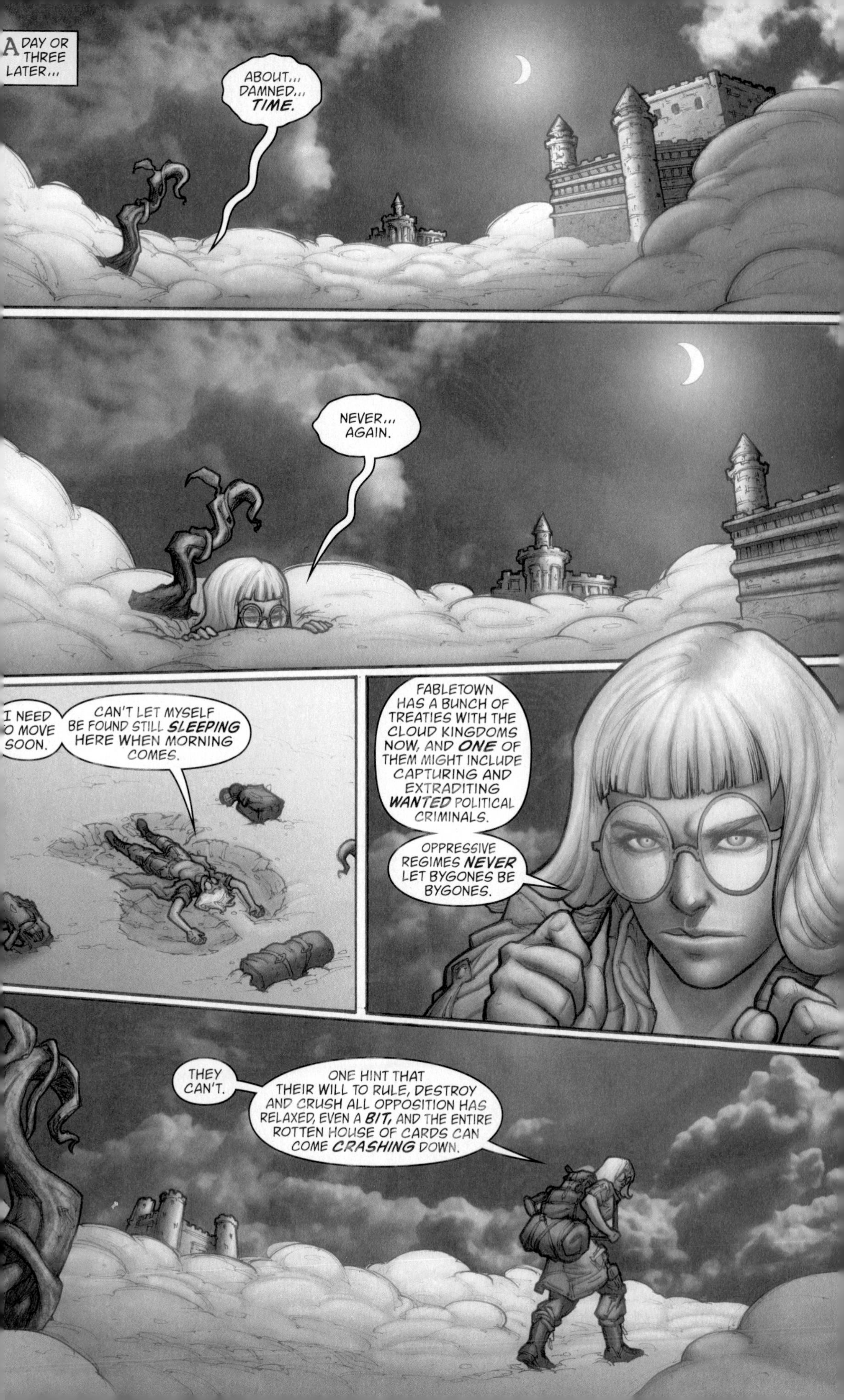
A DAY OR THREE LATER...
ABOUT... DAMNED... *TIME*.
NEVER... AGAIN.
I NEED TO MOVE SOON.
CAN'T LET MYSELF BE FOUND STILL *SLEEPING* HERE WHEN MORNING COMES.
FABLETOWN HAS A BUNCH OF TREATIES WITH THE CLOUD KINGDOMS NOW, AND *ONE* OF THEM MIGHT INCLUDE CAPTURING AND EXTRADITING *WANTED* POLITICAL CRIMINALS.
OPPRESSIVE REGIMES *NEVER* LET BYGONES BE BYGONES.
THEY CAN'T.
ONE HINT THAT THEIR WILL TO RULE, DESTROY AND CRUSH ALL OPPOSITION HAS RELAXED, EVEN A *BIT*, AND THE ENTIRE ROTTEN HOUSE OF CARDS CAN COME *CRASHING* DOWN.

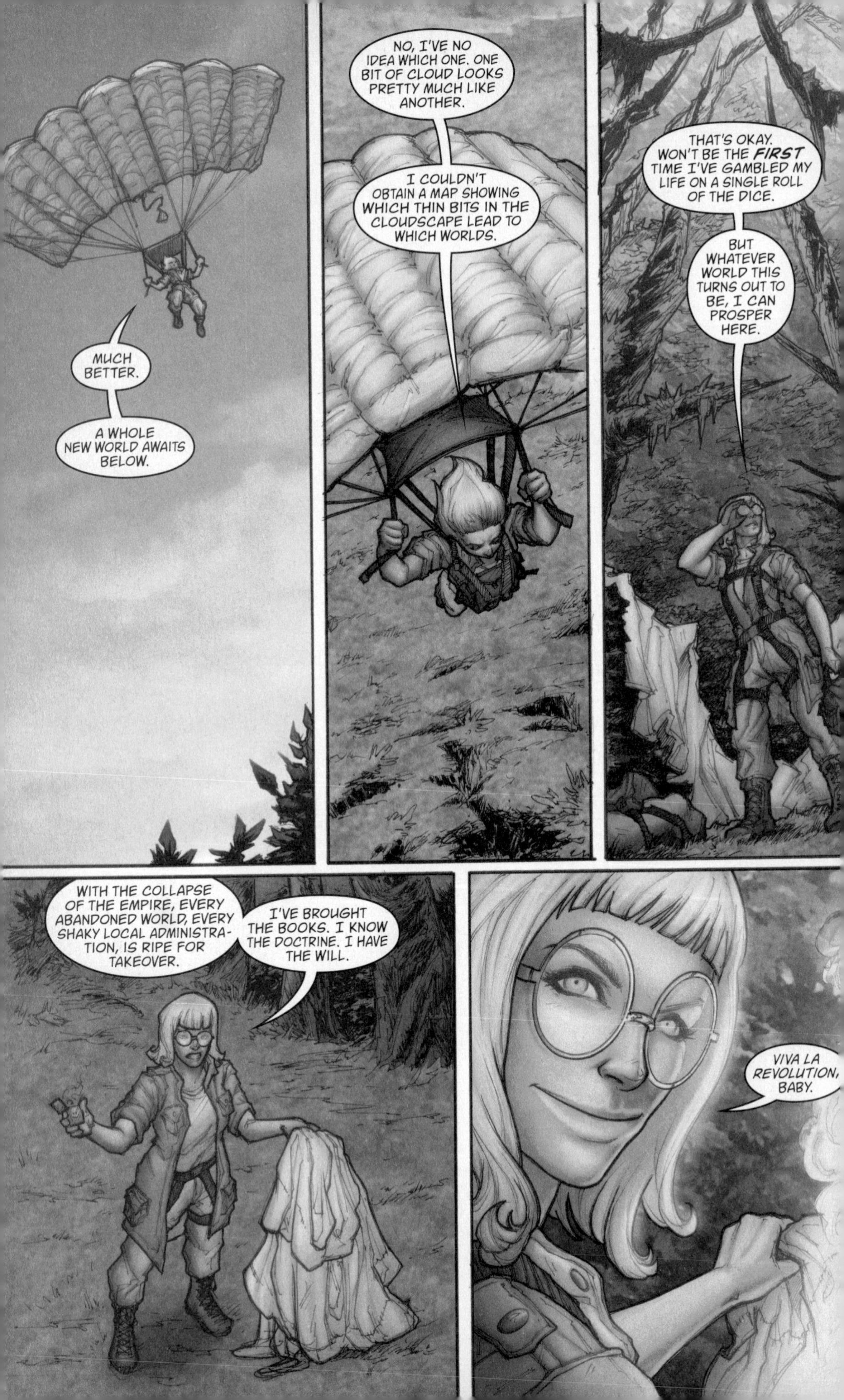
MUCH BETTER.
A WHOLE NEW WORLD AWAITS BELOW.
NO, I'VE NO IDEA WHICH ONE. ONE BIT OF CLOUD LOOKS PRETTY MUCH LIKE ANOTHER.
I COULDN'T OBTAIN A MAP SHOWING WHICH THIN BITS IN THE CLOUDSCAPE LEAD TO WHICH WORLDS.
THAT'S OKAY. WON'T BE THE *FIRST* TIME I'VE GAMBLED MY LIFE ON A SINGLE ROLL OF THE DICE.
BUT WHATEVER WORLD THIS TURNS OUT TO BE, I CAN PROSPER HERE.
WITH THE COLLAPSE OF THE EMPIRE, EVERY ABANDONED WORLD, EVERY SHAKY LOCAL ADMINISTRA-TION, IS RIPE FOR TAKEOVER.
I'VE BROUGHT THE BOOKS. I KNOW THE DOCTRINE. I HAVE THE WILL.
VIVA LA REVOLUTION, BABY.

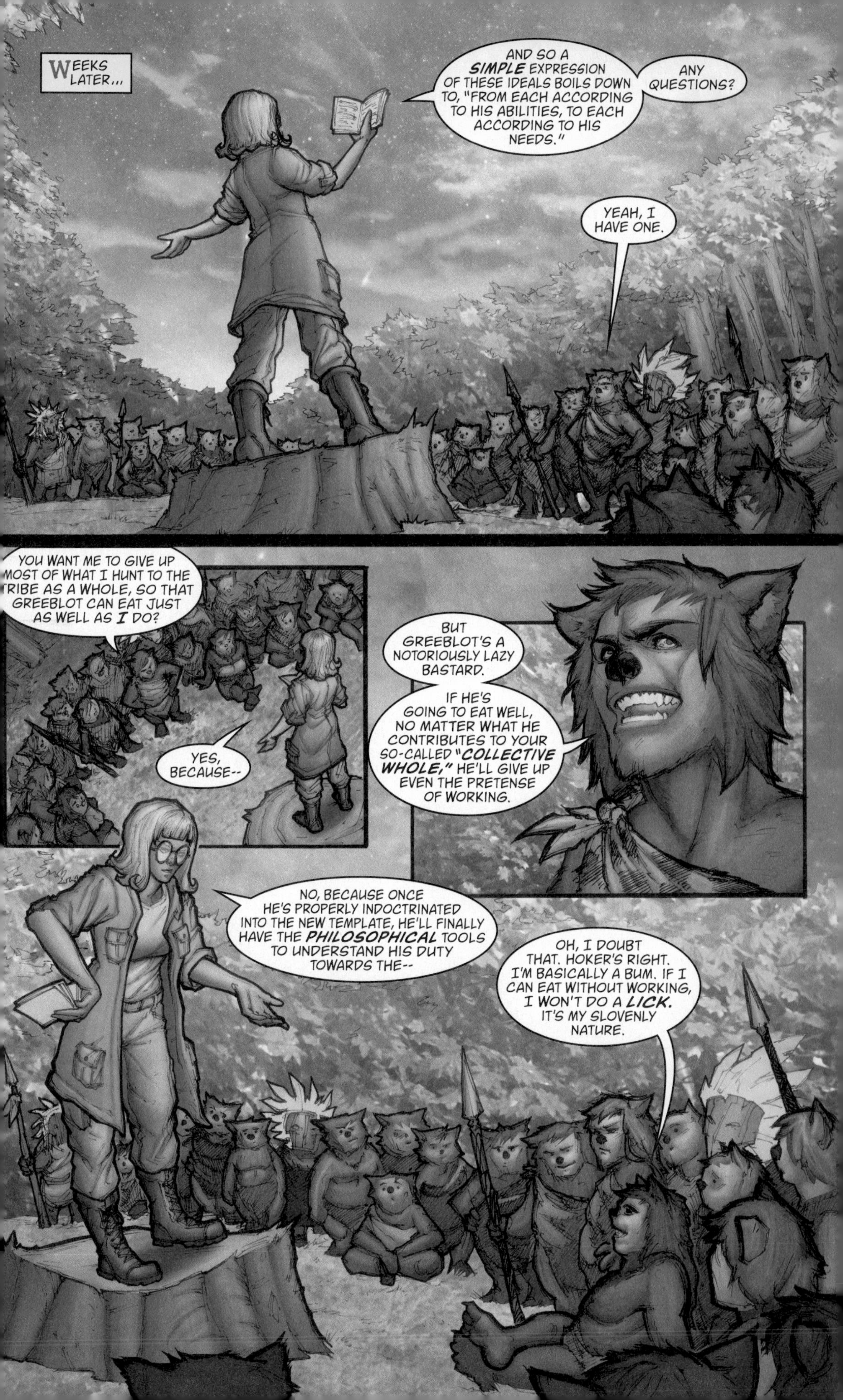
WEEKS LATER...
AND SO A SIMPLE EXPRESSION OF THESE IDEALS BOILS DOWN TO, "FROM EACH ACCORDING TO HIS ABILITIES, TO EACH ACCORDING TO HIS NEEDS."
ANY QUESTIONS?
YEAH, I HAVE ONE.
YOU WANT ME TO GIVE UP MOST OF WHAT I HUNT TO THE TRIBE AS A WHOLE, SO THAT GREEBLOT CAN EAT JUST AS WELL AS I DO?
YES, BECAUSE--
BUT GREEBLOT'S A NOTORIOUSLY LAZY BASTARD.
IF HE'S GOING TO EAT WELL, NO MATTER WHAT HE CONTRIBUTES TO YOUR SO-CALLED "COLLECTIVE WHOLE," HE'LL GIVE UP EVEN THE PRETENSE OF WORKING.
NO, BECAUSE ONCE HE'S PROPERLY INDOCTRINATED INTO THE NEW TEMPLATE, HE'LL FINALLY HAVE THE PHILOSOPHICAL TOOLS TO UNDERSTAND HIS DUTY TOWARDS THE--
OH, I DOUBT THAT. HOKER'S RIGHT. I'M BASICALLY A BUM. IF I CAN EAT WITHOUT WORKING, I WON'T DO A LICK. IT'S MY SLOVENLY NATURE.

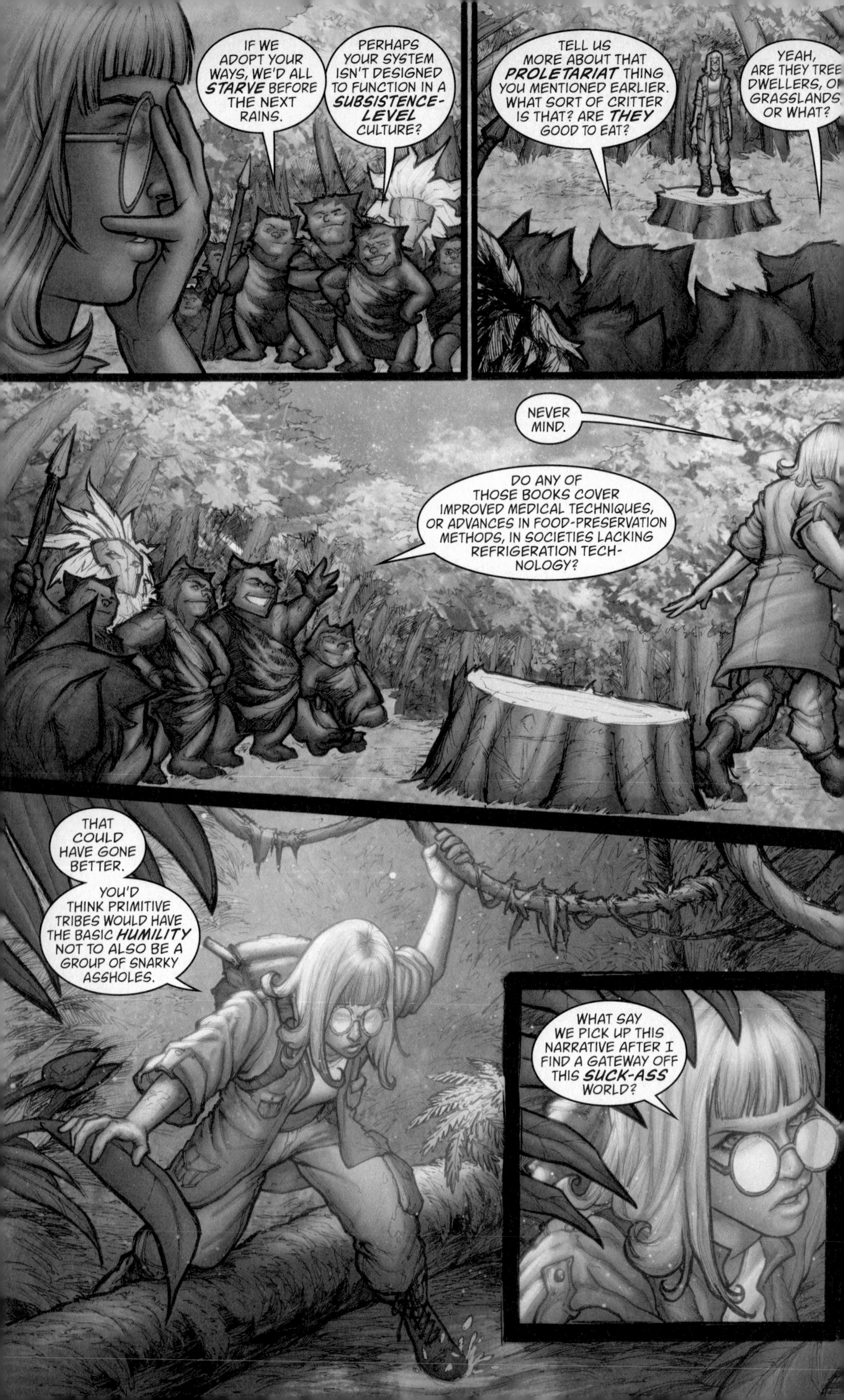
IF WE ADOPT YOUR WAYS, WE'D ALL STARVE BEFORE THE NEXT RAINS.
PERHAPS YOUR SYSTEM ISN'T DESIGNED TO FUNCTION IN A SUBSISTENCE-LEVEL CULTURE?
TELL US MORE ABOUT THAT PROLETARIAT THING YOU MENTIONED EARLIER. WHAT SORT OF CRITTER IS THAT? ARE THEY GOOD TO EAT?
YEAH, ARE THEY TREE DWELLERS, OR GRASSLANDS OR WHAT?
NEVER MIND.
DO ANY OF THOSE BOOKS COVER IMPROVED MEDICAL TECHNIQUES, OR ADVANCES IN FOOD-PRESERVATION METHODS, IN SOCIETIES LACKING REFRIGERATION TECHNOLOGY?
THAT COULD HAVE GONE BETTER.
YOU'D THINK PRIMITIVE TRIBES WOULD HAVE THE BASIC HUMILITY NOT TO ALSO BE A GROUP OF SNARKY ASSHOLES.
WHAT SAY WE PICK UP THIS NARRATIVE AFTER I FIND A GATEWAY OFF THIS SUCK-ASS WORLD?

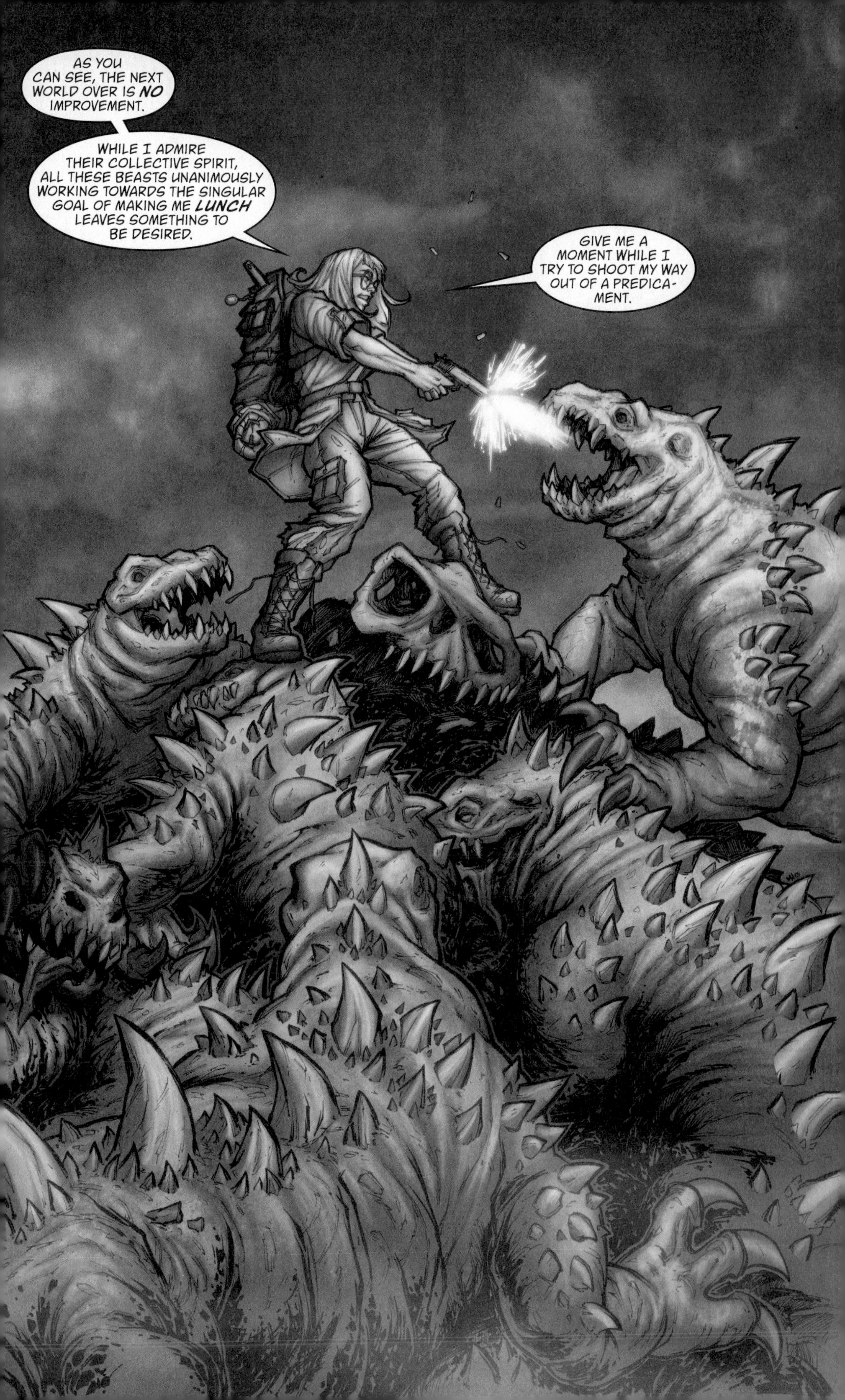
AS YOU CAN SEE, THE NEXT WORLD OVER IS ***NO*** IMPROVEMENT.
WHILE I ADMIRE THEIR COLLECTIVE SPIRIT, ALL THESE BEASTS UNANIMOUSLY WORKING TOWARDS THE SINGULAR GOAL OF MAKING ME ***LUNCH*** LEAVES SOMETHING TO BE DESIRED.
GIVE ME A MOMENT WHILE I TRY TO SHOOT MY WAY OUT OF A PREDICA-MENT.

I DIDN'T DIE.

THAT'S THE GOOD NEWS. THE BAD NEWS IS I BURNED UP MOST OF MY *AMMUNITION* GETTING OFF THAT WORLD OF NOTHING-BUT-HUNGRY MONSTERS.

THOSE WERE BULLETS I PLANNED TO LAST A LIFETIME, OR AT LEAST SPEND *OVER-THROWING* THE RIGHT KINGDOM, WHEN IT CAME ALONG.

OLD MAN GEPPETTO KEPT GUNS AND THEIR RELATED TECHNOLOGIES OUT OF HIS SPRAWLING EMPIRE.

SO THERE'S NO CHANCE OF A *RESUPPLY,* SHORT OF HEADING HOME AGAIN.

THAT'S ODD.

WHEN DID I START THINKING O THE MUND WORLD AS *HOME?*

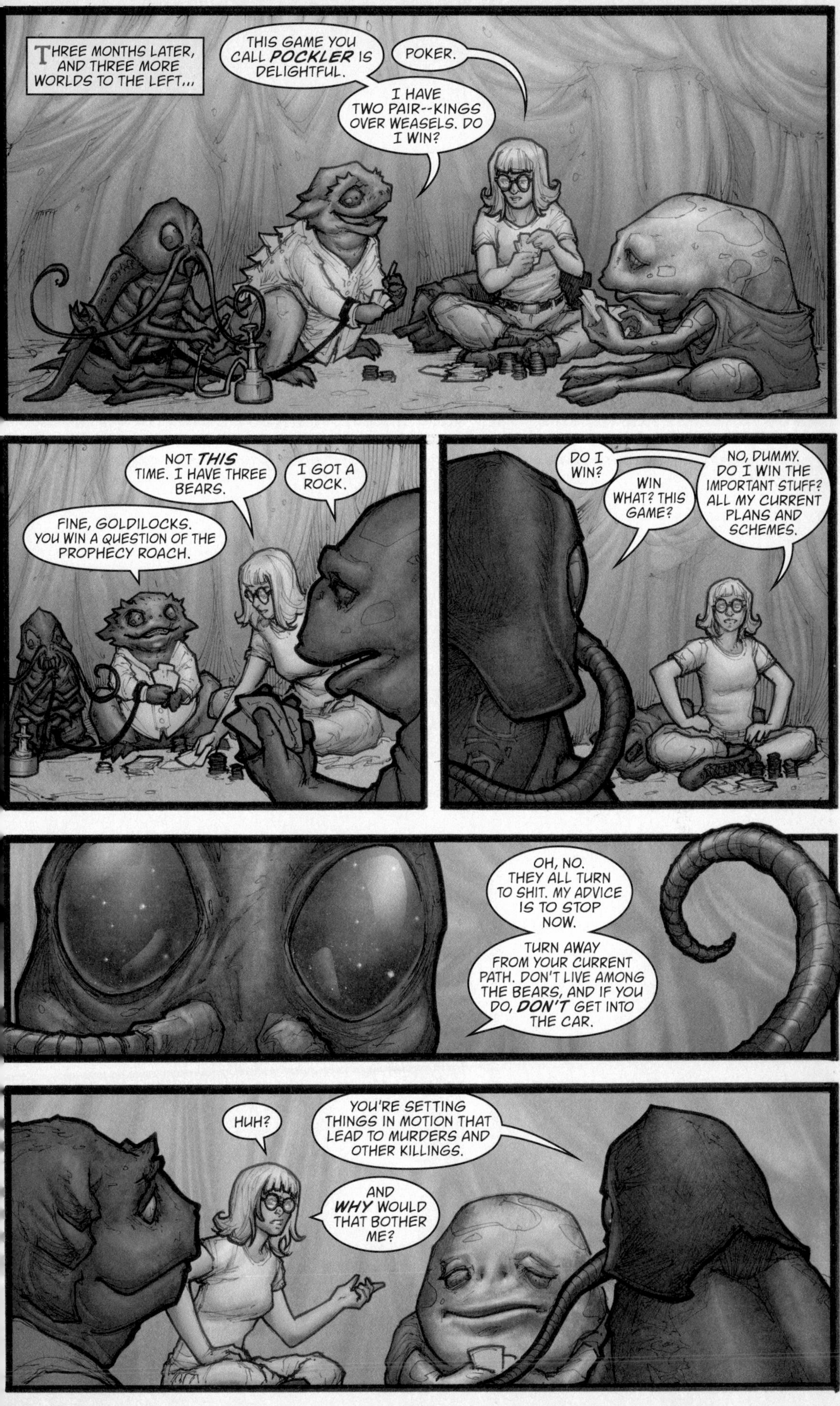
THREE MONTHS LATER, AND THREE MORE WORLDS TO THE LEFT...
THIS GAME YOU CALL POCKLER IS DELIGHTFUL.
POKER.
I HAVE TWO PAIR--KINGS OVER WEASELS. DO I WIN?
NOT THIS TIME. I HAVE THREE BEARS.
I GOT A ROCK.
FINE, GOLDILOCKS. YOU WIN A QUESTION OF THE PROPHECY ROACH.
DO I WIN?
WIN WHAT? THIS GAME?
NO, DUMMY. DO I WIN THE IMPORTANT STUFF? ALL MY CURRENT PLANS AND SCHEMES.
OH, NO. THEY ALL TURN TO SHIT. MY ADVICE IS TO STOP NOW.
TURN AWAY FROM YOUR CURRENT PATH. DON'T LIVE AMONG THE BEARS, AND IF YOU DO, DON'T GET INTO THE CAR.
HUH?
YOU'RE SETTING THINGS IN MOTION THAT LEAD TO MURDERS AND OTHER KILLINGS.
AND WHY WOULD THAT BOTHER ME?

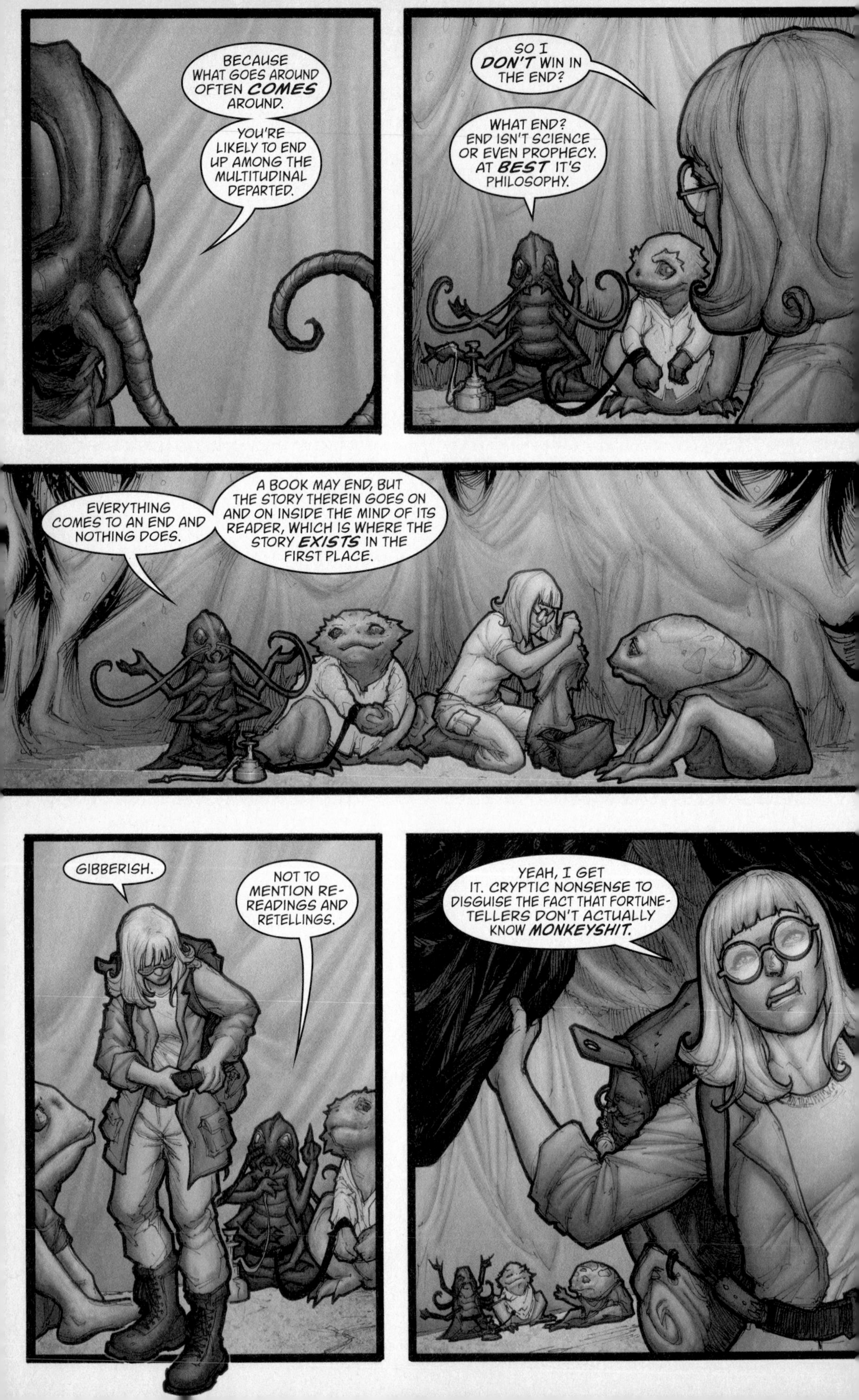
BECAUSE WHAT GOES AROUND OFTEN COMES AROUND.
YOU'RE LIKELY TO END UP AMONG THE MULTITUDINAL DEPARTED.
SO I DON'T WIN IN THE END?
WHAT END? END ISN'T SCIENCE OR EVEN PROPHECY. AT BEST IT'S PHILOSOPHY.
EVERYTHING COMES TO AN END AND NOTHING DOES.
A BOOK MAY END, BUT THE STORY THEREIN GOES ON AND ON INSIDE THE MIND OF ITS READER, WHICH IS WHERE THE STORY EXISTS IN THE FIRST PLACE.
GIBBERISH.
NOT TO MENTION RE-READINGS AND RETELLINGS.
YEAH, I GET IT. CRYPTIC NONSENSE TO DISGUISE THE FACT THAT FORTUNE-TELLERS DON'T ACTUALLY KNOW MONKEYSHIT.

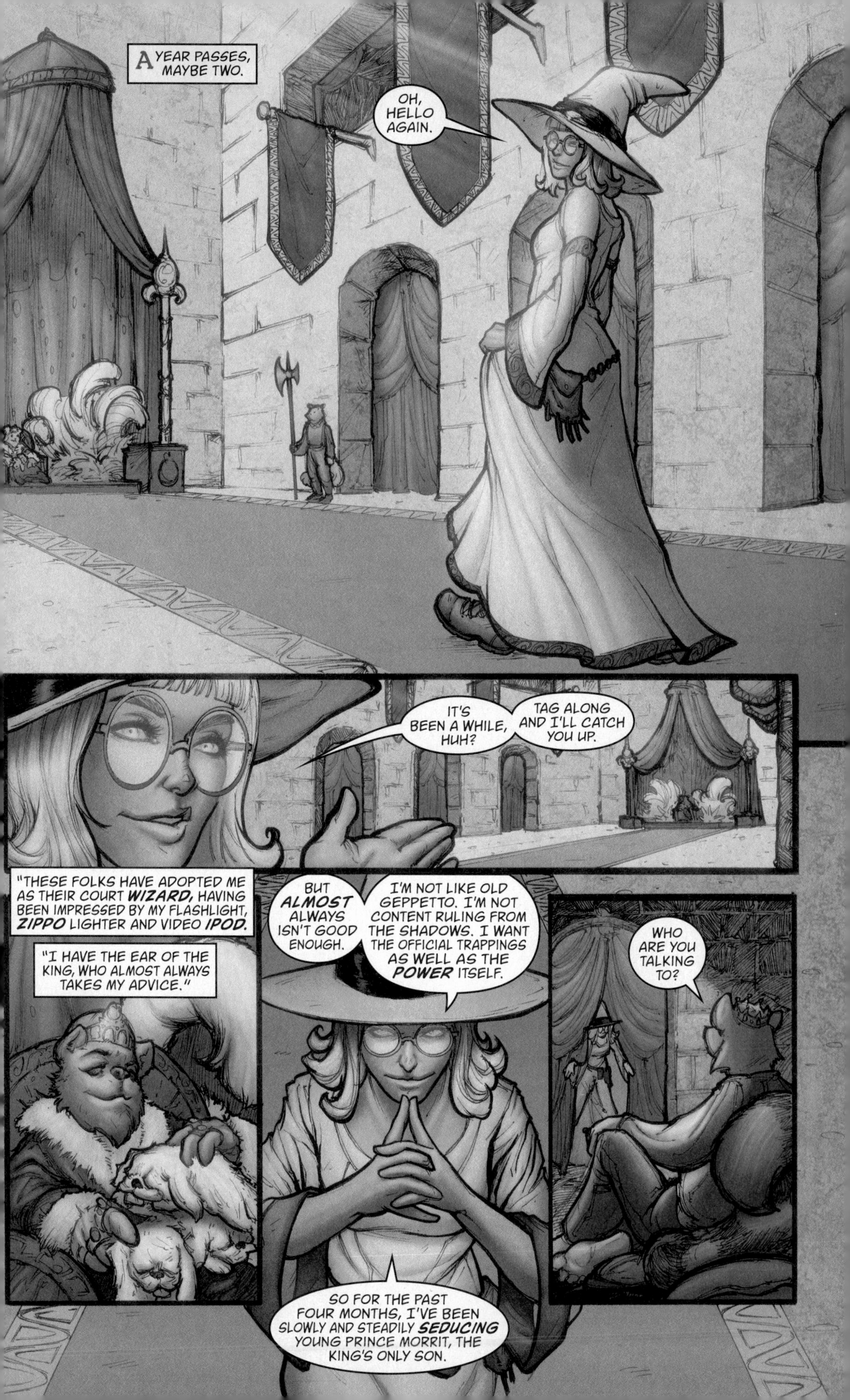
A YEAR PASSES, MAYBE TWO.
OH, HELLO AGAIN.
IT'S BEEN A WHILE, HUH?
TAG ALONG AND I'LL CATCH YOU UP.
"THESE FOLKS HAVE ADOPTED ME AS THEIR COURT WIZARD, HAVING BEEN IMPRESSED BY MY FLASHLIGHT, ZIPPO LIGHTER AND VIDEO IPOD.
"I HAVE THE EAR OF THE KING, WHO ALMOST ALWAYS TAKES MY ADVICE."
BUT ALMOST ALWAYS ISN'T GOOD ENOUGH.
I'M NOT LIKE OLD GEPPETTO. I'M NOT CONTENT RULING FROM THE SHADOWS. I WANT THE OFFICIAL TRAPPINGS AS WELL AS THE POWER ITSELF.
SO FOR THE PAST FOUR MONTHS, I'VE BEEN SLOWLY AND STEADILY SEDUCING YOUNG PRINCE MORRIT, THE KING'S ONLY SON.
WHO ARE YOU TALKING TO?

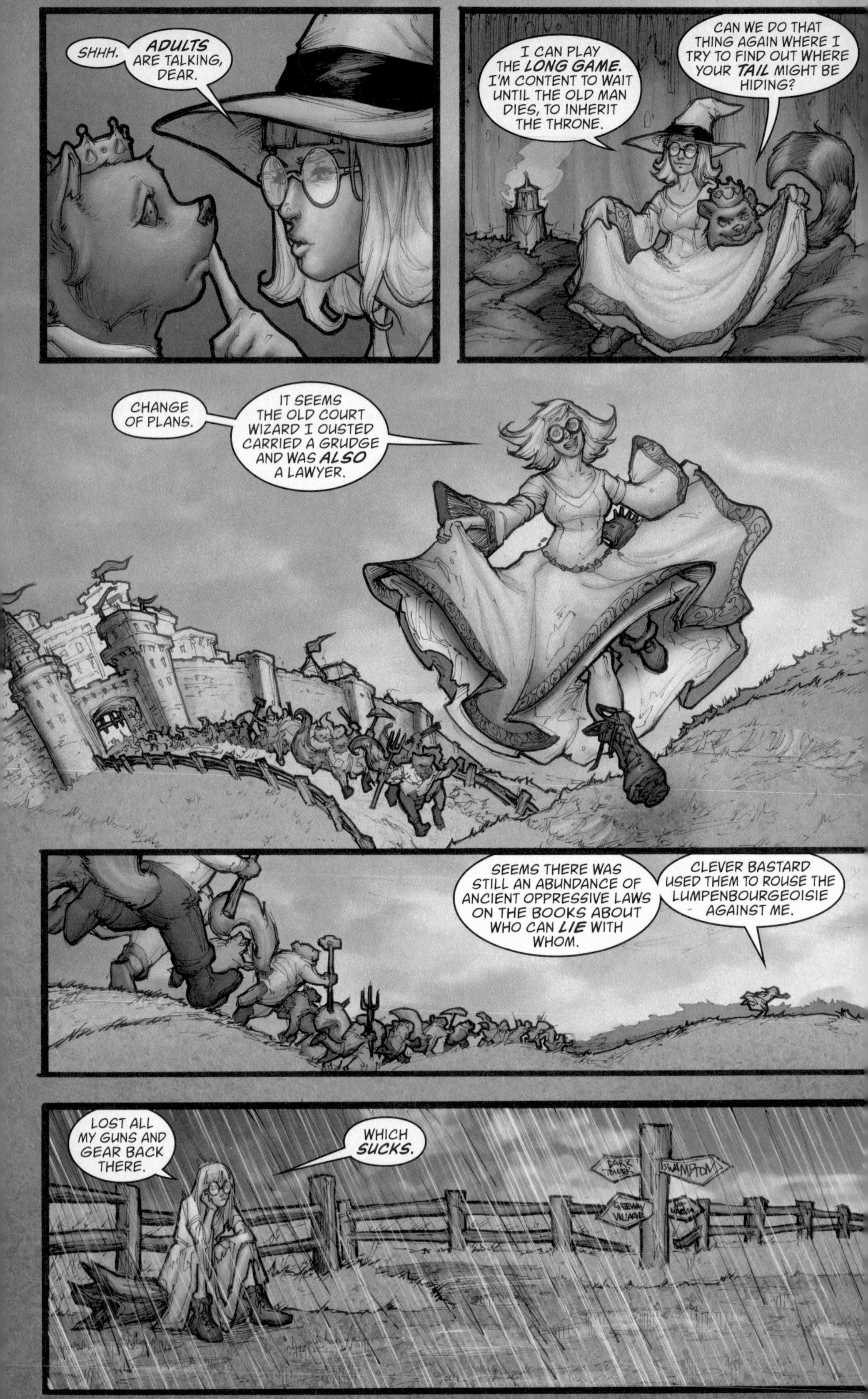
SHHH.
ADULTS ARE TALKING, DEAR.
I CAN PLAY THE LONG GAME. I'M CONTENT TO WAIT UNTIL THE OLD MAN DIES, TO INHERIT THE THRONE.
CAN WE DO THAT THING AGAIN WHERE I TRY TO FIND OUT WHERE YOUR TAIL MIGHT BE HIDING?
CHANGE OF PLANS.
IT SEEMS THE OLD COURT WIZARD I OUSTED CARRIED A GRUDGE AND WAS ALSO A LAWYER.
SEEMS THERE WAS STILL AN ABUNDANCE OF ANCIENT OPPRESSIVE LAWS ON THE BOOKS ABOUT WHO CAN LIE WITH WHOM.
CLEVER BASTARD USED THEM TO ROUSE THE LUMPENBOURGEOISIE AGAINST ME.
LOST ALL MY GUNS AND GEAR BACK THERE.
WHICH SUCKS.
SWAMPTON

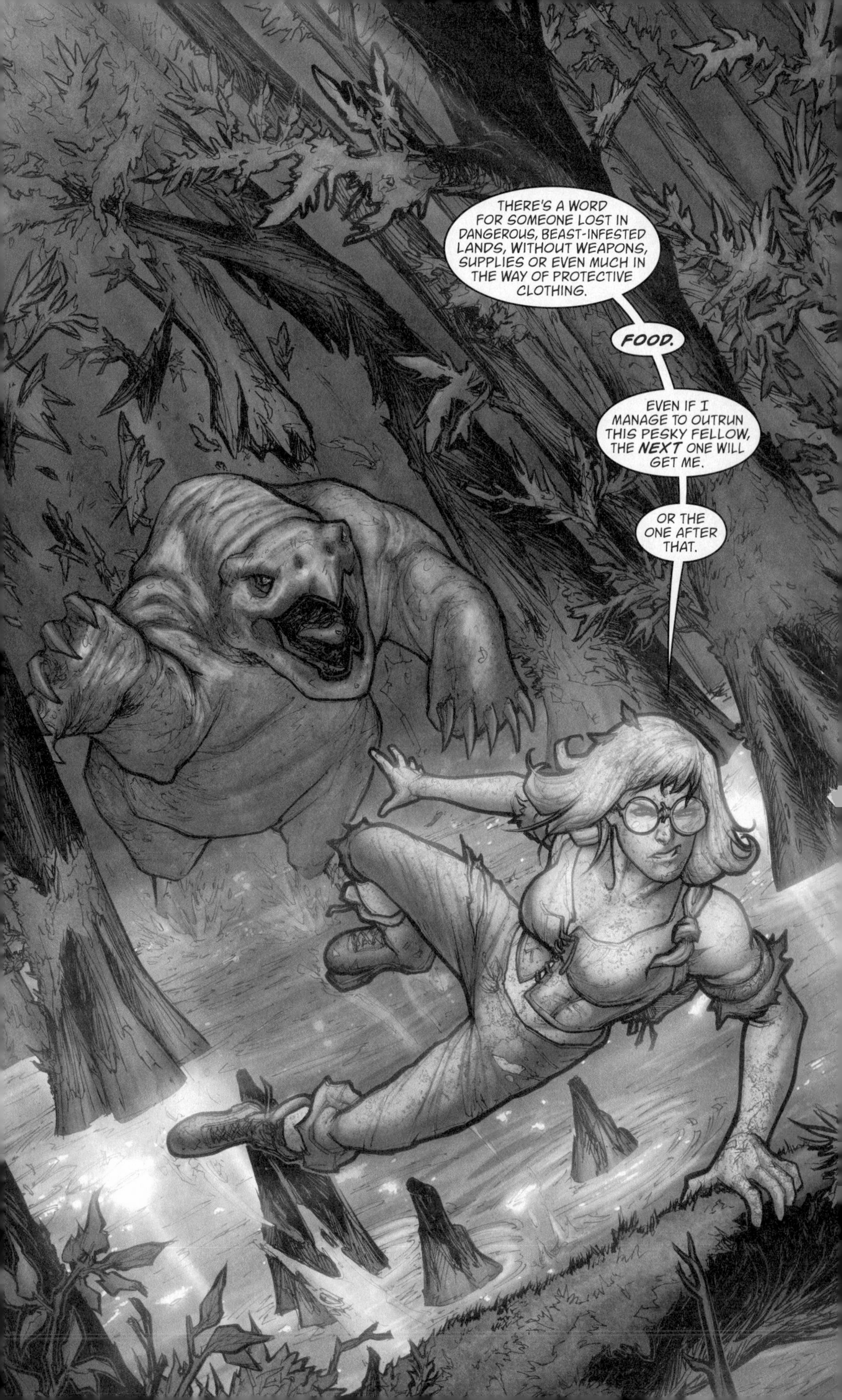
THERE'S A WORD FOR SOMEONE LOST IN DANGEROUS, BEAST-INFESTED LANDS, WITHOUT WEAPONS, SUPPLIES OR EVEN MUCH IN THE WAY OF PROTECTIVE CLOTHING.
FOOD.
EVEN IF I MANAGE TO OUTRUN THIS PESKY FELLOW, THE NEXT ONE WILL GET ME.
OR THE ONE AFTER THAT.

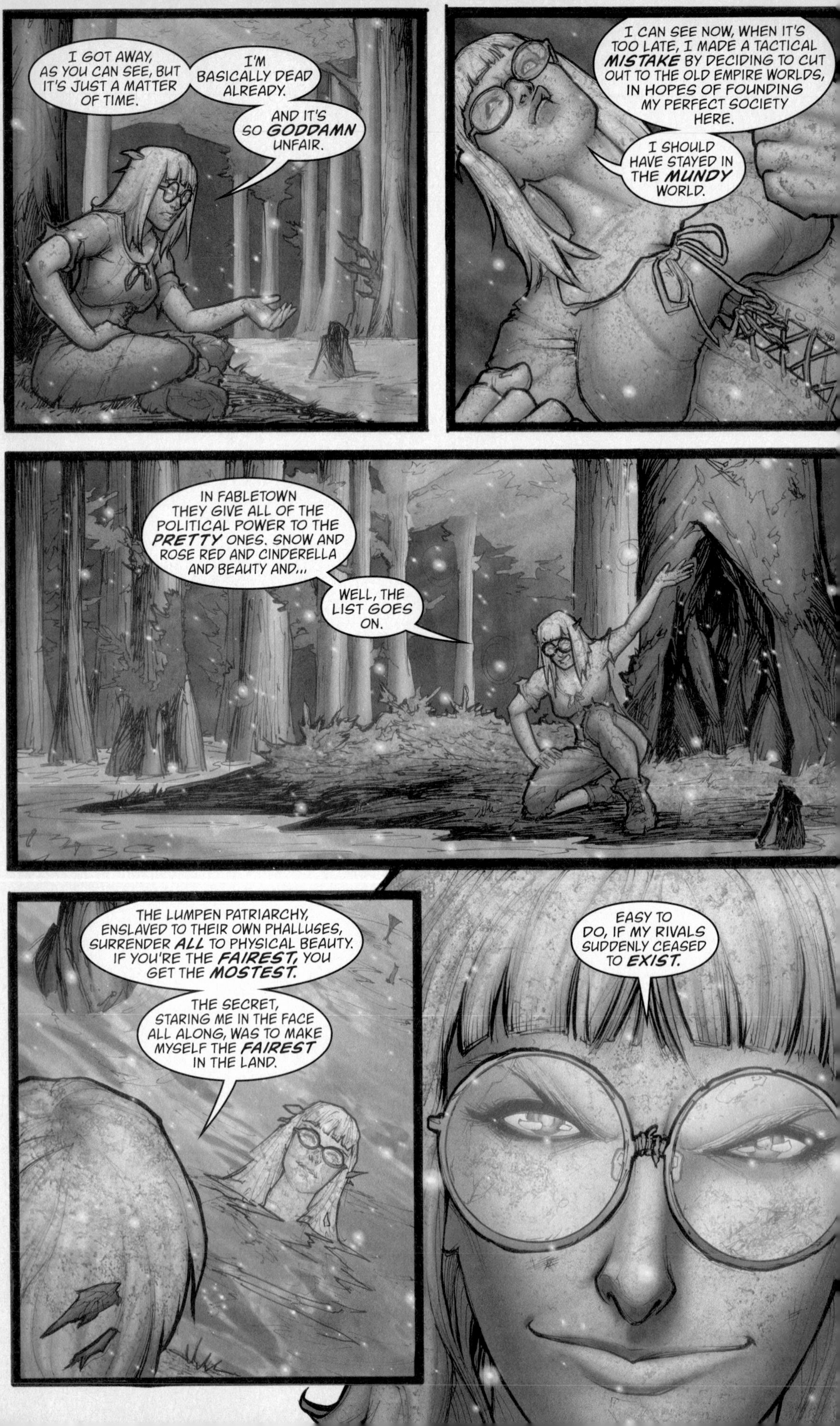
I GOT AWAY, AS YOU CAN SEE, BUT IT'S JUST A MATTER OF TIME.
I'M BASICALLY DEAD ALREADY.
AND IT'S SO GODDAMN UNFAIR.
I CAN SEE NOW, WHEN IT'S TOO LATE, I MADE A TACTICAL MISTAKE BY DECIDING TO CUT OUT TO THE OLD EMPIRE WORLDS, IN HOPES OF FOUNDING MY PERFECT SOCIETY HERE.
I SHOULD HAVE STAYED IN THE MUNDY WORLD.
IN FABLETOWN THEY GIVE ALL OF THE POLITICAL POWER TO THE PRETTY ONES. SNOW AND ROSE RED AND CINDERELLA AND BEAUTY AND...
WELL, THE LIST GOES ON.
THE LUMPEN PATRIARCHY, ENSLAVED TO THEIR OWN PHALLUSES, SURRENDER ALL TO PHYSICAL BEAUTY. IF YOU'RE THE FAIREST, YOU GET THE MOSTEST.
THE SECRET, STARING ME IN THE FACE ALL ALONG, WAS TO MAKE MYSELF THE FAIREST IN THE LAND.
EASY TO DO, IF MY RIVALS SUDDENLY CEASED TO EXIST.

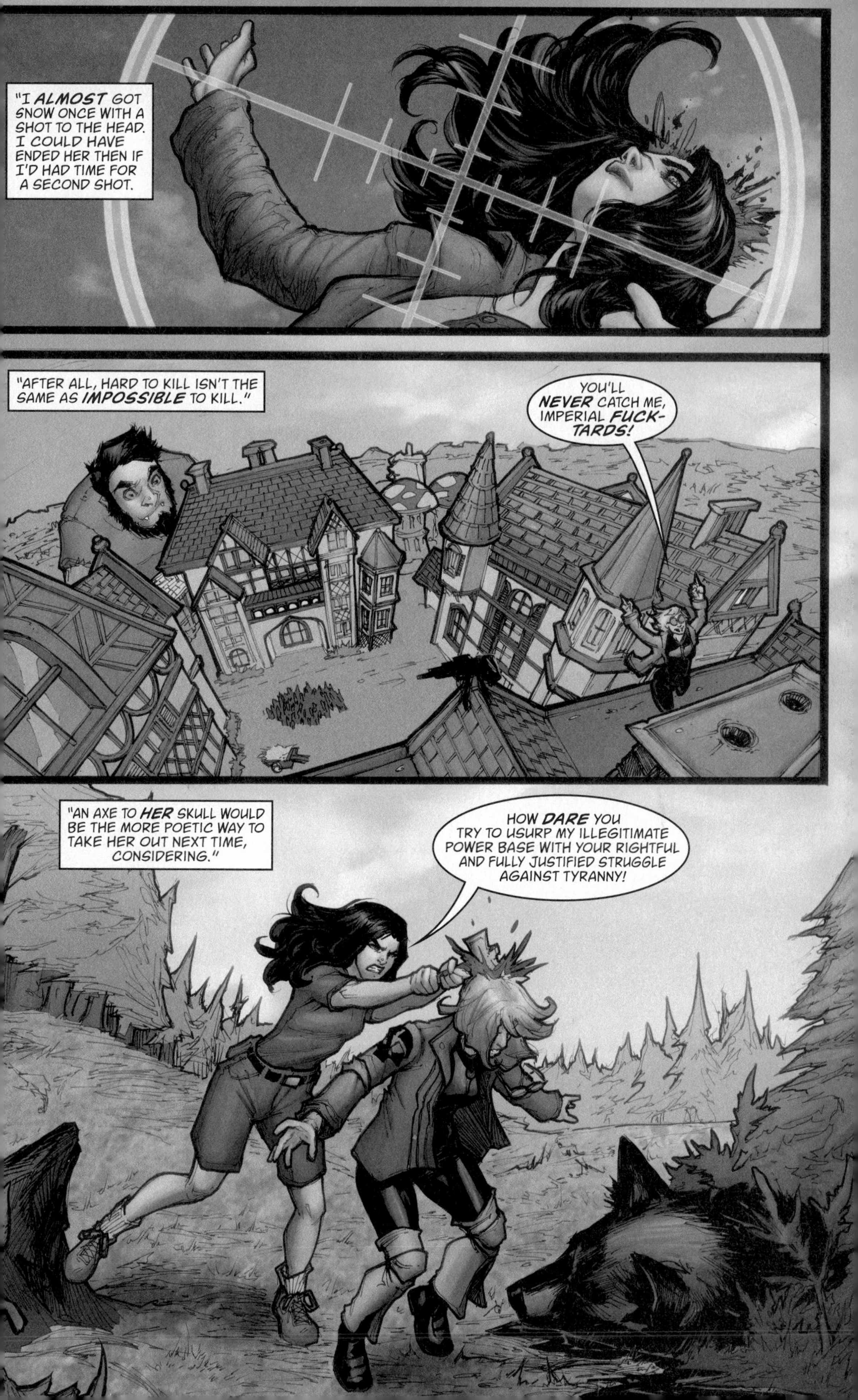
"I ALMOST GOT SNOW ONCE WITH A SHOT TO THE HEAD. I COULD HAVE ENDED HER THEN IF I'D HAD TIME FOR A SECOND SHOT.
"AFTER ALL, HARD TO KILL ISN'T THE SAME AS IMPOSSIBLE TO KILL."
YOU'LL NEVER CATCH ME, IMPERIAL FUCK-TARDS!
"AN AXE TO HER SKULL WOULD BE THE MORE POETIC WAY TO TAKE HER OUT NEXT TIME, CONSIDERING."
HOW DARE YOU TRY TO USURP MY ILLEGITIMATE POWER BASE WITH YOUR RIGHTFUL AND FULLY JUSTIFIED STRUGGLE AGAINST TYRANNY!

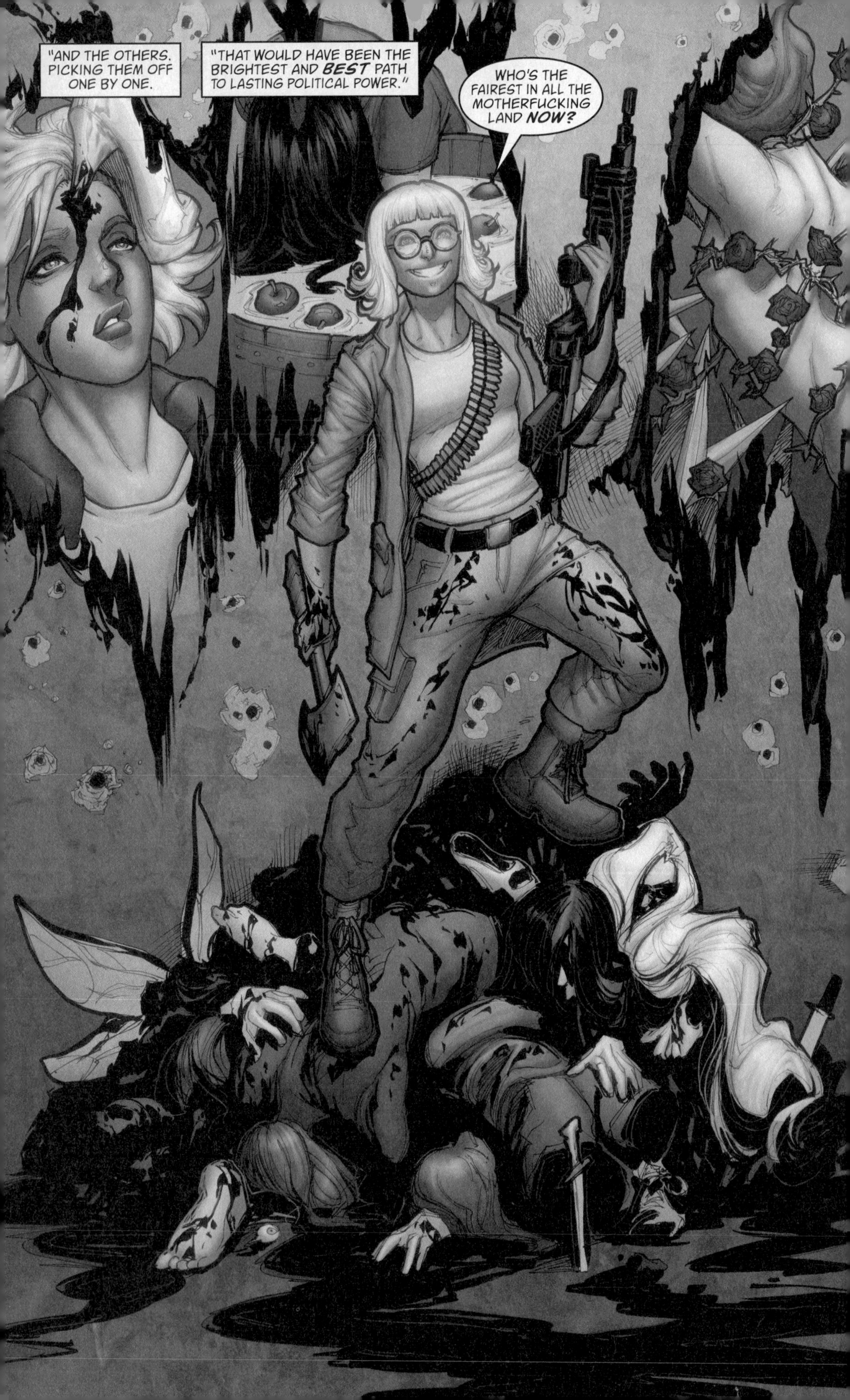
"AND THE OTHERS. PICKING THEM OFF ONE BY ONE.
"THAT WOULD HAVE BEEN THE BRIGHTEST AND BEST PATH TO LASTING POLITICAL POWER."
WHO'S THE FAIREST IN ALL THE MOTHERFUCKING LAND NOW?

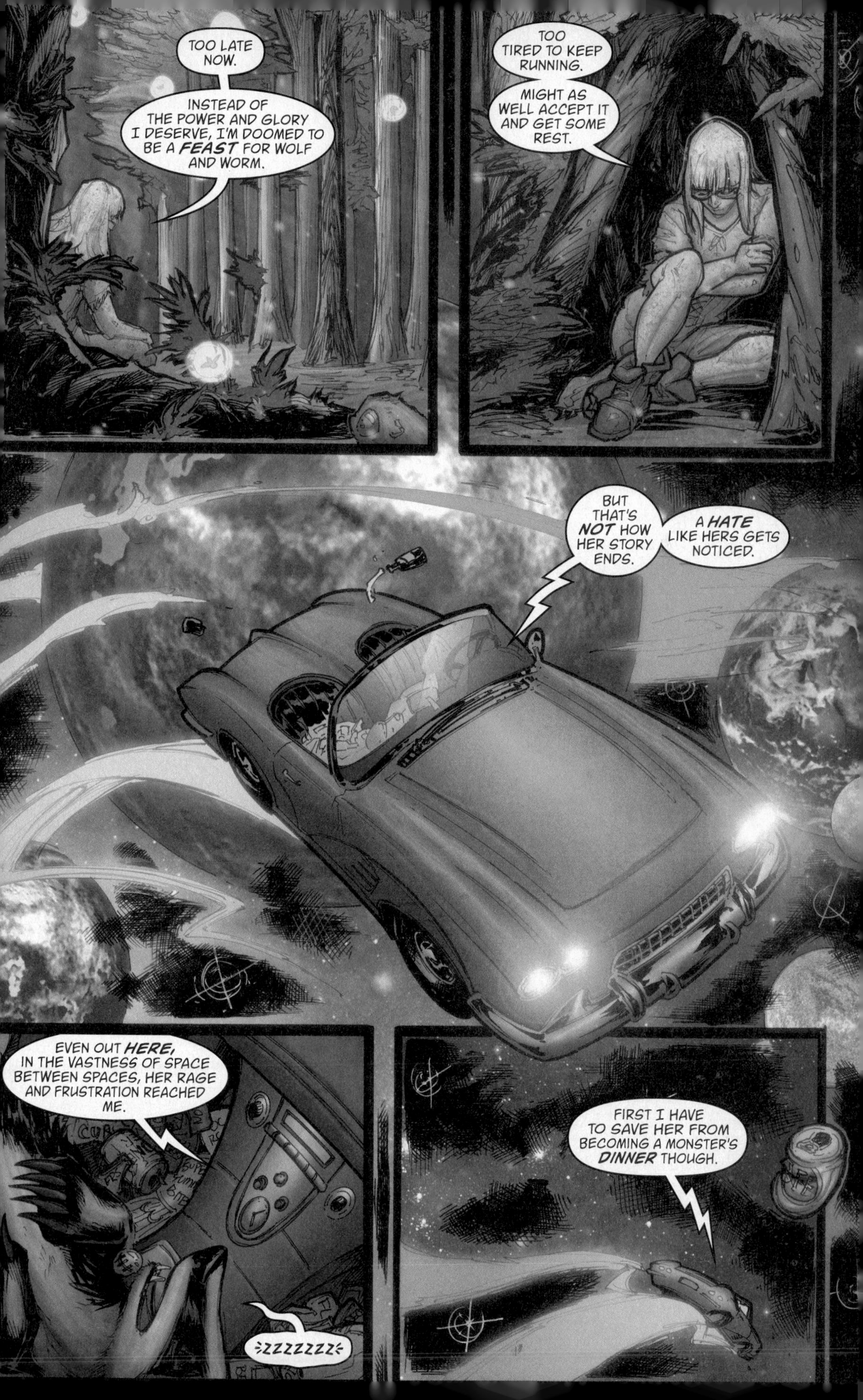
TOO LATE NOW.
INSTEAD OF THE POWER AND GLORY I DESERVE, I'M DOOMED TO BE A FEAST FOR WOLF AND WORM.
TOO TIRED TO KEEP RUNNING.
MIGHT AS WELL ACCEPT IT AND GET SOME REST.
BUT THAT'S NOT HOW HER STORY ENDS.
A HATE LIKE HERS GETS NOTICED.
EVEN OUT HERE, IN THE VASTNESS OF SPACE BETWEEN SPACES, HER RAGE AND FRUSTRATION REACHED ME.
ZZZZZZZ
FIRST I HAVE TO SAVE HER FROM BECOMING A MONSTER'S DINNER THOUGH.

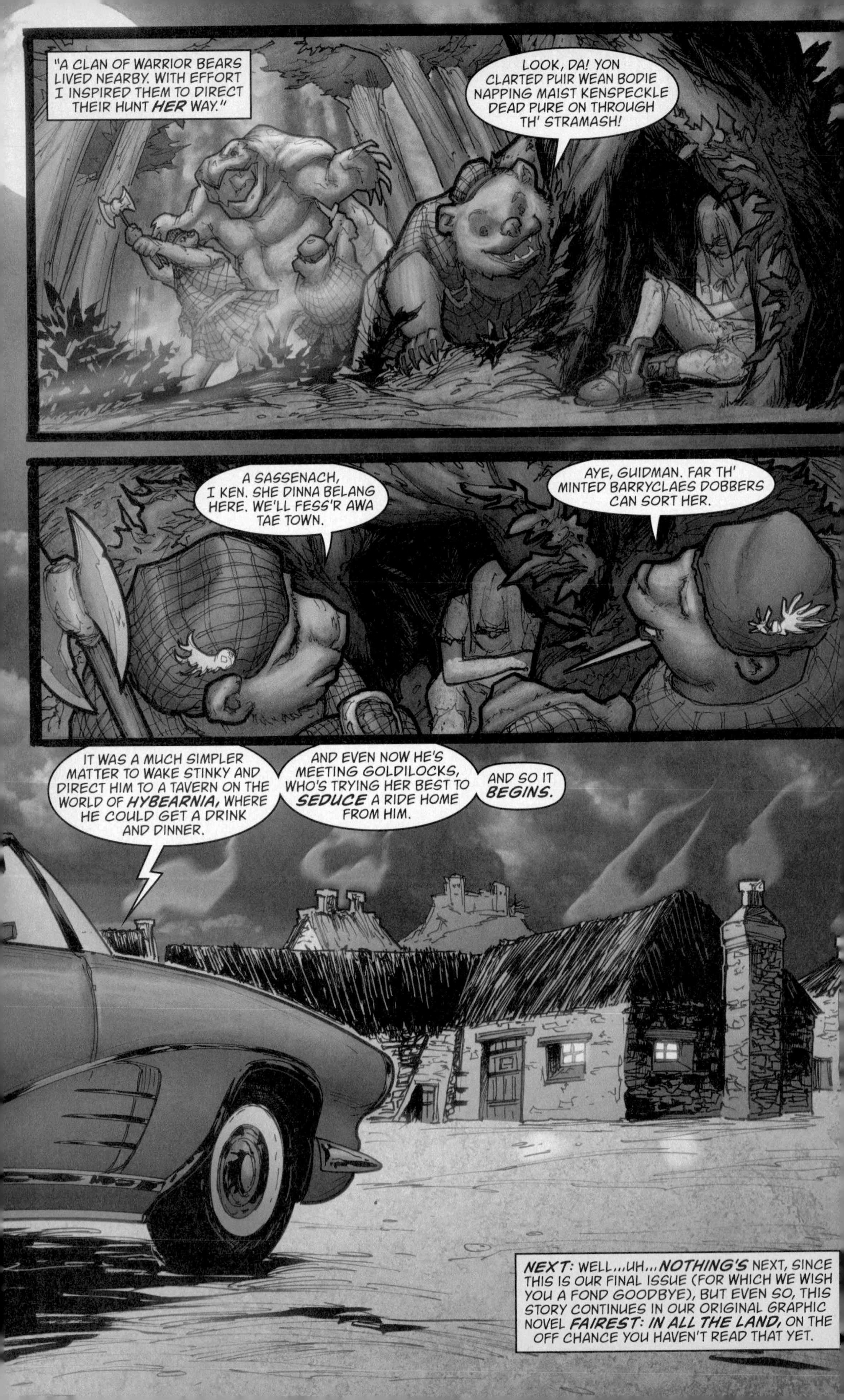
"A CLAN OF WARRIOR BEARS LIVED NEARBY. WITH EFFORT I INSPIRED THEM TO DIRECT THEIR HUNT HER WAY."
LOOK, DA! YON CLARTED PUIR WEAN BODIE NAPPING MAIST KENSPECKLE DEAD PURE ON THROUGH TH' STRAMASH!
A SASSENACH, I KEN. SHE DINNA BELANG HERE. WE'LL FESS'R AWA TAE TOWN.
AYE, GUIDMAN. FAR TH' MINTED BARRYCLAES DOBBERS CAN SORT HER.
IT WAS A MUCH SIMPLER MATTER TO WAKE STINKY AND DIRECT HIM TO A TAVERN ON THE WORLD OF HYBEARNIA, WHERE HE COULD GET A DRINK AND DINNER.
AND EVEN NOW HE'S MEETING GOLDILOCKS, WHO'S TRYING HER BEST TO SEDUCE A RIDE HOME FROM HIM.
AND SO IT BEGINS.
NEXT: WELL...UH...NOTHING'S NEXT, SINCE THIS IS OUR FINAL ISSUE (FOR WHICH WE WISH YOU A FOND GOODBYE), BUT EVEN SO, THIS STORY CONTINUES IN OUR ORIGINAL GRAPHIC NOVEL FAIREST: IN ALL THE LAND, ON THE OFF CHANCE YOU HAVEN'T READ THAT YET.

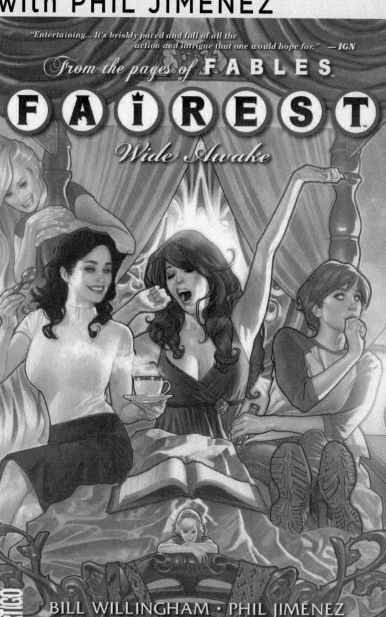

VERTIGO

> "FABLES is an excellent series in the tradition of SANDMAN, one that rewards careful attention and loyalty."
> —PUBLISHERS WEEKLY

> "[A] wonderfully twisted concept...features fairy tale characters banished to the noirish world of present-day New York."
> —WASHINGTON POST

> "Great fun." —BOOKLIST

BILL WILLINGHAM
FABLES VOL. 1: LEGENDS IN EXILE

THE #1 NEW YORK TIMES BEST-SELLING SERIES

FABLES

Legends in Exile

"A top-notch fantasy comic that is on a par with SANDMAN."
Variety

DIRECTOR

BULLFINCH STREET

Bill Willingham
Lan Medina
Steve Leialoha
Craig Hamilton

VERTIGO